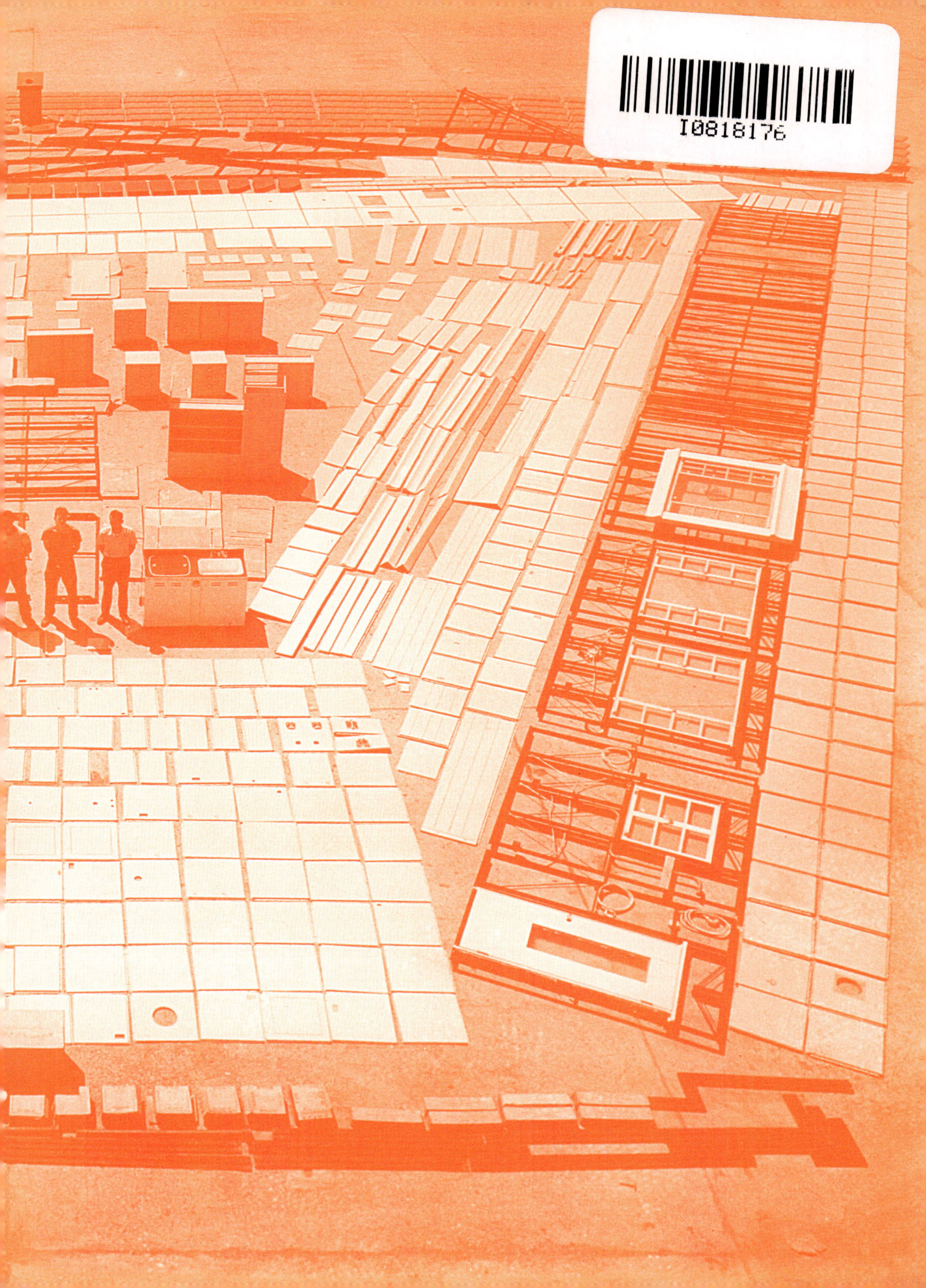
I0818176

JUST
MARRIED
DIRECTIONS
HOME
PORTABLE HOUSE Co.

SIKORSKY S-64
N6979R

ARNT COBBERS
OLIVER JAHN
PETER GÖSSEL (Ed.)

SIKORSKY SKYCRANE

PREFAB HOUSES

TASCHEN

POPULAR SCIENCE
MONTHLY
MAR. 1946
25 CENTS
STOP GAP
HOUSING – p. 66
Circulation This Issue Over 1,000,000

CONTENTS

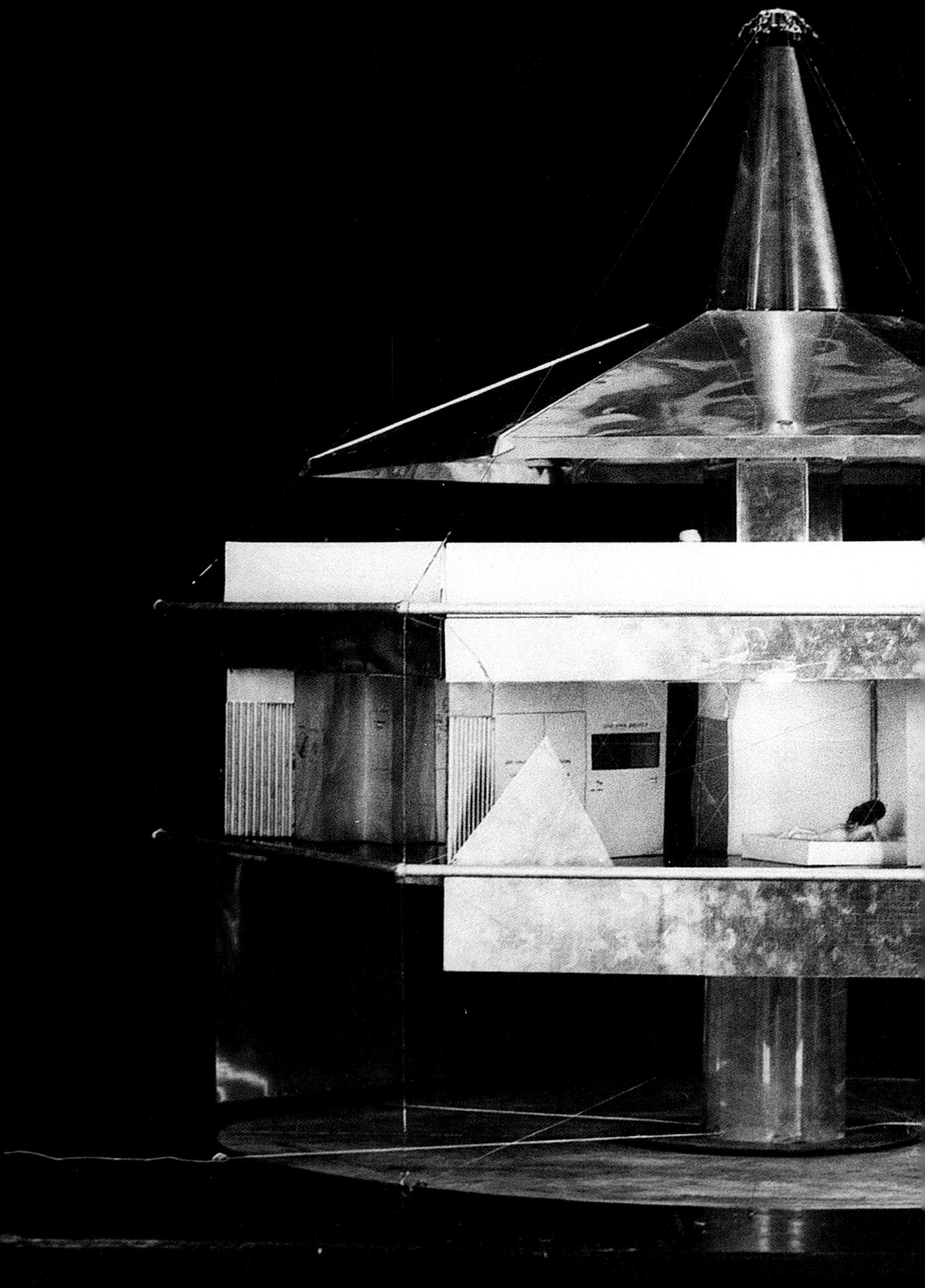

FACTORY-MADE HOUSES

A PORTABLE TOWN FOR AUSTRALIA,
ERECTED at HEMMING'S PATENT PORTABLE HOUSE MANUFACTORY, CLIFT HOUSE, BRISTOL,
Shewing the CHURCH and PARSONAGE HOUSE as ordered to be sent out to THE BISHOP of MELBOURNE.

A young couple receives a house as a wedding present. A prefabricated house. Still dressed in a tuxedo and bridal gown, the couple drives to the building site. A truck driver tosses the last of several casket-like boxes from the deck of his truck and races away. What then begins is an ill-begotten attempt on the part of the groom to put the numbered pieces of wood spilling out of the wooden boxes together to build an attractive little house. *One Week* is the title of this 1920 film classic, with Buster Keaton in the role of the young man. He saws, hammers, and stacks, and in the end he and his wife are completely perplexed when they take stock of the structure, which is more reminiscent of a Cubist sculpture—with its slanted walls, crooked windows, and entrance on the upper floor—than of a house. With this film Buster Keaton not only created a masterpiece of slapstick comedy, he also satirized a topic widely discussed in the United States and many other countries in the early 1920s: the prefabricated house. All over the world, innovative architects were developing concepts for houses that could be produced in assembly-line style.

However, not everything that looks like a prefabricated house, really is a prefabricated house. A prefabricated house, in the narrower sense, is either produced in a factory and set on

Opposite: A portable town for Australia, erected at Hemming's Patent Portable House Manufactory, Clift House, Bristol, c. 1853

Below: Miners' huts at the Blackwater gold mine in Waiuta, West Coast, New Zealand, c. 1910

the building site as a complete unit, or it consists completely of components that are industrially prefabricated before they are delivered to the building site, where the final assembly of the house is completed. Because more effort is involved in the preliminary planning, it makes sense to produce building components in standardized sizes beforehand. The boundary between prefabricated houses, in the narrower sense, and building methods that make only partial use of prefabricated elements cannot be clearly drawn.

Building block systems are usually used to ensure that building components are prefabricated at low prices, and that construction on site is as quick and as easy as possible. Hence, most prefabricated housing construction was based on wood or steel frames enclosed using prefabricated panels made of the most diverse materials. However, there were many experiments with the industrial production of complete units, including even the interior fixtures, that were arranged side by side on the building site.

Prefabrication is a child of nineteenth-century industrialization. The use of mass-produced nails, rather than expensive hand-wrought nails, made it possible to construct a house solely out of boards that any sawmill could deliver by using

Below: Patent for Portable Houses by D.N. Skillings, patent No. 33758

Opposite: The first Sears Homes catalog, issued in 1908

Following spread: Page from Sears 1923 catalog

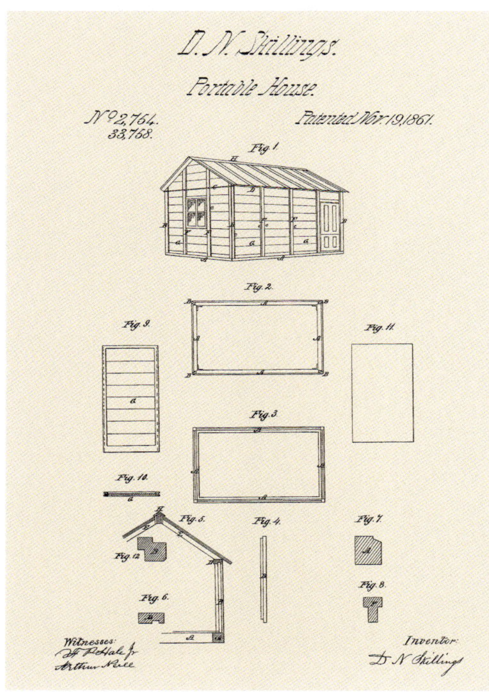

nailed joints. Mortise and tenon joints, as used in timber-frame houses, were no longer necessary. The emergence and spread of prefabrication is also closely related to the life of pioneers in those days, i.e. the occupation of extensive areas of land by European settlers. This gave rise to a need for houses that could be built quickly and at low cost, transported easily, and, considering the lack of trained craftsmen, built by people with no special skills. Hence, prefabrication was initially more common in North America and Australia.

The year 1833 was destined to mark a milestone in prefabrication; it was when the first historically documented prefabricated house was produced in Great Britain. The London carpenter Herbert Manning developed a complete building kit for emigrants headed for Australia, which could be assembled in one day. His Portable Colonial Cottage for Emigrants would eventually become famous.

This was also the year that "balloon frame" construction, which is still common in North America, was developed, presumably by the Chicago master builder Augustine Taylor. It was a precursor of prefabrication. The structures consist of narrowly placed studs and correspondingly arranged horizontal ceiling beams, with their broader sides in the vertical, encased in wooden boards on the outside and paneled on the inside. Basically it was a case of the re-adoption and adaptation of the traditional form of timber-frame construction with continuous studs previously used in Europe for centuries. The system was based on partial prefabrication; it still required considerable work at the building site, but this could be performed by untrained laborers.

The construction method based on this wooden skeleton was derisively referred to as "balloon frame" since it seemed as if a strong gust could blow the houses away. However, the system was practical and cheap, and the result was a permanent structure that was still highly variable in size and layout. It soon became widespread and contributed to a boom in the American wood industry. In the second half of the nineteenth century, a large proportion of all houses built in the United States had balloon frames. In the Western United States, entire cities were built using this type of house.

When the Glaswegian company Thomas Eddington and Sons developed a rolling process to produce corrugated sheet metal in 1844, a new material began to compete with all wood prefabricated post-and-beam construction. In order to produce housing for the hundreds of thousands of gold diggers who came to California between 1848 and 1854 to try their luck during the gold rush, entrepreneurs like Peter Naylor, from New York, made use of English corrugated sheet metal technology. Companies like Edward Bellhouse in Manchester, Charles Young in Glasgow, and Samuel Hemming in Bristol produced thousands of prefabricated houses out of corrugated sheet metal for California, Australia, and South Africa. The number of prefabricated houses only began to decline when an indigenous building industry began to emerge in the colonies around 1860.

At the beginning of the twentieth century, companies in the United States, like Sears, Roebuck and Co., Gordon van Tine, Montgomery Ward, The Hodgson Company, and Aladdin, began to market prefabricated houses through mail-order catalogs. Cut-to-measure wooden beams, as well as façade and roofing elements, were offered for houses built using the balloon frame widely accepted in the New World; customers could also opt for plumbing and heating, while the nails and paint were even included. Everything was precisely numbered and delivered, along with the assembly instructions, by rail or truck. The first product sold in this manner was the Readi-Cut House by Aladdin in 1906. Aladdin offered a total of 450 different models, and a total of roughly 65,000 houses were sold.

However, Sears, Roebuck and Co. enjoyed the greatest success. Between 1908 and 1940, the company was able to sell between 70,000 and 100,000 houses through its catalog and sales offices. The first catalog, printed in 1908, already offered 22 different models at prices between $650 and $2,500. Sears's strongest point was its ability to offer precision-built components for a surprisingly wide range of house models, all of which were packed and shipped along with

GREATER ECONOM

By Building Two or More Houses at the Same Ti
Are Now Building on a La

DO LIKE THE LARGEST REAL ESTATE OPERATORS ARE NOW DOING. Improve your property by building on a little larger scale and reap the big benefits either in the way of increasing your profits or doubling percentage of earnings on your investment. Houses built one at a time under ordinary conditions which would earn you 10 per cent would easily earn you 15 or 50 per cent more profit if the same quality of house was built six at one time.

THERE ARE MANY REASONS WHY YOU CAN LOWER YOUR BUILDING COSTS by this procedure. Here are just a few illustrations. For instance, excavating. While laborers, horses, scoops and other implements are on the ground, six basements can be excavated at a slight advance over a lesser number. As much as 25 per cent can be saved on this procedure alone. The cost of foundation walls, especially when made of concrete, can be considerably reduced in price when the forms for concrete work can be used for a number of houses, as the cost of lumber for making the forms, and the labor, can be entirely saved for all additional houses, and by placing a larger order for concrete or masonry work, any up to date contractor is willing to make big concessions in price.

BUILDING ON A LARGER SCALE enables the various contractors and subcontractors to proceed from one building to the next without loss or delay. Carpenters can lay out their framing work for six houses at one time. While one house is in the course of framing, another house will be under its roof, and carpenters during inclement weather can always be worked to the very best possible advantage, which means low building cost for carpenter labor. Plasterers and painters proceed in a like manner, all of them doing the work to the very best advantage and at the very lowest cost. Furthermore, much closer supervision can be had when a number of houses are built close together at one time, as the contractor or foreman can carefully watch the work as it progresses, making every penny paid for labor count to the very best advantage.

WE ARE SELLING MANY OF THE HOUSES SHOWN IN THIS BOOK in lots of fifteen to twenty-five houses, all of which are built in numbers of five to ten at one time. Realty operators and contractors building in this manner claim an actual saving of from 10 to 25 per cent, and claim to give the owner far better satisfaction than would be possible if building one house at a time. On pages 100 and 101 we show these very same houses separately with a larger illustration and quote a

=BIGGER PROFITS

All Live Real Estate Operators and Contractors Scale Wherever Possible.

total price for all the material to complete these houses. In designing these houses it has been our aim to have Modern Homes No. 193, No. 194 and No. 196 with foundations of exactly the same dimensions, thus enabling a contractor when laying out his work and making his form to use the same forms on the three different houses, all different in design from an exterior viewpoint yet similar in foundation and arrangement on the inside. We also have planned Modern Homes No. 192, No. 195 and No. 197 in a similar manner, which enables realty operators or individuals who are building on a larger scale for the purpose of renting, speculation or selling, to do the work in the most economical manner at the very lowest possible cost and still be in position to erect the six houses one next to the other without being confronted with the monotony that is found in many localities where the same scheme has been followed out by making slight changes in the front elevation, but not sufficient to make the house look as though each one was an entirely different pattern or design, as we aim to do, and as illustrated above. The above illustration shows six modern homes shown on pages 100 and 101 erected one next to the other on adjoining lots. One can see at a glance that there is no monotony or similarity in their appearance, yet they are constructed on similar foundations and three of each have identical interior arrangements.

IMPROVE YOUR VACANT PROPERTY. If you adopt this scheme of building two or more houses at a time your houses will be sold long before they are completed or, if rented, they will double the interest on your money. Investments of this kind are readily financed by banking institutions or money lenders, as they realize that the security is the best that can be had.

DON'T FORGET that when building in this manner you are cutting out all delays, you are saving in the cost of bringing the scaffolding and tools from one job to the other, you are practically building six houses with the same amount of trouble and attention that is necessary when building one.

TO THOSE WHO ONLY WANT TO BUILD ONE HOUSE FOR RESIDENCE OR OTHER PURPOSES, you can make no mistake in selecting any one of the designs on the following pages. Each one of them is considered very good, of a convenient arrangement, and the excellent material used puts these houses on a par with any other house we show in this book. We simply have pointed out the advantages of building more than one house at a time, which is now being practiced by all the largest and most up to date realty operators in this country.

simple assembly instructions. A Sears house was delivered by rail, packed in two freight cars. Most of the customers took advantage of the opportunity to seek advice in local sales offices. This enabled them to select a model, clarify the question of financing, and decide whether they wanted to order furniture from the Sears Roebuck catalogue all at the same time. The company even offered maintenance contracts.

The house kit essentially consisted of the pre-cut, marked wooden beams out of which the supporting frame was constructed according to the plan. The windows, doors, cladding elements, roofing shingles, nails, and paint were included; plumbing and electrical installations came at additional cost. The company advertised that roughly 40 % of the labor costs incurred in conjunction with traditional housing construction was saved in the production of their prefabricated houses, while the quality was considerably better. No architect was ever named for any of the roughly 450 different models offered by Sears Roebuck, although the company did have an architecture department, directed by David S. Betcone, while a woman named E. L. Meyer was responsible for interior decorating components for a certain period.

Since there was a shortage of housing in the vicinity of expanding production facilities, it made sense for many companies to build their own housing estates, thus enabling them, in times of labor shortages, to attract employees and tie them to the company. For example, after Standard Oil purchased a coal mine in Carlinville, Illinois, in 1917, the company ordered building kits for a million dollars from Sears—which was, at the time, the largest order in the history of mail-order sales. Railway tracks were even laid down solely for the purpose of unloading the freight cars that carried the 156 houses to this location.

An important step in the development of prefabricated houses was marked by the emergence of mass production at the beginning of the twentieth century, which was closely connected to the invention of the automobile and the assembly line. This process was made famous by the production of Henry Ford's Model T, which had been produced on an assembly line since 1913. The new production method did not result in advantages in terms of the quality or durability of automobiles, when compared with traditional assembly methods. However, the production costs could be reduced and the volume of production considerably increased. In terms of production, the focus was shifted from the optimization of the individual product to the optimization of the production process. Industrial production processes also opened up new possibilities for the building industry.

At the beginning of the twentieth century prefabrication had already attracted the interest of the young architectural avant-garde. Frank Lloyd Wright and Walter Gropius associated prefabricated building techniques not only with a new lifestyle, but also with the solution of social questions. Wright believed that every American was entitled to own a house that fulfilled high

Below: Cover of the Aladdin Houses catalog, 1913

Following spread: Page from the Hodgson Houses catalog, 1920

aesthetic standards, but was still affordable. In 1911 he designed American System Built Houses for the real estate developer Arthur L. Richards of Milwaukee. His "Ready Cut" prefabricated house, designed as a simple building kit in 1915 and based on the balloon frame system, is also worth mentioning.

After the First World War, prefabricated construction also finally reached the European continent. Almost over night, architects of the still young modernist movement became enthusiastic about new building materials and what seemed like unlimited technological progress. Industrial production became a model, both in terms of material aesthetics as well as production technology. The machine became one of the central metaphors of Modernism. It dominated design practice of architects and designers to the smallest detail. It is no wonder that innovations in the field of industrial mass production piqued the interest of architects.

One of the pioneers in this context was the German architect Walter Gropius. While working in Peter Behrens's office as a young architect he had already planned to establish a building company in order to both reduce costs by means of industrial prefabrication and to improve the quality of the buildings through meticulous development and extensive testing. As the director of the Bauhaus, he collaborated with Fred Forbat and Adolf Meyer between 1920 and 1923 in developing the *Baukasten* (building block) system of residential units based on concrete elements that would make it possible to build standardized flat-roofed houses—a concept that was not widely accepted. The *Metalltypenhaus* (metal model house) designed by Bauhaus artist Georg Muche and the architectural student Richard Paulick—a steel skeleton to which 3 mm steel plates were affixed—was only built as a prototype by a company in Leipzig that built safes, the Carl Kästner AG. The metal house can still be seen today in Dessau. The plans by the young architect Philipp Tolziner to expand the Törten Estate by building steel houses also failed. Nevertheless, all of these

Permanent Exhibits of Hodgson Portable Houses in Boston, New York and Dover

Outdoor Exhibit at (

HOW TO GET TO DOVER.—Dover, Mass., is about 15 miles south
and Hartford R. R., in about half an hour; or by automobile through p
railroad station, which our plant occupies, over an acre is set aside fo
houses. You'll find one of our representatives right at the exhibit re

Boston Office and Show Room, 71 Federal Street

Our Bo

You'll find this
Station, at 71-73
portable cottage,
houses, some bir
nels and other s
give you a good
tion and quality
in and talk to so
tives in the offic
you intend to er

Our New

Both show roo
Craftsman Build
ninth Street, just
only a few min
Grand Central S
in our exhibit-
houses, bird hous
lot of other inte
up for your insp
able to get all th
sire first-handed
tive in the office.

ıctory, Dover, Mass.

Boston. It can be reached from Boston on the New York, New Haven
/ country and over good roads. Of the several acres adjoining the
outdoor exhibit. You will find here a most interesting group of our
to show you around and give you any information you might desire.

ı Office

e near the South
deral Street. A
y house, poultry
ıses and dog ken-
er buildings will
of the construc-
ur houses. Step
f the representa-
out any building

rk Office

l office are in the
6 East Thirty-
Fifth Avenue, and
walk from the
n. You will find
cottage, poultry
og kennels and a
ıg houses all set
n. You will be
ormation you de-
ı the representa-

New York Office and Show Room, 6 East 39th Street

Metal model house by Bauhaus student Richard Paulick and artist Georg Muche, 1926–1927 for Carl Kästner A.G.

projects brought the Bauhaus the reputation of being one of the pioneers of the modern prefabricated house movement.

Another pioneer in the field of prefabricated construction was the French architect Jean Prouvé. In the mid-1930s he designed prefabricated buildings made of sheet metal that were never reproduced, but nevertheless represented a milestone. This included his building for the Aeroclub "Roland Garros" in Buc (Yvelines), which was prefabricated in Prouvé's workshop and can be seen as a manifesto of Modernism. Prouvé recognized the need to restructure the building industry and called for buildings to be produced like automobiles or airplanes in a process subject to continual refinement, optimization, and renewal.

The European avant-garde approach was transported to America in 1930 by the Swiss architect Albert Frey, who had worked on the Villa Savoye in Le Corbusier's Paris office, thus gaining familiarity with the design vocabulary of the movement from direct experience. At the *Architectural and Allied Arts Exhibition* in 1931, he presented his Aluminaire, a three-story house made of aluminum, glass, and steel, which

he had designed in collaboration with Alfred Lawrence Kocher. Companies like Bethlehem Steel, Alcoa (Aluminum Company of America), Westinghouse, and Pittsburgh Plate Glass made the materials used for the steel frames, the corrugated aluminum panels, as well as other components, available for the sake of advertising.

In the United States Frey encountered an increasingly prosperous market. After the World Economic Crisis in 1929, and the subsequent Great Depression, hope was burgeoning that the production of prefabricated houses would help to revive the desolate economy. With much aplomb, the architect Howard T. Fisher established the General Houses Corporation in 1932, which cooperated with diverse supply companies in their intention to play a leading role in the market for prefabricated houses. Companies like General Electric, Pittsburgh Plate Glass, or Pullman Car & Manufacturing were taken on board in order to be able to offer houses at prices of between $3,000 and $4,500. Fisher simply applied the production processes of the automobile industry to the production of prefabricated houses.

In the United States, the cooperation between innovative architects and the steel industry led

Walter Gropius, "Large-scale Building Blocks," 1923

to the development of remarkable ideas. One of the most experimental designers was the autodidactic engineer, architect, and futurist Richard Buckminster Fuller, who ceaselessly developed visions of new ways of living. Fuller's first model of a prefabricated housing unit was presented to the public at a Chicago department store in 1929; it was destined to make history as the Dymaxion House. The design was nothing less than an attack on every traditional concept of what houses should look like: Fuller proposed a central mast in the middle of the hexagonal floor plan that would support the entire structure via high-tension steel cables, thus rendering load-bearing walls unnecessary. The house was planned with a living room, dining room, two bedrooms, two bathrooms, a library, and even a sun terrace on the roof, but no one was interested in buying it. In 1936, he had a prefabricated bathroom patented under the name Dymaxion Bathroom. However, the only version to ever be produced was a living capsule, designed in 1944, called the Dymaxion Deployment Unit; it was deployed, in relatively small numbers, by the United States armed forces as officers' quarters, radar barracks, and infirmaries.

The "House of Tomorrow," designed by George and William Keck for the 1933 *Century of Progress Exposition* in Chicago was a product of the collaboration between architects and industry. Some 750,000 visitors viewed the prototype, which had been erected as a three-story steel skeleton structure clad in sheet steel in only three days. People marveled at features such as air conditioning and custom installations, which included a dishwasher in the kitchen and an aquarium in the children's room, but still no one wanted to buy the house.

The Chicago real estate tycoon Robert Bartlett purchased the prototype of the Keck House in 1935, along with four other models shown at the fair, and had them reassembled in Beverly Shores, where he intended to market premium building sites to his wealthy clientele. The plan backfired, but the former exhibition houses are still standing and now being restored: the Keck House can be found alongside a two-story flat-roofed building with a roof terrace by Robert Law Weed, the Florida Tropical House, a house made completely of cypress by Murray D. Heatherington, the Cypress Log Cabin, and a steel skeleton building by Walter Scholer, the Wieboldt-Rostone-House, which was clad in a material called Rostone (a mixture of slate, limestone, and alkali). The only house to fulfill the exhibition organizers' criteria of being low enough in cost for the average American family and suited for serial production was the Armco-Ferro House by Robert Smith Jr. His façade, made of riveted and enameled corrugated metal panels, served as a model for the Lustron Homes, produced from 1948 to 1950.

The designs by Fuller, Gropius, Frey, Weed and the Kecks were examples of Modernism. However, the public at large in America was not willing to accept factory-built houses, thus orders were rare. The idea of building a house out of metal, as if it were a car chassis, was

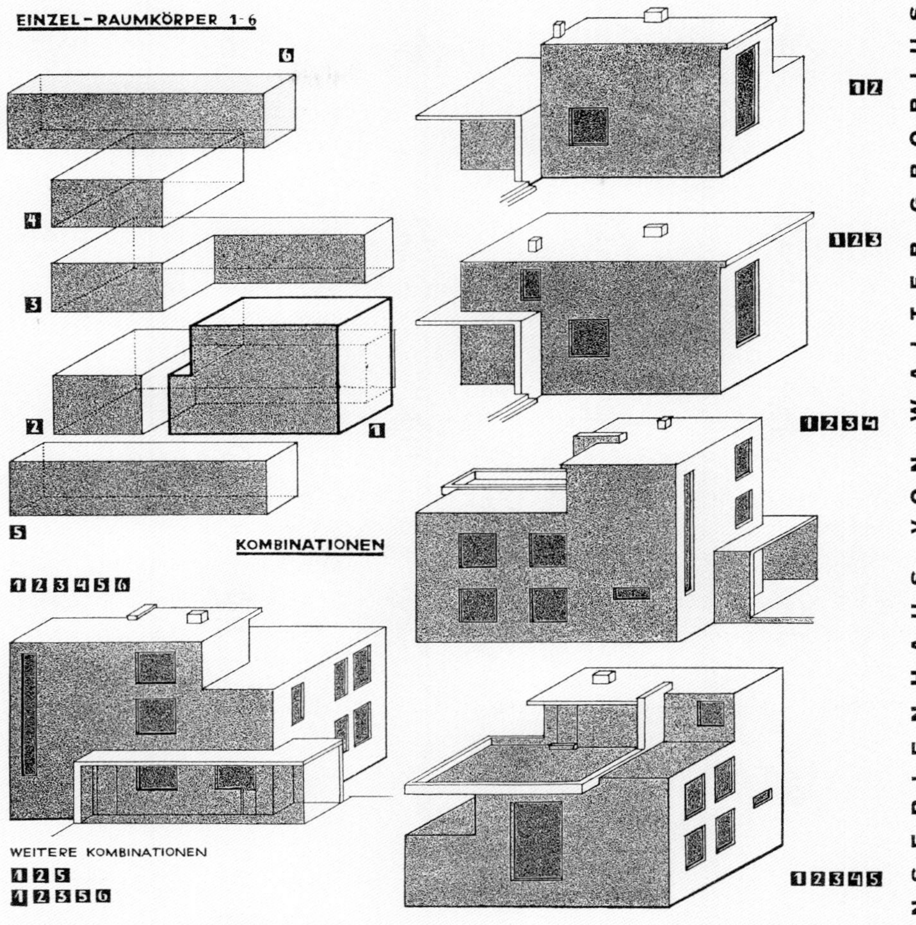

TYPENSERIENHAUS VON WALTER GROPIUS

BAUKASTEN IM GROSSEN, AUS DEM SICH NACH VORBEREITETEN MONTAGEPLÄNEN JE NACH KOPFZAHL UND BEDÜRFNIS DER BEWOHNER VERSCHIEDENE „WOHNMASCHINEN“ ZUSAMMENFÜGEN LASSEN

Below: Richard Buckminster Fuller, Dymaxion House, project, c. 1927

Opposite: George Fred Keck and William Keck, "House of Tomorrow" at the *Century of Progress Exposition*, Chicago, 1933

Following spread: A prefabricated house with carport by Erik Georg Friberger, Sweden, 1936

something new that people were not used to. It is therefore not surprising that a critic for the New York Sun snidely referred to it as a "canned house," arguing, "If father wants a new door cut through to his room he doesn't get a saw. He gets a can opener." Innovative companies founded in the 1930s, like American Homes, American Houses, Inc., or the Homosote Company, soon went bankrupt. The building industry in those years focused mainly on the task of erecting living space as quickly, cheaply, and simply as possible. The order books of Sears and Aladdin were full, and they saw no need to adapt the traditional formal language of their house models to Modernism.

While the prefabricated steel house continued to play a subordinate role in private residential construction, the situation in the military context was quite different. In order to create easily transportable housing for the troops

of the United States Army, the engineers Peter Dejongh and Otto Brandenberger designed the so-called Quonset Hut for the George A. Fuller Construction Company in 1941. Reminiscent in its tunnel-like shape of the Nissen Huts used by the British military in the First World War, it was named after the naval air base at Quonset Point, Rhode Island, where it was originally produced. The prefabricated hut consisted of a skeleton of round arches, clad in galvanized corrugated sheet metal, and had a plywood floor. Many of the roughly 170,000 housing units that were produced have survived to this day in the United States: as factory halls, simple churches, or shops. The concept was never accepted for the construction of private houses. However, the modernistic church that Bruce Goff designed in 1945 on the basis of one of them in Camp Parks, California, did become famous, as did the studio house that the French avant-garde architect

The Armco-Ferro-Mayflower House, a steel structure designed by Robert Smith Jr. and presented at the *Century of Progress Exposition* in Chicago, 1933, was presumably the first house to feature porcelain enamel siding

Pierre Chareau designed for the American painter Robert Motherwell on the basis of two Quonset building kits in 1946, which featured full-length windows flooded with light.

The prefabricated housing industry received tremendous impetus after President Roosevelt established the Federal Housing Agency in 1942, which was responsible for creating housing for the many workers in the defense industry who were deployed at locations far from home. After the war, the agency was responsible for promoting building programs to satisfy the demand for living space on the part of soldiers returning from Europe and the Far East. This is where the two German architects Walter Gropius and Konrad Wachsmann saw a chance for the panel system they had developed in the early 1930s for Christoph & Unmack, one of the largest producers of wooden barracks in Europe. After emigrating to the United States, they had developed a prefabricated house out of preassembled panel elements for General Panel Corporation, a company they jointly founded in 1941. However, the hope that they would be able to sell 10,000 units per year was never fulfilled. Fewer than 200 houses were produced, and even fewer of them were sold.

After the Second World War there was a regular prefabricated housing boom in the United States. Some 70 companies were active in this market segment in the postwar era, ultimately leading to the construction of roughly 200,000 prefabricated houses. However, companies such as Vultee, Lustron, and the Spartan Aircraft Company, which offered buildings built on the basis of steel frames or clad in sheet metal, were still not able to survive. Companies that limited themselves to more conventional forms and materials were more successful, and, correspondingly, most of the prefabricated houses were clad in shingles and had pitched roofs. When Gropius's student Carl Koch developed his first prefabricated house in 1948, he equipped it in the best Bauhaus tradition with a flat roof. When it failed to sell, he developed his Techbuilt House, this time of course with a pitched roof—and he was soon successful.

The situation in Europe was more difficult: although millions of people had no place to live on the Old Continent due to the destruction of the Second World War, people were reluctant to accept prefabricated construction. In Germany, which had not only lost 25 % of its entire housing stock to bombing, but also had to integrate 12 million refugees from former German territories in Eastern Europe, one form of prefabricated housing was used extensively: the Nissen Hut. This was a barracks-like emergency shelter made of corrugated sheet metal with an arched roof, which had already been developed during the First World War by the Canadian engineer Peter Norman Nissen. Thousands of them were erected on the periphery of cities and towns and became the architectural symbol of the misery of postwar Germany. A sense of the provisional and of desperation associated with those years is possibly what later prevented people in Germany from believing in prefabricated houses—people wanted nothing more than a secure roof over their heads and to be surrounded by sturdy walls.

An attempt was also made in postwar France to combat housing shortages with the help of prefabricated houses. In 1944, Jean Prouvé was already commissioned by the Ministry of Reconstruction and Urban Planning to build 800 houses as emergency shelters that could be easily disassembled. However, only 400 of these Maisons à portique (Porch Houses), which were equipped with an axial steel frame, were ever erected. Again commissioned by the government, Prouvé developed a series of aluminum clad lightweight steel houses based on the same principle, but only a few were ever erected because they were more expensive than expected. Prouvé's Alba houses, developed for the Abbey Pierre's homeless organization in 1956, were also not a success.

The 1960s were a period of social transition in which attitudes towards prefabricated housing also changed. During this era, which was marked by space travel, the moon landing, and even children's books that predicted weekend trips to

Below: Prefabricated houses for workers on a dam in Victoria, Australia, 1947

Opposite: Quonset Huts in London, UK, 1944

distant galaxies, prefabricated construction was discovered both as a form of artistic expression and as a technical means of creating houses to provide a basis for new lifestyles, which seemed to be imminent in a society characterized by an extremely optimistic view of progress. One of the houses of the era of space travel was La Bulle six coques (Bubble of six shells) by the French architect Jean Maneval, which was used for an entire colony of holiday homes in the Pyrenean Mountains in 1967, literally making it look like the site of an invasion from outer space. The spaceship-like pavilions, called Futuro, made of fiberglass reinforced polyester and designed by the Finnish architect Matti Suuronen in 1968, also look somehow intergalactic.

These approaches led to the ideal of creating megastructures out of residential capsules: the architect Moshe Safdie, who was only 24 at the time, presented his megastructure Habitat 67 at the *Expo 67* in Montreal: 158 housing units consisting of 354 concrete modules assembled as a conglomerate. The British architectural group Archigram developed building structures made of residential capsules as an architectural utopia, which could be expanded at will and joined to-

gether to form entire cities. In 1972, the Japanese architect Kisho Kurokawa built the Nakagin Capsule Tower in Tokyo; housing cells were layered around a prefabricated concrete core to form a fourteen-story residential tower. The idea of residential capsule megastructures was repeatedly revived, as in Zvi Hecker's Ramot housing development in Jerusalem in 1974.

In addition, architects given to experimentation developed studies for houses that included elements of prefabricated construction, but which nevertheless remained one of a kind. Representatives of British high-tech architecture such as Alison and Peter Smithson, Richard Rogers, and Norman Foster developed concepts for building techniques aimed at greater flexibility and technical refinement as a result of their fascination with factory-produced metal and plastic components, without seriously being interested in seeing their designs produced in series. This was true of Richard Rogers's Zip-Up House (1968), a bright yellow residential box resting on pink legs, which featured aluminium panels connected by neoprene gaskets and reminded one of the Beatles' "Yellow Submarine." In 1984 Richard Horden adopted the aluminium

Below: Demountable employee housing by the Tennessee Valley Authority: houses were constructed in fully equipped slices, which were transported individually and connected to each other on the site

Opposite: Trailer House, as demountable employee housing, commissioned by the Tennessee Valley Authority and built between 1933 and 1945

Following spread: Case Study House No. 8, the Eames House, was designed by Charles and Ray Eames for their own use and erected in Pacific Palisades, California, 1945–1949

mast used as a load-bearing element in his Yacht House, a lightweight grid structure, from shipbuilding and suspended the roof and wall panels from it.

The ecology movement of the 1970s brought an end to this euphoria with regard to technological progress and futuristic architectural dreams. Now, highly modern building materials that did not seem to be in harmony with a return to nature—such as plastic or aluminum—fell into disrepute. This was further exacerbated by the fact that prefabricated elements had often been used to build high-density housing, which was now generally viewed negatively. Hence, prefabricated building now came to be associated with the aesthetic and social failure of de-individualized, megalomaniac, prefabricated slab housing blocks clustered on the periphery of large cities.

Thus, the acceptance of the prefabricated house in large parts of Europe remained

Below: Paul Rudolph's Wilson Residence, dubbed the Honeycomb House, in Sarasota, Florida, 1953, was built using prefabricated honeycomb panels made of paper

Opposite: Poster for a prefab exhibit 1947 in Stuttgart, Germany

low up until the 1990s. Nevertheless, many very successful prefabricated houses were built. Manufacturers of prefabricated homes in Germany repeatedly hired ambitious architects for individual series, such as Otto Leitner, who developed the Ideal Haus for the Kaufhof chain of department stores in 1961. It was built by the Johann Huf carpentry workshop as a flat-roofed building resting on supports, clad in wood, with a panorama window, a porch swing seat, and an outdoor pool. In 1972, Manfred Adam, a student of Sep Ruf's, also designed the equally successful and timelessly beautiful model called the Fachwerkhaus 2000 for Huf. The prefabricated house called Tanja, designed in 1970 by Heinrich B. Hellmuth for the Schneckenburger company in Rottenburg, represented an interesting approach with its spacious layout and expressive pitched roof. However, such ambitious prestige projects cannot conceal the fact that many prefabricated

EXPORTMUSTERSCHAU - VERSUCHSSIEDLUNG
DAS
FERTIGHAUS
STUTTGART-ZUFFENHAUSEN
TÄGLICH GEÖFFNET VON 10-21 UHR

The "House of the Future" at Disneyland in Anaheim, California, 1957, was an experiment in building with plastics

houses seemed provisional, banal or akin to barracks; the producers often attempted to make the product appear to be unique by adding elements that seemed to be individual.

Prefabricated construction only gradually began to again emancipate itself from a homespun, cheap, mass-produced image during the 1990s. This is mainly due to the use of computer-operated programs in the design and production processes. The prefabricated housing industry now stands at a juncture reminiscent of the dynamism of the 1920s and 1930s. In the meantime, even star architects such as Daniel Libeskind have designed prefabricated houses, and these are produced and equipped according to state-of-the-art ecological criteria. Unlike the case during the early modernist period, planners' visions are now no longer threatened by failure due to inadequate building technology. Today it is a very short path from computer-aided design (CAD) to the computer-controlled production of building components with previously

unimaginable precision. It is now impossible to build a passive house, for example, without using prefabricated components that can only be produced within tolerances of less than a millimeter by using CAD. The tools used in industrial production are so flexible that the components no longer need to be slavishly standardized as was the case in traditional production, and measurements can now be easily varied.

In the meantime, houses are emerging in Europe, Asia, and in North and South America, that are particularly interesting in terms of design. Rocio Romero's LV House (2000) for instance, or the weeHouse by Alchemy Architects (2003), appear to be the most recent reinterpretations of Ludwig Mies van der Rohe's Farnsworth House. For many years now, companies like Muji in Japan or BoKlok in Scandinavia—and more recently also in Poland and England—have been supplying prefabricated houses in large numbers. In Sweden alone, with only nine million inhabitants, 14,000 units are

Below: A standard 20 ft. shipping container was recycled for Adam Kalkin's Push-button House, 2007

Opposite: Single family houses by IKEA/BoKlok in a conservative style

sold every year. Muji offers models designed by Kengo Kuma and Kazuhiko Namba that are as simple as they are elegant, and far more interesting than the building-kit houses offered by the multinational concerns Mitsubishi, Toyota, and Panasonic. Katsu Umebayashi of F.O.B. Architects in Kyoto established the company F.O.B. Homes along with his colleague Kazu Kobayashi in Tokyo in 1999 in order to develop a modernistic prefabricated house that can be individually adapted to the clients' requirements, in terms of both the building's volume and the layout of the rooms, by the company's own team of designers.

In view of questions regarding energy consumption, recycling, sustainability, and cost efficiency, ideas like Adam Kalkin's concept of constructing houses entirely out of decommissioned shipping containers emerge. The basic version of his Quik House consists of six reusable cargo containers. The individual modules are assembled using a crane in one day; the house is ready for habitation within three months. The perforations required for doors and windows are made beforehand in consultation with the customer. Including heating and plumbing fixtures, the basic version of the Quik House, with three bedrooms, two bathrooms, and a total of 2,000 sq. ft. of floor space, costs roughly $184,000. Kalkin does not really act as an architect, but instead offers the customer a system that allows them to assemble their own living containers. However, concepts of this type have their limits. A decommissioned container can be purchased for roughly €2,000, while a new one from the factory costs roughly €4,000. An old container intended for conversion is dented and rusty and requires extensive refurbishment: doors and windows must be cut out and sufficient insulation must be provided. Transportation ultimately costs roughly €9.00 per mile, and a crane is needed to install the container modules on site. This is a clear indication of how an idea, which is interesting from the standpoint of recycling, becomes problematic not only in economic terms, but also ecologically, in terms of the carbon footprint made by refurbishment and transport.

What will the prefabricated house of the future look like? Will it have a steel frame or be a wooden structure, built as a skeleton or panel system? Or will there be yet again a greater tendency to shift to the old idea of the "residential cell" and to favor residential units that can be easily moved and quickly deployed anywhere? The modernist ideals of producing intelligently designed, bright, and low-cost living spaces are currently being revitalized. In 1929, the visionary architect Richard Buckminster Fuller was asked whether the mass production of residential buildings would ultimately lead to architects' losing their jobs. Fuller responded: "The architect's efforts today are spent in the gratification of the individual client. His efforts of tomorrow, like those of the composer, the designer of fabrics, silver, glass and whatnot may be expanded for the enjoyment of vast numbers of unseen clients. Industrial production of housing, as contrasted with the present industrial production of raw materials and miscellaneous accessories, calls for more skill and a higher development of the design element, not its cessation."

FROM 1830s
PORTABLE COTTAGES

TO TODAY'S
ESSENTIAL HOMES

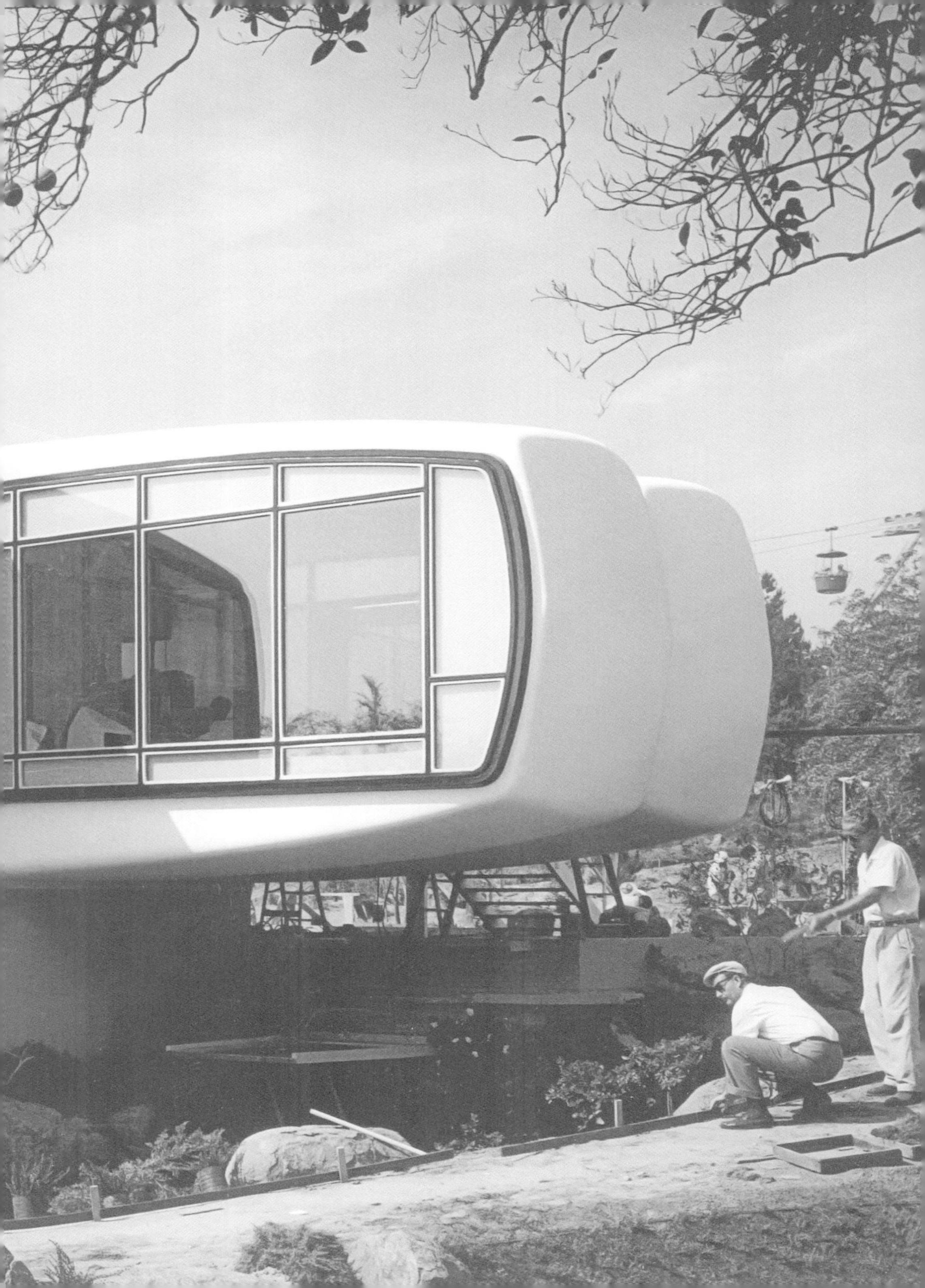

MANNING PORTABLE COLONIAL COTTAGE

Herbert Manning
London, Great Britain, 1833–1840

Around 1833 a London carpenter named Herbert Manning designed a portable, easy-to-assemble wooden house for his son, who intended to emigrate to Australia. The cottage had a wooden frame and a pitched roof. The supporting posts and beams were already cut to length and could be screwed together on site. The roof was made of tent canvas. Grooves were cut into the posts, which stood about a yard apart, so that the prefabricated full-length wall, door, and window panels could be fitted into them.

Since the wave of immigration from England to Australia began to swell in the years after 1833, there was suddenly a great demand for portable, easy-to-assemble housing of the type that Manning had developed. An advertisement for Manning's "Portable Colonial Cottages" published in the *South Australian Record* on November 27, 1837, is the first evidence of his entrepreneurial initiative, and Manning actually did ship dozens of prefabricated cottages to Australia in subsequent years. The fact that the building components could be easily transported over great distances contributed to the success of the cottages. In the Australian city of Melbourne, the Manning Cottage built in 1839 for Charles La Trobe, who later became the Lieutenant Governor of Victoria, can still be viewed with many of its original furnishings. Long before the word "prefabrication" even

existed, Manning had developed a system that worked by precisely adhering to standard measurements. With panels, posts, and plates that each had the same length, breadth, and thickness, and thus could be easily installed, Manning created the prototype of the modern prefabricated house.

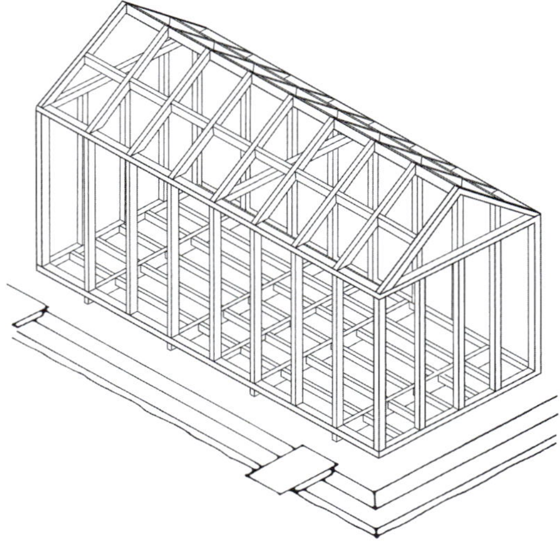

Opposite: Lieutenant Governor Charles La Trobe's house, Jolimont (Melbourne), 1839–1840

Above: Watercolor of Lieutenant Governor Charles La Trobe's house by R. A. Bastow, 1913

Following spread: Quaker Meeting House, North Adelaide, 1840

HODGSON HOUSES

Ernest Franklin Hodgson
E. F. Hodgson Company
Dover, Massachusetts, USA, 1894–1944

Ernest Franklin Hodgson, the son of a farmer from Massachusetts, began breeding poultry at an early age and was soon building his own brooders and chicken coops. In 1891, at the age of 21, Hodgson began producing his "Peep-o'-Day portable coops and brooders" in series on his father's property in the town of Dover, near Boston. Using a simple building system based on prefabricated wooden elements joined by wedge key bolts instead of nails, he soon began building dog houses, pigeon coops, tool sheds, and, finally, the one-room "Hodgson Camp Cottage," which he offered in his first mail order catalog in 1894. The introduction of a garage that could be built quickly and easily in 1900, the "Hodgson Auto Stable," was particular successful. In 1902, Hodgson brought his "Portable Vacation Cottages" onto the market, and they were soon followed by larger houses.

Despite the rapidly growing competition—e.g. as of 1908 from the Sears Roebuck mail-order catalog company—business flourished. A Hodgson Bungalow was even depicted in newspaper advertisements published by the Boston Edison Company in 1908, illustrating the advantages of electricity. A year later, Hodgson delivered 20 prefabricated houses to Messina, Sicily, in order to provide shelter for the victims of a flood. Hodgson built hospitals, schools, churches and, above all, residential buildings that were attractively presented to customers in Boston, New York, and other large cities in newspaper advertisements and at exhibitions.

The catalog ultimately offered four different models with designates that reflected their floor plans, namely I, T, L, and H. They all had one-story and were based on the same system of 6 × 12 ft. wooden elements used for the walls (with a window or a door where needed), the roof, and the floor. The walls and ceilings consisted of red cedar rabbeted boarding backed with a heavy fiber lining, and the floors were of hard pine. All of the elements were either of exposed wood or painted: if the customer did not choose otherwise, the walls were gray, the window frames ivory, and the decorative ornaments leaf green. All that was needed to build the house was a hammer in order to connect the building parts by means of the wedge key bolts.

Clients could opt to have Hodgson or a local company install heating, bathrooms, toilets or even an open fireplace, features that, even by the 1930s, were by no means considered basic amenities in houses in rural America.

Ernest Franklin Hodgson, who proudly referred to himself as "America's First prefabricator," sold the Hodgson Company in 1944. He died four years later; the company he founded continued to exist under various names until 1995.

Opposite: Wedge key bolts used to assemble a house

Below: Hodgson House in Reedsville, West Virginia, around 1936

Following spreads: Pages from the Hodgson Houses catalogs for 1920 and 1908

All the 12 foot wide houses shown in this catalog are made
porches, ells, valley roofs, etc., it is possible to make up most a
the catalog you can figure out any special combination, or ma

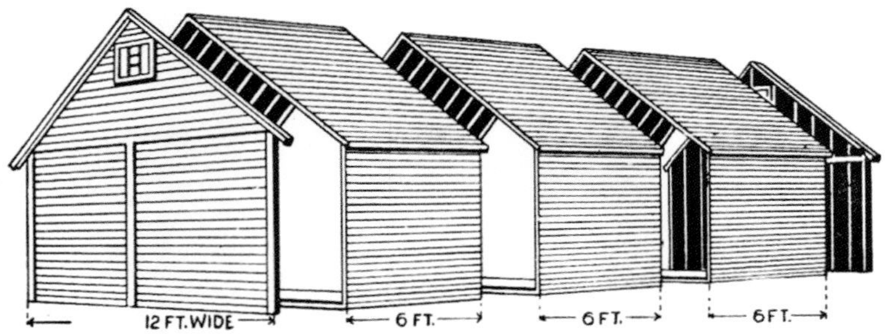

Blank Units (disjointed)

This drawi
12 units an
If put tog
make a hou
prices of th
are in the
the prices o
should be a
the windo
etc., these d
below. All
back of the

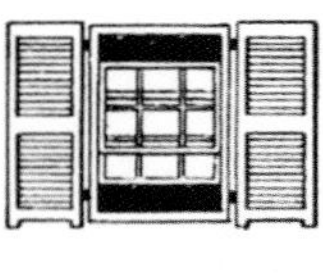

SRW B W B DW CW DCW

These drawings show the different styles of windows, door
where desired, and the prices will be found in the back of the

Window and Door Detail:—S. R. W.—Sunroom Window;
C. W.—Casement Window; D. C. W.—Casement Window Dia
Glass Door; D. G. D.—Dutch Glass Door; F. G. D.—French
—Crescent shutters hinged like blinds.

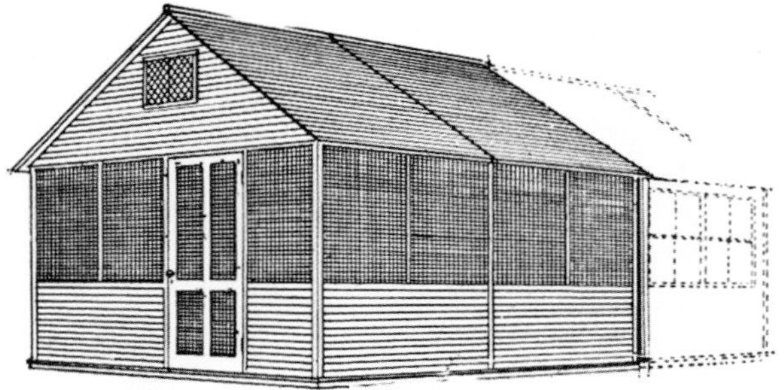

Screened Room Unit 12 x 12 ft.
See pages 26-28-32-50

SCREENED ROOM UNIT

Screened room units are the same size and price as the regular units and the prices include the screens made of galvanized netting. They can be attached to the regular units or made into buildings by themselves as shown on pages 82 and 83. With Storm Awnings, as shown on page 50 will give protection from sun and storms.

PRICES IN BACK

ıit System

6 x 12 ft. units as shown and described here, so that with the
rangement of rooms desired. With the price list in the back of
anges in those shown.

ws three 6 x
12 ft. ends.
they would
x 18 ft. The
its and ends
list, and to
e blank units
the prices of
oors, blinds,
being shown
s are in the
log.

PARTITIONS

These 12 ft. partitions can be used at any of the junctions of the 6 ft. units, thereby forming rooms 6, 12, and 18 ft. in length. The opening is furnished with a curtain pole, but if a door is preferred consult the price list. The opening can be at either side or centre of the partition and can be changed at will.

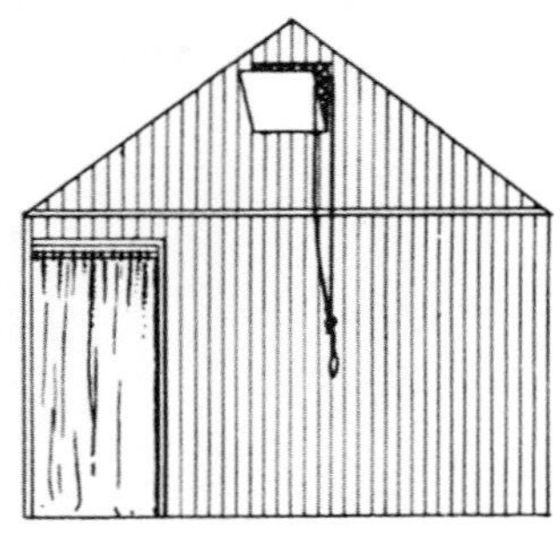

Partitions—See pages 43 and 50

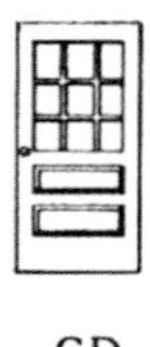
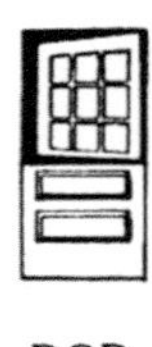
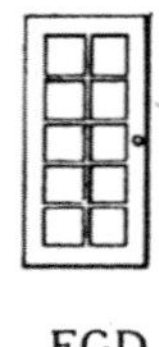

PD GD DGD FGD SS CS

. that are used in our houses. These can be located in the units
og.
—Regular Window; B.—Blinds; D. W.—Diamond Light Window;
Lights; T. W.—Transom Window; P. D.—Panel Door; G. D.—
Door; R. D.—Door to roll; S. S.—Solid Shutter to bolt on; C. S.

LEY ROOF UNIT

y Roof units are
to add rooms at
angles to other
s. If a house has
al rooms it is wise
se a valley roof
r than to run too
rooms in one line.
s use a more prac-
arrangement of
s may be had.

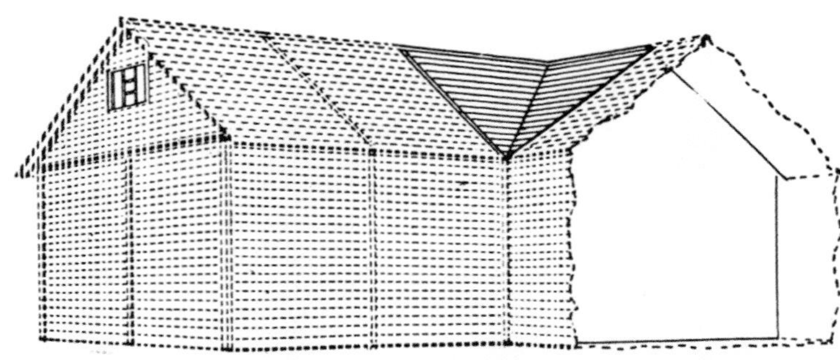

Valley Roof Unit. See pages 34-40-44-46-49

For Hip Roofs, in place of gables, add $10.00 per end or $20 more for a complete hip roof. (See pages 40-46.)

Wigwarm Frame Construction

WIGWARM CONSTRUCTION

The Wigwarm construction is different from that of other portable houses. Practically speaking, it is a framed house, although lighter than the regularly built house, its frame work is much closer together, making a very strong construction. Washington ceder and fir are used with door and window frames moulded out of heavy fir stock.

Each house is made up of several sections and they are fastened together with Wigwarm key bolts of special design, and with one blow of a hammer the wedge key tightens up the bolt, saving much time and annoyance during erection or taking apart. The frames are covered with a very heavy waterproof fibre (Wigwarm lining) and then with the Wigwarm special milled, narrow, rabbeted siding not over three to four inches in width. This siding is milled especially for the Wigwarm houses out of California redwood, and is fastened to the frame with Wigwarm galvanized, cement-coated nails. In the construction of one of the small sized Wigwarm houses (10 x 12 feet) over three thousand nails are used. So rigid is its construction that they have withstood gales on the New England coast that have destroyed many staunch buildings about them. Many times sections of the Wigwarm Houses have remained out on the ground unprotected, for three days at a time, with heavy rains, yet when set up they have gone together without the slightest trouble. This construction, although expensive, will not warp or twist, so that a building can be set up any number of times without trouble.

Every house is set up at the factory and the sections stamped, and with the printed directions and plan it is easily put together by unskilled labor without other tools than a screw driver and hammer. All necessary hardware is furnished, and strap irons to fasten them to the foundation. All through the entire construction nothing but the best of lumber, free from defects and knots, is used. In order to make the most perfect portable construction known today practically all the materials entering into the Wigwarm construction are made especially for Wigwarm Houses. Cheaper construction and materials could be used, but the houses would not stand up and would disappoint the person buying them.

Detailed construction of the different sections used to make up a house is given on pages 10 and 11.

WIGWARM COTTAGES

These two combinations include three large rooms, an ell, and front and side porches. For description of porches and ell, see page 28. Cottage furnishings page 12. Freight rates page 46.

ELL 6½×6
ROOM 10×12
ROOM 10×12
SIDE PORCH 6×12
ROOM 10×12
FRONT PORCH 10×6

Combination No. 85

Combination No. 85

One Room 10 x 12 feet	$130
Two Additional Rooms each 10 x 12 feet	220
One Front Porch 6 x 10 feet	35
One Side Porch (one door) 6 x 12 feet	30
One Ell 6 x 6½ feet	40
Total weight, 4,150 lbs. Total,	$455

Combination No. 86

One Room 12 x 12 feet	$155
Two Additional Rooms, each 12 x 12 feet	260
One Front Porch 6 x 12 feet	45
One Side Porch (one door) 6 x 12 feet	30
One Ell 6 x 8½ feet	50
Total weight, 5,050 lbs. Total,	$540

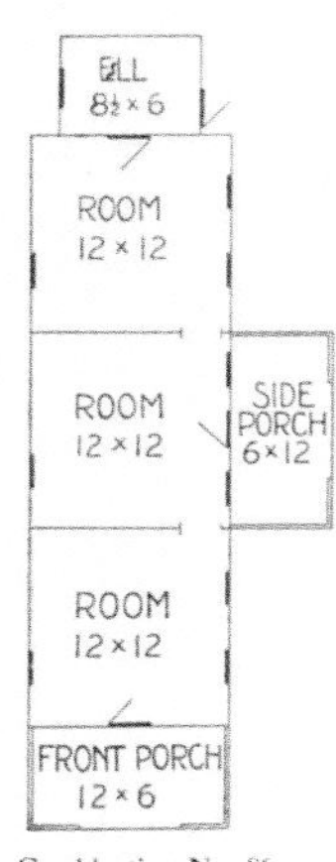

Combination No. 86

Wigwarm Cottage—Three Rooms, Front and Side Porch and Ell

Above: Hodgson House in East Dennis, Massachusetts

Below and opposite: Hodgson Houses in Bristol, Maine

EINSTEIN HOUSE

Konrad Wachsmann
Christoph & Unmack AG
Niesky, Germany, 1929

In early 1929 the City of Berlin launched a plan to honor Albert Einstein on his fiftieth birthday by presenting the avid sailor with a lakefront site, on which he could build a summer house. The young architect Konrad Wachsmann read about the plans in a newspaper, which also reported that the Nobel laureate favored wooden houses. As an employee of Christoph & Unmack, a company in Niesky specialized in the construction of wooden barracks, he saw this as the chance of a lifetime and contacted the Einsteins. He was actually able to win their confidence, and within a few weeks he advanced to the position of their most trusted advisor in questions of building sites and housing construction. While the city fathers' plans to give the famous scientist a building site fell victim to all sorts of infighting, Einstein bought a piece of land on his own

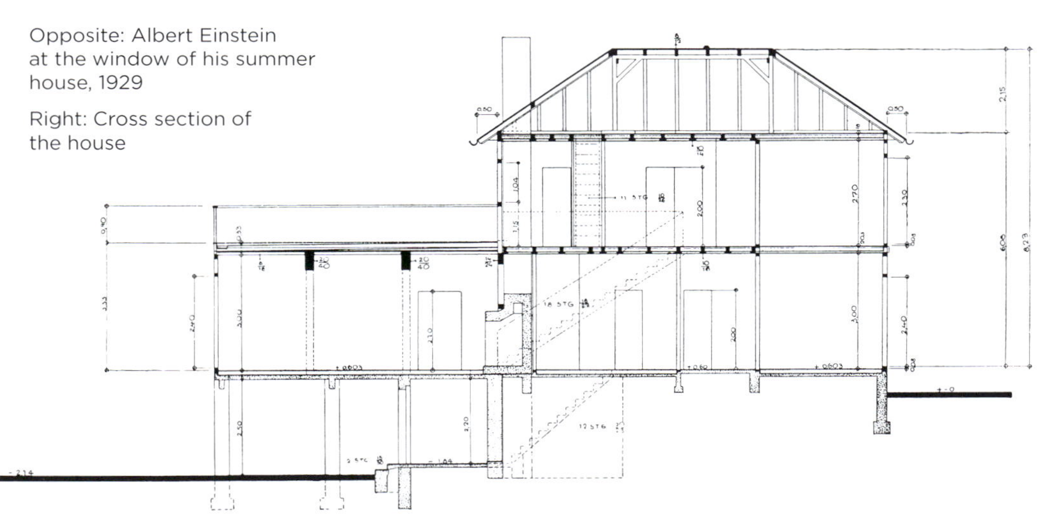

Opposite: Albert Einstein at the window of his summer house, 1929

Right: Cross section of the house

on a hill near Caputh, a town south of Potsdam between two of the Havel lakes. In Konrad Wachsmann he already had the architect for his house.

Wachsmann's structure combined stationary timber framing with a wooden panel construction. The architect used fir from Galicia for the outer cladding; the interior walls were clad in plywood and panels made with a lignin resin. Slabs of peat were sandwiched in between these two layers as insulation. Particularly striking were the two 30 ft. supporting beams of Oregon pine, imported from America, that ran through the living room. The full-length, white French doors made the house seem elegant and airy. The house was not one of those produced in series, but essential elements were prefabricated by Christoph & Unmack, assembled in a trial run in a production hall in Niesky, and then taken apart again before being transported to the building site.

In September of 1929 Einstein was able to move into his new abode. Although planned as a summer house, Einstein spent more time there than in his city flat, before emigrating to the United States (1932). The Einstein House was recently renovated and now serves as a center for scientific conferences.

Opposite: View of the garden

Above: View over the terrace

Right: Longitudinal section of the house

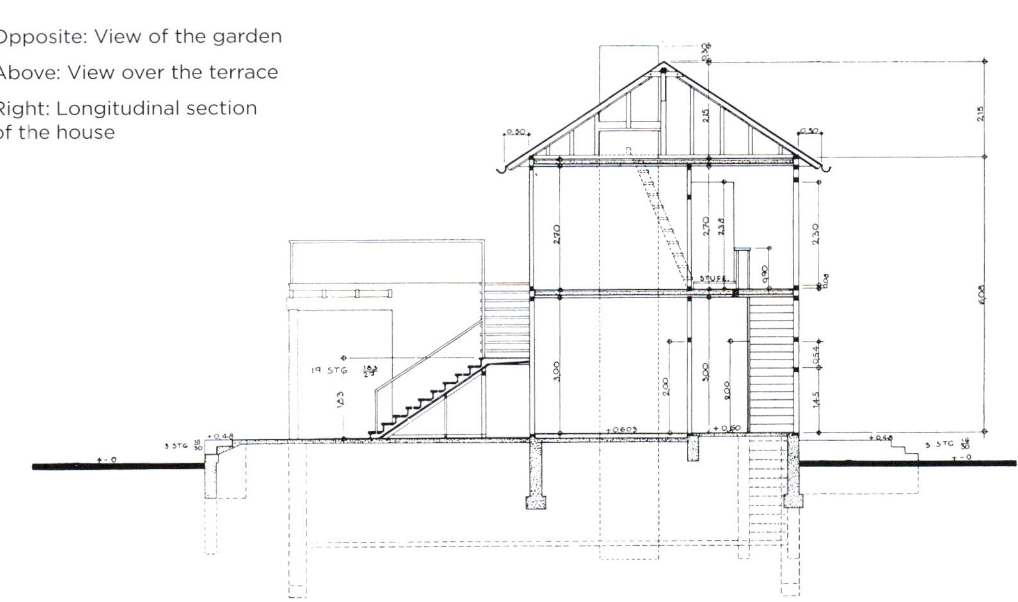

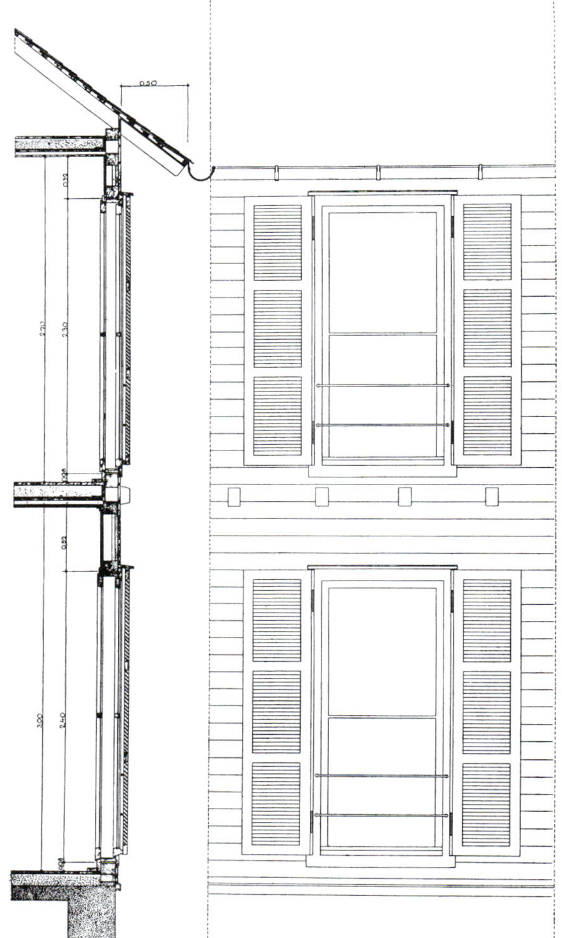

The kitchen with the serving hatch (opposite) and the built-in cupboard in the living room with the serving hatch closed and open (above)

Left: Elevation and section of a façade element

Following spread: View of the terrace from the living room

ALUMINAIRE

Albert Frey, A. Lawrence Kocher
New York, USA, 1931

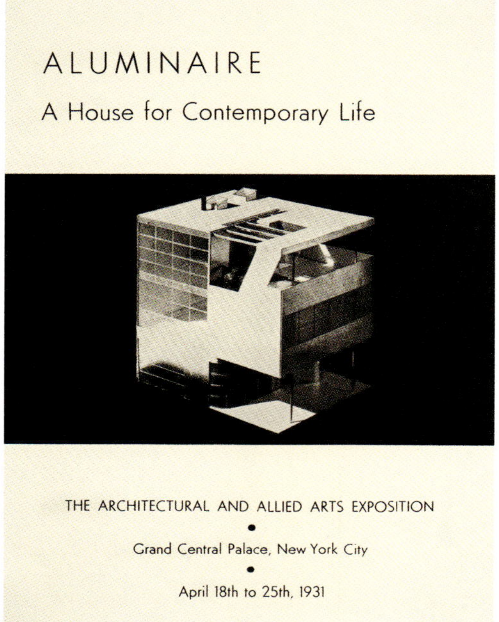
ALUMINAIRE

A House for Contemporary Life

THE ARCHITECTURAL AND ALLIED ARTS EXPOSITION

•

Grand Central Palace, New York City

•

April 18th to 25th, 1931

The Aluminaire house by Albert Frey was first shown in an exhibition hall. The three-story building made of aluminum, glass, and steel was shown at the *Allied Arts and Building Products Exhibition*, which was staged at the Grand Central Palace in New York from April 18—25, 1931. According to contemporary reports, it was the only exciting item exhibited at an otherwise rather boring building trade show.

Albert Frey was born in Switzerland and had worked in Le Corbusier's Paris office between 1928 and 1930, where he also helped to draw the building plans for the Villa Savoye. The creative roots and the experimental character of the Aluminaire are easily recognizable against this background. At the same time, the house was an advertisement for modern building materials from a variety of manufacturers.

The three-story steel skeleton frame structure was clad in low-gauge corrugated aluminum to which panels of insulation were attached. The doors and the frames of the ribbon windows were made of steel, the floors were made of rolled steel plates covered with insulation and black linoleum. The entire load was distributed onto six support pipes, strongly reminiscent of Le Corbusier's *"pilotis."* The two-story living room on the first floor was particularly impressive: measuring over 16 ft. in height, it was fully glazed on one side.

The Aluminaire was designed as a prefabricated house that—if roughly 10,000 were produced—could be offered at a price of $3,200.

Page 62, top: Brochure presenting the house at the 1931 *Architectural and Allied Arts Exhibition*

Page 62, bottom: Perspective view

Page 63 and below: The Aluminaire on the grounds of Wallace K. Harrison's country house in Syosset, New York

However, it never was produced in series. Directly after the exhibition, the New York architect Wallace K. Harrison, who was known for having designed the Rockefeller Center and the Lincoln Center, purchased the prototype for $1,000 and installed it on the grounds of his country home in Syosset on Long Island. A year later, Henry-Russell Hitchcock and Philip Johnson presented photographs and drawings of the Aluminaire in their seminal *International Exhibition of Modern Architecture* at the Museum of Modern Art in New York. Along with Richard Neutra's Lovell House (1927–1929), it was one of only two works in the exhibition by an American architect.

The house has had a turbulent history. It was repeatedly moved and reconstructed on Harrison's property. After Harrison's death in 1981, his country home was sold and the new owner rented the Aluminaire to tenants who had to be evicted by force five years later so that it could be torn down. On the initiative of the architectural historian Joseph Rosa, who was working on a book about Frey at that time, the house was saved and painstakingly restored on the Central Islip Campus of the New York University of Technology. However, the Aluminaire's odyssey did not end there: in 2003 the architectural department at Central Islip was closed. The search for a new location culminated in its dismantling and reassembly in Palm Springs, California, in 2024.

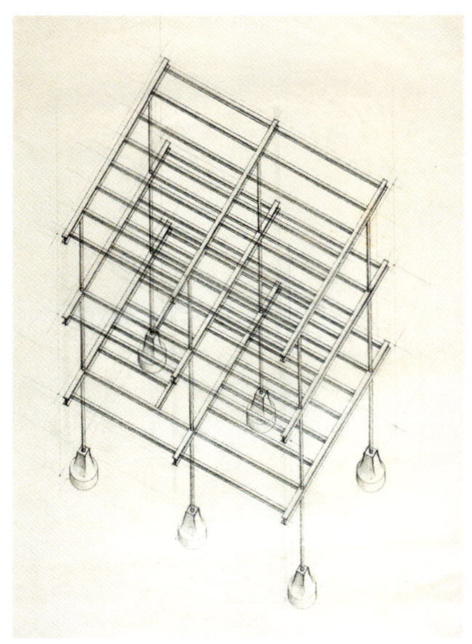

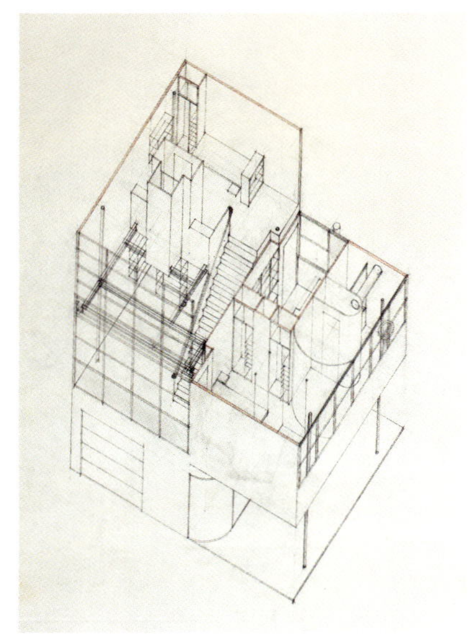

Above left: Axonometric drawing showing structural framework

Above right: The axonometric drawing shows the two story living room

Right: Reconstruction of the Aluminaire on the Central Islip Campus of the New York Institute of Technology in 1991

A rendering of the house appeared in a 1931 issue of *Popular Mechanics*

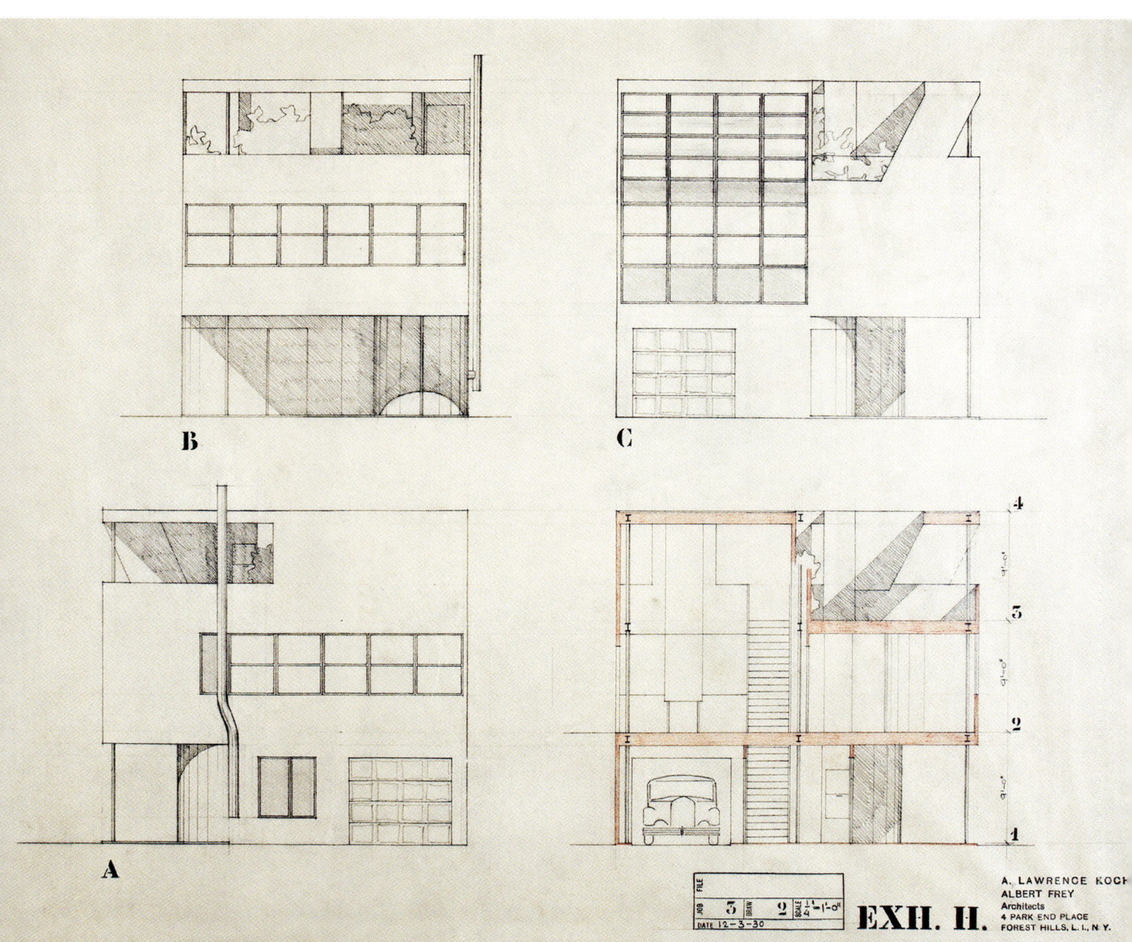

Above: Elevation and cross section

Opposite: Roof terrace of the Aluminaire in Syosset, 1932

Above: Sketch of the entryway (above) and the kitchen (below)

Opposite: Perspectival sketch of the library and the dining room

Following spread: Plans and roof elevation

glass

LIBRARY

DINING ROOM

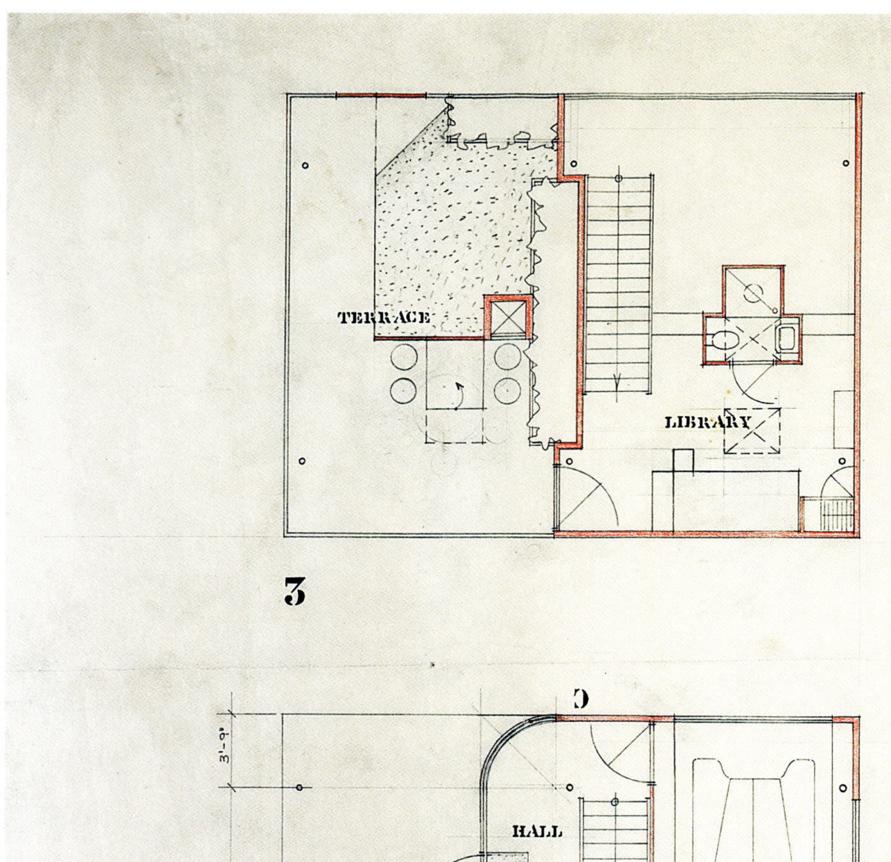

TERRACE
LIBRARY
3
C
3'-9"
15'-0"
3'-9"
B
HALL
PORCH
GAR.
HEAT.
STOR.
A
11"
13'-5½"
13'-5½"
11"
1

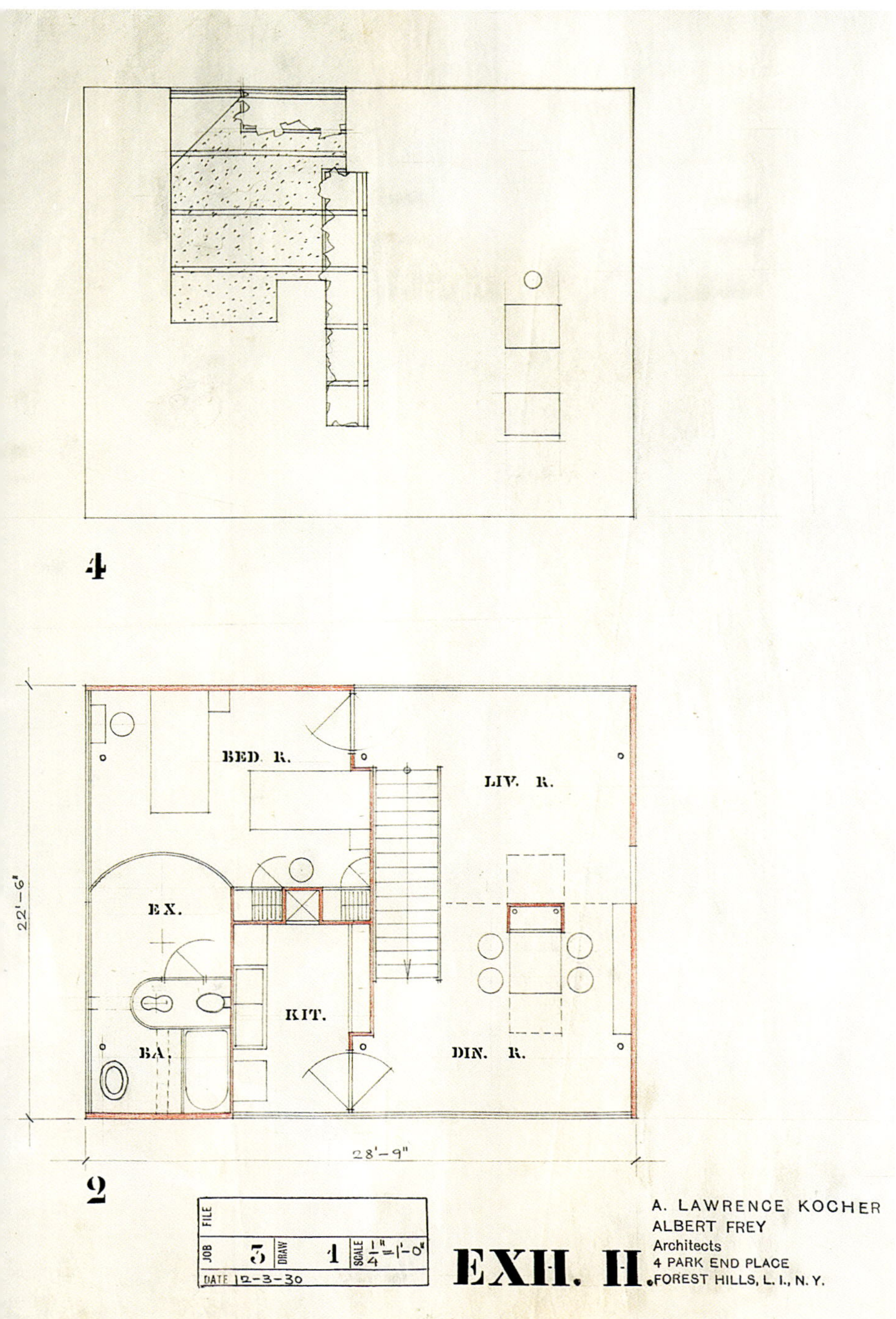
4
BED. R.
LIV. R.
EX.
KIT.
BA.
DIN. R.
22'-6"
28'-9"
2
FILE
JOB 3
DRAW 1
SCALE 1/4"=1'-0"
DATE 12-3-30
EXH. II.
A. LAWRENCE KOCHER
ALBERT FREY
Architects
4 PARK END PLACE
FOREST HILLS, L. I., N. Y.

KUPFERHAUS

Robert Krafft, Friedrich Förster, Walter Gropius
Hirsch Kupfer- und Messingwerke
Eberswalde, Germany, 1931–1934

Opposite: The house models *Juwel* (Jewel), *Kupfermärchen* (Copper Fairy Tale) and *Maienmorgen* (May Morning) in front of the water tower in Eberswalde, 1931

Following spread: Catalog of the Hirsch Copper and Brass Works, 1931

The Hirsch Kupfer- und Messingwerke (Hirsch Copper and Brass Works) in Eberswalde began producing prefabricated all-copper houses developed by the architect Robert Krafft and the engineer Friedrich Förster in 1930. Because of its relatively light weight and high resistance to fire and corrosion, copper is particularly suitable for prefabricated house construction, and it is as easy to assemble as it is durable. A façade of narrow Eternit panels was built up over wooden framing and then covered with ribbed sheets of copper and insulated with aluminum foil. A patented universal end piece made the panels easy to screw together; the edges were then concealed by copper molding. Originally, sheet copper—with a diamond pattern—was also used for the roof.

The interior walls were clad in embossed sheet metal. The purchasers were able to enjoy a completely furnished kitchen, pre-installed plumbing fixtures, and central heating; they were also able to choose six different diamond patterns embossed into the sheet metal wall cladding in colors such as pastel blue, Nile green, or coral red. The heat build-up originally feared by contemporaries was not a problem, but there was interference with radio reception, since the building acted as a Faraday cage. It also offered little acoustic insulation.

The copper houses cost between 5,000 and 20,000 *Reichsmark*; between 1931 and 1934 fifty-one of them were produced—and ten of these have been preserved in their original form in Berlin. As can be seen in the sales catalog from

1931, the company advertised its various models with names like *Kupfercastell* (Copper Castle), *Juwel* (Jewel), *Frühlingstraum* (Spring Reverie), *Lebenssonne* (Sunshine), and *Eigenscholle* (Source of Life). The range extended from a little garden house to models with six rooms.

In 1932, Walter Gropius was commissioned by the Hirsch Works to design two prototype houses: *Sorgenfrei* (Carefree) and *Kupferstolz* (Copper Pride). He made a few changes in the appearance of existing models, substituted aluminum panels for the sheet steel interior cladding, and optimized the mechanical design of the corner joints.

In 1933 new models were added with names like *Haifa*, *Jerusalem*, and *Sharon*, along with the flagship model *Libanon* (Lebanon). The Jewish company developed these models especially for the Middle East and advertised among Jews forced to emigrate with the slogan, "Take a copper house with you to Palestine," claiming that "Even when it's very hot, your rooms will stay cool!" Fourteen of these houses actually did make their way to the British Mandate of Palestine, not least because they offered refugees a reminder of home. Today there are still eleven of these houses left in Haifa.

ALL KUPFERHAUS

DAS IDEALE EINFAMILIENHAUS

HIRSCH KUPFER- & MESSINGWERKE A.-G. BERLIN

HARDENBERGSTR. 43 / FERNSPR.: SAMMEL-NR. C1 STEINPLATZ 8091 / FÜR FERNVERKEHR: SAMMEL-NR. C1 STEINPLATZ 4536

Ihr Heim!

Haus „Kupfermärchen“

Dieses ist ein wundervolles Kupferhaus

4 Zimmer, Küche, Bad und Kammer . . . . . **siehe Seite 10**

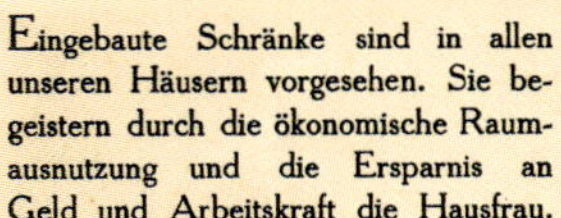

Eingebaute Schränke sind in allen unseren Häusern vorgesehen. Sie begeistern durch die ökonomische Raumausnutzung und die Ersparnis an Geld und Arbeitskraft die Hausfrau.

Eine unerlässliche Einrichtung für den Haushalt ist unser in die Wand eingelassenes Bügelbrett. Die dauernde Dienstbereitschaft verbunden mit der leichten Handhabung ist in der Tat wirklich praktisch!

In allen unseren Typen ist ein Badezimmer vorgesehen. Wir halten es vom hygienischen Standpunkt aus für unerlässlich und haben es daher zum Prinzip gemacht, dass jedes Haus ein Bad besitzt.

Mit diesem Komfort sind alle unsere Häuser ausgestattet

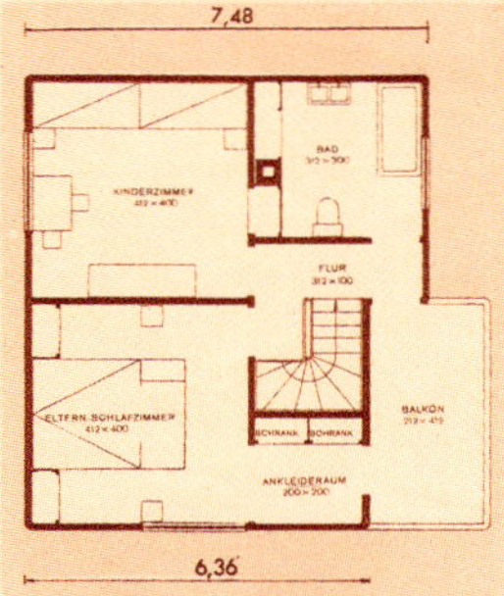

OBERGESCHOSS

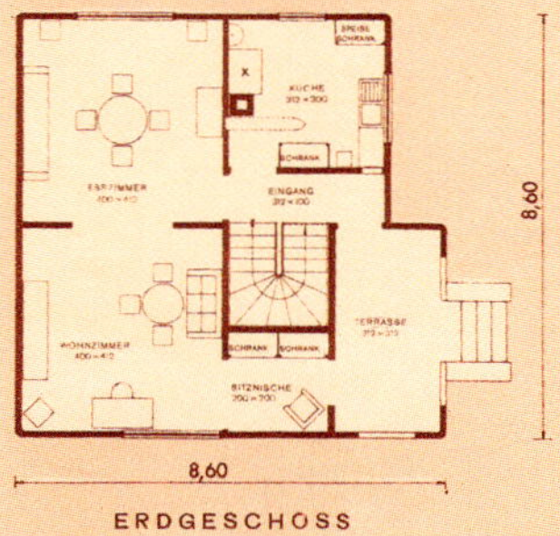

ERDGESCHOSS

Haus „Kupfercastell“

Hier ist ein entzückendes zweistöckiges Eigenheim, das durch sein gefälliges Aeussere und seine gelungene Linienführung mit Recht das Ideal eines zweistöckigen Einfamilienhauses genannt wird. Interessant ist die Anlage der Eingangsterrasse, die nach oben hin in einen grossen Balkon endigt, der auch vom Elternschlafzimmer aus zu betreten ist. Die Eingangsterrasse, die eine enge Verbindung mit den Innenräumen herstellt, ist ein beliebter Aufenthaltsort, eine Lebensfreude für den Besitzer. Ueber die Terrasse gelangt man zu dem seitlich gelegenen Eingang. Hier eröffnen sich die unteren grossen Räume. Links von der Diele sieht man eine bequem begehbare Treppe, die zu den oberen Räumlichkeiten führt. Das Esszimmer bietet durch eine reizvolle Oeffnung der Zwischenwand einen wirkungsvollen Durchblick zu dem geräumigen Wohnzimmer mit seiner idyllischen Sitznische. Die Anordnung der Fenster ermöglicht eine rasche Durchlüftung der Räume. Die Küche ist mit allem Komfort ausgestattet, um die häusliche Arbeit so angenehm wie möglich zu gestalten: passend eingebaute Schränke, eingebautes Bügelbrett, ein gut gewählter Platz für Herd und Abwaschtisch sind die besonders auffallenden Vorzüge. In unmittelbarer Nähe des Kücheneingangs bietet sich, falls eine Unterkellerung gewählt wird, die Möglichkeit zur Anlage eines Kellereinganges, der seine Beleuchtung durch ein Fenster von der Terrasse empfängt. Von der im ersten Stock gelegenen Diele führt ein separater Eingang zu den beiden Schlafzimmern, dem grossen Bad und dem Balkon. Einen ganz besonderen Komfort bildet die Ankleidenische im grossen Schlafzimmer mit den beiden eingebauten Wäsche- und Kleiderschränken. Ein Austritt zu dem Balkon ist auch hier vorgesehen. In den Schlafzimmern wie im Bad sind unsere eingebauten Schränke eine sehr willkommene Einrichtung. Der Bodenraum ist mit einer Umklappleiter von dem oberen Flur aus bequem zu erreichen.

BLICK IN DAS WOHNZIMMER

Opposite: The *Kupfercastell* (Copper Castle) model in the company's catalog

Right: Section and detail of the external walls

Above: Installation of wall elements (left), living room interior designed by Gropius (opposite)

Below: Variations of the expandable floor plan

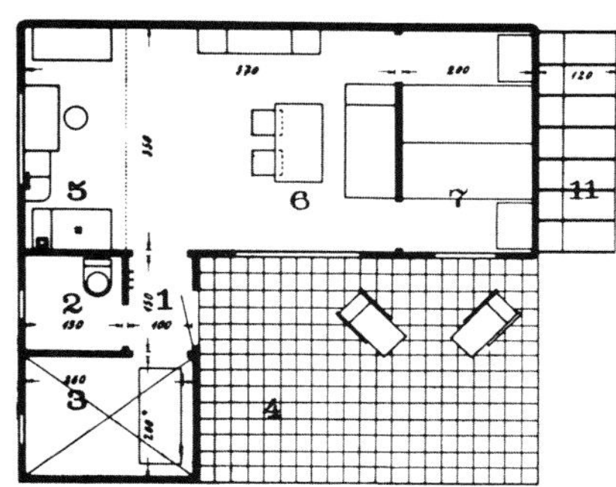

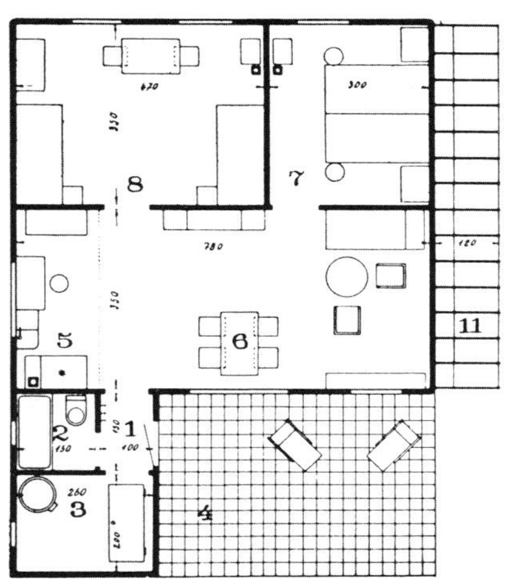
8
7
5
6
1
2
3
4
11

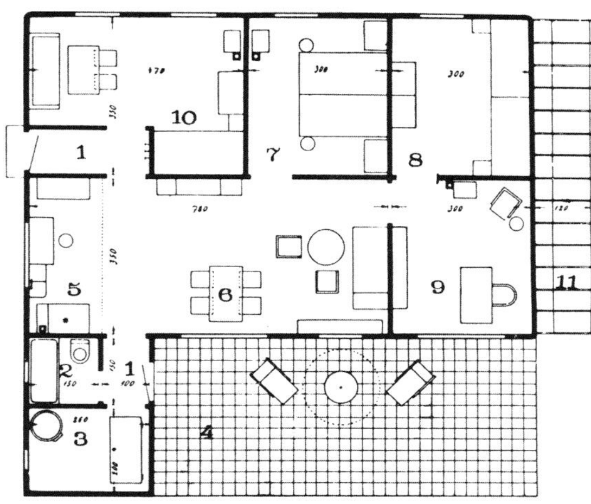
10
1
7
8
5
6
9
11
1
2
3
4

Haus „Maienmorgen“

Wir sind der Ueberzeugung, dass unser Haus „Maienmorgen“ die Erfüllung des Traumes aller derer bedeutet, die bei ihren bescheidenen Mitteln bisher nicht in der Lage waren, an den Kauf eines solchen Hauses zu denken. Wenn man in Betracht zieht, dass bei Verwendung von Ziegeln die Nutzfläche um etwa 20% verkleinert würde, so kann man verstehen, dass auf der verhältnismässig kleinen Baufläche von 37,5 qm viel Raum geschaffen ist. Besonders praktisch und ökonomisch ist der Grundriss angeordnet. Das Wohnzimmer mit der gemütlichen, gut beleuchteten Essnische erweckt einen warmen, behaglichen Eindruck. Für die in letzter Zeit besonders beliebt gewordene Kleinküche mit eingebauten Regalen und einer Abstellkammer sind die Ausmasse dennoch so gewählt, dass der Haushalt bequem versorgt werden kann. W.C. mit Dusche liegen zu ebener Erde. Ueber die separat liegende Treppe erreicht man die oberen Räumlichkeiten. Das lichtdurchflutete Schlafzimmer enthält zwei begehbare eingebaute Schränke und eine Abstellkammer. Der vorgelagerte durchgehende Balkon sowie der Erkerbau geben dem Hause eine reizvolle Note.

Haus „Juwel"

Dieser Dreizimmertyp eines Einfamilienhauses mit den praktisch angelegten grossen Räumen, dem besonders grossen Bad wurde in kurzer Zeit sehr beliebt. Der Eintretende wird von der Individualität und von den Ausmassen der Räume gleichermassen angenehm überrascht sein. In diesem Hause finden Sie, wie in allen unseren Häusern, das Ideal der Hausfrau: eingebaute Schränke. Der Ess-Wohnraum, 5×4 m gross, der von der gut beleuchteten Diele betreten wird, wirkt durch die drei Doppeltüren an der Stirnseite sehr repräsentativ. Der erkerartige Ausbau gewährt einen freien Ausblick nach drei verschiedenen Seiten. — Gleich am Eingang befindet sich eine Telefonnische, durch die das Telefon vom Esszimmer und von der Diele aus bedient werden kann. Eine Durchreiche von der Küche zum Speisezimmer ist eine wirkliche Bequemlichkeit. Vom mittleren Raum gelangt man in die angrenzenden hellen angenehmen Schlafzimmer, deren grösseres direkten Zugang zum Bad und W. C. hat. Eine bemerkenswerte Einrichtung ist das eingebaute Apothekerschränkchen. — Beim Projektieren der Küche waren wir auf Zweckmässigkeit und ökonomische Raumausnutzung besonders bedacht. Die geräumigen Vorratskammern bieten einen vollen Ersatz für einen etwa in Wegfall kommenden Keller und haben den weiteren Vorteil, das lästige Treppensteigen zu ersparen. Der für Abstellzwecke ausnutzbare Bodenraum ist durch eine Luke in der Küchendecke erreichbar.

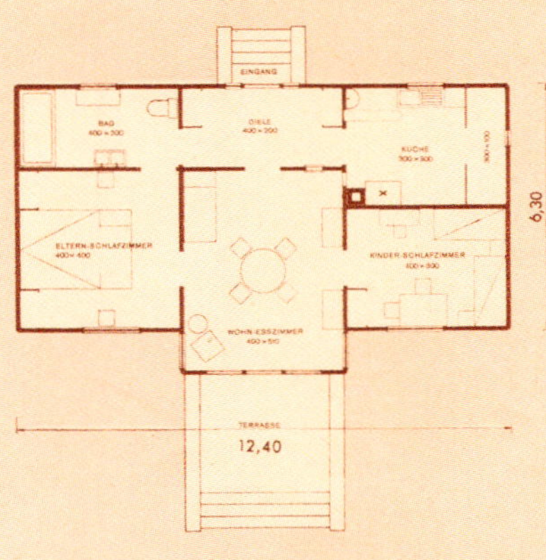

Wie arbeitet Ihr so angelegtes Kapital? Es bringt die höchsten Zinsen: Gesundheit, Glück und besseres Leben!

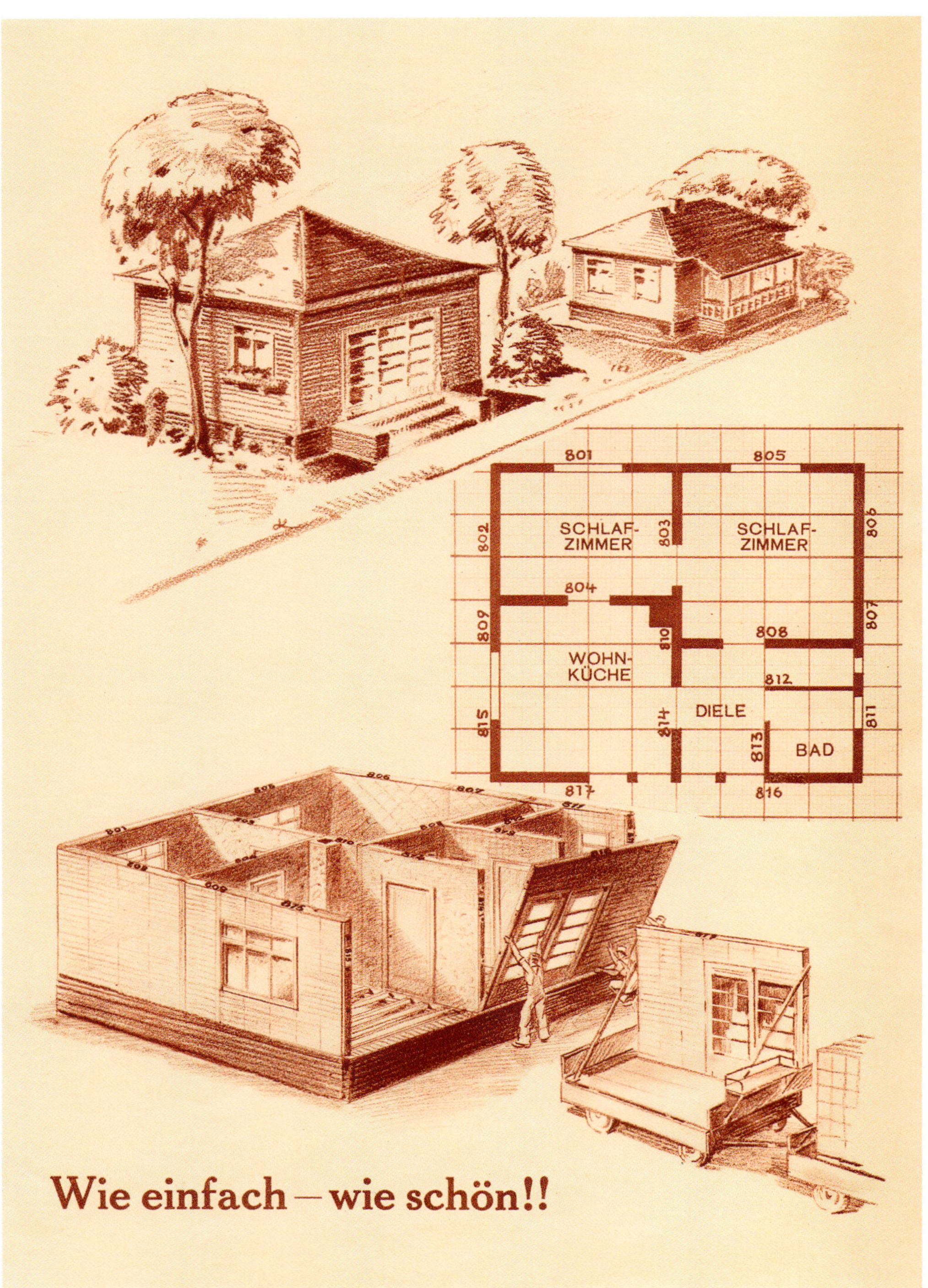
801
805
SCHLAF-
ZIMMER
803
SCHLAF-
ZIMMER
802
806
804
809
810
808
807
WOHN-
KÜCHE
812
815
814
DIELE
811
813
BAD
817
816
Wie einfach – wie schön!!

Farbenmuster für unsere Innenwände

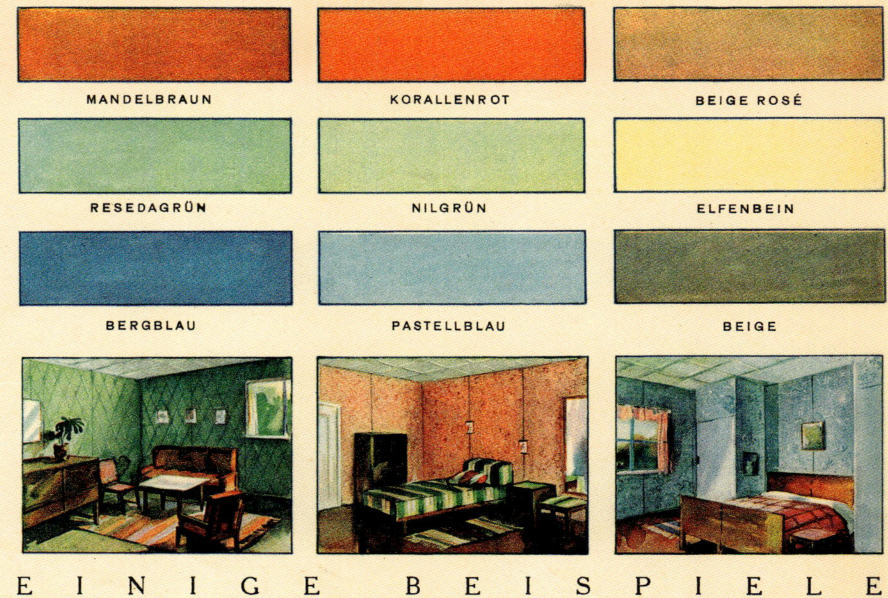

Reliefmuster für die Innenwände

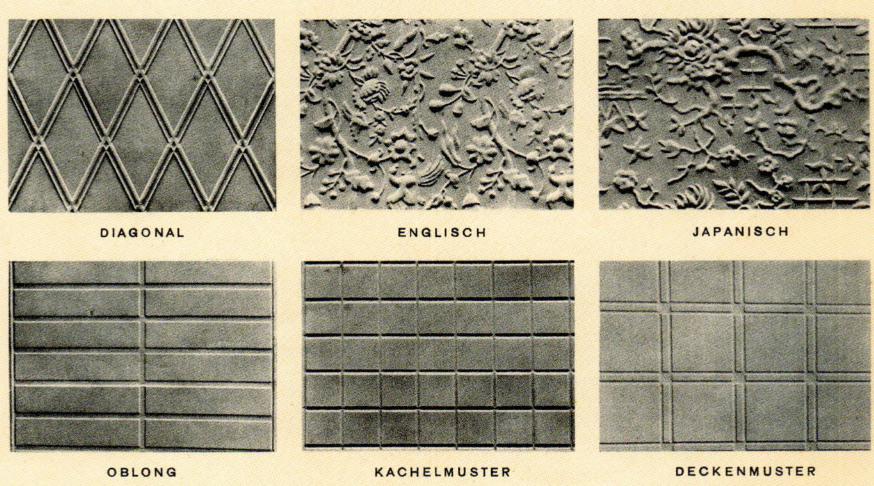

AMERICAN MOTOHOMES

Robert W. McLaughlin Jr.
American Houses, Inc.
Kearny, New Jersey, USA, 1932–1935

Like many of his colleagues, the American architect Robert McLaughlin believed that he could make money during the Great Depression of the 1930s by building low-cost, prefabricated homes. Hence, he founded American Houses, Inc. in 1932, the year he presented the prototype for a house that would eventually be produced in series under the name American Motohome.

The spectrum of these steel-skeleton houses ranged from a simple four-room model to a spacious version with six bedrooms, four bathrooms, and a two-car garage. The Motohome was clad in panels of asbestos and cement. Heating, plumbing, and electricity were combined in a central "Moto-unit." The house contained countertops made of stainless steel, built-in cabinets, and was equipped with a custom fit stove that included a vent, as well as a refrigerator, and even cigarette lighters.

Each of the homes, as McLaughlin explained, was characterized by "a hitherto unknown level of durability, beauty, economy, and comfort."

The components were produced in a factory in New Jersey and assembled on site. The one- or two-story flat-roofed houses paid tribute to International Style. They were advertised as "dwelling machines" and could even be delivered with a supply of food in the kitchen. However, the ostensibly attractive Motohomes did not appeal to a sufficient number of customers, so that the architect and his company turned to the production of more conventional prefabricated homes after barely three years, during which 150 models were delivered.

Winslow Ames House in New London, Connecticut, 1933 (opposite), house in Boston, Massachusetts, 1934 (above)

Following spread: "American motohomes: the prefabricated houses that come complete with food in the kitchen. Dedicated to the women of America by Sarah Delano Roosevelt, April 1, 1935." Brochure presenting 14 house models

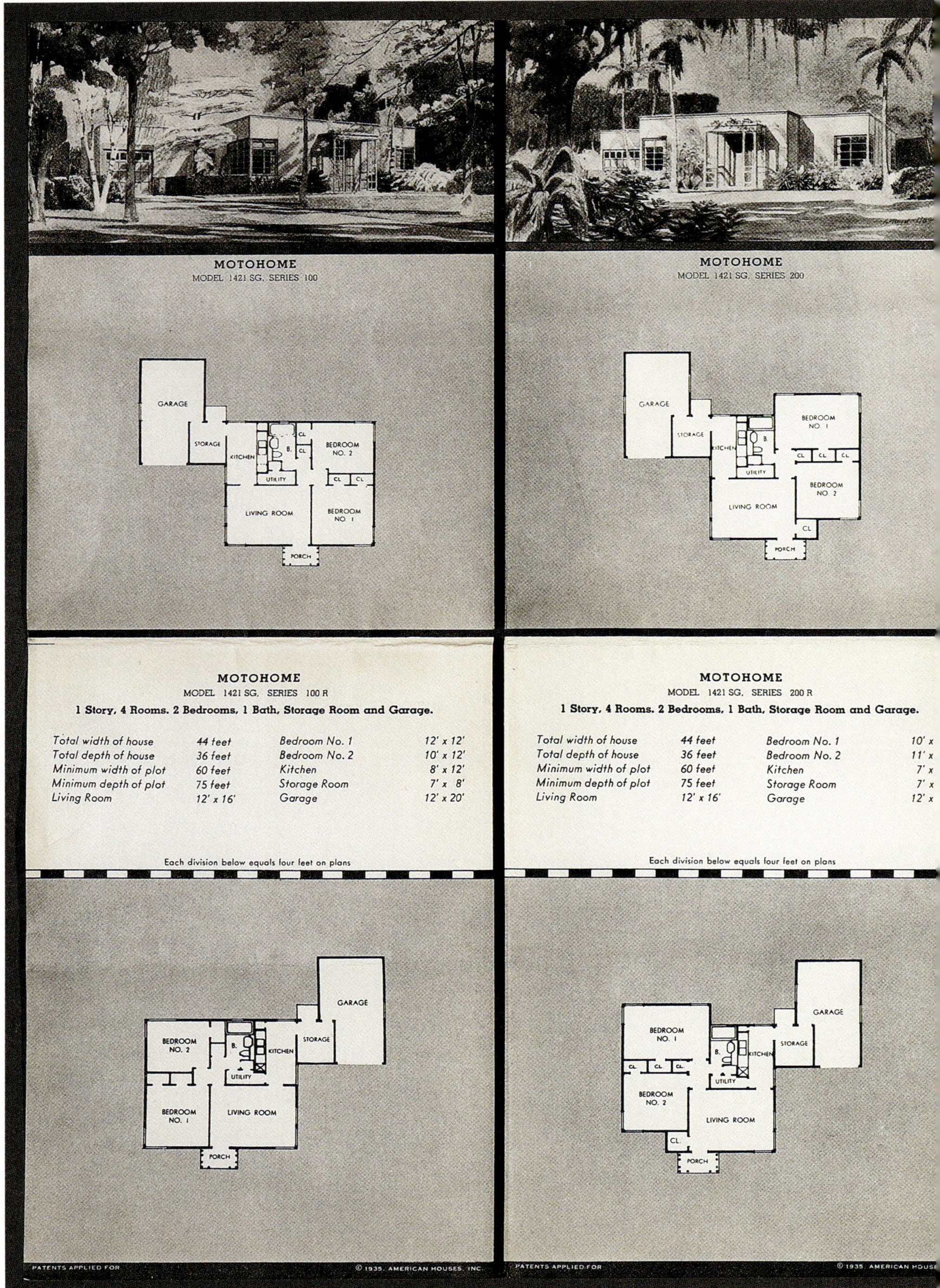

MOTOHOME
MODEL 1421 SG, SERIES 100

MOTOHOME
MODEL 1421 SG, SERIES 200

MOTOHOME
MODEL 1421 SG, SERIES 100 R

1 Story, 4 Rooms. 2 Bedrooms, 1 Bath, Storage Room and Garage.

Total width of house	*44 feet*	*Bedroom No. 1*	*12' x 12'*
Total depth of house	*36 feet*	*Bedroom No. 2*	*10' x 12'*
Minimum width of plot	*60 feet*	*Kitchen*	*8' x 12'*
Minimum depth of plot	*75 feet*	*Storage Room*	*7' x 8'*
Living Room	*12' x 16'*	*Garage*	*12' x 20'*

Each division below equals four feet on plans

PATENTS APPLIED FOR

MOTOHOME
MODEL 1421 SG, SERIES 200 R

1 Story, 4 Rooms. 2 Bedrooms, 1 Bath, Storage Room and Garage.

Total width of house	*44 feet*	*Bedroom No. 1*	*10' x*
Total depth of house	*36 feet*	*Bedroom No. 2*	*11' x*
Minimum width of plot	*60 feet*	*Kitchen*	*7' x*
Minimum depth of plot	*75 feet*	*Storage Room*	*7' x*
Living Room	*12' x 16'*	*Garage*	*12' x*

Each division below equals four feet on plans

PATENTS APPLIED FOR

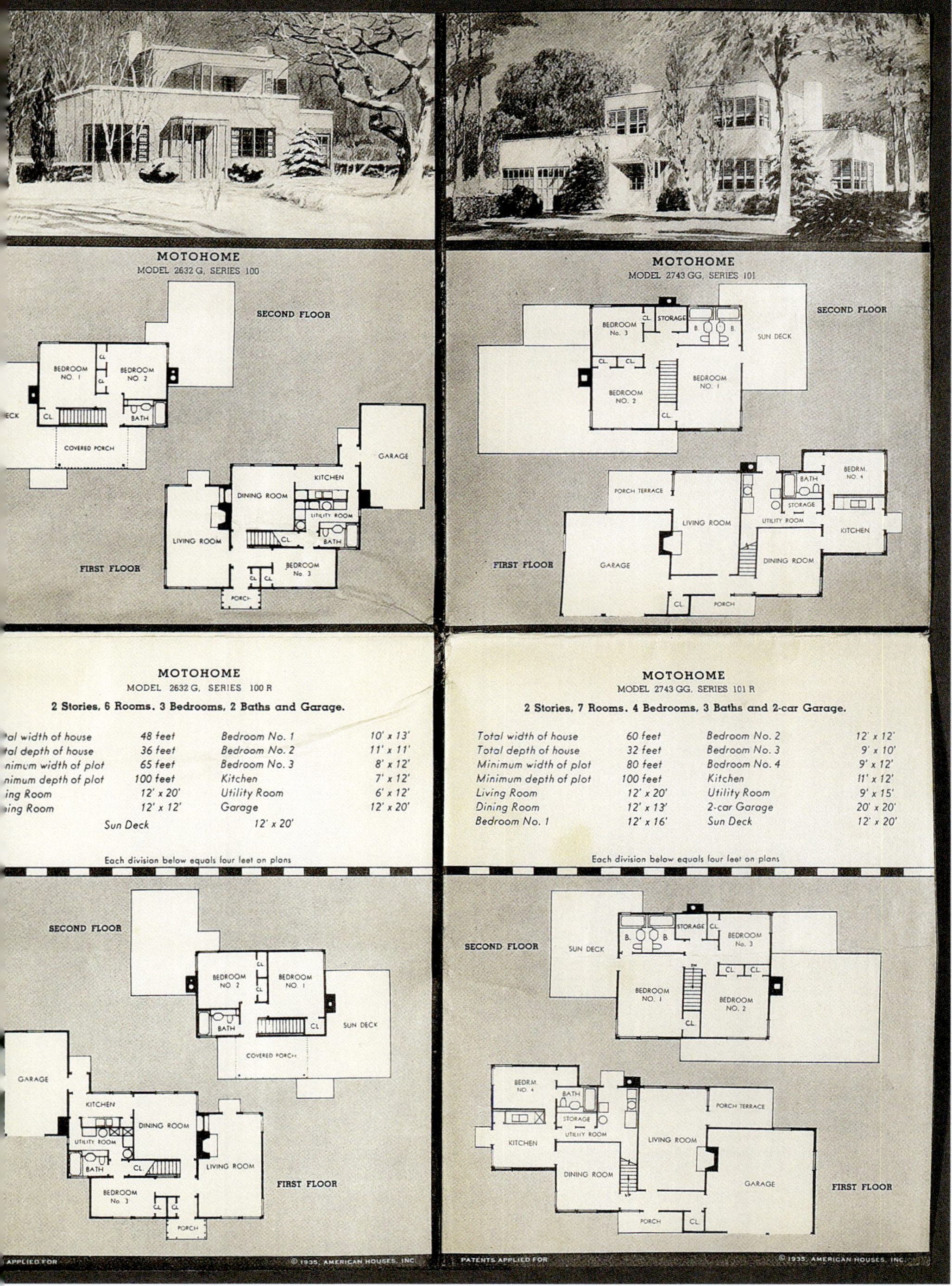

MOTOHOME

MODEL 2632 G, SERIES 100 R

2 Stories, 6 Rooms, 3 Bedrooms, 2 Baths and Garage.

·al width of house	48 feet	Bedroom No. 1	10' x 13'
·al depth of house	36 feet	Bedroom No. 2	11' x 11'
·nimum width of plot	65 feet	Bedroom No. 3	8' x 12'
·nimum depth of plot	100 feet	Kitchen	7' x 12'
·ing Room	12' x 20'	Utility Room	6' x 12'
·ing Room	12' x 12'	Garage	12' x 20'
Sun Deck	12' x 20'		

Each division below equals four feet on plans

MOTOHOME

MODEL 2743 GG, SERIES 101 R

2 Stories, 7 Rooms, 4 Bedrooms, 3 Baths and 2-car Garage.

Total width of house	60 feet	Bedroom No. 2	12' x 12'
Total depth of house	32 feet	Bedroom No. 3	9' x 10'
Minimum width of plot	80 feet	Bedroom No. 4	9' x 12'
Minimum depth of plot	100 feet	Kitchen	11' x 12'
Living Room	12' x 20'	Utility Room	9' x 15'
Dining Room	12' x 13'	2-car Garage	20' x 20'
Bedroom No. 1	12' x 16'	Sun Deck	12' x 20'

Each division below equals four feet on plans

GENERAL HOUSES

Howard T. Fisher
General Houses, Inc.
Chicago, Illinois, USA, 1933–1940

The first American architect to consider the idea of producing prefabricated steel houses in series was presumably Howard T. Fisher. As a one-time law student at Harvard, and the son of the former Secretary of the Interior and prominent Chicago lawyer Walter Lowrie Fisher, he had excellent contacts. In 1931 he was able to win the support of the president of the Pullman Car Company, which was able to supply the know-how in steel construction for his project. Other wealthy industrialists also joined in when Fisher founded General Houses Inc. in 1932, at the youthful age of twenty-six. The company's name being reminiscent of General Motors is not merely coincidental. Fisher believed that it should be possible to standardize houses, so that they could be produced and sold in large numbers. However, what Fisher envisioned was not the production of houses on a factory assembly line. On the contrary, various parts were to be produced by different companies and put together on the building site. Pullman, for ex-

Below: Model house at the *Century of Progress Exposition*, 1933

Opposite: Original design of the wooden panel as used in houses for the 1933 *Century of Progress Exposition*

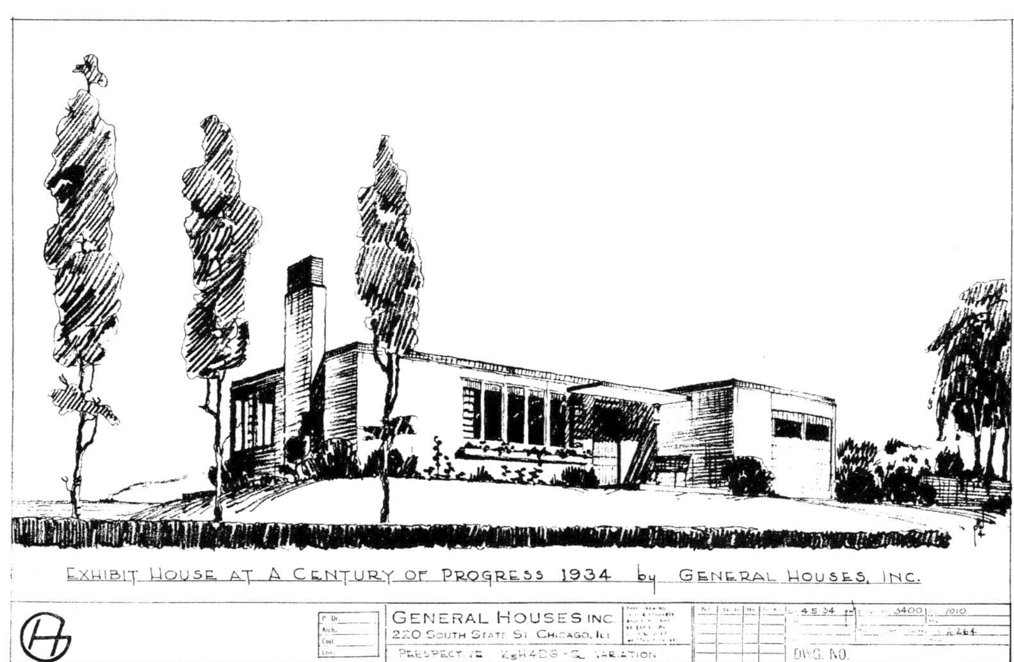

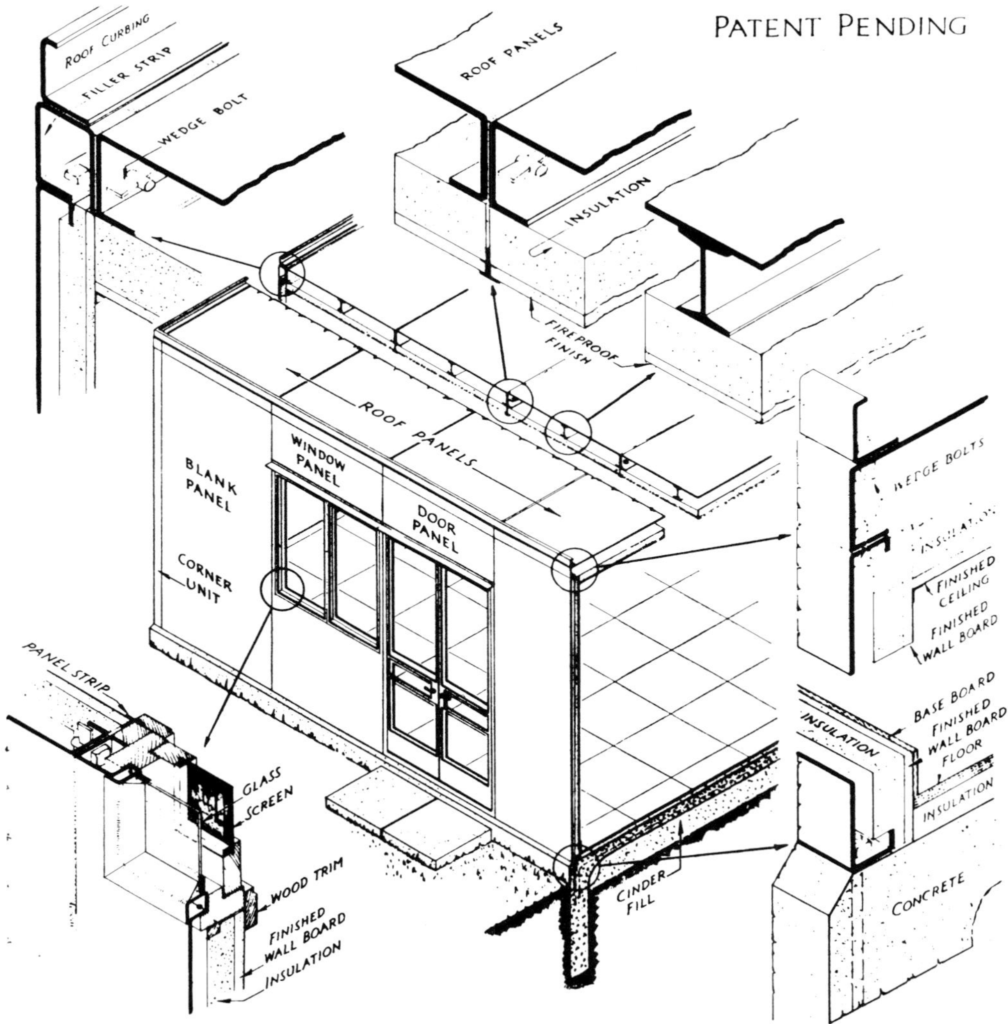

ample, would deliver the steel plates for the external walls. General Houses had no production facilities of its own.

In 1933, the first model house was presented during the five-month's of the Chicago *Century of Progress Exposition*. It aroused considerable interest on the part of the public and the press, but it was not widely accepted. Fisher was, after all, an ambitious architect and had given the house a modern form: a flat-roofed cube without any ornamentation. The walls were made of 4 ft. wide, floor-to-ceiling steel panels, which supported the weight of the roof. The internal walls were also made of exposed steel.

National sales began that same year. Models were offered ranging from a four-room house for $4,500 to a two-story, six-room house with a garage for $8,550 (1934 prices). When the

sales volume failed to increase, despite extensive marketing, moderate prices, and easy payment options (installments of $30 per month), the inside was made "cozier" by adding wooden paneling. Later, the outside was also revamped by replacing the flat roof with a pitched version. The mail- order catalog company Sears Roebuck and Co., which became a partner in the project in 1935, argued that the taste of the public at large should be taken into consideration. The system of load-bearing steel plates was first replaced by a steel frame structure fitted out with wood-clad panels of asbestos cement. Later, the entire structure was made of wood.

It is now impossible to determine how many steel houses the company was ever able to sell, presumably the figure is under one hundred. After Fisher, the company's founder, left General Houses in 1940, the modern forms were abandoned completely. The subsequent success was overwhelming: in 1943 General Houses produced roughly 2,000 prefabricated houses per month in a traditional style.

Above: McDougall Residence in Riverside, Illinois, 1930s

Opposite: House in Lake Delavan, Wisconsin, 1935

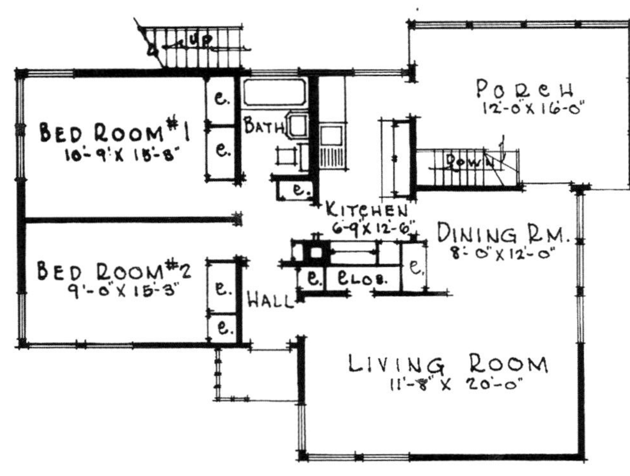

Left: First floor plan of the exhibition house at the *Century of Progress Exposition*, 1933

Below: Living room in a model house from the *Century of Progress Exposition*, 1933

Opposite: Kitchen in a model house from the *Century of Progress Exposition*, 1933

DYMAXION DEPLOYMENT UNIT

Richard Buckminster Fuller
Butler Manufacturing Company
Kansas City, Missouri, USA, 1944

In 1940, Richard Buckminster Fuller was commissioned by the United States government to design low-cost housing for troops that could be produced efficiently. The housing units were planned as a means of supporting the British forces, then at war with Germany. The multitalented inventor, who had already designed the Dymaxion House in 1927 and presented it in 1929, recognized the project as an opportunity to realize a similar, industrially produced building.

Fuller developed his Dymaxion Deployment Unit (DDU) in collaboration with the Butler Manufacturing Company in Kansas City, which then produced grain silos out of corrugated sheet metal. Using the circular floor plan of a silo, he constructed a housing unit that could be easily erected and taken down and in which the external wall and the supporting structure formed a single unit. The roof was a dome that consisted of convex sheets of steel.

The central mast, which had been designed to support the entire Dymaxion House as well as to contain the distribution and supply systems and the triangular lift, served mainly as

an assembly aid in the DDU: it could be used to hoist up the cupola after it was assembled on the ground. The plumbing unit was included in a separate cylindrical element. Fuller attempted to use the building's shape to promote air circulation in order to avoid overheating in what was essentially a tin can. Both the wind and installed ventilators played a role here.

The United States military initially ordered thousands of these sheet-metal units in order to use them as radar barracks and emergency housing. However, once metal was classified as a material of strategic importance to arms production after the United States entered the war in 1941, it was 1944 before a small number of these circular buildings were produced for deployment in Alaska, the Near East, and at Fort Monmouth near New York City. Fuller had also designed the DDU for private use, but there was no demand for it by civilians after the war.

Drawings for the patent #2343764 on the Dymaxion Deployment Unit

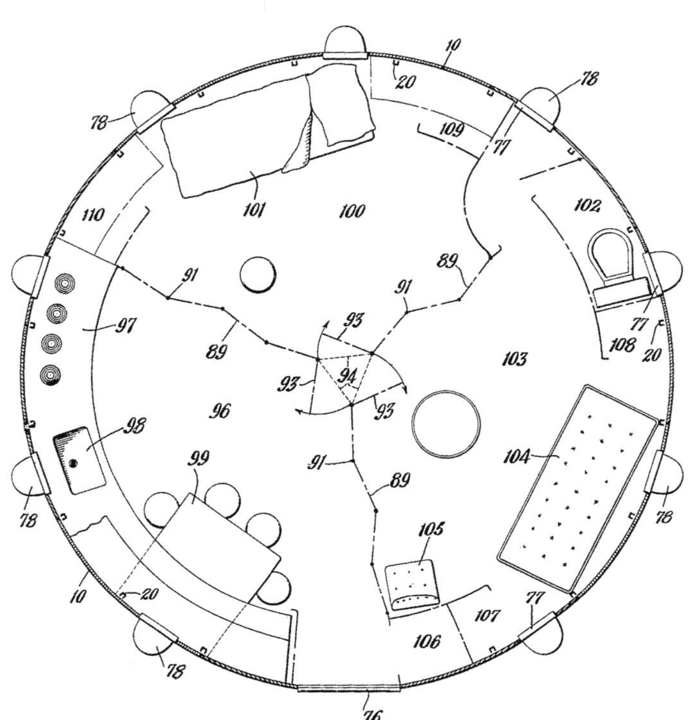

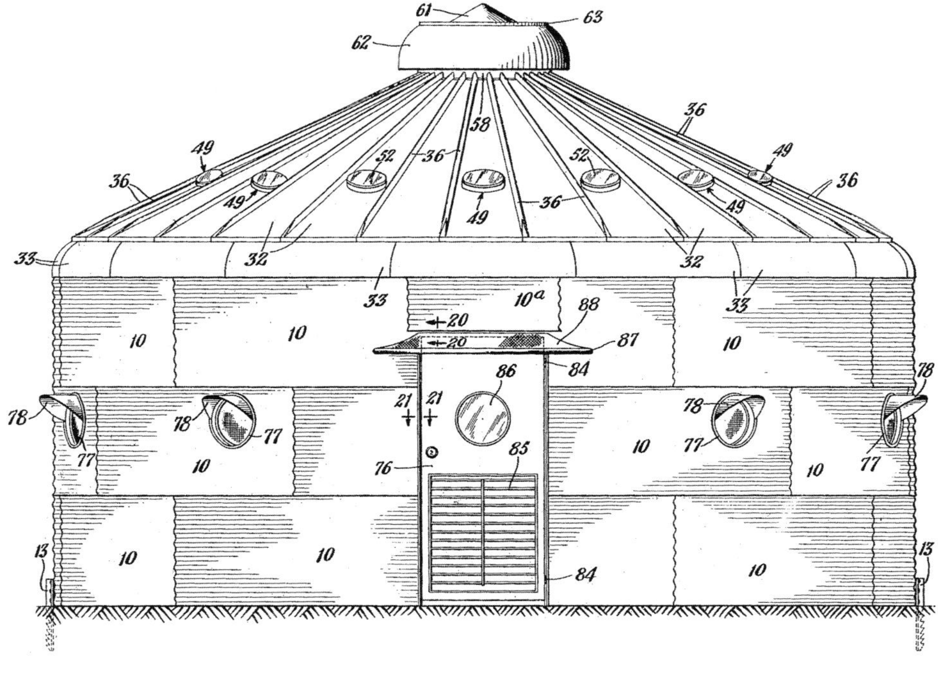

Page 96: Dymaxion Deployment Unit used as accommodation for troops, 1940

Page 97, above, and following spread: Publicity photos promoting the residential use of the Dymaxion Deployment Unit, 1941

PACKAGED HOUSE SYSTEM

Konrad Wachsmann, Walter Gropius
General Panel Corporation
Lincoln, Massachusetts, USA, 1947–1952

The General Panel Corporation was established by the German immigrants Konrad Wachsmann and Walter Gropius in 1941. They developed a system of building components for prefabricated wooden houses, which became known as the Packaged House System. According to company information, the prefabricated building panels made it possible for five untrained workers to erect a house in less than nine hours. The dimensions of the building elements were all adapted to fit the square grid on which the construction system was based. Hence, it was possible for all of the components, including the plumbing and electrical installations, to be produced in a factory.

The Packaged House System consisted of supporting wooden frames filled in with sheets of plywood and insulated with fiberglass. These sheets were connected to each other using special X-shaped wedge connectors developed by Wachsmann, which enabled the same type of building elements to be used both for the walls and the ceilings. This procedure made it possible to erect either single- or multi-story buildings. The façade was additionally clad in vertically arranged wooden boards. The windows, doors, fittings, electrical and sanitary installations were already integrated into the prefabricated building elements. Wachsmann developed a linear wedge system which made it possible to connect internal walls invisibly at the intersections.

Although the production facilities established in 1947 had already been shut down by 1952, due to the lack of demand, the construction and production principles continued to influence wooden construction in the United States.

Left: Hand-drawn cover of a contemporary documentation

Opposite top: Walter Gropius and Konrad Wachsmann

Opposite bottom: Assembly at the building site

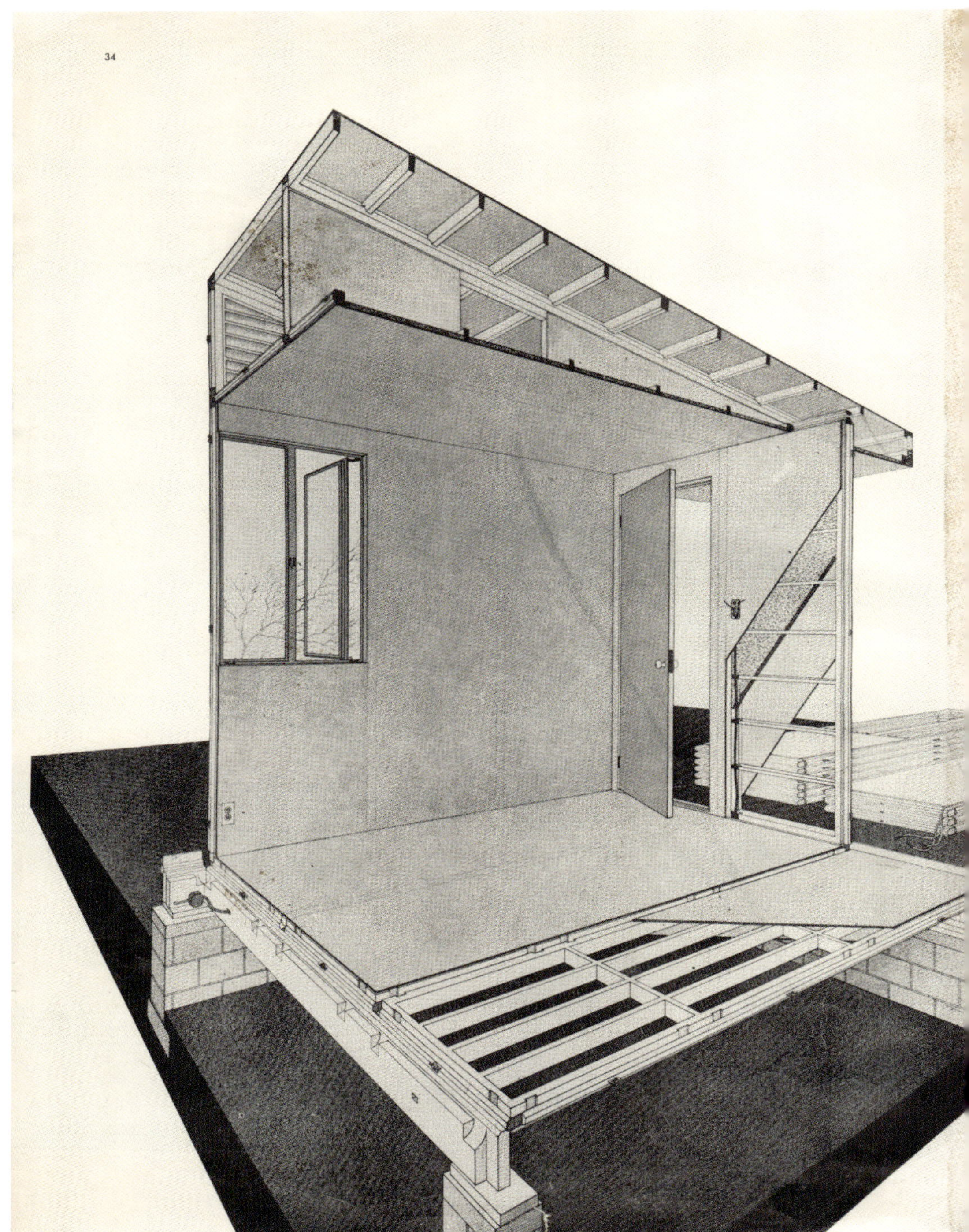

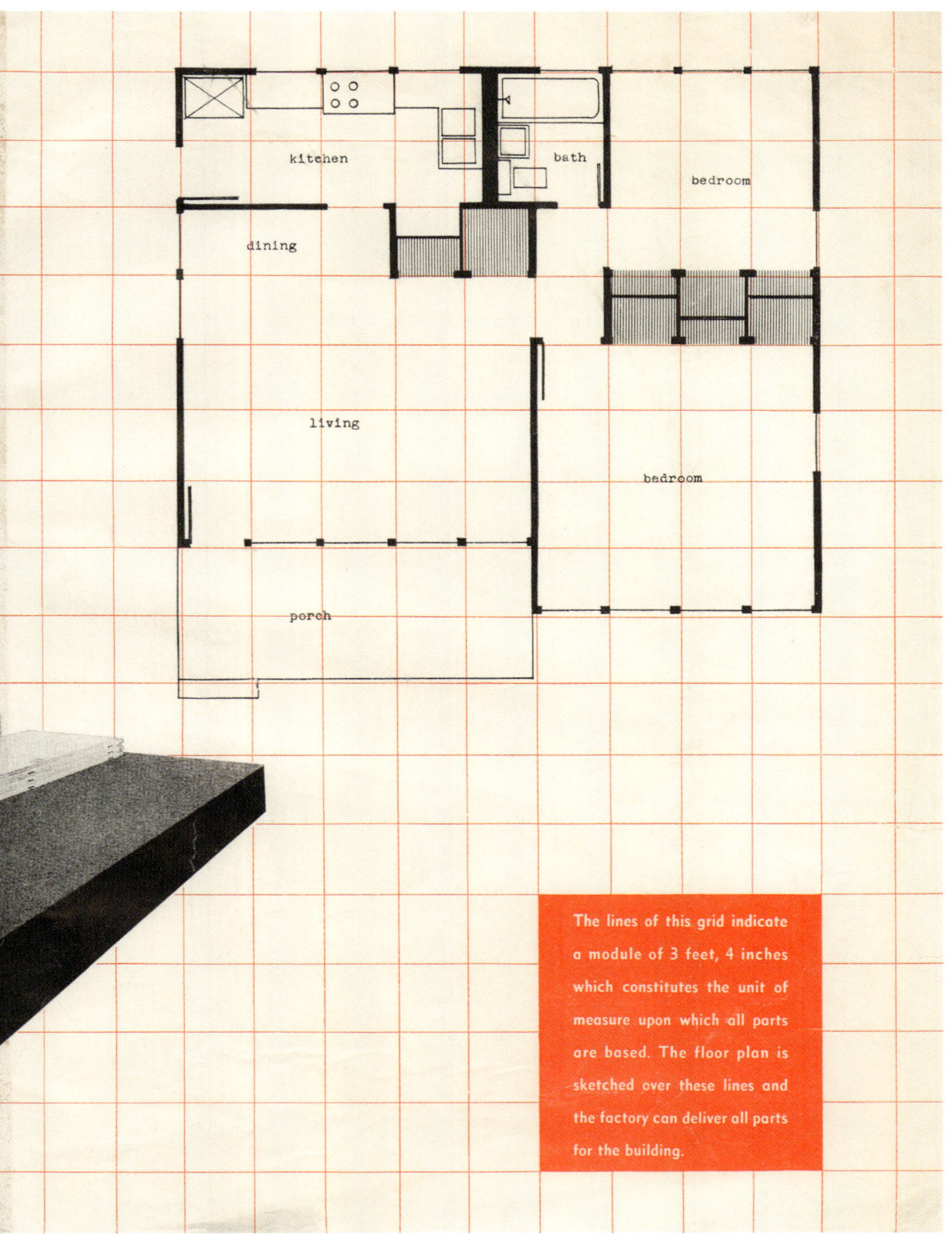

The lines of this grid indicate a module of 3 feet, 4 inches which constitutes the unit of measure upon which all parts are based. The floor plan is sketched over these lines and the factory can deliver all parts for the building.

Previous spread: The lines of the grid indicate a module of 3 ft., 4 in. which constitutes the unit of measure upon which all of the parts are based

Right: Model of the connection between the wall elements

Below and opposite bottom: Production in the factory

Above: One truck transports all of the prefabricated parts for a single-family house to the building site, including all of the built-in furniture and the fixtures for the kitchen and bathroom

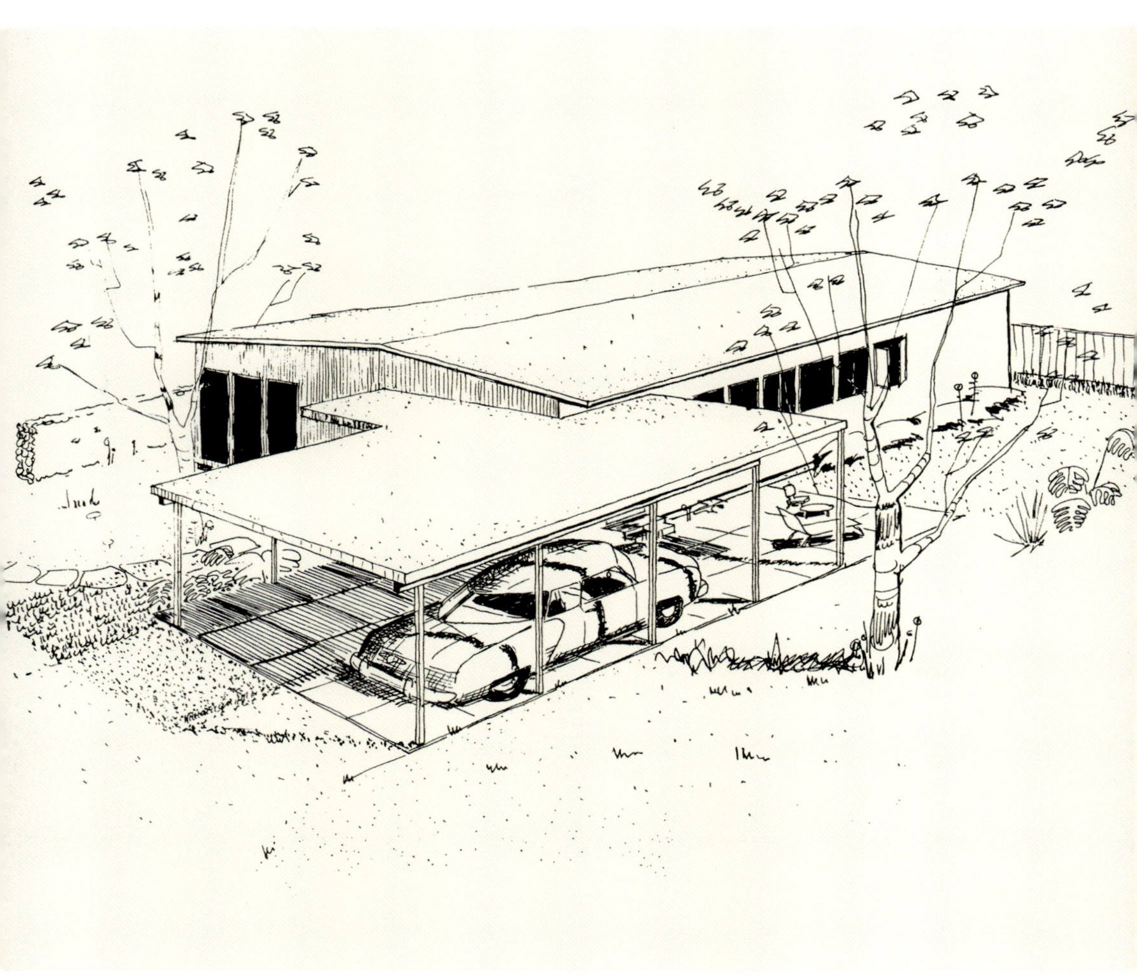

Perspective, one of many alternative design

The living room

DYMAXION HOUSE II

Richard Buckminster Fuller
Beech Aircraft Company/Fuller Houses Inc.
Wichita, Kansas, USA, 1947

The irrepressible inventor, Richard Buckminster Fuller, was given another opportunity to realise the Dymaxion House, which he had originally developed in 1927, in 1944. His partner was now the Beech Aircraft Company in Wichita, Kansas, which was looking to diversify its product line, since the company's order books were no longer full. For a full two years, the directors of the company gave Fuller a free hand in the factory so that he could develop an aluminum house, which they were hoping to sell at a volume of fifty to sixty thousand per year and at a price of $6,500 (roughly the price of a luxury car). Beech and Fuller jointly founded Fuller Houses Inc. for this purpose.

The new version of the Dymaxion, with a circular floor plan, was to be suspended slightly above the ground. The floor plate was to be held up by steel cables attached to a slender steel mast. The circular floor plan was intended to provide stability while simultaneously requiring the lowest possible volume of building material. The house measures 36 ft. in diameter and weighs 5,000 lbs. including the built-in furnishings.

The roof is a flat dome with a ventilator mounted in a cap on top in order to circulate the air within the house. The central mast contains all of the utility cables as well as the pipes for the kitchen and the two bathroom units, which were patented by Fuller in 1936 and designed to

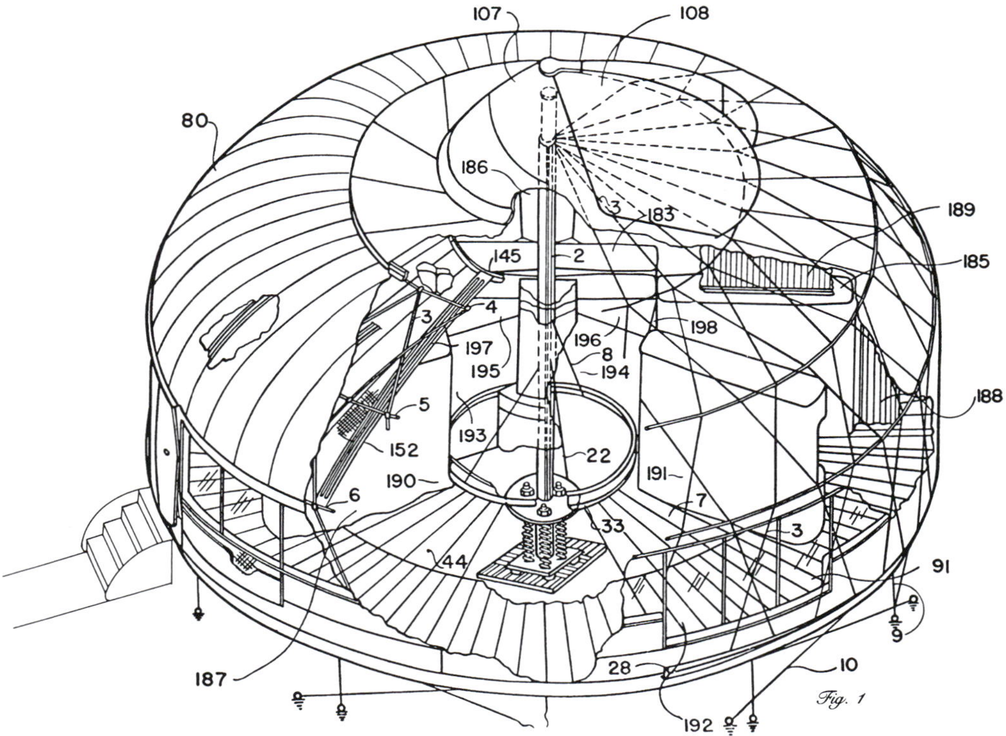

Fig. 1

Opposite and left: Conceptual model for a Dymaxion House colony and the interior of a house

Above: Drawing of a patent for the Dymaxion house, submitted but never granted

Following spread: Plan illustrating the flow of convection currents in the Dymaxion House

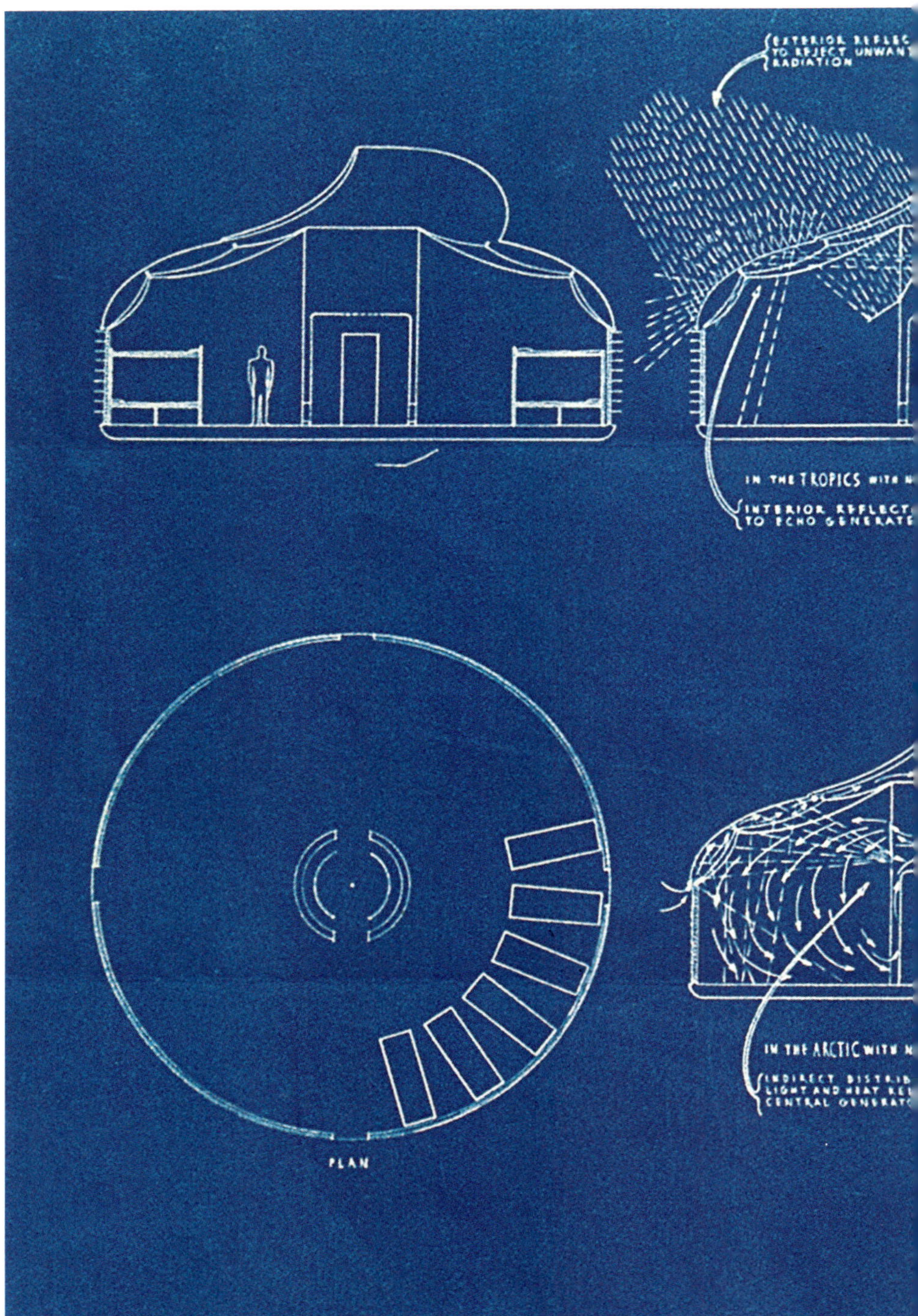
PLAN

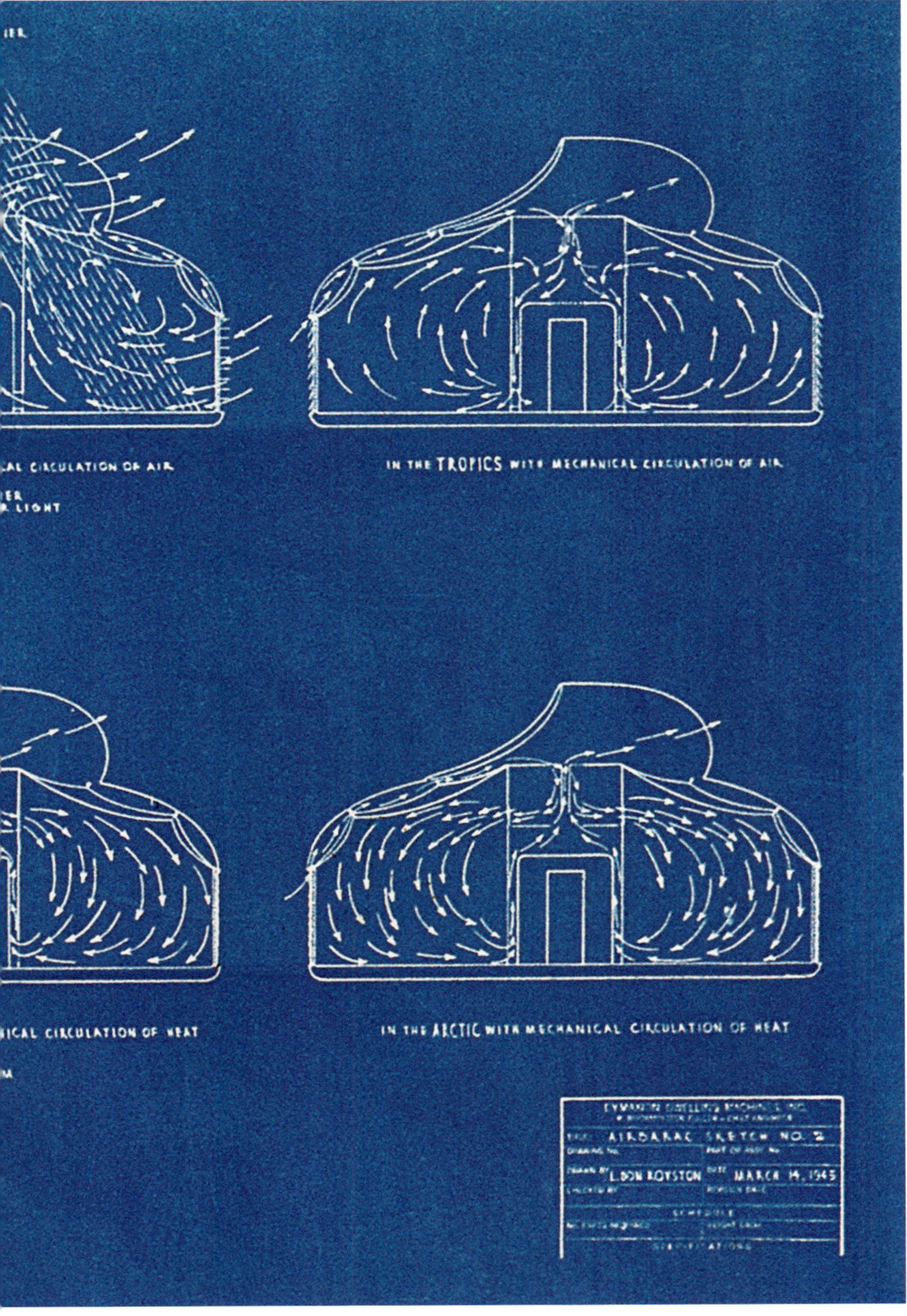
IN THE TROPICS WITH MECHANICAL CIRCULATION OF AIR
IN THE ARCTIC WITH MECHANICAL CIRCULATION OF HEAT
AIRDARAC SKETCH NO. 2
L. DON ROYSTON
MARCH 14, 1945

KANSAS-46
T2-1759

be highly water efficient. Rainwater could also be collected from the roof.

The 1,000 sq. ft. of living space also offeres enough room for a vestibule, a living room, two bedrooms, a dining room, and a pantry adjacent to the kitchen. Special features included folding doors and "o-volving shelves," storage cabinets that swing into the room at the press of a button. The wraparound panorama windows provided a perfect view in every direction.

After two prototypes, with which Fuller was not satisfied himself, the Beech Aircraft Company decided to abandon the project. A question that was never clarified was how the project should be marketed, particularly since there was so much resistance against it by local builders and trade unions, which saw their members' livelihoods threatened by it. Fuller left Wichita in 1947—thus another of his projects was stranded halfway towards completion.

The entrepreneur William Graham bought the prototype and had a "hybrid version" attached to his house in Wichita. Graham and his family used the building for roughly thirty years, although some of Fuller's innovations, such as the ventilator on the roof, were never operated.

In 1991, the family donated the Dymaxion House and all of its related parts to the Henry Ford Museum in Dearborn, Michigan, where it was restored to its original condition in years of painstaking work.

Previous spread, opposite and above: Assembly of the prototype

Right: Sketch of the installation of the rotating shelves based on the paternoster principle

Following spread: The house on William Graham's property, 1946

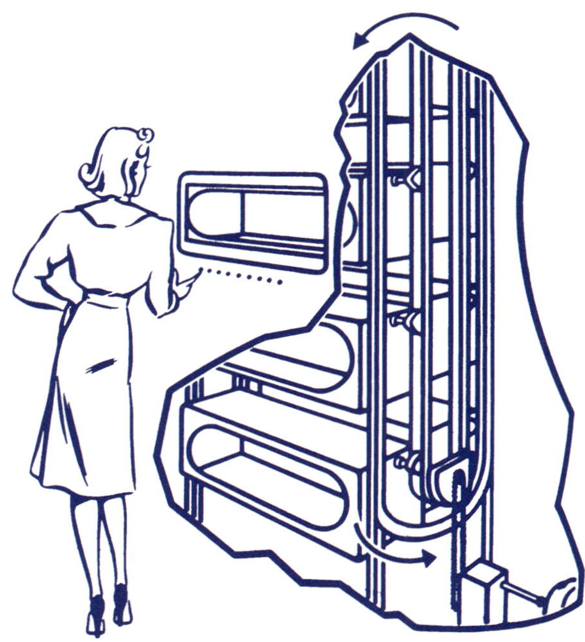

VULTEE HOUSE

Edward Larrabee Barnes, Henry Dreyfuss
Consolidated Vultee Aircraft Corporation
San Diego, California, USA, 1947

After the Second World War there were dozens of aircraft manufacturers in the United States with idle production facilities. At the same time, there was an enormous demand for new housing. Hence, it seemed to make perfect sense to use these dormant resources in order to develop and build prefabricated houses. One of these companies was the Consolidated Vultee Aircraft Company in California, which commissioned the industrial designer Henry Dreyfuss and the architect Edward Larrabee Barnes to develop two prototypes for a prefabricated house.

The Vultee House consisted of a series of factory-finished wall and roof elements. The building components had a stiff, honeycomb-like paper core with a thin sheet of aluminum on both sides. These panels were similar in structure to those used for the airplane bodies built by the workers in this same factory during the war. The sheet metal house consisted of 28 components. Since windows accounted for three quarters of the wall space, it seemed larger than the 800 sq. ft. it measured.

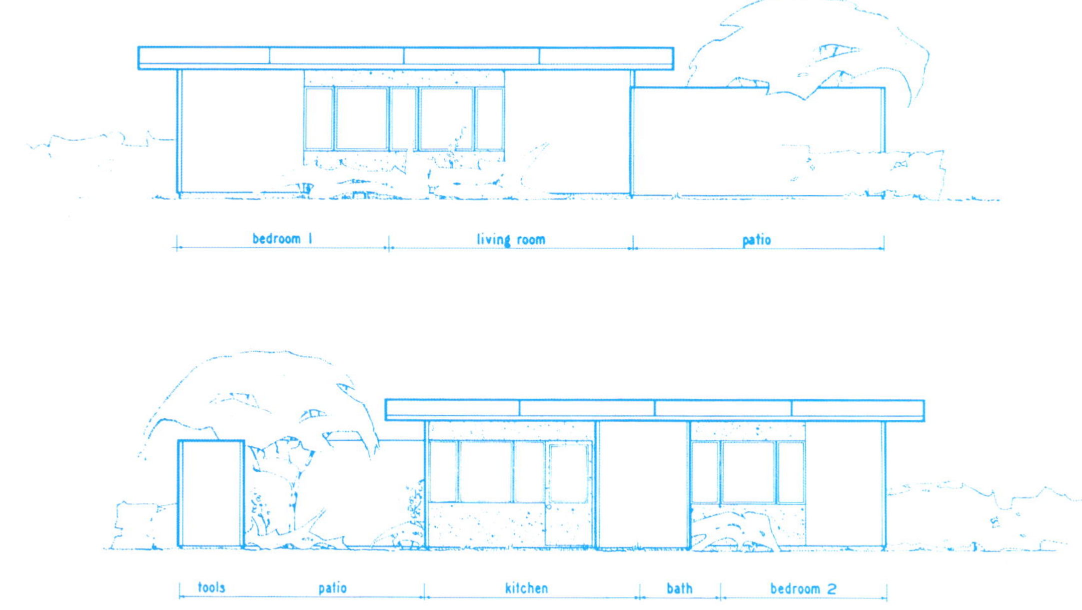

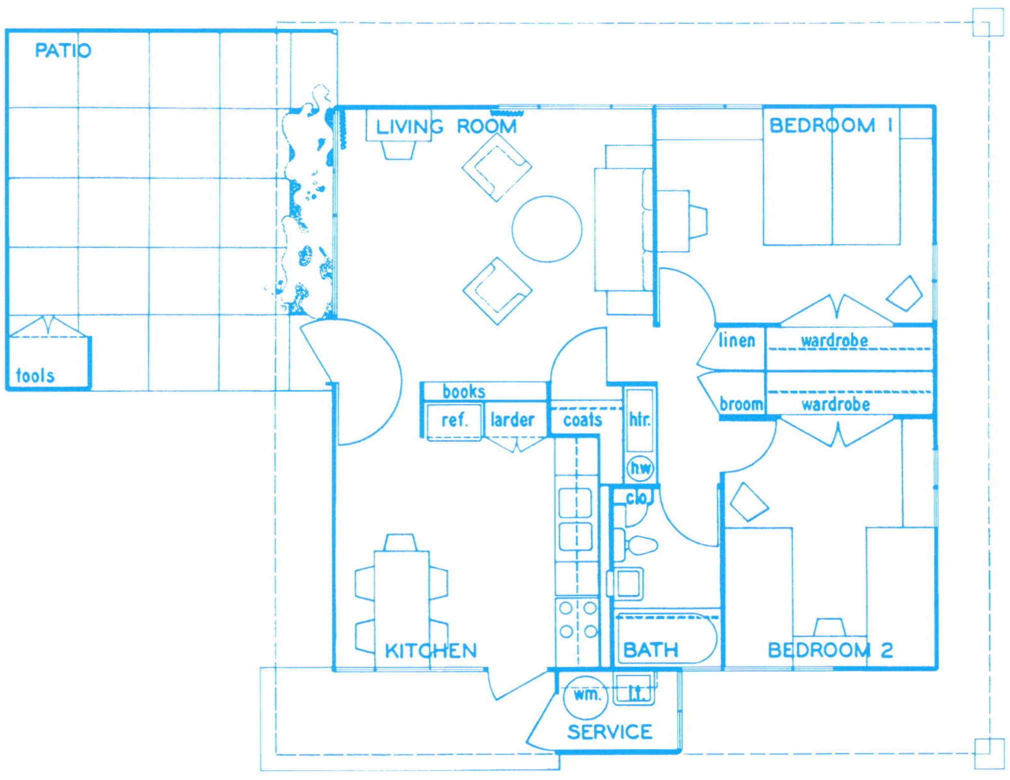

Elevations and plan

Excited by the innovative design, Reginald Fleet, who was the president of Southern California Houses, the company that marketed the house, moved into one of the two prototypes with his family in South Pasadena. It was his intention to demonstrate the advantages of a modern prefabricated home for potential buyers directly on site. Yet the Vultee House was still not a success; apparently people were not quite ready to live in a house that was reminiscent of an airplane.

Both prototypes were long considered to have been lost; however, the Fleet Family's house in South Pasadena, mentioned above, was rediscovered in 2006 and saved from demolition.

Opposite: Assembly of wall elements in the factory

Above: The model house in the factory

Below: Connection of walls with ground plate

Above and opposite: The interior of the model house erected in the factory

LUSTRON HOMES

Carl Strandlund
Lustron Corporation
Columbus, Ohio, USA, 1948–1950

After the Second World War, the United States government reacted to the housing shortage by granting generous loans to domestic builders. The intention was to promote the production of low-cost, quickly built, standardized houses. One of the builders was the Swedish-born inventor Carl Strandlund, who had already made a name for himself by producing prefabricated service stations. In 1947, he established the Lustron Corporation at a decommissioned airplane factory in Columbus, Ohio, in order to introduce a prefabricated house onto the market.

Like Strandlund's service stations, the Lustron Houses consisted entirely of metal. The supporting structure was made of steel, the wall segments and roofing elements were made of sheet steel, and the façade consisted of extremely durable and easy-to-clean enameled sheet steel panels. The roof was made of enameled steel shingles.

Production of the Lustron houses in series began in 1948. The assembly of the roughly 3,000 parts, which weighed 12 tons and were delivered on purpose-built flatbed trucks, took

Opposite:
A Lustron delivery truck

Above: Carl Strandlund posing in front of a Lustron transporter decorated with a large ribbon

about eight days. Of the many versions available, the "Westchester" was the most common model, with roughly 1,000 sq. ft. of floor space. The façade panels were offered in four colors: maize yellow, dove gray, surf blue, and desert tan. They were insulated with a thin layer of fiberglass between the wall elements. The built-in furnishings were also made of sheet metal. The color scheme was proposed by the interior decorator Herbert Ketchum, who had already made a name for himself by designing the interior of PanAm airplanes. The bathrooms and bedrooms were equipped with pocket doors. Pictures could be hung on the walls with magnets. The flooring laid down on the concrete foundation was usually marbleized dark brown linoleum.

Yet, the attraction of this new industrial product was apparently short-lived. The number of orders began to decline as early as 1949, after it became clear that the prices ranging between $10,000 and $12,000 were up to 50% higher

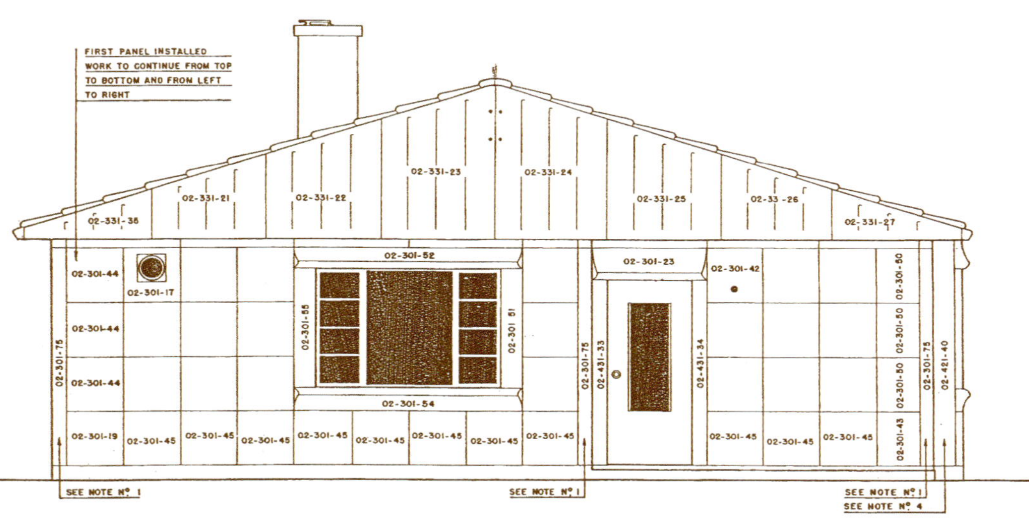

than originally advertised. Instead of producing 100 houses per day as planned, the daily output was generally only about twenty. *Time* magazine, in particular, derisively followed the rapid demise of the company and ridiculed the houses by comparing them to a "hot dog stand," while relishing in accounts of the company's losses and fuelling the public's skepticism by asking whether anyone really wanted to live in a steel house.

By 1950 the company was bankrupt, not least of all because of Strandlund's dubious business dealings. Particularly controversial was his deal with Joseph McCarthy, in the wake of which the senator wrote an article entitled "A Dollar's Worth of Housing for Every Dollar Spent" making a case for prefabricated housing in general and for the products of the Lustron Corporation in particular. Strandlund had paid the Republican senator, who later became known for his witch hunts against purported Communists, the generous sum of $10,000 and financed his exorbitant wagers on horses.

Of the roughly 2,500 Lustron Houses delivered to locations as far apart as Los Alamos and Alaska, roughly 1,800 still exist today, often lovingly cared for by owners who are aware of their history and significance.

Below: Elevations

Following spread: The many parts of a Lustron house in a promotional photo, 1949

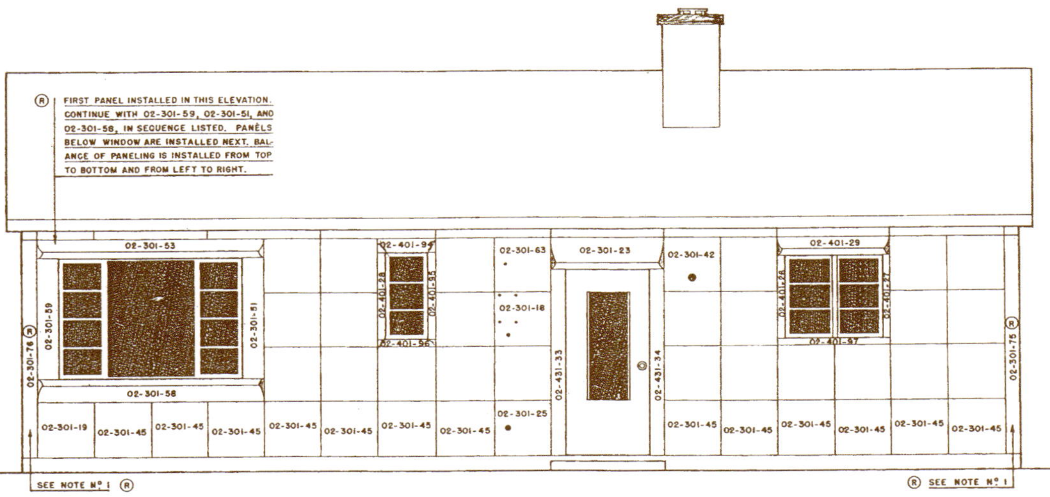

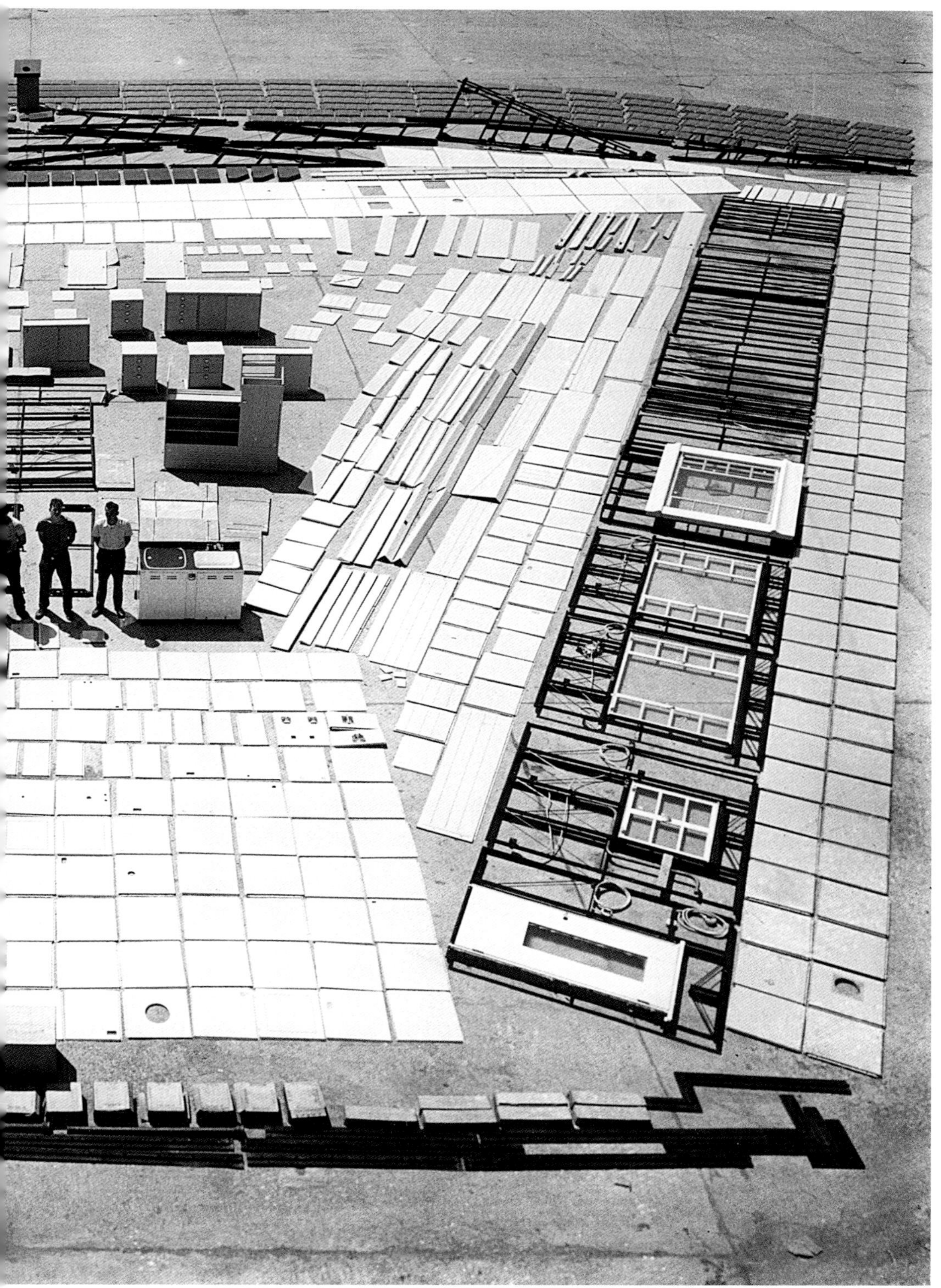

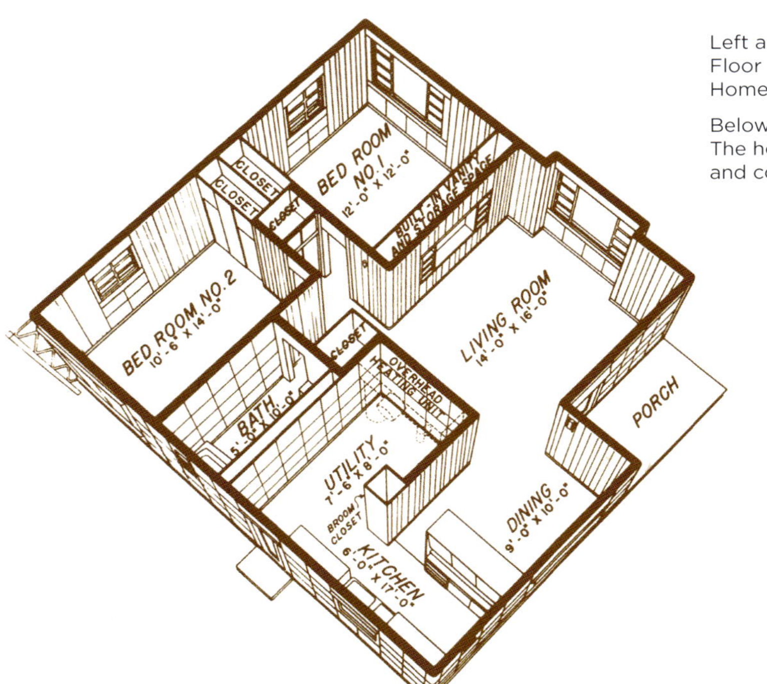

Left and opposite bottom: Floor plans from the Lustron Home Erection Manual

Below and opposite top: The house under construction and completed

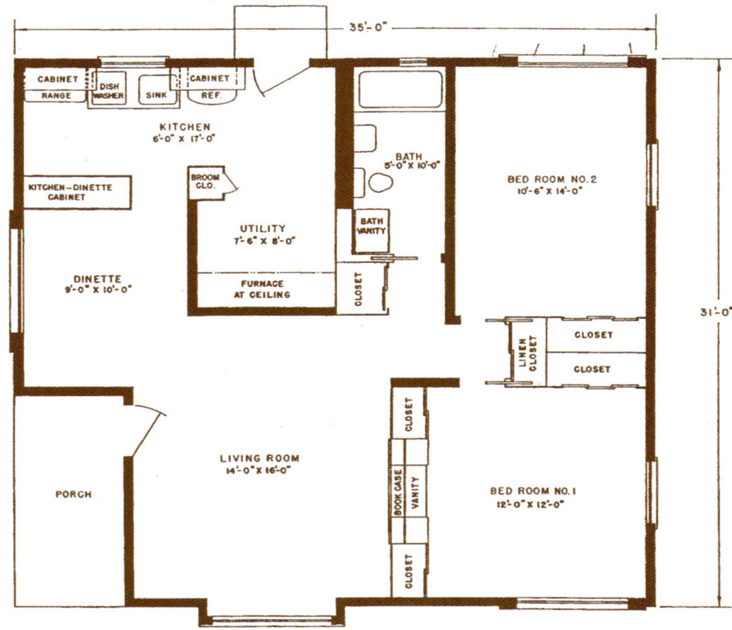
35'-0"
CABINET
RANGE
DISH WASHER
SINK
CABINET
REF.
KITCHEN
6'-0" X 17'-0"
BATH
5'-0" X 10'-0"
BED ROOM NO. 2
10'-6" X 14'-0"
KITCHEN-DINETTE CABINET
BROOM CLO.
UTILITY
7'-6" X 8'-0"
BATH VANITY
DINETTE
9'-0" X 10'-0"
FURNACE AT CEILING
CLOSET
31'-0"
CLOSET
LINEN CLOSET
CLOSET
CLOSET
LIVING ROOM
14'-0" X 16'-0"
PORCH
BOOK CASE
VANITY
BED ROOM NO. 1
12'-0" X 12'-0"
CLOSET

In a brochure Lustron recommended examples of modern interiors

When unrelated ornate forms are combined, they become confusing.

3. FORM . . .

is the shape of objects. It is form that distinguishes the various styles or periods in furniture. Well designed furniture is simple in form. Periods can be mixed with each other and with contemporary when the forms are good. The principles of form apply not only to furniture but to certain fabrics, lamp and lamp shades, picture frames, etc.

Related simple forms are restful in appearance.

Above: Bedroom with a dressing table

Left: Built-in cabinet between kitchen and dining space

Opposite: Lustron house utility room

MAISON STANDARD MÉTROPOLE

Jean Prouvé
Maxéville, France, 1949–1952

For Jean Prouvé it was only natural for things to be produced industrially, whether it was the furniture or the entire building. Having already designed simple wooden barracks for the military in 1939, he began to concentrate on the construction of residential structures in metal after the war. A common characteristic of his buildings was the use of central supports arranged in rows and rigidly joined to the ridge beam. In a 1946 design, these central supports resembled an upside down V, but he subsequently executed them at right angles, so that they could be more easily integrated into the interior design.

On the recommendation of Eugène Claudius-Petit, the French Minister for Reconstruction and Urban Development, Jean Prouvé and his workshops in Maxéville, near Nancy, were commissioned to design a prefabricated, lightweight steel-frame house that could be produced at low cost and assembled quickly and easily on site. After it became clear that the costs would overrun the proposed budget, the ministry distanced itself from the plan to purchase 25 of the Maisons standards métropoles. After long negotiations, it was agreed that ten of the standard houses, and four additional houses of the coque (Case) type, would be erected in a park-like area in the Paris suburb of Meudon. Construction was overseen by the architects André Sive and Prouvé's brother Henri, who also designed some of the foundations on which the houses were set. Four of the standard houses built in Meudon had 26 × 26 ft. of floor space, the other six had 26 × 39 ft. The remaining 15 of the 25 standard houses prefabricated in Maxéville were later distributed throughout France; a few of them were even sent to Algeria.

Depending on the size of the house, the supporting structure consisted of one or two frames made of folded sheet steel shaped like an upside-down U with a groove into which the roof beam fit. This support system was a refinement of the framing system that Prouvé had already designed during the war, together with Pierre Jeanneret and Charlotte Perriand, for the Maison à portique (Porch House) and also used for the Maisons tropicales (Tropical Houses) exported to Niamey, in Niger, and Brazzaville, in the Congo, in 1949.

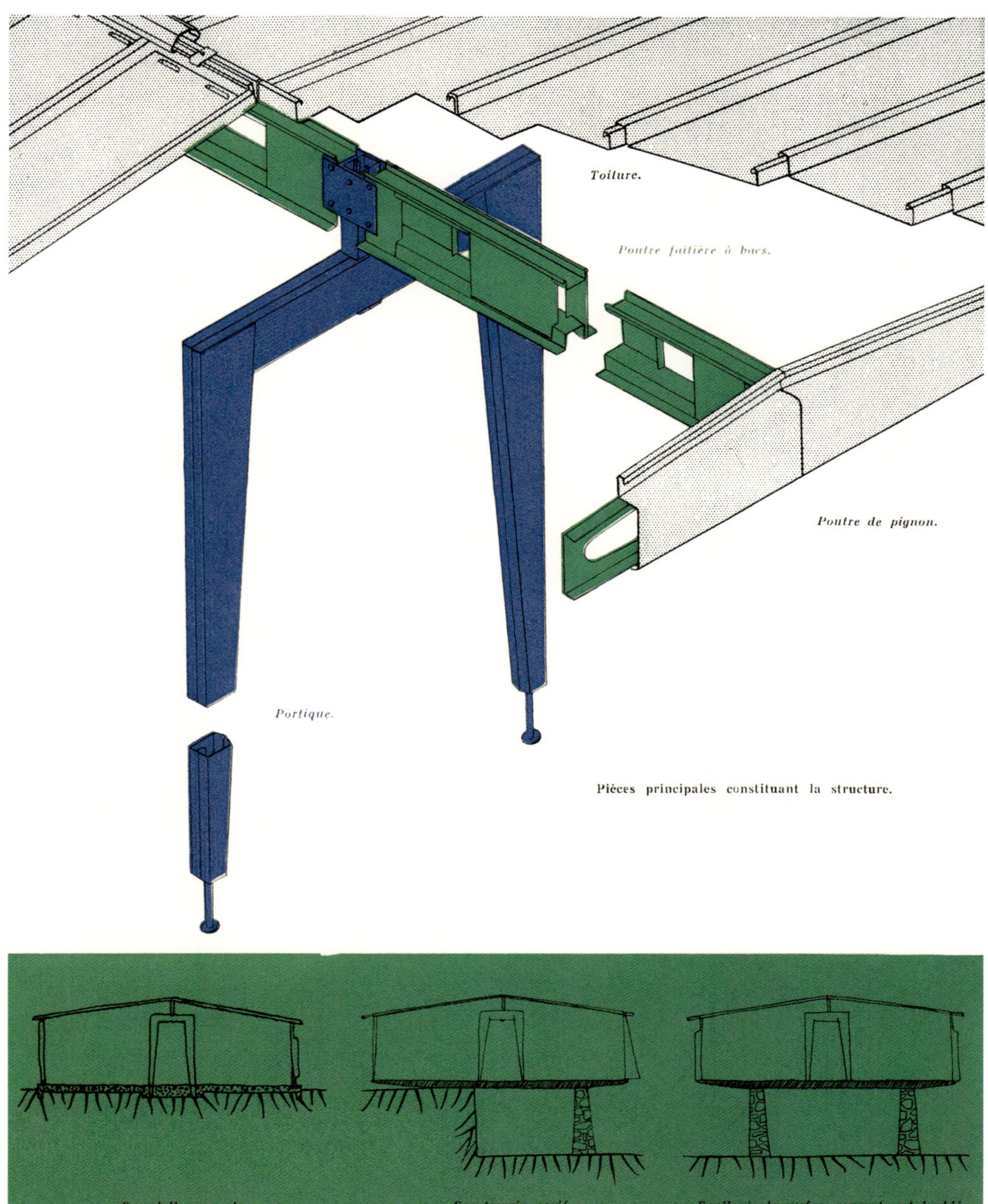

Advertising brochure with a detail drawing of the connection between the frame, roof beam, and roof

Below: Assembly in Meudon, 1949

Bottom: The Maison standard métropole at the *Salon des arts ménagers*, 1950

Opposite: The Maison standard métropole in Meudon, France, 1949

The façade consisted of 3 ft. 3 in. panels of sheet aluminum. Doors and windows were integrated as modules, and their arrangement could be determined by the customer. Sheet steel segments connected the elements. A filling of glass wool provided thermal insulation, with steel springs between the inner and outer walls to ensure stability. To this day, the ensemble consisting of 14 houses in Meudon has been well preserved, and many of the owners have lived in these lightweight metal icons for over half a century.

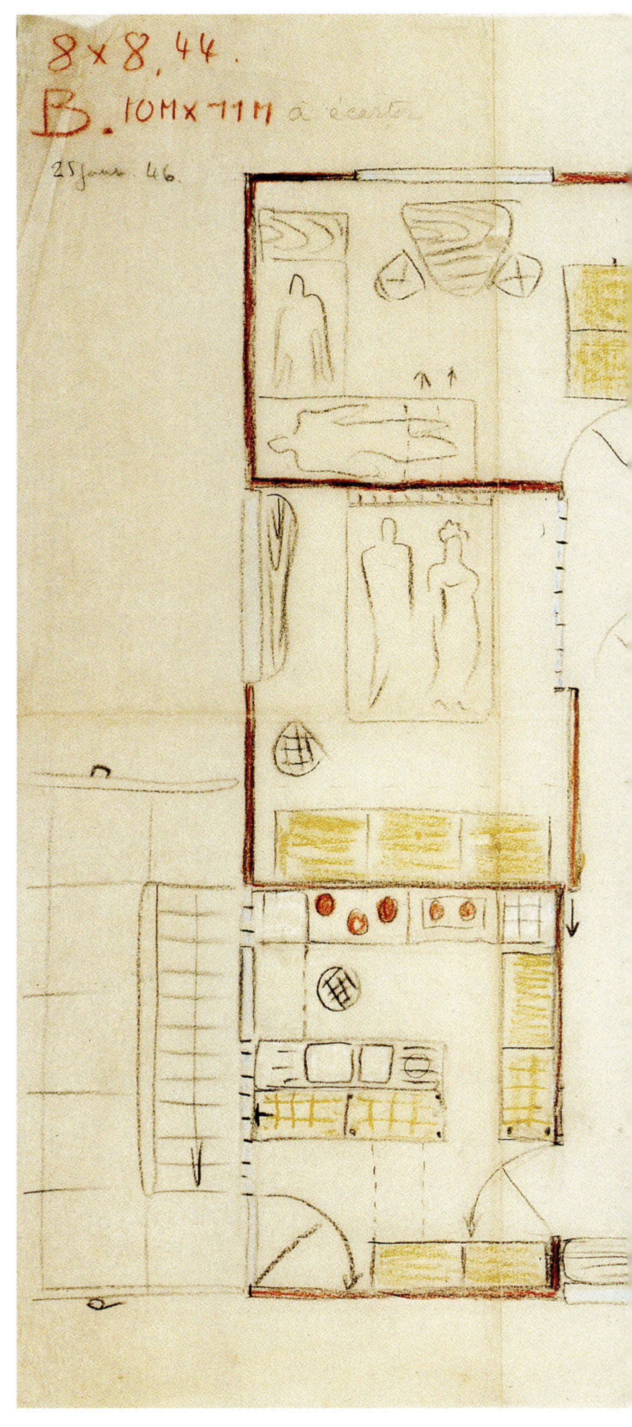

Right: Plan of the 26 ¼ × 26 ¼ ft. prefabricated house, Maison à portique, developed in 1945, drawing by Pierre Jeanneret

Following spread: The colony in Meudon, France, 1949

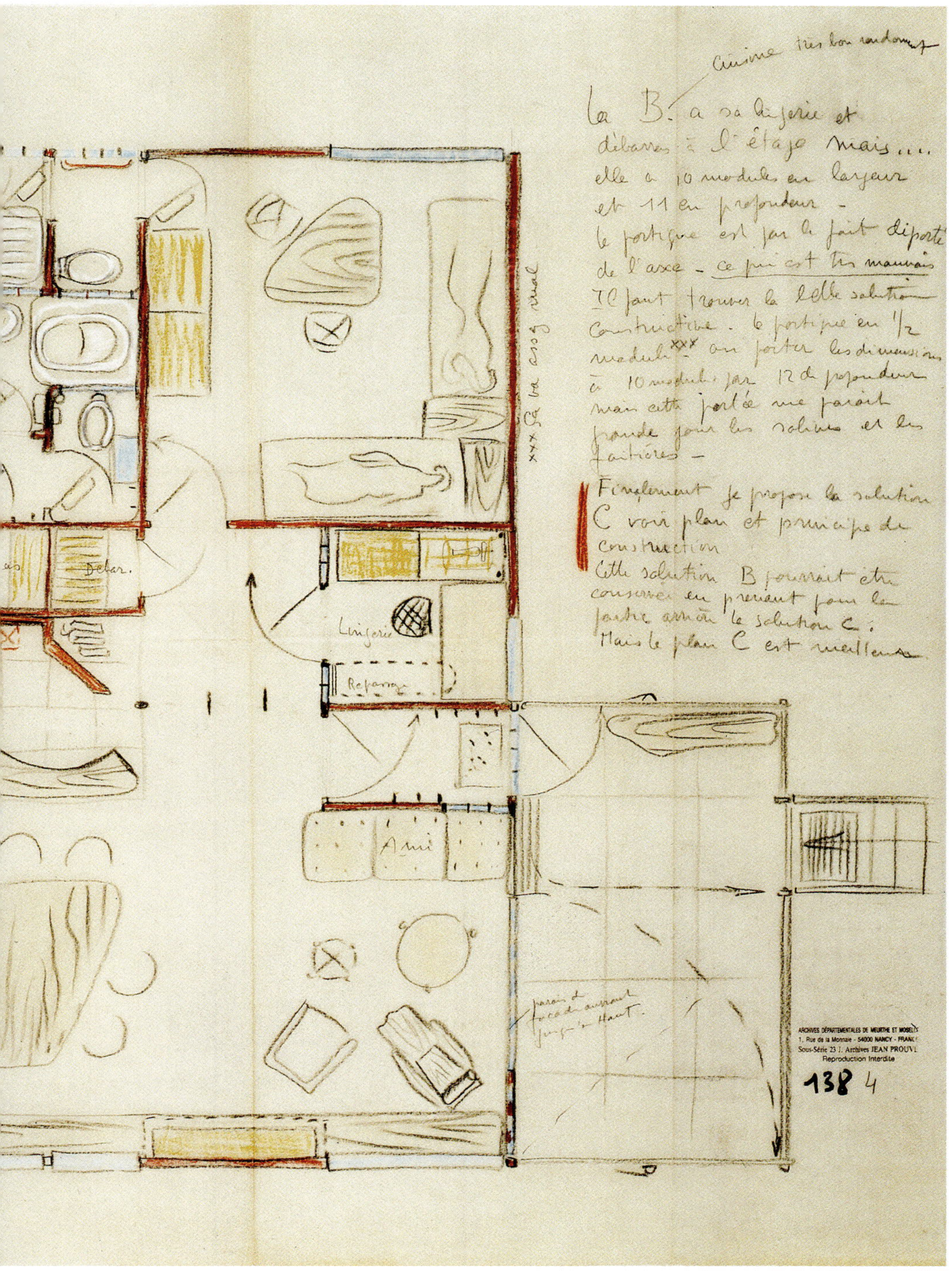
Cuisine très bon rendement
la B. a sa lingerie et
débarras à l'étage mais....
elle a 10 modules en largeur
et 11 en profondeur –
le portique est par le fait déporté
de l'axe – ce qui est très mauvais
Il faut trouver la belle solution
constructive. le portique en 1/2
module xxx ou porter les dimensions
à 10 modules par 12 de profondeur
mais cette portée me paraît
grande pour les solives et les
faîtières –
Finalement je propose la solution
C voir plan et principe de
construction
Cette solution B pourrait être
conservée en prenant pour la
partie avant la solution C.
Mais le plan C est meilleur
Débar.
Lingerie
Repassage
Ami
ARCHIVES DÉPARTEMENTALES DE MEURTHE ET MOSELLE
1, Rue de la Monnaie - 54000 NANCY - FRANCE
Sous-Série 23 J. Archives JEAN PROUVÉ
Reproduction Interdite
138 4

MAISON TROPICALE

Jean Prouvé
Maxéville, France, 1949–1951

Prouvé's attempts to utilize the extensive production capacity of the plant he established after the Second World War in Maxéville by building prefabricated houses proved to be unexpectedly difficult. Hence, the request he received from Paul Herbé, who had been appointed as a town planner for Niger, must have been more than welcome. Herbé was interested in a house that was not only suited to the tropics but could also be transported by airplane. The first of these houses was intended for the director of the University of Niamey, and others were to follow—but, it never came to that. Prouvé's factory was only ever able to deliver two additional houses—to Brazzaville two years later, and these had already been revised.

Instead of standing on a flat ground plate, the houses in Brazzaville stood on stilts and were connected to each other by a bridge. They served as the office and residence of the director of the local office of the Bureau d'Information de l'Aluminium Français. The reason for putting

Floor plan, elevation and section of both houses in Brazzaville

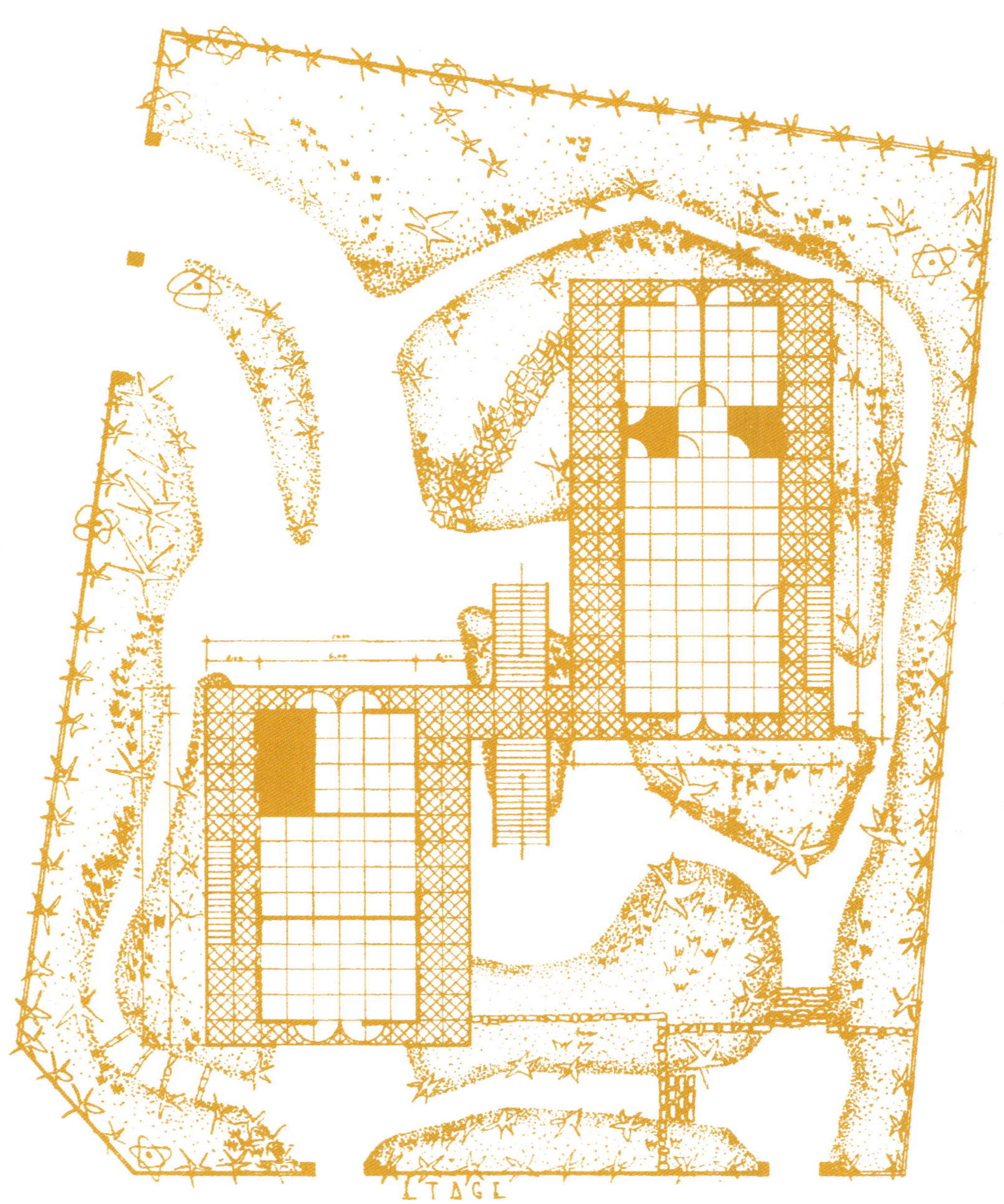

the buildings up on stilts was the steep slope of the terrain along the street. Prouvé had considered various means of adapting the building to the climate: the inner core consists of various fixed and sliding aluminum walls with circular perforations; there is also a narrow wraparound veranda, which is enclosed by a railing and adjustable blinds for solar protection. The roof also adheres to the two-layer principle; natural ventilation between the two layers is meant to reduce the heat from the tin roof in the sun. All of the load-bearing components were made of folded sheet steel; all of the others, particularly the roof, were made of sheet aluminum.

Unfortunately, there were never any subsequent orders, because the houses were simply too expensive. Yet the prototype houses, with their grid structure and obviously industrial character on open display, became prominent examples of successful modern architecture. All three of the houses have been preserved. In the meantime, they have been taken apart and restored, and one of them was sold by Christie's at an auction in 2007.

Opposite top: Assembly of the house on a concrete ground plate in Niamey, Niger, 1949

Opposite bottom: Unloading building parts from the plane in Niamey, Niger, 1949

Above: Construction of the houses in Brazzaville on stilts

Previous spread: Trial assembly of a part of the building on the premises of the factory in Maxéville, 1949

Below: The section shows the structure of the central support and the chimney-like ventilation opening in the roof

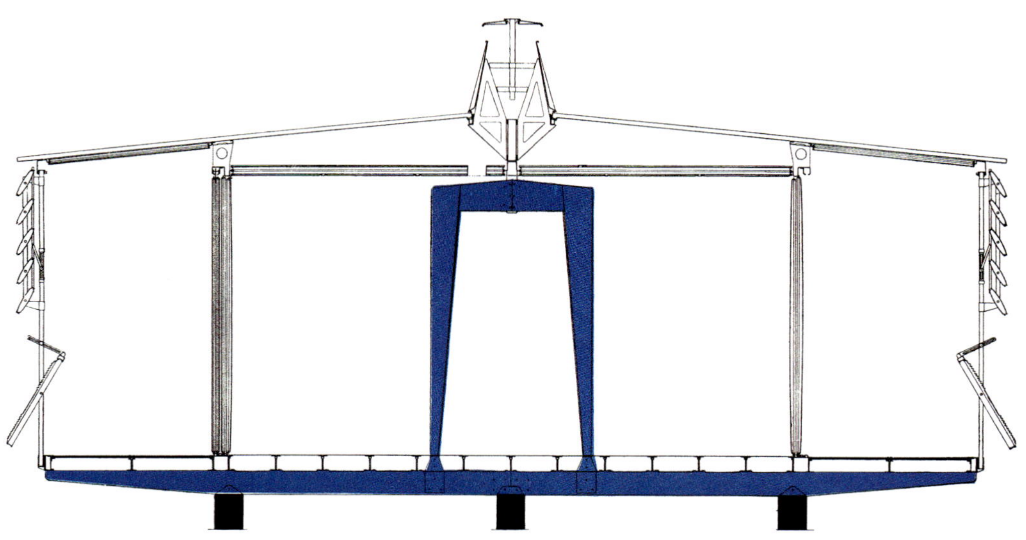

LE BUREAU D'INFORMATION DE BRAZZAVILLE

Le Bureau d'Information de Brazzaville a été officiellement inauguré le 3 décembre 1951 par M. Jean Dupin, président du Conseil d'Administration de L'Aluminium Français, entouré de MM. Marcel Pubellier, directeur de la Cégédur, Roger Voisard, directeur de Studal, et Jacques Piget, directeur de ce bureau africain. A cette manifestation assistaient les personnalités les plus marquantes de l'A. E. F. On notait la présence de MM. Bordier, chef de cabinet de M. Chauvet, Haut-Commissaire de la République; Mestre, représentant le Gouverneur Cédile; Cabou, directeur général des Affaires Économiques; Puech, directeur général des Douanes, ainsi que la plupart des autorités militaires et des dirigeants des affaires industrielles, commerciales, bancaires, etc.

Cette réception ayant eu lieu à la tombée de la nuit. il a été impossible de recevoir les personnalités du Congo belge par suite des horaires des vedettes traversant le fleuve. A leur intention, une deuxième réception a été organisée le mercredi 5 décembre à laquelle une quarantaine de personnes de tous les milieux assistaient.

La présentation du nouveau Bureau d'Information de L'Aluminium Fran-

58

TECHBUILT HOUSE

Carl Koch
Techbuilt, Inc.
Cambridge, Massachusetts, USA, 1954–1967

Carl Koch was one of the first architects in America to be influenced by European Modernism. While still at Harvard, where he was taught by Walter Gropius and Marcel Breuer, among others, he was inspired by the idea of the Bauhaus and worked in the office of the Functionalist architect Sven Markelius from 1940 to 1941 in Stockholm. In the post-war period, Koch became convinced that the housing shortage could be alleviated by the construction of prefabricated houses that could be easily assembled and disassembled. In 1948 he created the box-like Acorn House, his first prefabricated house, on which *Life* magazine reported extensively, but this did not ensure financial success.

The prefabricated house developed in 1952 by Techbuilt, Inc. was an entirely different case: Koch placed less emphasis on the formal austerity of the Bauhaus and more on a pleasant exterior, to which the deeply overhanging eaves of the pitched roof, inspired by Japanese architecture, made a considerable contribution. It was presumably the first prefabricated house to be marketed on television. Millions saw the

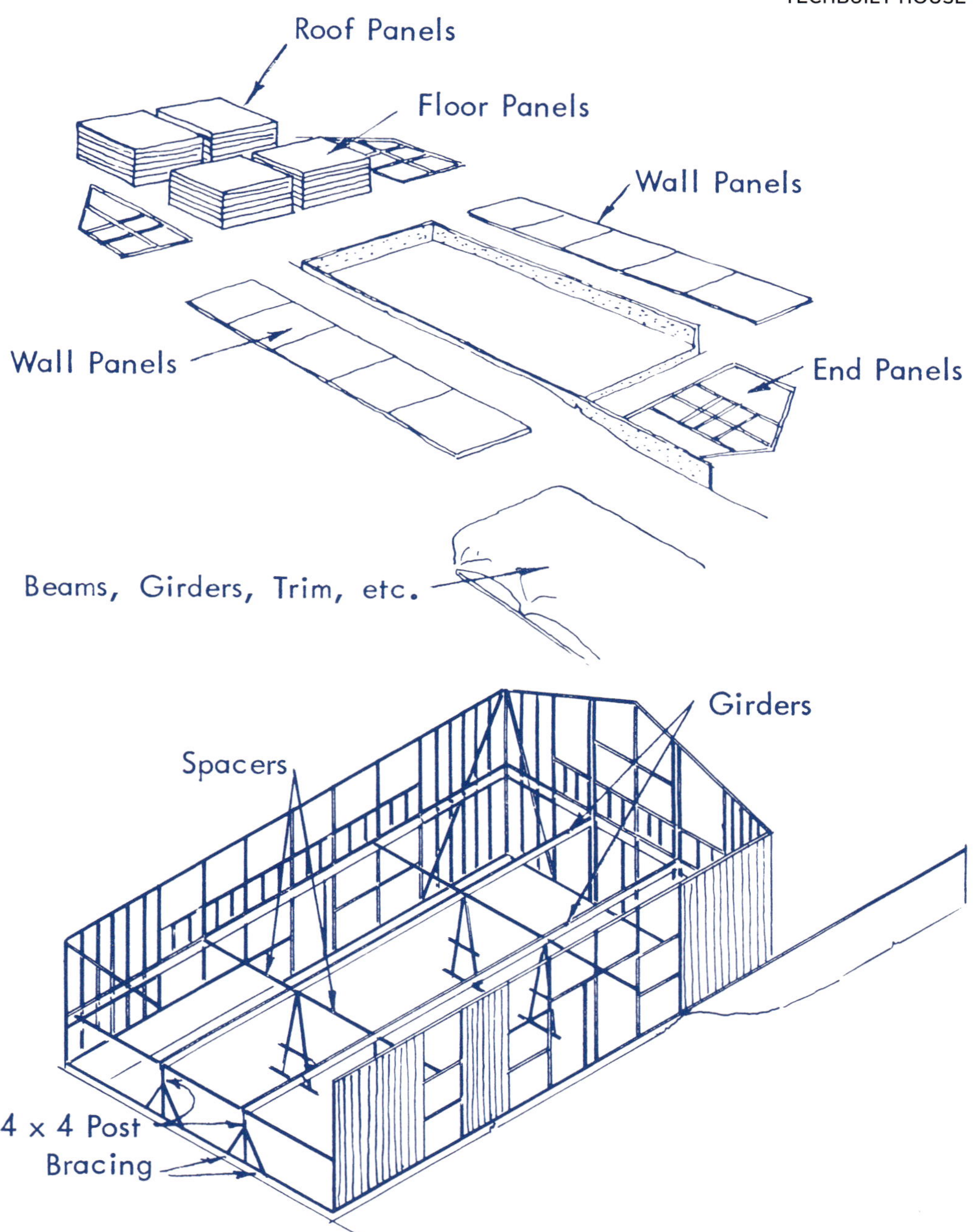

Opposite: Cover of Carl Koch's 1958 book *At Home with Tomorrow*

Above: A single truckload delivers the shell of a house. Four men can set up the shell and roof in two days' time

Below: The Techbuilt Cottage was a simpler, one-story addition to the program

Opposite top: Floor plan

Opposite bottom: Unlike most houses built in the United States, the ground floor of Techbuilt Houses was slightly below ground level

Following spread: Interior view

broadcast in February 1954 in which the assembly of a Techbuilt kit was minutely demonstrated. After the broadcast the company was swamped with orders.

Koch soon established a franchise system with offices throughout the country. On Eastern Long Island alone, more than 50 Techbuilt Houses were erected in the early 1960s. The houses had between 570 and 775 sq. ft. of floor space, and even the least expensive version cost less than $20,000. The building components were delivered on a truck and could be easily assembled in just a few days. The pre-assembled wall panels, insulated with fiberglass, pre-cut beams, windows, and the sliding doors, were all assembled on the basis of a simple post-and-beam structure.

Roughly 100 of the 500 Techbuilts delivered within the United States are still standing.

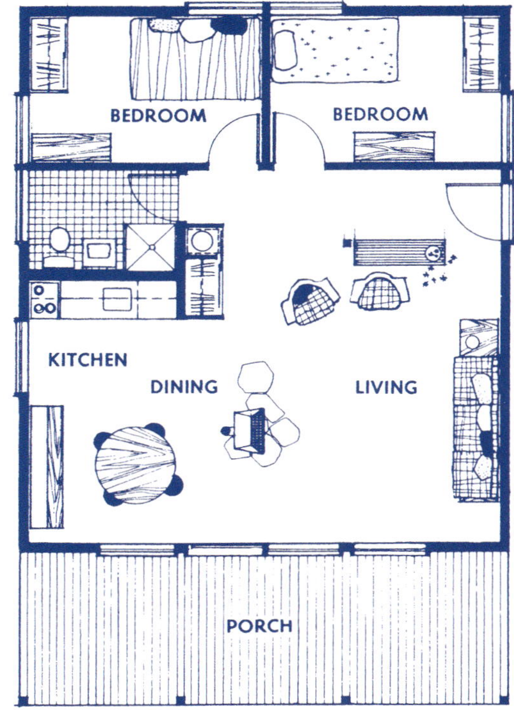
BEDROOM
BEDROOM
KITCHEN
DINING
LIVING
PORCH

ERDMAN PREFAB NO. 1

Frank Lloyd Wright
Marshall Erdman and Associates, Inc.
Madison, Wisconsin, USA, 1956–1961

This was not the first collaboration between Frank Lloyd Wright and Marshall Erdman. Wright had already put this master builder of Lithuanian extraction in charge of executing his designs for the First Unitarian Society Church in Madison, Wisconsin, between 1949 and 1951. Hence, after Erdman had established a company to build prefabricated houses in 1951, Wright saw an opportunity to resume their successful collaboration in what he recognized as the important field of prefabricated residential construction in 1954. However, it was 1956 before he submitted the plans for his three prefab versions of the Usonian Houses that he had developed for the American middle class in the 1930s. The first Prefab No. 1 was built that same year, and this new type of prefabricated house was presented in a cover story by *House & Home* magazine.

The Prefab No. 1, however, can only be partially seen as a prefabricated house, since it is a combination of prefabricated parts and brickwork. The house is laid out as an elongated L. It is divided into a sleeping area under the pitched roof on the long side and a carport under a flat roof on its short side. These two segments, which are made of prefabricated parts, are connected to each other by a brick-built living area with a kitchen and a fireplace. The Prefab No. 1 is a one-story building and, depending on its configuration, provides between 1,860 and 2,400 sq. ft. of floor space.

Opposite: Perspective drawing

Above: Catherine and William Cass House, "The Crimson Beech" on Staten Island, New York, 1959

The façades of the prefabricated parts are clad in cream-colored Masonite panels and decorated with strips of American redwood, emphasizing the horizontal orientation of the building. The house looks closed from the front, while wide windows in the back open up to the garden. The roof is covered with terneplate, rolled iron coated with a tin-lead alloy. The furnishings were also designed by Wright. Nearly all of the built-in elements are made of mahogany. Before Wright began his work, he asked the clients to submit a topographical map and photos of the lot in order to gain a better understanding of the building site. He also insisted on inspecting the houses after they were completed.

It is obvious that with this level of individual involvement, similar to what would be expected in conventional building practice, only eleven prefabs were ever built. Two of them, however, proved to be surprisingly mobile: in 1985 one was moved over a distance of 40 miles from its original location in Madison to Beaver Dam, Wisconsin, the other one was moved over a distance of 525 miles from the Greater Chicago area to a location in Pennsylvania in 2007, where it is now used as a guest house.

Opposite: Cass House, garden front

Below: Interior of the Cass House

MAISON ALBA

Jean Prouvé
Maxéville, France, 1956–1962

The "seed" from which the single-family house called Alba (Aluminium-béton armé) developed was the prefabricated small bathroom unit that Jean Prouvé built in 1935 for the Aero Club in the French town of Buc. In his workshops in Maxéville, he collaborated with his employee Maurice Silvy in further developing the Alba single-family house, which contained a "monobloc"—a prefabricated kitchenette, bathroom, and toilet—at its core, which simultaneously served as a supporting element in the construction of the house. This monobloc was made of reinforced concrete and set down on a foundation trough of in-situ concrete.

A modified version of the Maison Alba, with a simplified floor plan and monobloc made of metal, was built within the context of a charitable program: Abbé Pierre of Paris, who had dedicated his life to fighting homelessness, approached Prouvé in 1955, asking him to develop a system for building low-cost single-families houses. On February 21, 1956, a model of the Alba was erected in the middle of Paris, on the banks of the Seine, in a spectacular publicity event witnessed

Opposite: Seynave House in Beauvallon, France, 1962, floor plan

Below: Terrace view

by numerous onlookers. On only 560 sq. ft. of floor space the Alba boasted two bedrooms and a multifunctional living room, which one entered directly through the front door. However, the innovative model was never produced in series since the building authorities refused to grant approval of the central sanitary unit in the middle of the living room.

However, between 1961 and 1962 Prouvé erected two more of the Alba houses. Working with the architect Neil Hutchinson, he constructed the holiday home "Seynave" in Beauvallon for a paper manufacturer from Lorraine. Horizontal support beams bearing the ceiling load rest on a number of concrete cores that contain parts of the kitchen, the toilet, and storage space. Slender red steel pipes provide additional stability, while the façade and the remaining interior walls were executed in sheets of laminated wood. In 1962 Prouvé built the other Alba in Saint-Dié, together with the architects Baumann and Remondino, as a home for his daughter Françoise and her husband Pierre Gauthier. Here, however, unlike the holiday home in Beauvallon, both the inside and the outside of the two-layer wall structures were clad in corrugated aluminum panels and thermally insulated with polystyrene.

Seynave House in Beauvallon, France, 1962

Seynave House in Beauvallon, France, 1962

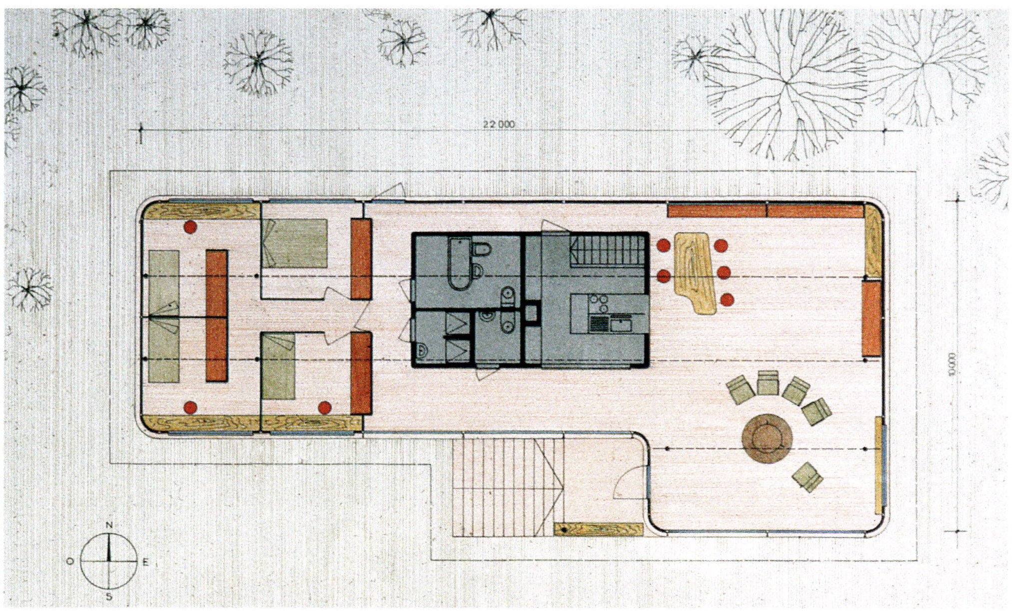
22 000
10 000
N
O
E
S

Opposite: Gauthier House, Saint-Dié, France, 1962, overall view (top) and and plan (bottom)

Below: House for Abbé Pierre on the banks of the Seine in Paris, France, 1956

PRE-BUILT HOUSE

Norman Cherner
U.S. Department of Housing
Washington, D.C., USA, 1957

Norman Cherner (1920–1987) was a famous furniture designer; his best-known design is the Plycraft Cherner Armchair, a softly curving chair made of plywood, which he introduced in 1958. The prominent role that chairs came to play within Cherner's oeuvre is reflected in the name of the company his two sons established in 1999 in order to market their father's products: The Cherner Chair Company. Yet Cherner also designed tables, storage units, textiles, glassware, lamps—and houses. In the 1950s, he spent an extended period concentrating on prefabricated housing, publishing his thoughts and designs in several books. *Fabricating Houses from Component Parts* was published in 1957 and presents, as the fifth of fifteen designs, the "Bent House," commissioned by the U.S. Department of Housing. After having been shown at an exhibition in Vienna, the house was erected in Ridgefield, Connecticut, where it served Cherner as a residence and workplace. Technical literature today refers to it as "Cherner's Pre-Built."

It is a one-story flat-roofed building on stilts, with a floor plan determined by the construction method: "Bent Construction" uses a number of wooden frames consisting of two supports, ceiling and roof beams, which are connected to each other by wall elements. Hence the walls are not load-bearing. The house, mounted on pillars, rests on foundation pads. The "bents" were produced in a factory in a variety of shapes. Cherner's own pre-built house consists of six

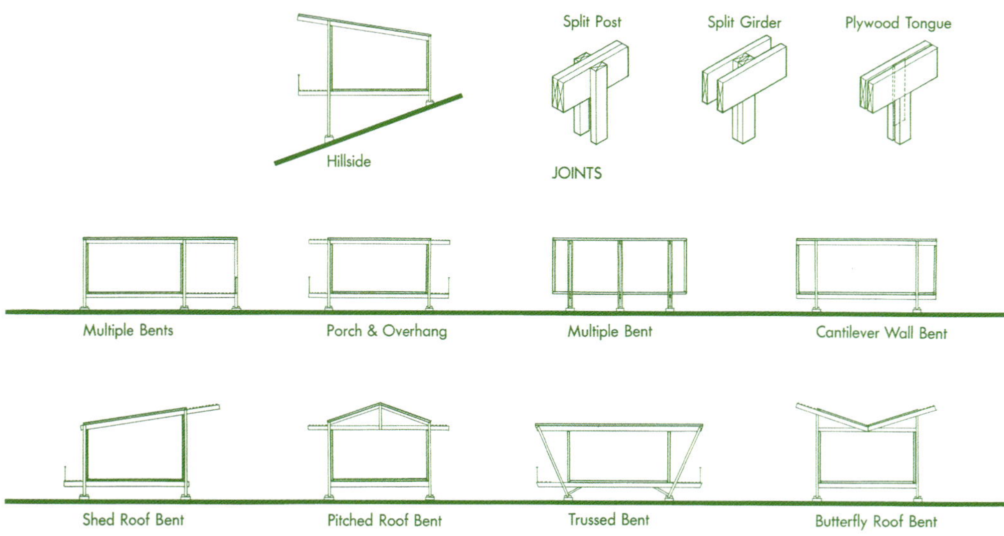

Opposite: Diagram showing different types of bent construction

Below: Isometric drawing showing bent construction

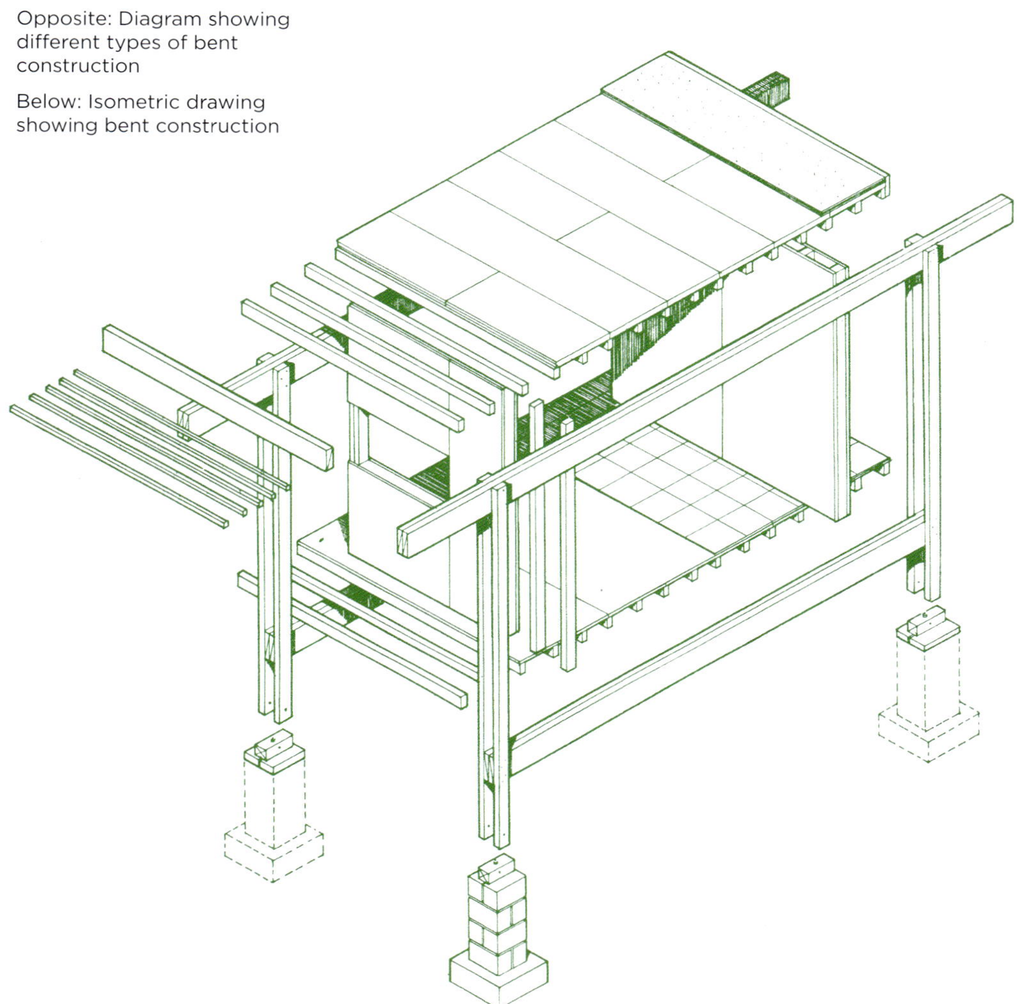

bents, each 16 ft. in length, which are assembled with an axial distance of 8 ft. Hence, the house is 5 × 8 = 40 ft. long and 16 ft. wide. The middle section of the house, accessible by an outdoor stairway, contains the hallway, bathroom, and the kitchen unit, jutting out of the living room. The square living and dining area is located to the right of the entrance, the two bedrooms are to the left. The house has 7 ft. ceilings, with the floor 3 ft. above the ground.

The "Girder House" is another one of the structures presented by Cherner. Here, two or more beams installed in parallel are borne by supports and connected to each other by rafters. Non-load-bearing walls, glass façades, or wide sliding doors can be hung from the beams across the entire length of the house.

Above: Woodlands House, Ramapo, New York, 1948

Below: Details of girder construction

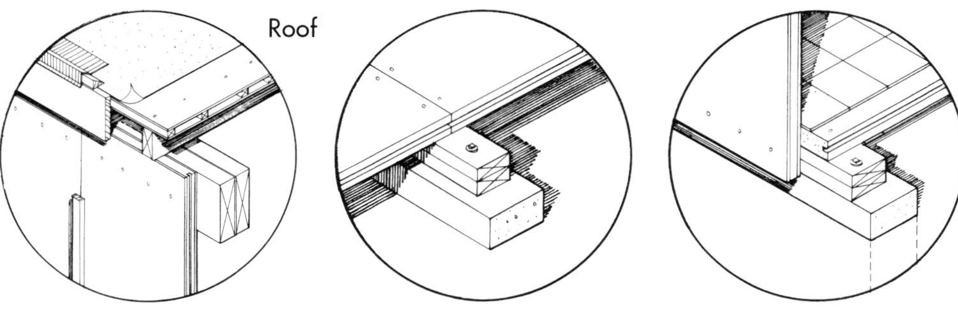

Right: Pre-Built House No.5, manufactured in Camden, Maine, 1957

Below: Woodlands House, interior

Fredric Bensen Summer Residence, Saltaire, Fire Island, New York, 1958. Exterior photo, axonometric drawing, section and plan

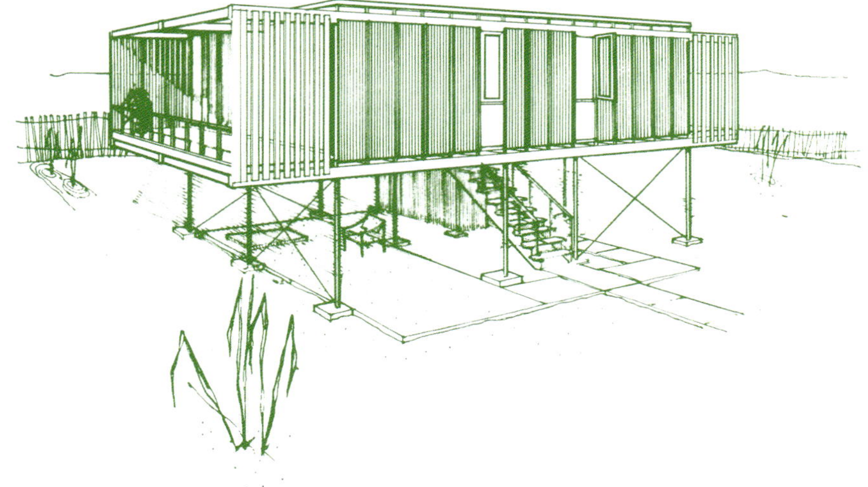

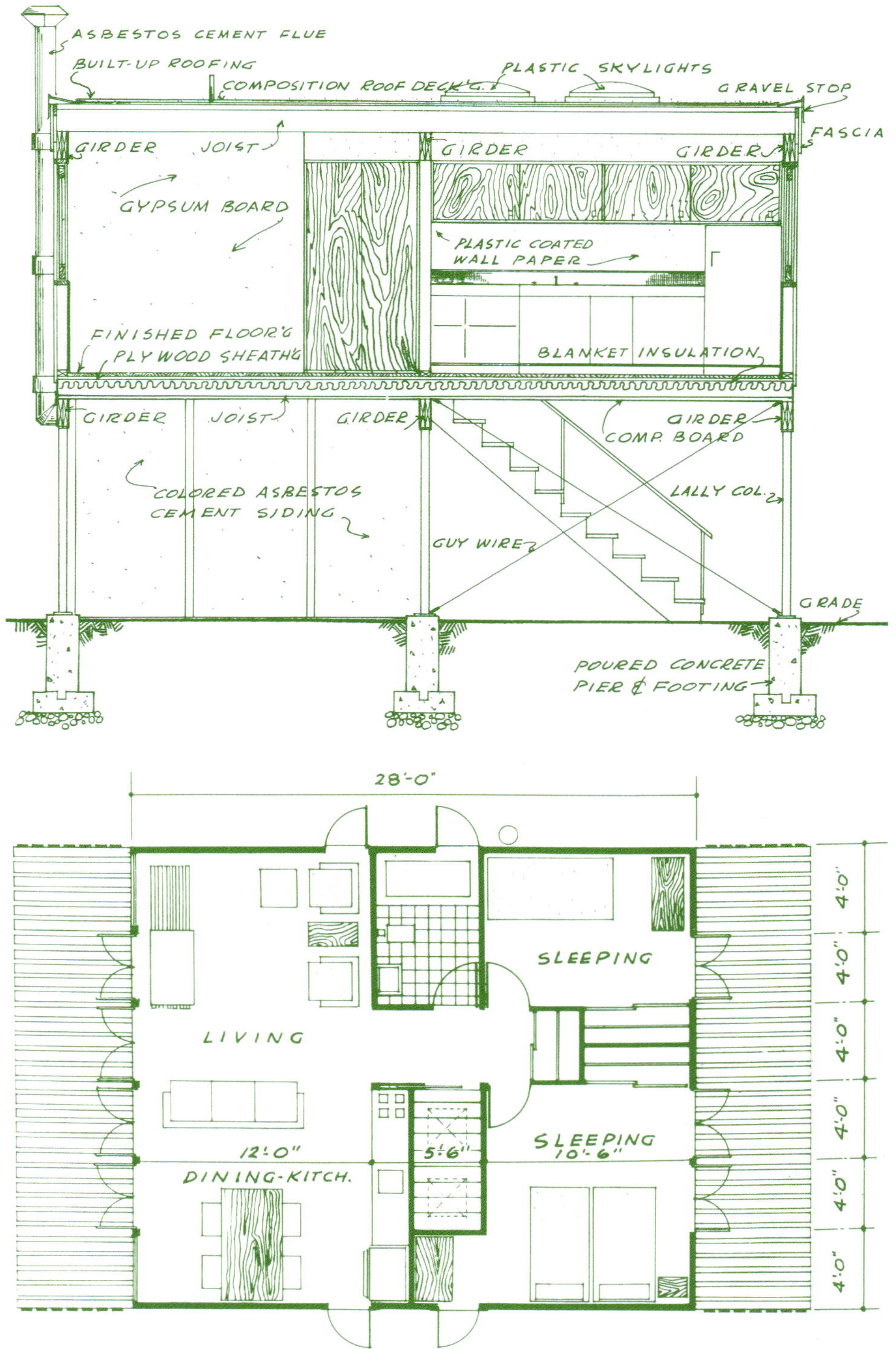
ASBESTOS CEMENT FLUE
BUILT-UP ROOFING
COMPOSITION ROOF DECK'G.
PLASTIC SKYLIGHTS
GRAVEL STOP
FASCIA
GIRDER
JOIST
GIRDER
GIRDER
GYPSUM BOARD
PLASTIC COATED WALL PAPER
FINISHED FLOOR'G
PLYWOOD SHEATH'G
BLANKET INSULATION
GIRDER
JOIST
GIRDER
GIRDER
COMP. BOARD
COLORED ASBESTOS CEMENT SIDING
LALLY COL.
GUY WIRE
GRADE
POURED CONCRETE PIER & FOOTING
28'-0"
4'0"
4'0"
4'0"
4'0"
4'0"
4'0"
SLEEPING
LIVING
SLEEPING
10'-6"
12'-0"
5'-6"
DINING-KITCH.

MARIHOUSE

Aarno Ruusuvuori
Marikylä Corporation
Bökars, Finland, 1966

When the visionary textile designer Armi Ratia and her husband Viljo established the Marimekko company in 1951, it could hardly have been anticipated that just a few years later the small textile manufacturer would become a label for which there would be a great demand throughout the world. After Jacqueline Kennedy bought seven of their dresses in 1960, Marimekko shops were opened in the United States, Europe, Japan, and Australia. In 1962 the couple began to cooperate with the architect Aarno Ruusuvuori, known for the modernity and asceticism of his designs, who took charge of designing the Marimekko shops. However, the Ratias were not only interested in printing and selling textiles, but also in creating a new lifestyle. In 1963 Ruusuvuori was commissioned by Marimekko to design a model development for 3,500 inhabitants, including company staff, near Porvoo, a country town 31 miles east of Helsinki. In order to produce the prefabricated houses that were planned for this project, Ruusuvuori established the Marikylä Corporation that same year.

The building components of the model house were produced in Bökars near Porvoo, the headquarters of the Marimekko company.

Contemporary color photographs, made for advertising purposes, show a wood-clad one-story residential box full of colorful interiors in the middle of a forest of birch and pine trees. The 520 sq. ft. block was assembled on site out of four prefabricated room units: one contained the bedroom, another the bathroom and kitchen, two others contained the living room. Brightly

Below and following spread:
The model house, 1963

Opposite: Axonometric drawing

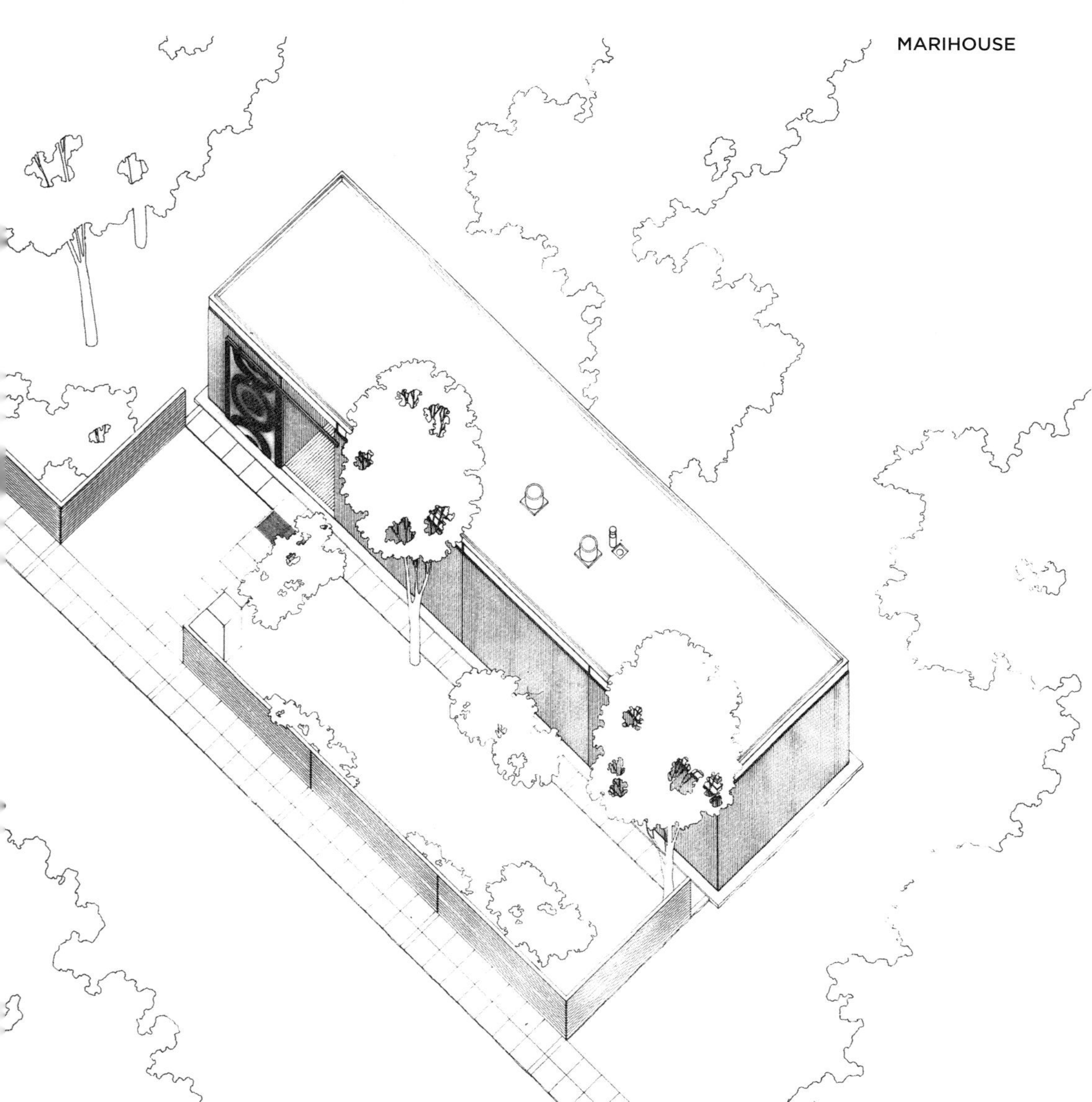

visible in the large windows of this “blue submarine” (a title bestowed upon it by the contemporary press) were curtains of natural materials in patterns designed for the company by Marimekko’s head designer Maija Isola.

The press reacted enthusiastically, celebrating Marimekko’s project as a departure into new architectural territory. But all of the enthusiasm was to no avail. The very first inhabitants—of all people Armi and Viljo’s son and his family—found the living quarters too cramped. The failure of this residential utopia was ultimately due to the cost, and even more so to the reluctance of the company’s employees to live in an isolated development deep in the woods.

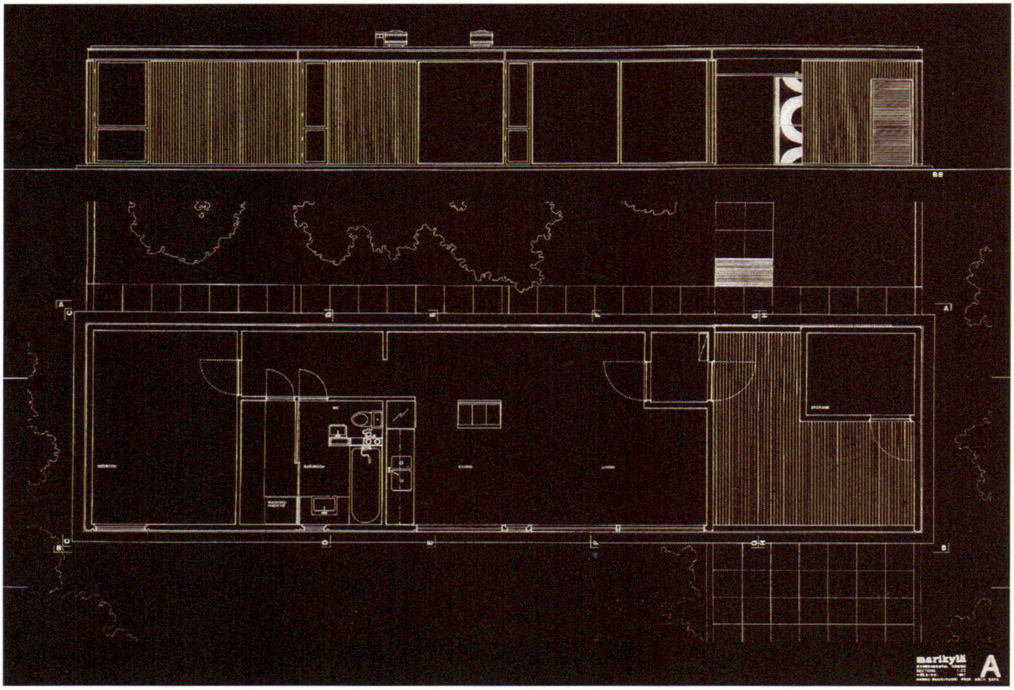

Opposite top and above:
The kitchen in the Marihouse

Opposite bottom: Elevation
and floor plan

Above: Aarno Ruusuvuori designed a sauna for Marimekko intended for the international market, but—like the Marihouse Project—it never went into serial production

Opposite: Planned, but never realized, version with more floor space

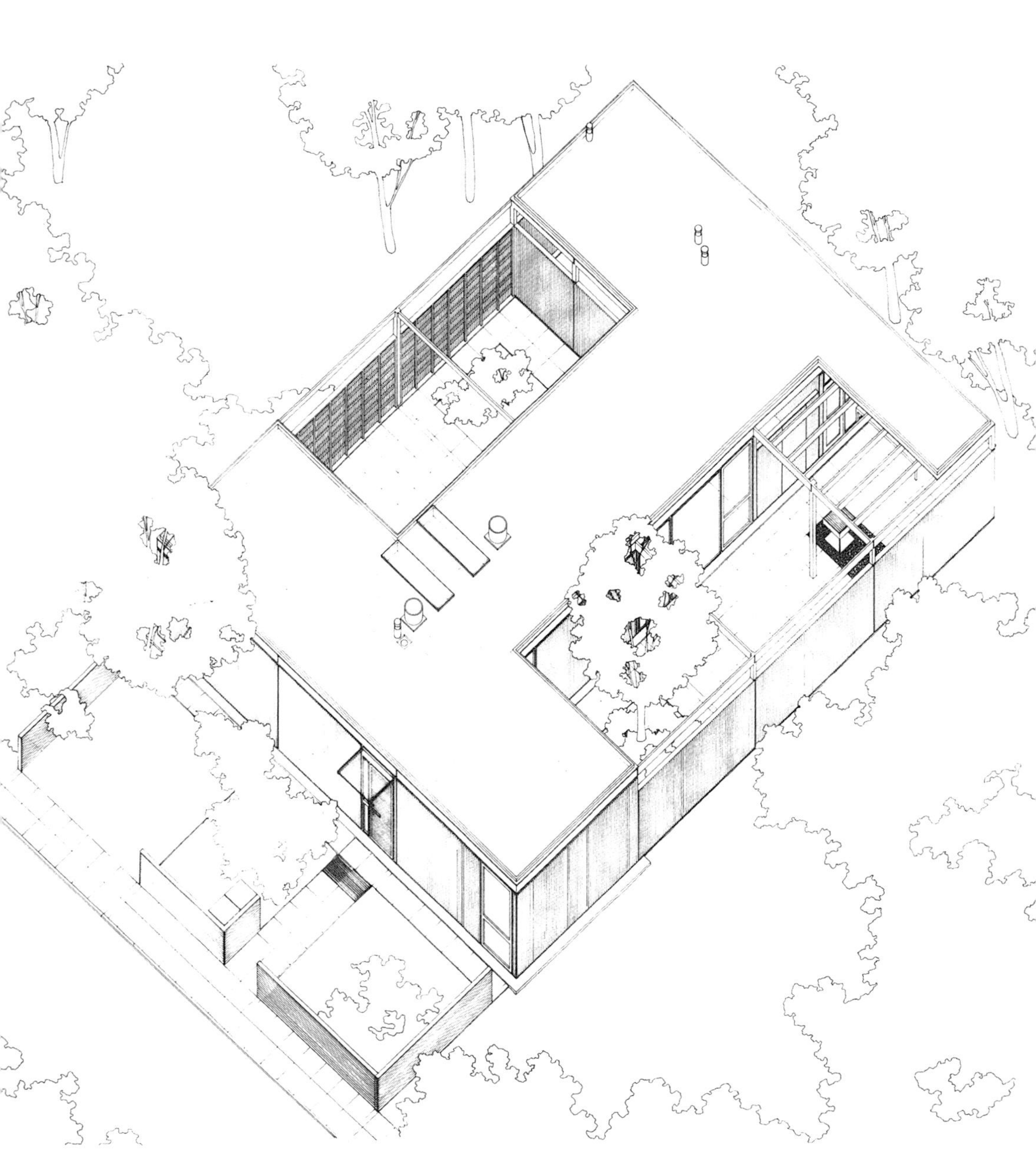

BULLE SIX COQUES

Jean Maneval
Bati-Plastique, Chantiers Dubigeon
Nantes, France, 1967–1970

The excellent tensile characteristics of fiber-reinforced plastics have been familiar to us since the 1940s, due to their use in airplane, automobile, and boat construction. However, it took until the 1960s for a number of architects to discover plastic as a building material. Fiber-reinforced plastic resins are very lightweight and therefore perfectly suited for use in lightweight supporting structures spanning broad distances, as well as for houses that are to be transported. In 1964, the French architect and city planner Jean Maneval (1923–1986) designed a mini weekend house measuring only 390 sq. ft. Twenty of these houses were erected in Gripp, in the Campan region of the Département Hautes-Pyrénées, in 1967. There they formed an experimental vacation village.

As the name indicates, the house Bulle six coques (Bubble made of six shells) consists of six "shells" (coques) made of polyester and grouped in the shape of a star around a central element (bulle = bubble). They are screwed to each other as well as to the steel skeleton that supports the floor. The house floats on a support just over 3 ft. above the ground. Every shell is roughly 6 ½ ft. wide, the diameter of the building is roughly 22 ½ ft., and the ceiling height is just over 8 ft. There are two basic models, which can be freely combined with each other: shells with full-length windows at the front, or shells with a completely closed front but with one or two small windows on the narrow side. The entrance to the house is reached over an outdoor stairway leading to a door on the narrow side of the shell.

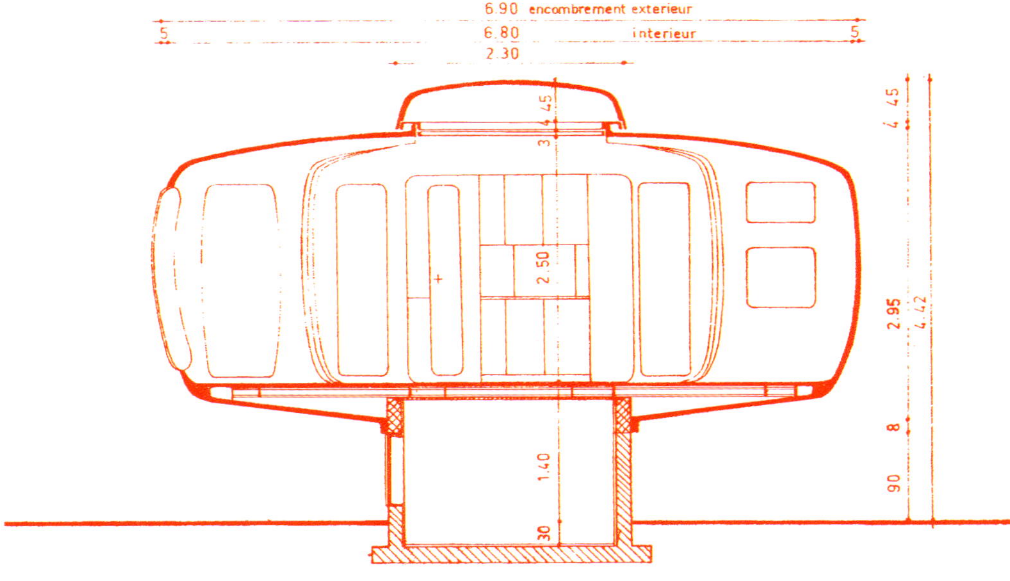

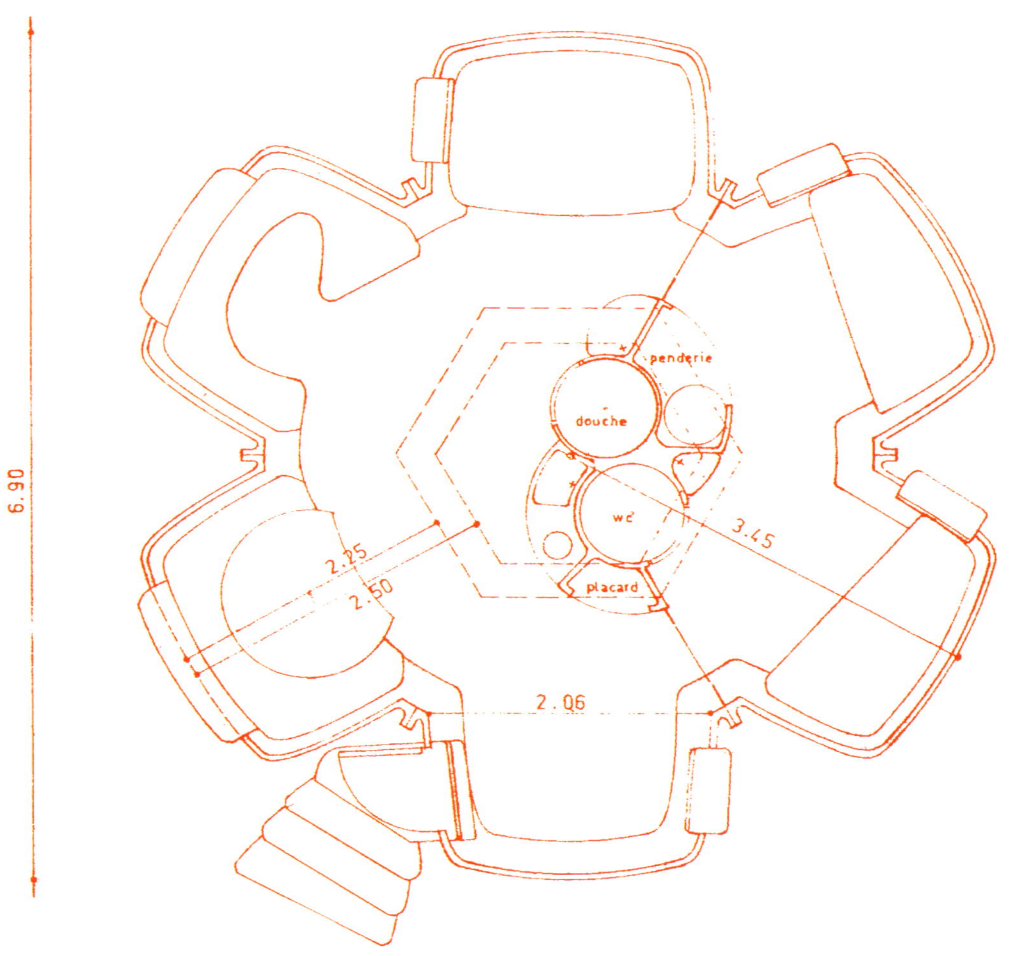

Section (opposite) and plan (above)

The water and power supply lines run through a shaft in the support column. Consequently, Maneval installed the kitchen unit, and the toilet and shower unit in the middle of the house, separated from each other by walls. The remainder of the space could be used as dining, living, or sleeping areas. The storage units at the center of the house and the other furniture were executed in wood and metal, according to designs by Maneval.

The house went into production in series in 1968. It was available in three colors, white, green, and chestnut brown. The six shells, each weighing 463 lbs., were delivered by truck. Only a very few of the houses were ever sold—the figures range between 30 and 100—before production was discontinued in 1970. The holiday complex in Gripp was dismantled in 1998, but some of the houses were preserved.

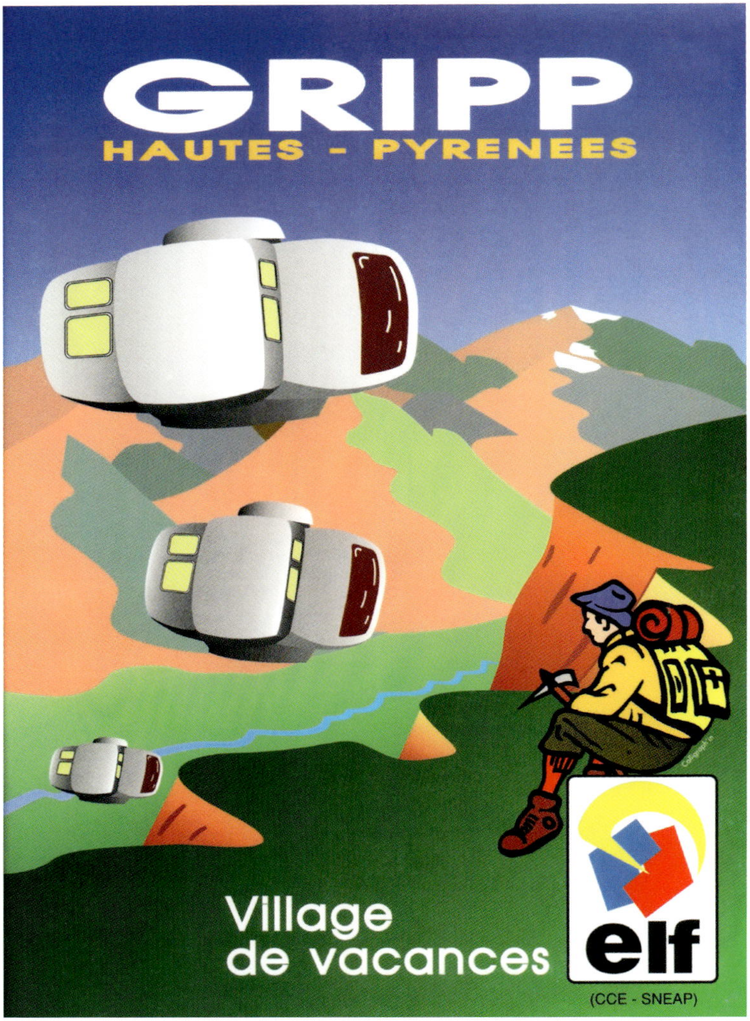

GRIPP
HAUTES - PYRENEES

Village
de vacances

elf

(CCE - SNEAP)

Above: Advertisement for the holiday village owned by the Elf oil company in the French Pyrenean town of Gripp

Opposite top: In 1971 the Bulle six coques was presented at the *International Plastics Exhibition* (IKA) in Lüdenscheid, Germany, under the name "Orion"

Right and opposite bottom: Assembly and interior of the model house, 1967

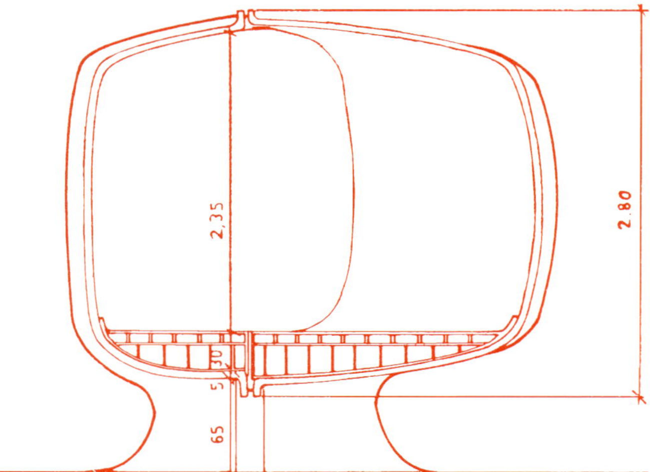

Above and below: Plan and section of the Minibulle: Bulle trois coques (Bubble of three shells)

Opposite top: The Elf oil company's holiday village in Gripp

Opposite bottom: Cross section perspective

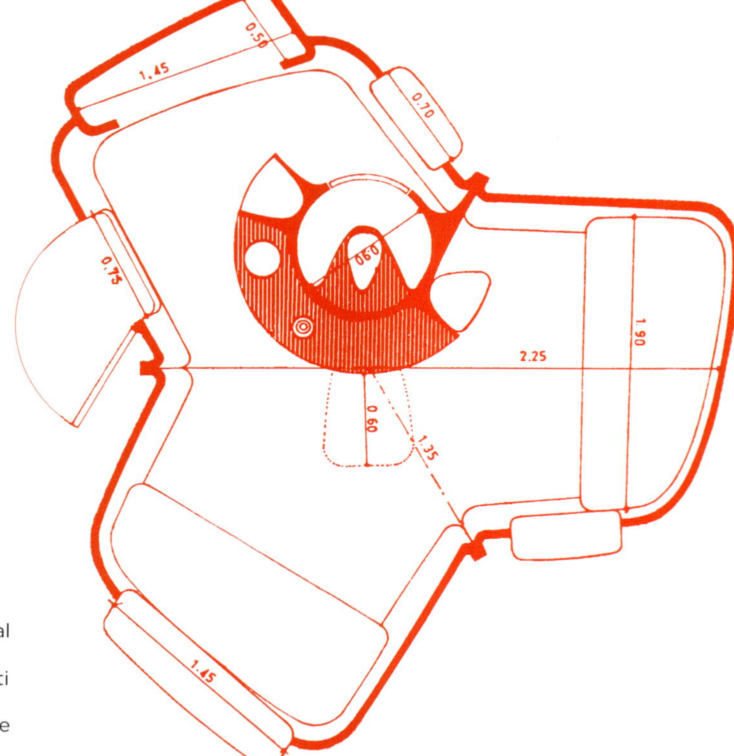

Following spread: Invasion from outer space: the Bulle six coques at the International Plastics Exhibition in Lüdenscheid, Germany, in 1971. Matti Suuronen's Futuro can be seen on the left and the space capsule-like Rondo house by Casoni & Casoni on the right

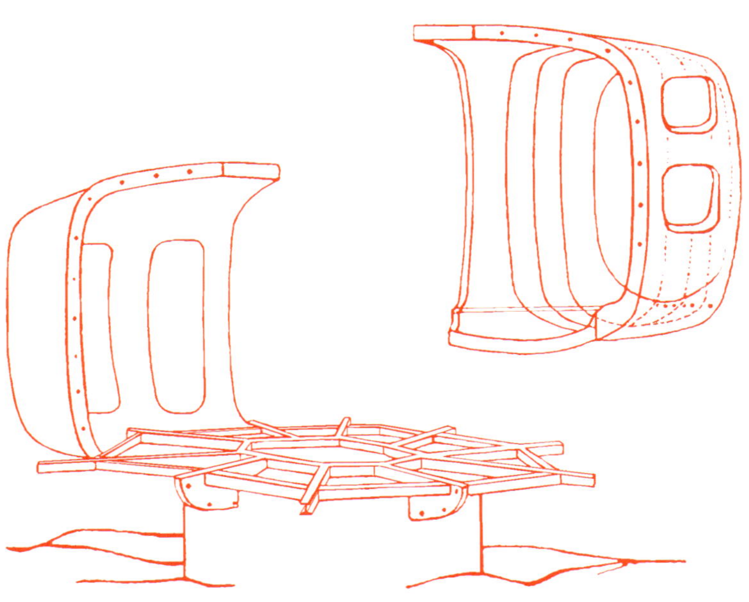

rondo

RISOM HOUSE

Jens Risom
Stanmar, Inc.
Wayland, Massachusetts, USA, 1967

In 1967, the Risoms decided to build a vacation home on Block Island, just off the coast of Rhode Island. In order to save money and time, Risom chose a prefabricated wooden house built by Stanmar Inc., a company from Wayland, Massachusetts, but altered a few details in the plans. After a two-month building period—according to the building company an earlier completion date was delayed by heavy fog—the Risoms were able to take possession of their "custom-made prefab." Up until this point, this is a relatively unspectacular story. Yet this house became famous for three reasons: one is that Jens Risom, who was born in Copenhagen in 1916 and had been living in or near New York since 1938, was already a famous designer. Secondly, this inspired *Life* magazine to publish a photo essay on the Risoms' house in 1967, and, thirdly, the house really is very special.

Opposite and above: Whether viewed from inside the living room, or from the surrounding landscape, pictures of both the completed house, and the house while under construction, show the glazed gable to be the frame of a distinctly dramatic feature

Following spread: In contrast to the standard version, the house has been extended and opened up in the front by means of extensive glazing

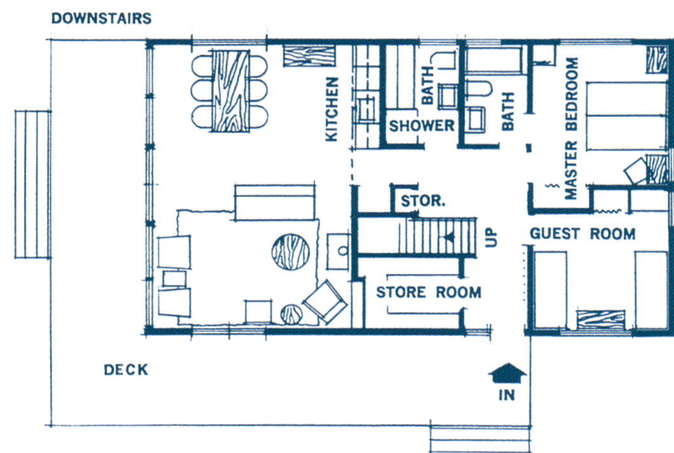

Kitchen, dining room, and living room area

The frontal view printed in *Life* is quite spectacular. Surrounded on two sides by a wooden terrace built on stilts, both the house and terrace seem to be floating over the green grass of the island—an effect that is amplified by the open flight of stairs. Its form is as simple as possible: one story with a pitched roof. Through the gable end of the house, which is fully glazed from top to bottom, there is a view of the living room with a comfortable sitting area, a dining table, an open kitchen, and the son's loft up on a gallery at the back. The rich green of the surroundings shimmers through a window at the back. Two additional bedrooms and bathrooms, which cannot be seen, are located at the rear on the ground floor, under the loft. A highly dramatic 20 ft. wall extending all the way up to the peak of the roof is made of wooden boards stained gray; it provides a counterpoint to all this transparency and a backdrop for the chimney pipe from the wood-burning stove. The walls on either side of the living area are the same color—while the wood of the floors and on the underside of the roof has been left naturally light.

The view from the house is no less spectacular; it overlooks a lighthouse and the ocean. Seen from the back, however, the house is far less exciting: here its origin in a catalog is more obvious—narrow windows in between vertical wooden siding on the outside. The walls, which were partially prefabricated in a factory, are anchored to the concrete foundation using massive bolts to keep the house safe during storms. The roof is covered with wooden shingles. The overall floor space of the house is 24 × 42 ft., the greater part of which (16 × 24 ft.) is taken up by the living room.

FUTURO

Matti Suuronen
Oy Polykem AB
Helsinki, Finland, 1968–1978

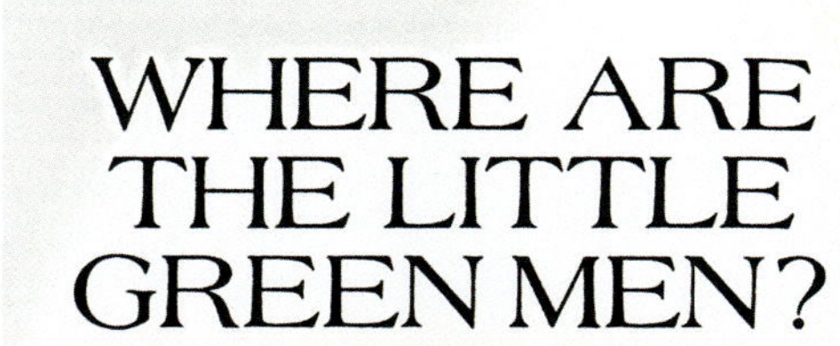

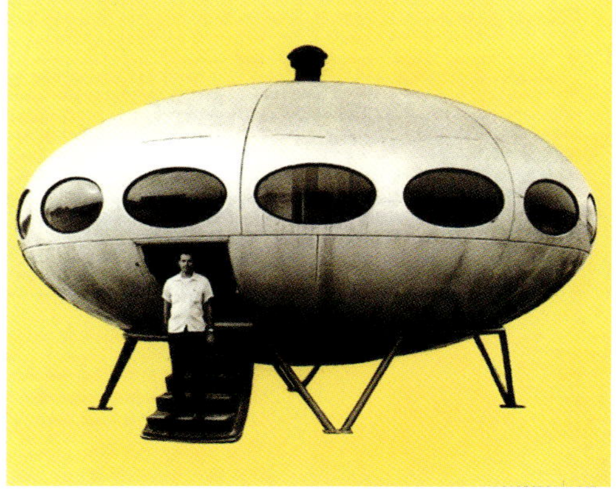

It was a simple ski house that the Finnish architect Matti Suuronen was asked to design for a friend in 1965. It was supposed to be easy to build in difficult terrain and quick to heat. What ultimately resulted was an icon of the belief in progress predominant in the age of space travel during the late 1960s; it attracted worldwide attention, for its creator had made a ski house that looked more like a UFO: an ellipsoid on four legs. The structure was made of fiberglass reinforced polyester. The architect had already gained experience building with plastic while fulfilling a commission to design a plastic dome for the top of a grain silo. The solution he adopted also made it possible for the capsule to be transported by helicopter, since it weighed relatively little.

The prototype he presented on the grounds of the Polykem company in 1968 measured over 26 ft. in diameter and 11 ft. 6 in. in height. Even in cold weather, the barely 540 sq. ft. of space in the capsule could be brought up to a comfortable indoor temperature within half an hour, thanks to its electric heating and polyurethane insulation. The most fascinating pieces of furniture were the pull-out lounge chairs, which were grouped around the fireplace in the middle. However, the price of $12,000 was exorbitant at the time.

After tremendous success in London at the *Finnfocus Export Fair* in October 1968, Polykem Ltd. decided to start producing the house in series. Within a short time, over 400 inquiries had been received from foreign companies interested in procuring production rights; licenses were granted in 25 countries. The Futuro house came on a truck in the form of 16 curved, fiberglass reinforced composite shells, which were screwed together on site and set onto a foundation ring. An even more effective advertising measure proved to be the option of having the complete Futuro delivered by helicopter.

In the 1970s, the photographer and advertising guru Charles Wilp had a Futuro erected on the roof of his own house in Düsseldorf, where he received guests like Andy Warhol and Christo, who also later wrapped the plastic ellipsoid during one of his art actions. The Futuro with the serial number 13 was purchased by the GDR and

A Futuro being delivered to its final location by a Swedish air force helicopter in 1969

installed in the Cultural Park in the Berlin district of Treptow in 1969. The "space capsule" soon became an attraction there, although some people suspected that it was a Stasi monitoring station. In fact, it only served as an information center and as a radio studio from which music was broadcast throughout the park. In the meantime it has been sold and removed from the now neglected park. It has since been transported to a nearby site on the banks of the Spree River.

Between 1968 and 1978, 20 Futuros were built in Finland alone. The website *thefuturo-house.com* documents 67 surviving units out of 96 that are known to have been produced.

Above: The Futuro at the 1971 *International Plastics Exhibition* (IKA 71) in Lüdenscheid, Germany. The Rondo house by Casoni & Casoni can be seen on the right

Opposite: The Futuro in Philadelphia, Pennsylvania, 1970

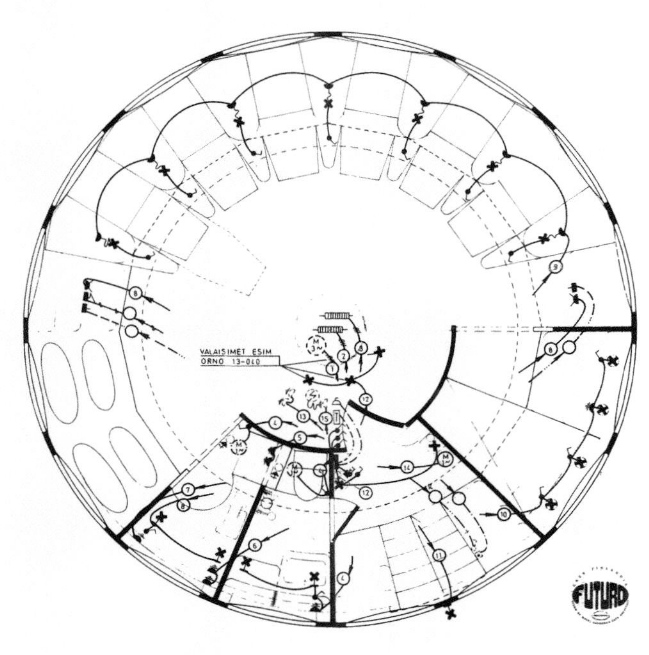
VALAISIMET ESIM
ORNO 13-040
FUTURO

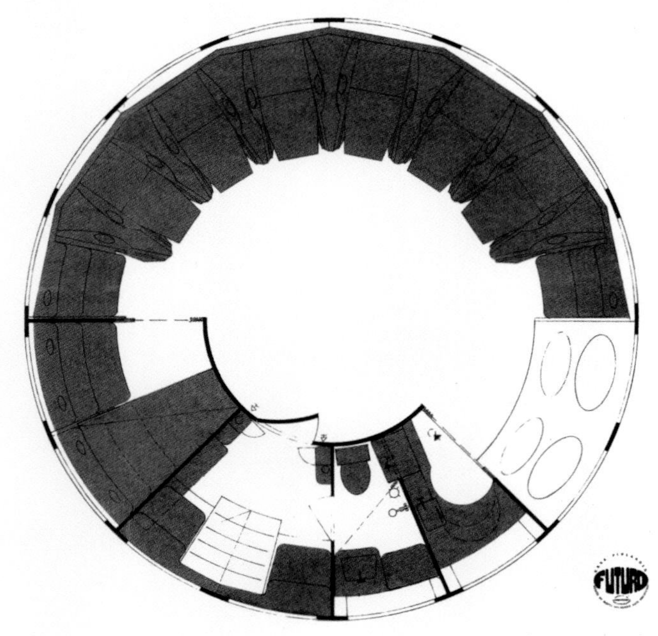
FUTURO

Opposite: Plans with installation instructions

Above: The permanently installed seating does not allow for any changes

Right: One of C. G. Hagström's fashion photos for Vuokko

Following spread: The publicity photo shows the fireplace and, in the background, niches for the kitchen (right) and a double bed (left)

KUNSTSTOFFHAUS FG2000

Wolfgang Feierbach
Altenstadt, Germany, 1968–1970

Wolfgang Feierbach was always fascinated by plastics. After training as a model builder, he passed his examination as a master craftsman at the age of 24, then went into business for himself. He began to design not only switchboxes, protective hoods and similar money-bringing items, but also plastic furniture. And since fiberglass reinforced polyester resin, or fiberglass, has tremendous tensile strength, he asked himself whether he could build an entire house out of the material—a house in which he and his family could feel at home.

Feierbach was already considering the possibility of production in series when he decided not to build the house in one piece, but out of individual elements instead. Since there is always a danger of the fiberglass parts warping during the production process, he designed the supporting wall elements with a slight curvature from the outset. In a number of experiments he determined the thickness and the length of the roof elements. In one test he left a truck parked on prototypes for the elements which he had laid across saw-horse-like supports—it had no

NORDANSICHT

WESTANSICHT

Moderne Formgebung und technische Qualität prägen die Vorbilder für neue Wohnideen. Im Wandel zum progressiven Stil stehen Fiberglasmöbel aus dem Programm fg design Wolfgang Feierbach an führender Stelle. Ein Gestaltungsbeitrag zu Leitbildern für modernes Wohnen in der Gegenwart und Zukunft.

design · wolfgang feierbach

effect on them. Thus, Feierbach was finally convinced that his concept would work.

At seven o'clock in the morning on July 18, 1968, under the watchful eyes of numerous journalists, ten of Feierbach's employees began to assemble 13 roof and 26 wall elements, including six with windows: two wall elements and one roof element were put in place on the reinforced concrete roof of the Feierbach office building and screwed together—without using a crane or hoists, but instead only hydraulic lifts. The windows were fitted into the front and back façades and by around five o'clock the shell of the largest plastic house ever built was completed. The wall and ceiling elements that opened up to the interior were clad with upholstered plywood. In

Previous spread: A brochure for fiberglass furniture, Feierbach's main product

This spread: Like the house itself, the roof elements were installed without lifting equipment. The lightweight wall elements could be set into their foundations by four workmen

order to provide insulation, the thin walls were constructed in two layers with a core of insulating hard plastic foam.

The layout is divided into two parts: one combines the living, dining, and cooking areas; the other, at the back, holds the master bedroom, children's room and bathroom, separated either by closets or by folding textile doors. The interior was decorated according to original designs, using some of the company's own custom products. A control panel is found at the heart of the house's technical installations, located between the living and sleeping areas. It includes a digital clock, weather station, thermostat to regulate the room temperature, and switches to operate the lighting, motorized curtains, awning, and small side windows. Over the course of a year, hundreds of visitors viewed the model house, then Feierbach moved in with his family of five. In 1979 they moved into a new plastic house; while the original model house is still standing without ever having to be repaired. It is still used as an office.

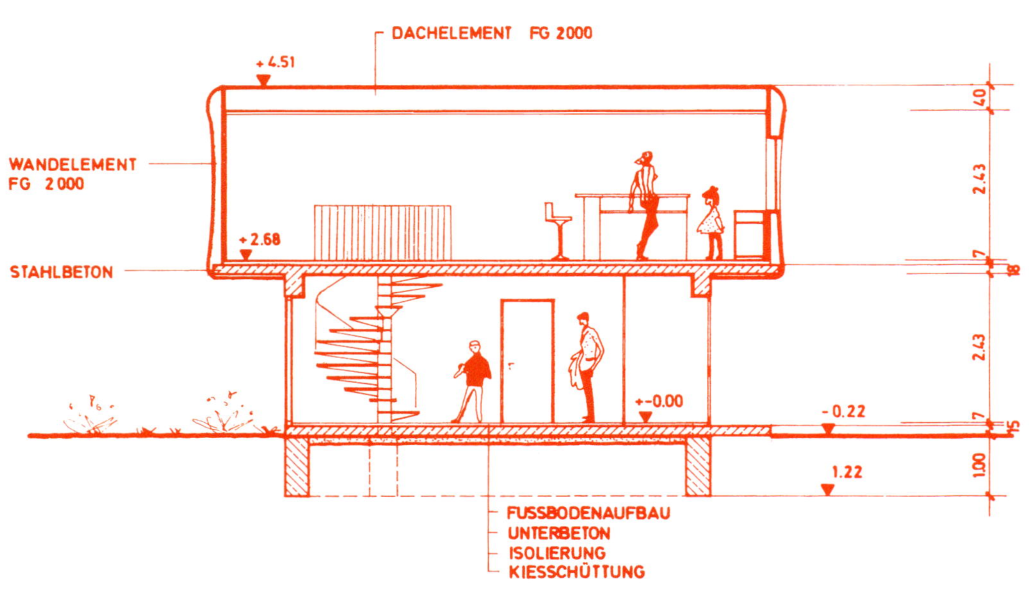

Below: The above ground foundation was built in a conventional manner and served as a substitute for a cellar and a garage

Following spread: The ceiling was decorated with colorful shag carpeting and the walls were upholstered

The isometric drawing shows the interior of a room divided only by furniture

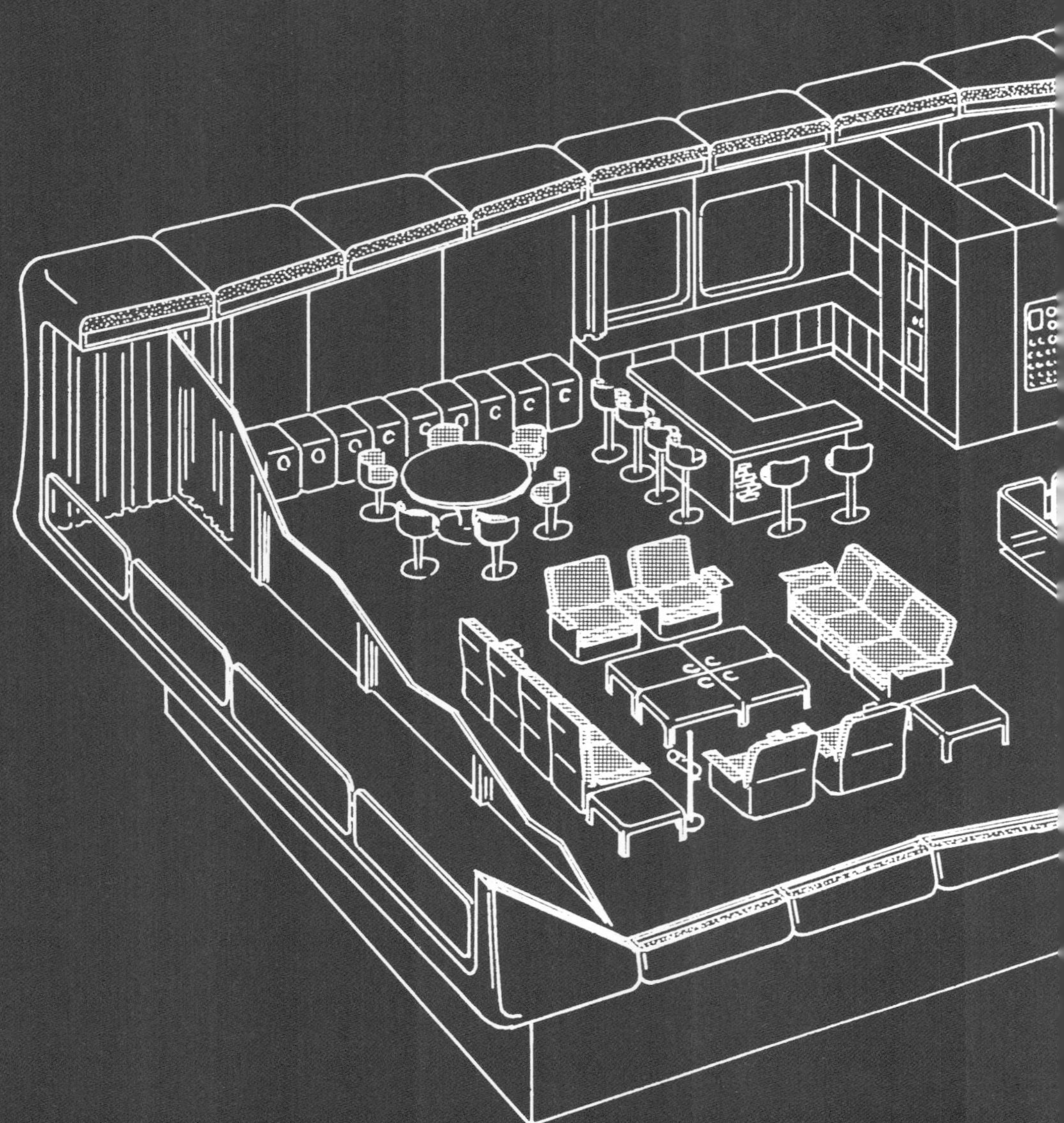

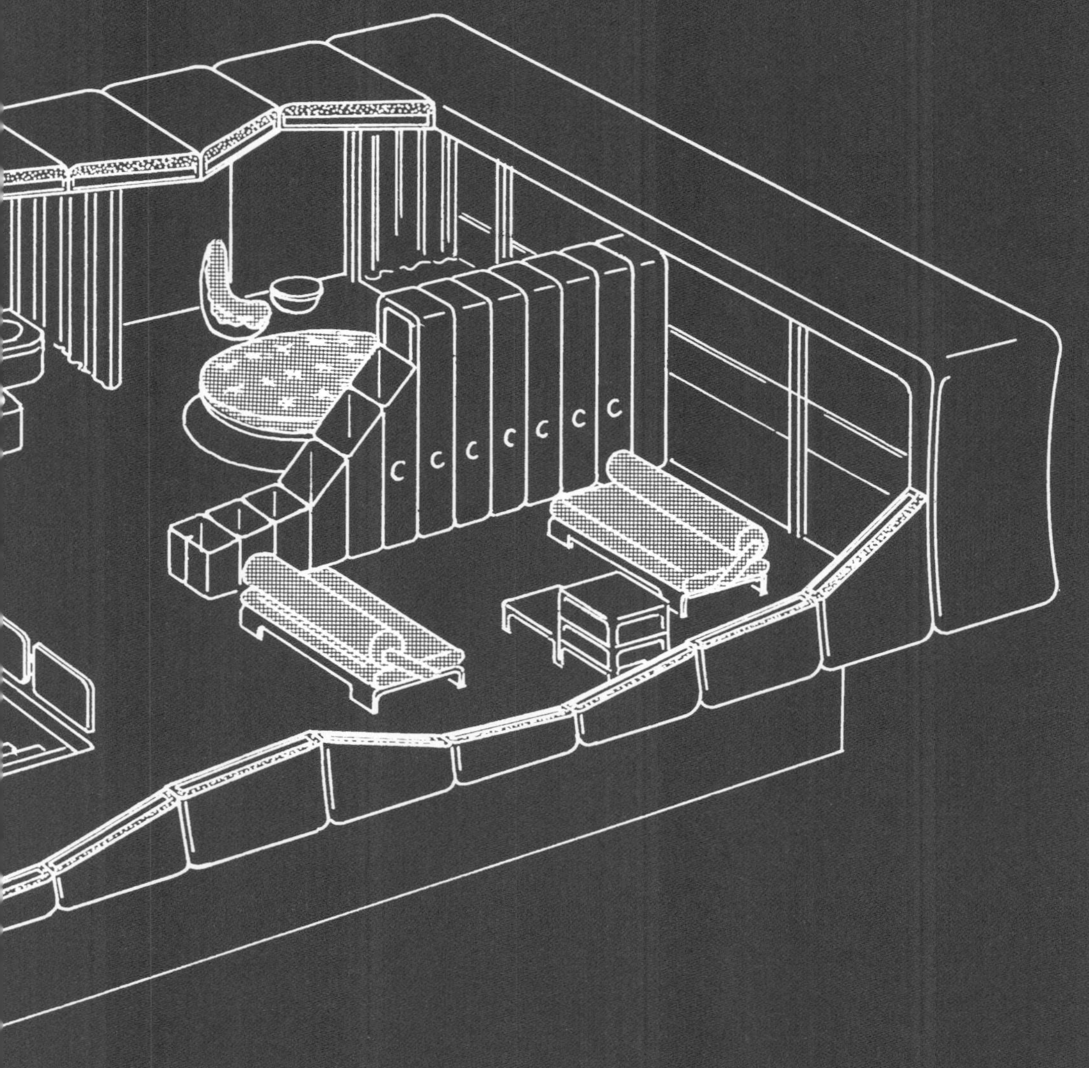

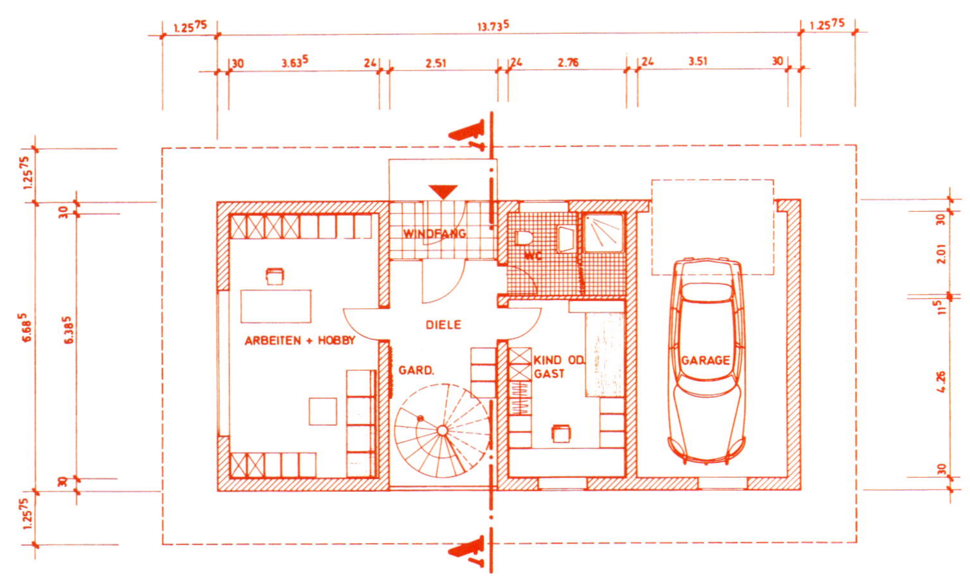
1.25^75
13.73^5
1.25^75
30
3.63^5
24
2.51
24
2.76
24
3.51
30
WINDFANG
WC
DIELE
ARBEITEN + HOBBY
GARD.
KIND OD.
GAST
GARAGE
1.25^75
30
6.68^5
6.385
30
1.25^75
30
2.01
115
4.26
30
ERDGESCHOSS

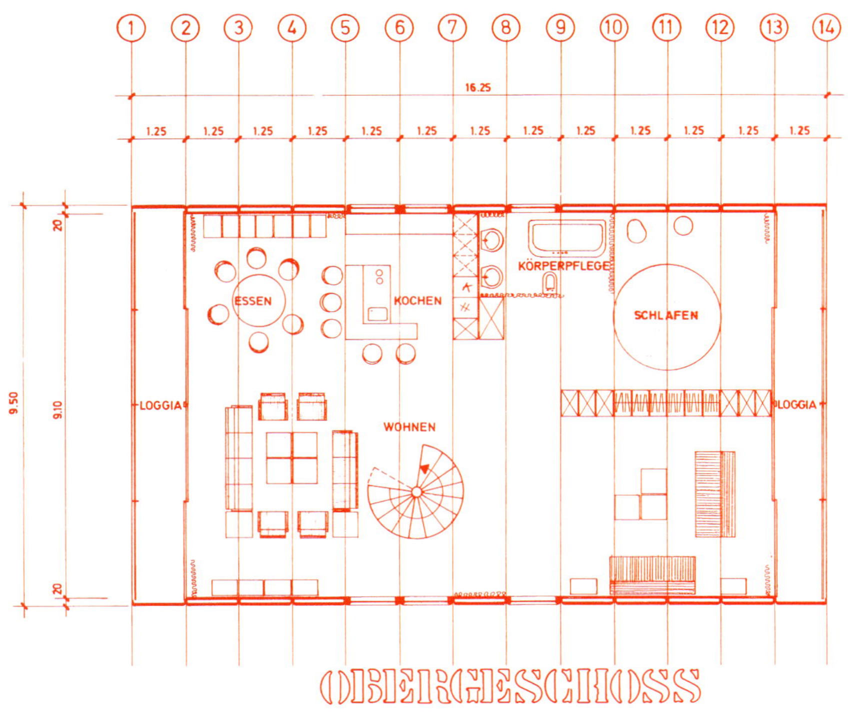
1
2
3
4
5
6
7
8
9
10
11
12
13
14
16.25
1.25
ESSEN
KOCHEN
KÖRPERPFLEGE
SCHLAFEN
LOGGIA
WOHNEN
LOGGIA
9.50
9.10
20
20
OBERGESCHOSS

The fiberglass furniture determined the character of the interior

The bedroom with a round, free-standing bed (below) and the bathroom (opposite)

FERTIGHAUS TANJA

Heinrich Bernhard Hellmuth
Schneckenburger & Co.
Rottenburg am Neckar, Germany, 1970–2009

The homes designed by Heinrich Bernhard Hellmuth and built by Schneckenburger & Co. of the Swabian town of Rottenburg provide proof that a freelance architect committed to design excellence can work effectively with a prefabricated housing builder who is forced to take economic constraints into consideration. Hellmuth produced the first designs for prefabricated houses in the early 1960s; the collaboration ended in 2009 when Schneckenburger closed the company due to his age. The house model was named after Hellmuth's older daughter Tanja and developed in 1970; over 40 of these houses were built. A subsequent smaller model was named after his younger daughter Katja.

Hellmuth developed the prototype as his own home in the town of Bieringen. He established his architectural office on the ground floor, which receives natural light from one side due to its location on a slope.

The "studio house" has a number of different faces. The floor plan describes nearly a perfect square, with one exciting variation: the living area extends beyond the limits of the otherwise compact layout. When the house is approached from the valley, it seems compact and enclosed under a slightly asymmetrical pitched roof. Seen from the slope behind the house, the entire back opens up to the garden; the roof also extends down over the living room. Hence, the dark line

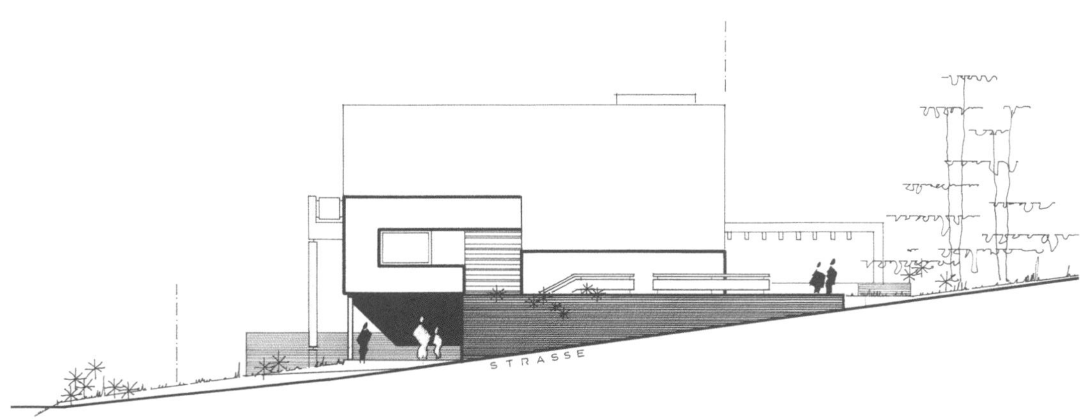

Elevations

of the slate-clad edge of the roof leads from the ground up over the peak to the other side, where it doubles back to underline the balcony; the white brick chimney makes for an effective vertical counterpoint.

The house encompasses a total of 1,800 sq. ft. of living space on two floors. On the ground floor, there is a living room and a children's area: the two children's rooms and a bathroom overlook the valley. The hallway with stairs to the lower level serves as a buffer zone—also against possible noise from the children's rooms—between the nearly 430 sq. ft. "Grand Room" under the slanted roof and the dining room, which is connected to the kitchen via a "breakfast bar." The roofed terrace with an open fireplace is located in front of the dining room. On the upper floor there is a "quiet zone" that includes the master bedroom, bathroom, and a large gallery, which also has an open fireplace and is reached from the living room via a straight flight of stairs. The interior rooms prominently feature wooden paneling.

The house is built as a wooden structure. Schneckenburger offered Tanja models in different variations, including with different roofs, with or without a cellar, and with or without a recessed balcony.

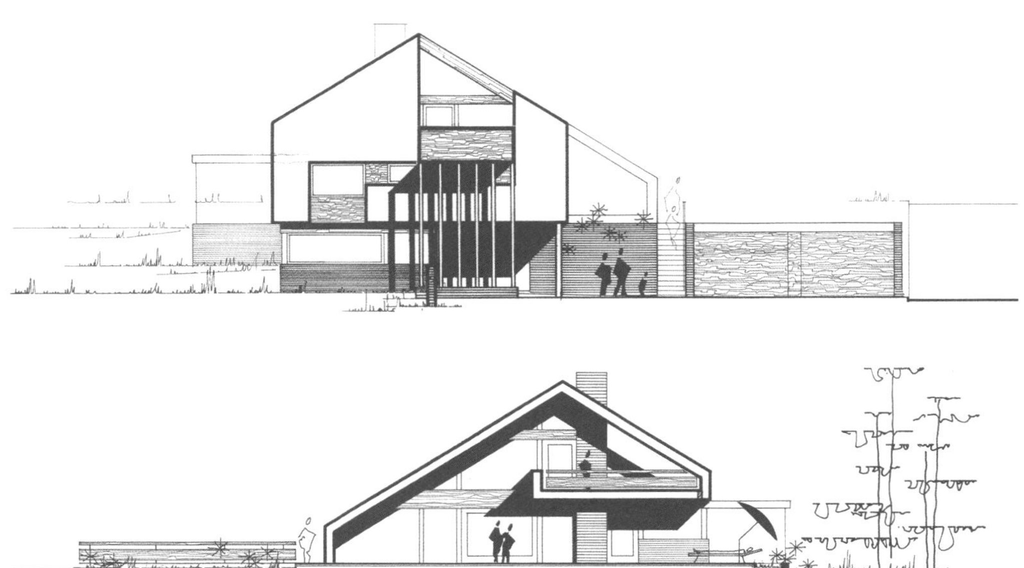

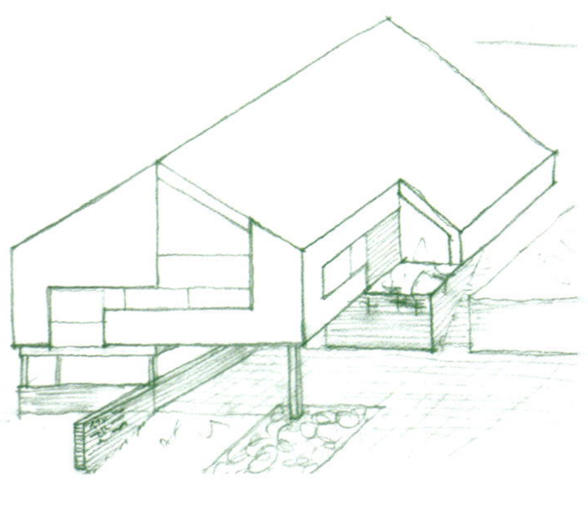

The open side of the house facing the garden differs considerably from the closed side facing the driveway

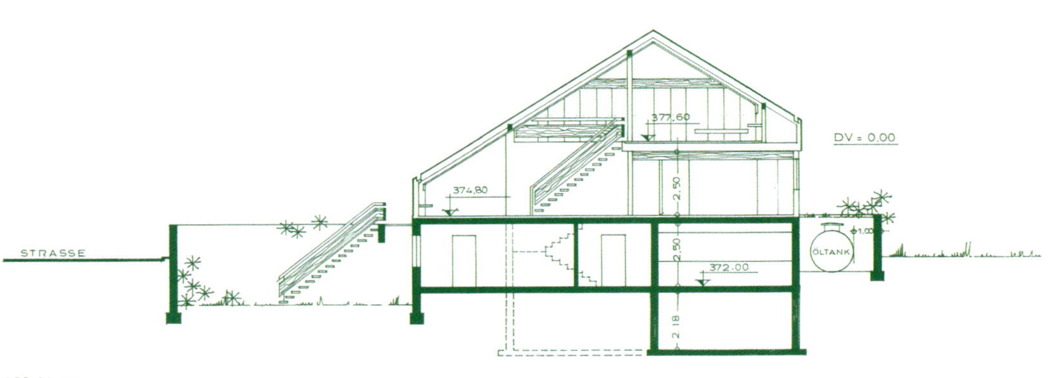

The gallery with the master bedroom is reached from the spacious living room, while the children's rooms form a separate area on the ground floor

A variety of materials in the house, wood paneling on the slanted ceiling in the bedroom (opposite) and a carpet clad wall in the entryway (above)

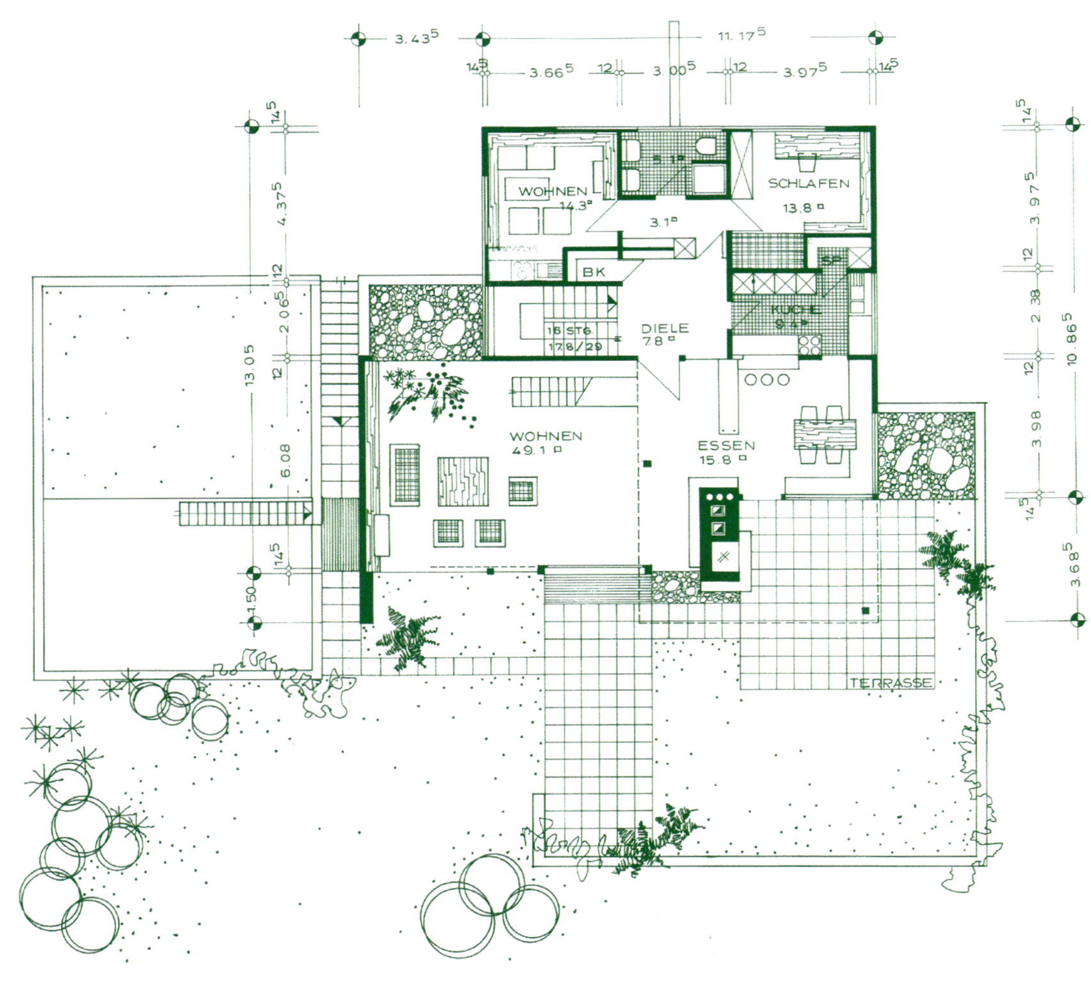

Plans of the ground floor (above) and the upper level (opposite top)

Opposite bottom: Laminated cabinet doors in the kitchen and tile in the bathroom

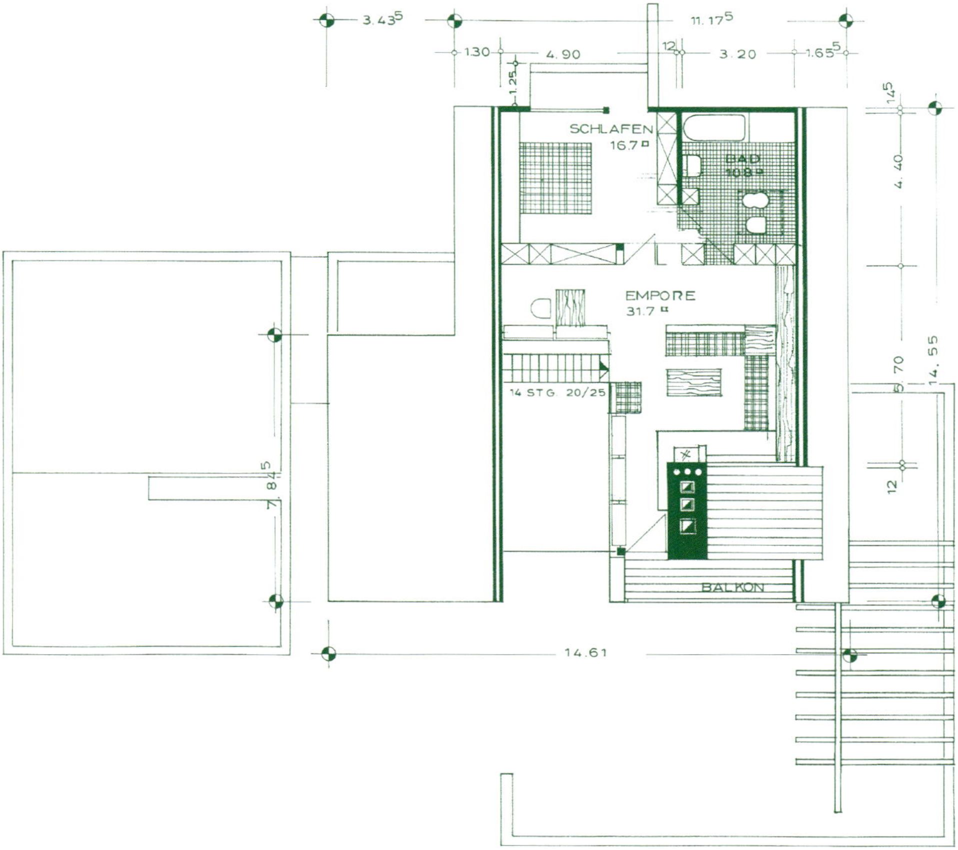

3.43⁵ 11.17⁵
130 4.90 12 3.20 1.65⁵
1.25 145
SCHLAFEN 16.7 ㎡
BAD 10.8 ㎡
4.40
EMPORE 31.7 ㎡
14 STG. 20/25
5.70 14.55
7.84⁵
12
BALKON
14.61

VENTURO

Matti Suuronen
Oy Polykem AB
Helsinki, Finland, 1971

In Polykem's brochure for its Casa Finlandia prefabricated house program, Suuronen's famous Futuro by no means stood alone. The CF Futuro, often called the UFO, was flanked by the FF-12 plastic tunnel for commercial car washes, the CF-100/200 shell roof for restaurants or railway stations, the smaller CF-10 and CF-16 for kiosks, as well as the Venturo CF-45 for leisure homes or smaller branch offices. The model numbers also indicate the floor space in square meters. Once it became obvious that the Futuro would not be a commercial success, marketing efforts concentrated on the Venturo.

The name Venturo is programmatic: an Italian word, it can be translated as "next" or "coming." In contrast to the Futuro, which suggested a radical departure into a distant future in space, the Venturo still appeared to be a contemporary house, designed to be at home on planet Earth. This was reflected not least of all in the fact that it was possible to furnish the house in a conventional manner; unlike the Futuro, it even allowed the inhabitants to bring their own furniture with them. Thus, the transformation from the aesthetics of futuristic space travel to trendy Modernism was complete, and this expanded the options for use considerably. One brochure shows the house being used by fashionably dressed vacationers in Marimekko outfits. Plans for the house, in addition to its use as a leisure home, included combining multiple units to form larger ensembles.

The Venturo is not made entirely of plastic: there are aluminum supports within the rounded shell. The Venturo, which could be assembled on site from just a few parts, weighed only four tons, hence it could be erected on very simple foundations. The house consisted of three modules, which could be delivered on two trucks. The two-layer fiberglass structure had 2 in. foam panels installed as insulation. The production of thousands of the Venturo houses was planned, but ultimately only 19 of them ever left the plant, and half of those came to be used as service stations.

Brochure from 1971

The "Venturo" is a modular, easily transportable building system, having excellent insulation, low weight and designed for minimum assembly on site.
It is built of high quality materials in order to ensure maximum weathering properties for use in arctic as well as tropical climates and is almost maintenance free.
Being of low weight and factory preassembled, the Venturo means very low erection and foundation costs, where heavy equipment can be avoided.
The basic unit (fig. 1) is usually delivered to the site on a truck with trailer in two major sections, a and b, one containing the bathroom/kitchenette, the other with the centre sections (c) packed inside.
For easy transportation all sections are 2,3 m (appr. 7' 6'') wide; length 6,9 m (appr. 23 ft). Then basic unit (fig. 1) is when assembled, 6,9 m x 6,9 m (23 x 23 ft), giving a floor area of appr. 45 sq. m. (509 sq.ft.). This basic unit can be enlarged by adding extra centre sections; to make still larger buildings two or more basic units are linked. In this way an unlimited variation of buildings in size and plans can be formulated.
The height of the preassembled sections (a and b) is appr. 290 cm (9.1/2 ft), inside height of room 240 cm (appr. 8 ft).
The roof and corner sections are large double skin mouldings of fibreglass with off-white gel-coated exterior surface as standard, with a 2" polyurethane foam insulation.
The floor is an insulated composite beam construction of marine grade plywood and wood with all facia parts showing. covered with fibreglass mouldings.
The facades, available as standard in several colors and designs as per fig. 2, consist of prefabricated anodized aluminium framing with insulated prepainted aluminium exterior panels in various attractive colors.
Glazing may be either insulated glass or single or double sheet glazing.

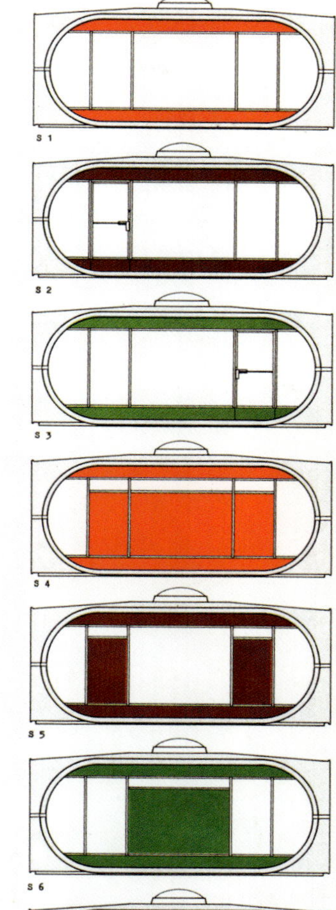

Design and Engineering

The structural calculation is made by Mr. Matti Sihvonen, Civil Eng. RIL.
Design loads 180 kg/sq.m. (36 lbs/sq.ft) snowload and windload 100 kg/sq.m. (21 lbs/sq.m), (W = 40 m/sec., appr. 80 mph).
Designer of the house is Mr. Matti Suuronen, Arch. SAFA.
The design is registered in most Patent offices throughout the world.

Manufacturer

The Venturo is manufactured and developed by Oy Polykem Ab, Finland, and manufactured under license in several countries by local manufacturers.

Assembly and site preparations

The preassembled sections, delivered to the site by a truck with trailer, are, depending on ground conditions, installed on a flat surface or on 16 small piers. The basic unit weighs appr. 4 tons.
Electricity, water and waste-line are hooked up under the floor. Where electricity, water or sewerage are not obtainable prophane gas and/or gasoline motor driven generators can be used. For sewage septic tanks may be used. Please specify local conditions for further advice on nonstandard deliveries.
Kindly make your color choice for the facades among the below standard colors.

COLOR Y	COLOR G	COLOR B	COLOR O

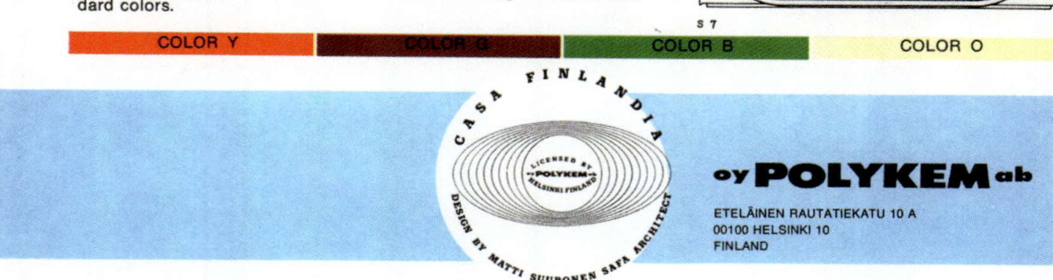

Previous spread and below: Publicity photos from 1971

Opposite: In contrast to the Futuro, the Venturo was intended to appeal to a somewhat more traditional clientele

The historical photos depict the house in such a clever way that it appears surprisingly spacious despite its modest footprint of 484 sq. ft.

HEXACUBE

Georges Candilis, Anja Blomstedt
Dubigeon Plastiques
Leucate, France, 1972

Hexacube was an experimental modular housing prototype designed by the Franco-Greek architect George Candilis in collaboration with the Finnish interior designer Anja Blomstedt. It was developed and tested in Leucate, which is about 15 miles from the Spanish border in southwestern France. Conceived in the context of post-1960s research into flexible, low-cost leisure housing, the Hexacube reflects Candilis's long-standing interest in adaptable architecture and collective living. In the early 1970s, Candilis was responsible for tourist and housing developments in the Leucate/Port-Leucate area, where the Hexacube was tested.

The project takes its name from its hexagonal geometry. Each Hexacube is a 75 sq. ft. autonomous module composed of two molded fiberglass-reinforced polyester shells. Large openings provide light, ventilation, and views of the surroundings. A simple connection system allows several modules to be joined horizontally, enabling users to assemble larger living units. The interior layout, designed by Blomstedt, incorporates built-in furniture, sleeping areas, and storage, emphasizing compactness and multifunctionality. Conceived as a temporary or seasonal habitat, particularly suited to seaside environments, several prototype units were installed on the beaches of Port-Leucate in 1972. Manufactured with industrial partners (Dubigeon Plastiques) and briefly patented, the Hexacube was never mass-produced.

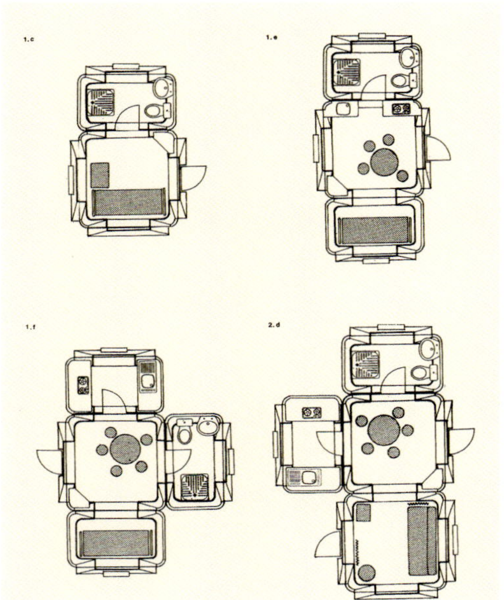

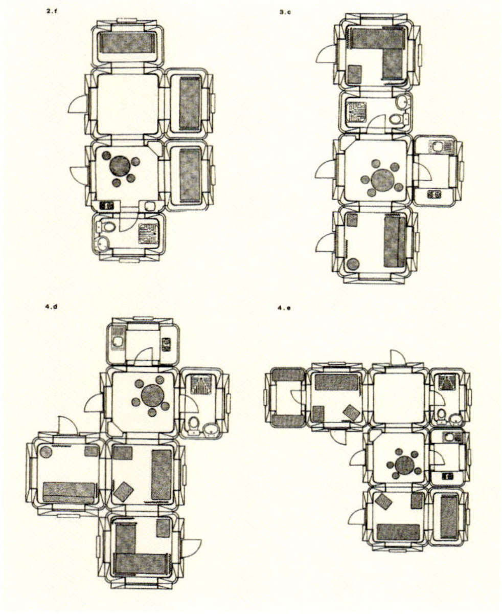

HEXACUBE
BREVET 7438006
GEORGES CANDILIS
ANJA BLOMSTEDT
18 rue DAUPHINE 75006 PARIS

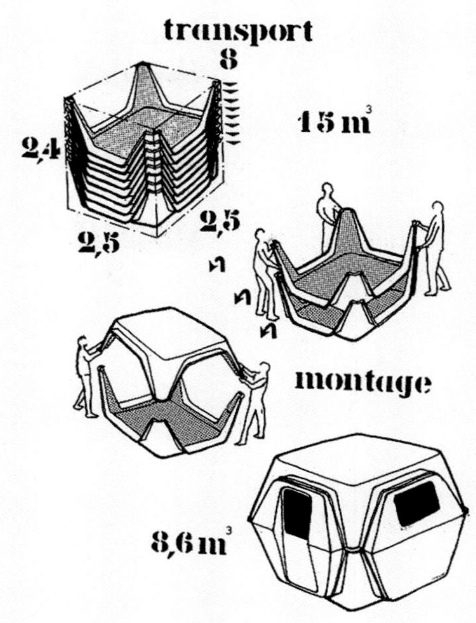

CIFAM
2 RAMELET MOUNDI
31300 TOULOUSE
LARDENNE
TEL: 42 70 43

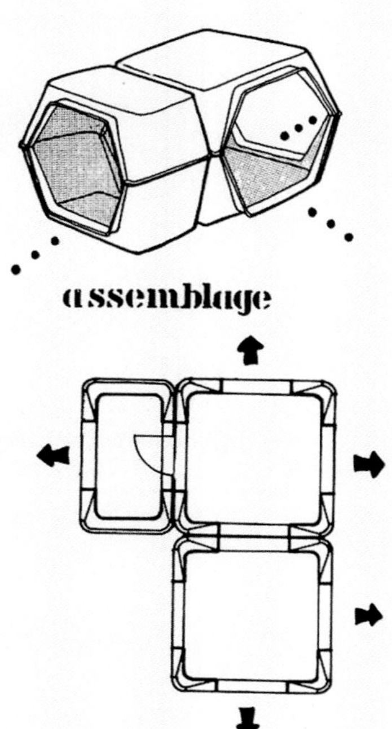

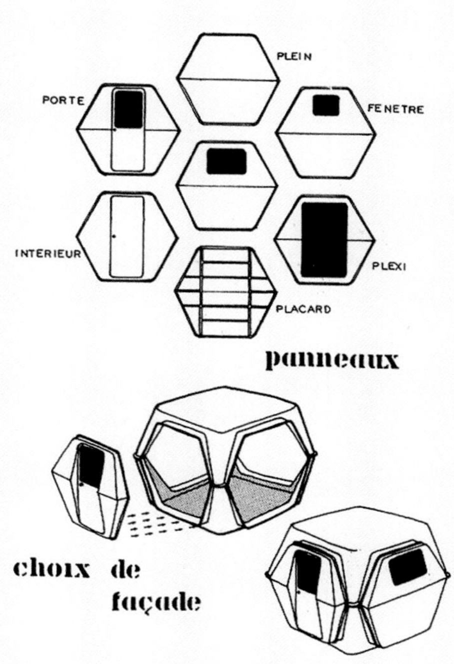

une nouvelle manière de vivre ...

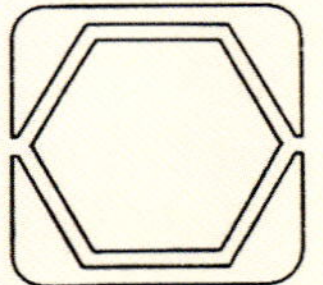

LE CUBING

photo yan

avec l'HEXACUBE de Georges Candilis et Anja Blomstedt.

CIFAM s.a. **Compagnie Internationale des Fabrications Modernes**
2, chemin Ramelet - Moundi - 31300 Toulouse

SOCIÉTÉ ANONYME AU CAPITAL DE 300.000 FRANCS

TEL. : (61) 42.70.13 R.C. TOULOUSE 73 B 15 INSEE 735 31 555 0106 C.C.P. TOULOUSE 3132 56 M

Previous spread: The drawings show the assembly and transportation options for the cubes

Above: Assembly of cubes creating a sheltered patio

Opposite: Easily moved and put together, the structures also required no excavation or foundation work

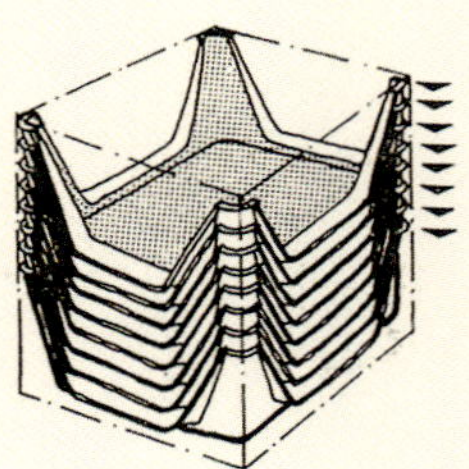

photo yan

photo yan

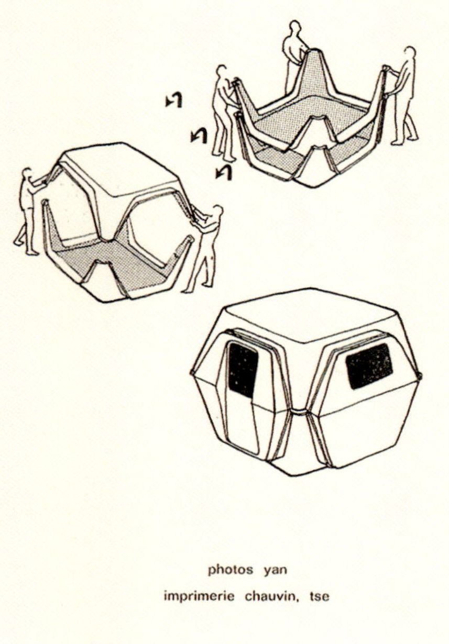

photos yan

imprimerie chauvin, tse

Above and opposite:
The hexagonal shape of the units made assembly and transportation easy while creating a modern, livable interior

photo yan

Trois personnes inexpérimentées peuvent assembler trois Hexacubes en six heures.

Les percements désirés s'obtiennent selon leurs dimensions par l'emploi de forets et scies appropriés et permettent à la demande les branchements : électrique, eau, l'évacuation des effluents, ainsi que les aérations en application des règlements en vigueur.

Les « HEXACUBES », par la nature et la qualité de leurs matériaux, ne nécessitent aucun entretien autre que de propreté.

La longévité des RESINES POLYESTER employées depuis près de 20 ans pour la construction de bateaux est maintenant définitivement établie ainsi que leur résistance aux agents extérieurs.

Acquérez nos pièces détachées « CUBING » et construisez à votre goût la maison que vous souhaitez.

Votre maison vous accompagnera si vous changez votre lieu de résidence-loisir.

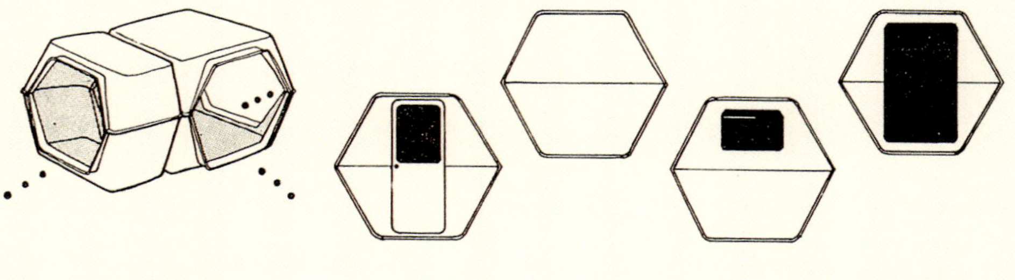

Following spread: Larger hexagonal units could be used to create a central volume to which several smaller modules could be attached

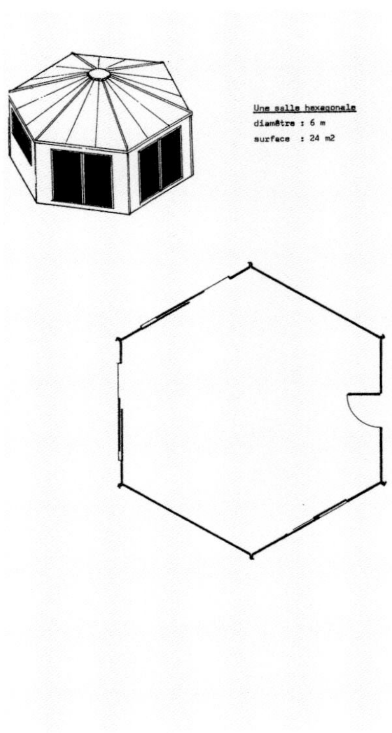

<u>**Une salle hexagonale**</u>

diamètre : 6 m

surface : 24 m2

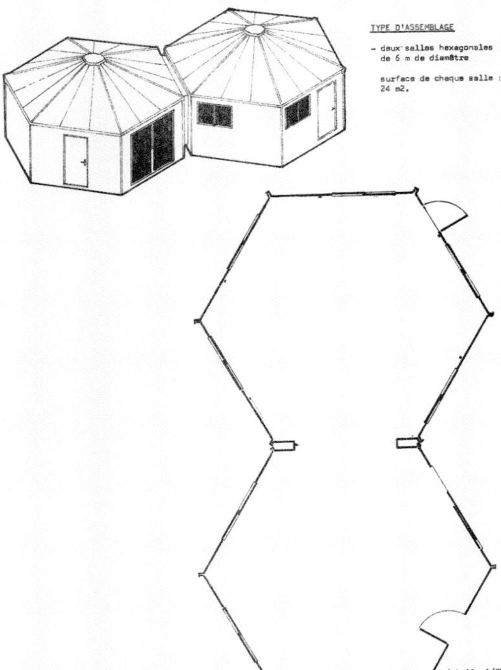

<u>TYPE D'ASSEMBLAGE</u>

- deux salles hexagonales de 6 m de diamètre

surface de chaque salle : 24 m2.

échelle 1/5[illegible]

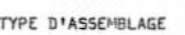

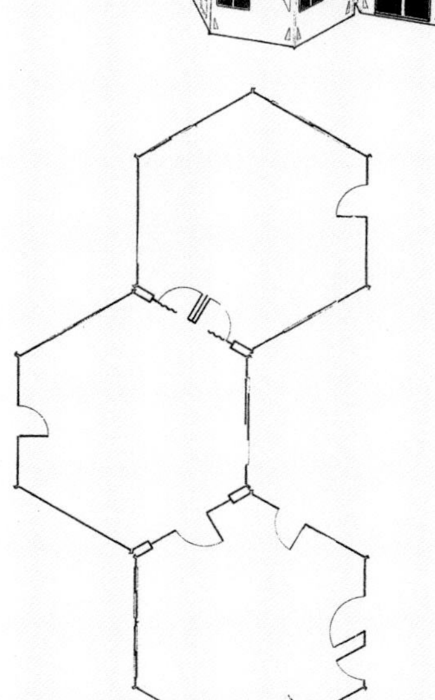

TYPE D'ASSEMBLAGE
-=-=-=-=-=-=-=-

3 salles hexagonales

diamètre pour chaque salle :
- 6 m

surface pour chaque salle :
- 24 m2

<u>TYPE D'ASSEMBLAGE</u>

- 1 salle hexagonale de 6 m de diamètre
- 1 module de 1.65 x 2.50

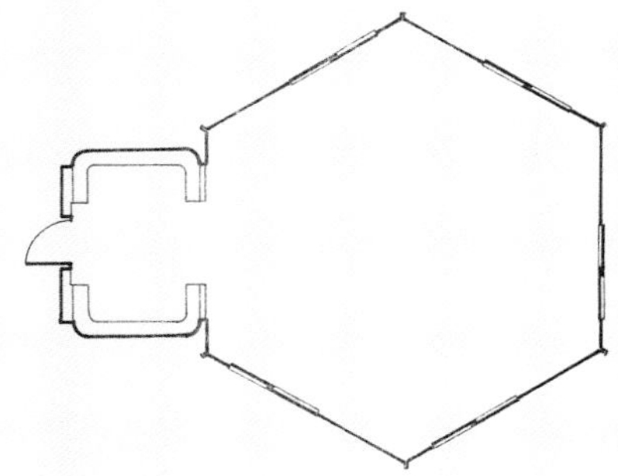

TYPE D'ASSEMBLAGE

- 1 salle hexagonale de 6 m de diamètre
- 1 module 2.50 x 2.50

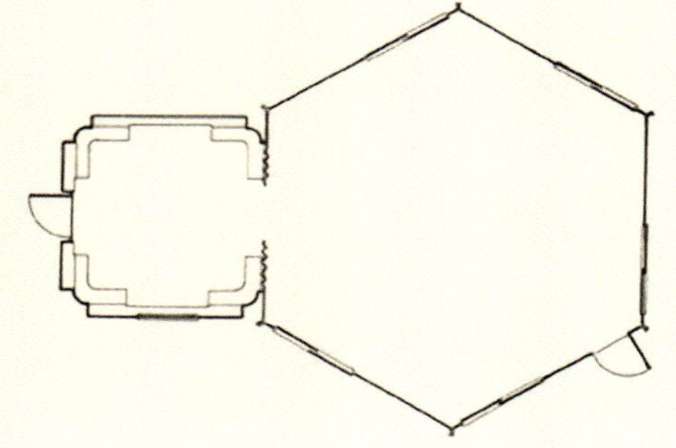

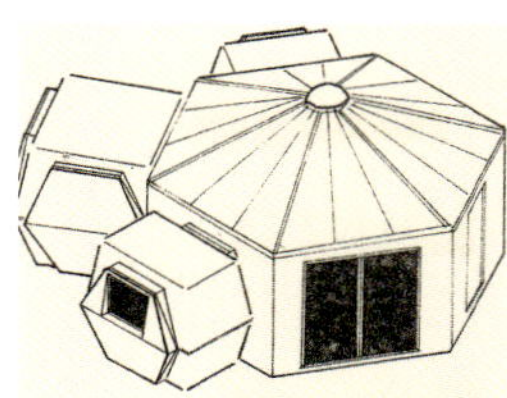

TYPE D'ASSEMBLAGE

- une salle hexagonale de 6 m de diamètre
- un hexacube 2.50 m x 2.50 m
- deux blocs polyvalents 2.50 m x 1.65 m

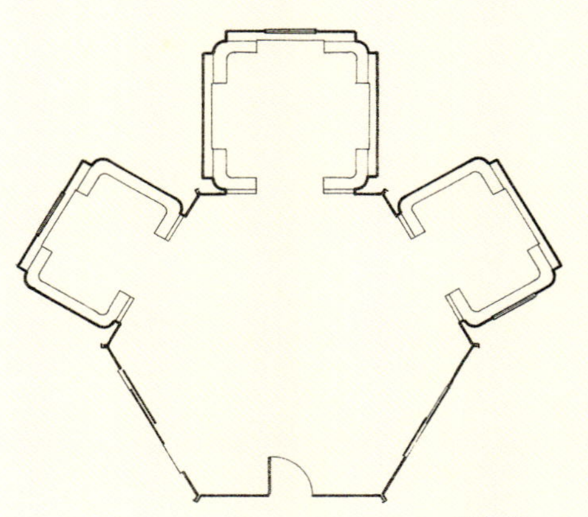

échelle 1/50e

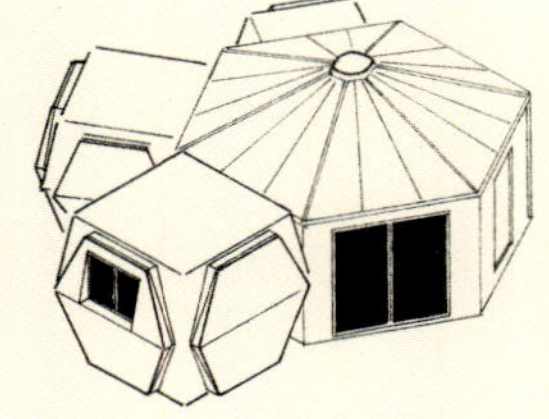

TYPE D'ASSEMBLAGE :

- 1 salle hexagonale de 6 m de diamè-tre
- 1 hexacube de 3.00 m x 3.00 m
- 1 hexacube de 2.50 m x 2.50 m
- 1 bloc polyvalent de 2.50 m x 1.65 m

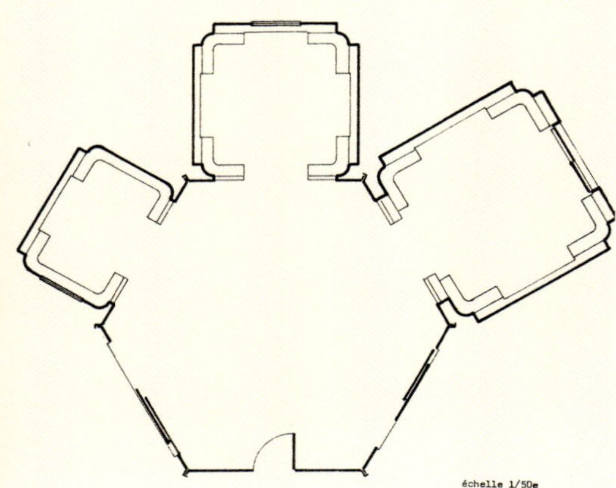

échelle 1/50e

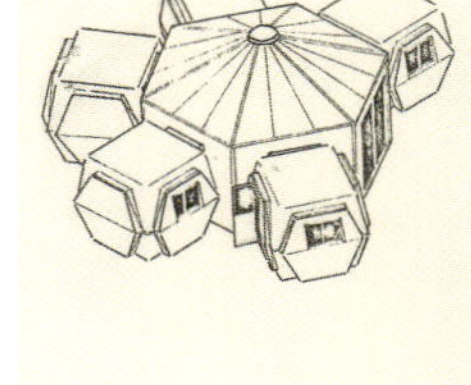

TYPE D'ASSEMBLAGE

- salle hexagonale de 6 m de diamètre
- 5 HEXACUBES de 2.50 x 2.50
- 1 baie vitrée coulissante sur une face

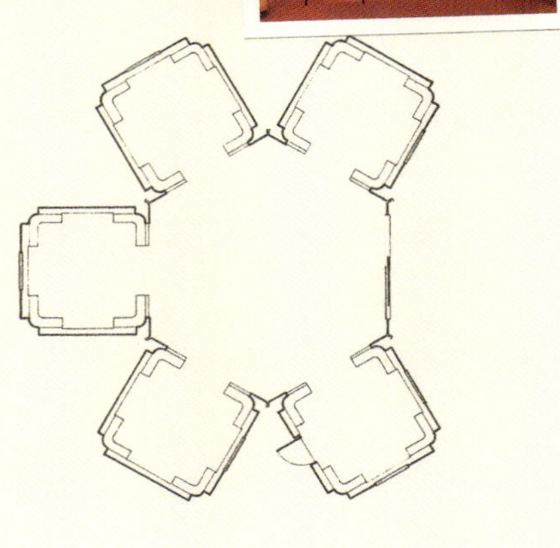

Opposite top: Assembly drawings for the chairs designed in the same spirit as the housing modules

Opposite bottom: Interior image showing the larger central space leading to smaller modules

Below: A larger assembled dwelling with the large central unit in the middle as seen from the interior

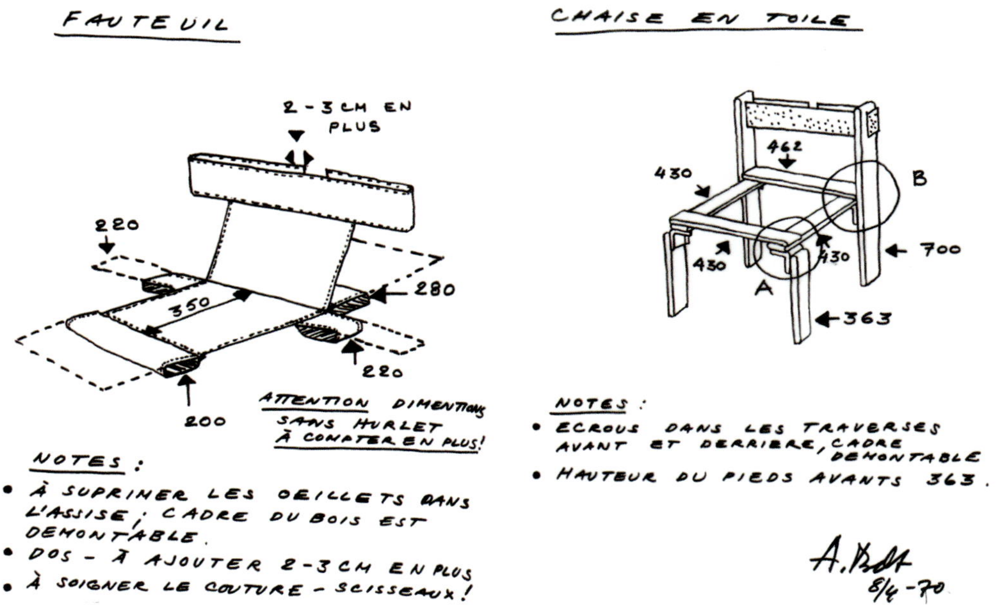

FAUTEUIL

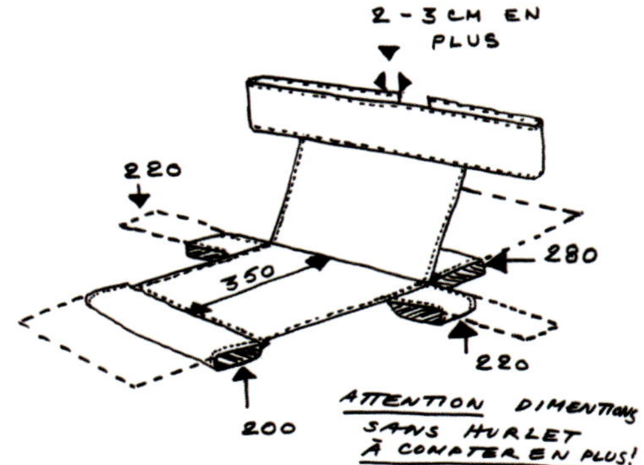

NOTES :

- À SUPRIMER LES OEILLETS DANS L'ASSISE; CADRE DU BOIS EST DEMONTABLE.
- DOS – À AJOUTER 2-3 CM EN PLUS
- À SOIGNER LE COUTURE – SCISSEAUX!

CHAISE EN TOILE

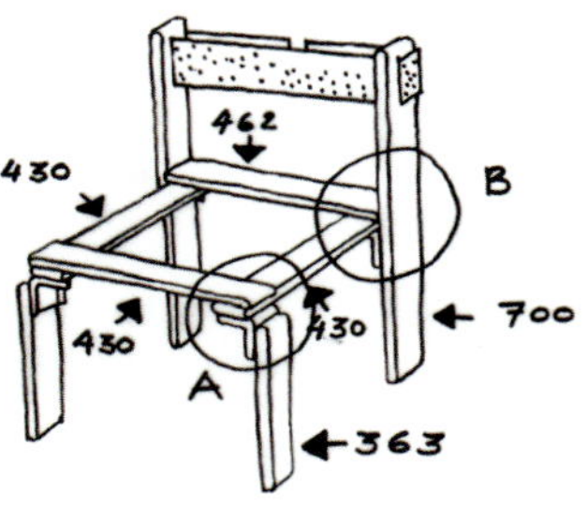

NOTES :

- ECROUS DANS LES TRAVERSES AVANT ET DERRIERE, CADRE DEMONTABLE
- HAUTEUR DU PIEDS AVANTS 363.

8/4-70

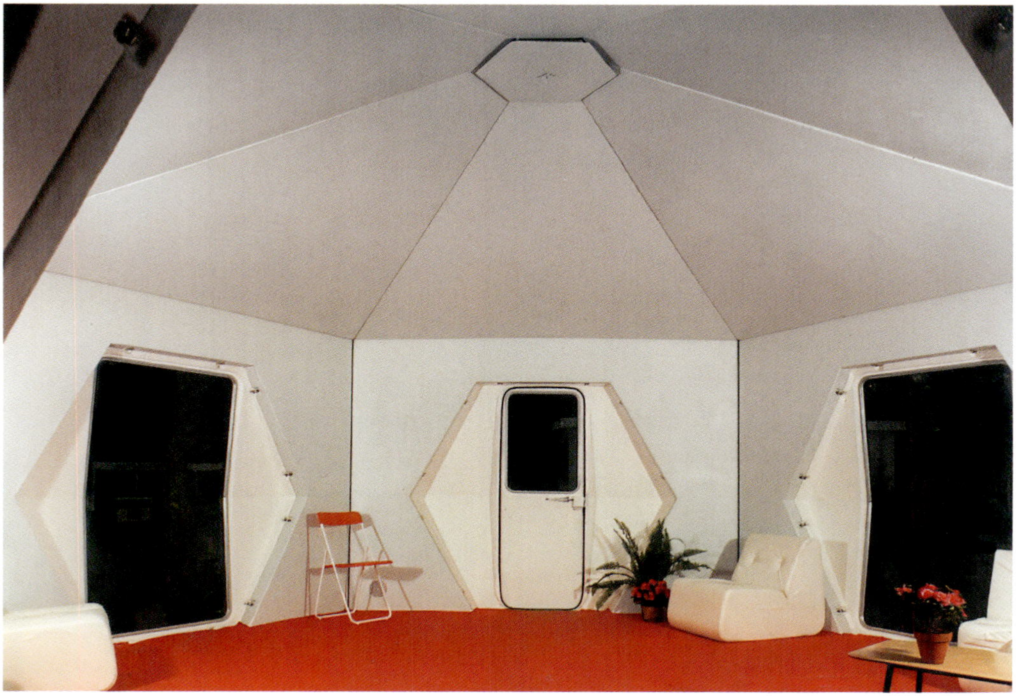

HUF FACHWERKHAUS 2000

Manfred Adams
Huf Haus GmbH & Co. KG
Hartenfels, Germany, 1972–

The founding of the company dates back to a carpentry shop established by Johann Huf in the village of Krümmel in the Westerwald in 1912. A year later, the workshop had already moved to the nearby town of Hartenfels, where the company still has its headquarters. After the Second World War, Johann's son Franz Huf expanded the company's operations beyond the region. Huf made its first appearance in an international context after being commissioned by Sep Ruf and Egon Eiermann to do the woodwork for the Arabian and German pavilions at the Brussels *World's Fair* in 1958. In 1972, Manfred Adams, a student of Sep Ruf's, designed the Huf Fachwerkhaus 2000. It marked the cornerstone of a new orientation for the company: the fundamentals of the design developed by Adams in this context are still applied to every Huf model today.

Wood and glass are the decisive materials in a Huf Haus, which is built as an open wooden skeleton structure with characteristically deep eaves and an amply overhanging pitched roof. The half-timbered structure made of laminated wood has floor-to-ceiling glazing; the remainder of the façade consists of thermally insulated stuccoed composite panels. The floor plan is spacious; on the ground floor there is an open kitchen with a bar and a dining and living area; the upper floor features a gallery, the master bedroom, two children's rooms, and two bathrooms.

Since 1996, the grandsons Georg Huf and Thomas Huf have been in charge of the company, which in the meantime operates globally.

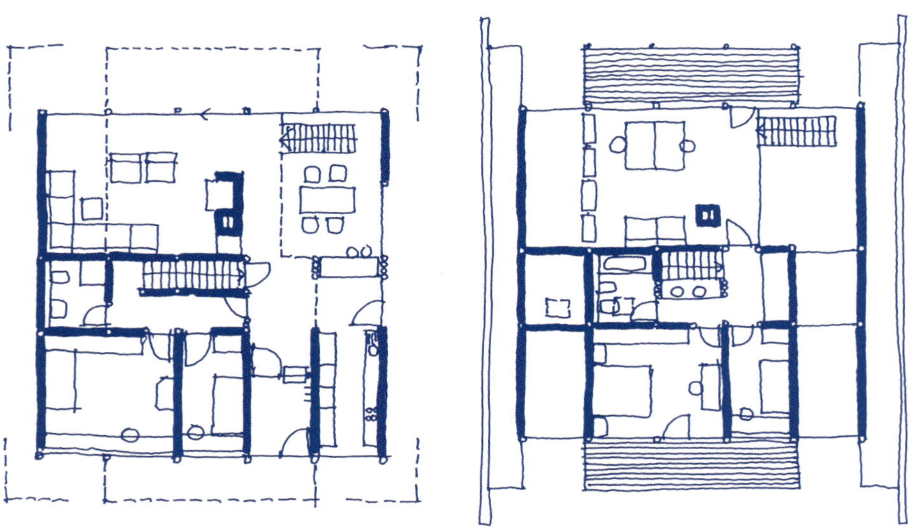

Opposite: Floor plans of the ground floor (left) and the upper floor (right)

Above: Clients can choose to have the houses delivered with white or dark wood

Following spread: Initially, a version with a flat roof was also offered

These prefabricated houses from the Westerwald have already been delivered to England, France, Austria, and Switzerland. There has even been interest in the houses in China, where an electronics company ordered five Huf houses for a small residential development.

The customers gladly travel to Hartenfels in order to view the model houses and make their selections from hundreds of carpets and all sorts of flooring at the Huf showrooms. In the meantime, there is even a "Huf Haus Owners' Group" in England, the members of which share information concerning their experience with this German product. At roughly one million euros, a Huf Haus is hardly one of the cheapest prefabricated houses on the market, but they do set new standards, particularly in terms of their energy balance.

TBS TROPICAL BUILDING SYSTEM

Frank Huster, Peter Hübner
Staudenmayer Bauproduktion
Salach, Germany, 1976–1977

Like Jean Prouvé's Maisons tropicales, the tropical building system (TBS) developed by Frank Huster and Peter Hübner was intended to provide an effective solution to a number of building tasks in countries with tropical heat. The components of this system for buildings with one or more stories for a variety of uses were required to withstand extreme weather conditions, be as extensively prefabricated as possible, easy to transport, and able to be assembled by untrained workers in a short time. The finished building had to provide protection against outdoor temperatures often in excess of 50° C (122° F) while being cooled by refrigeration units—it was basically a refrigerator under a beach umbrella.

Hollow steel sections are used to support the structure, their dimensions can be adapted to the tensile requirements. Solid caps attached to the ends of these sections contain the bores and threads for connecting the support grid in which prefabricated reinforced concrete elements are laid to form the floor slabs. The components that fill in the walls and the vaulting of the sunroof are made of fiberglass reinforced polyester; the wall elements were paneled with plasterboard on the inside. The sanitary facilities are made of prefabricated polyester elements.

Aerial photograph of the Huster House in Neckartenzlingen, Germany

Below: Detail of the hub between the supports illustrates the principle of the interlocking joints

Opposite: The solar protection roof on steel girders and the building system for the space created using fiberglass reinforced plastic panels are two separate elements

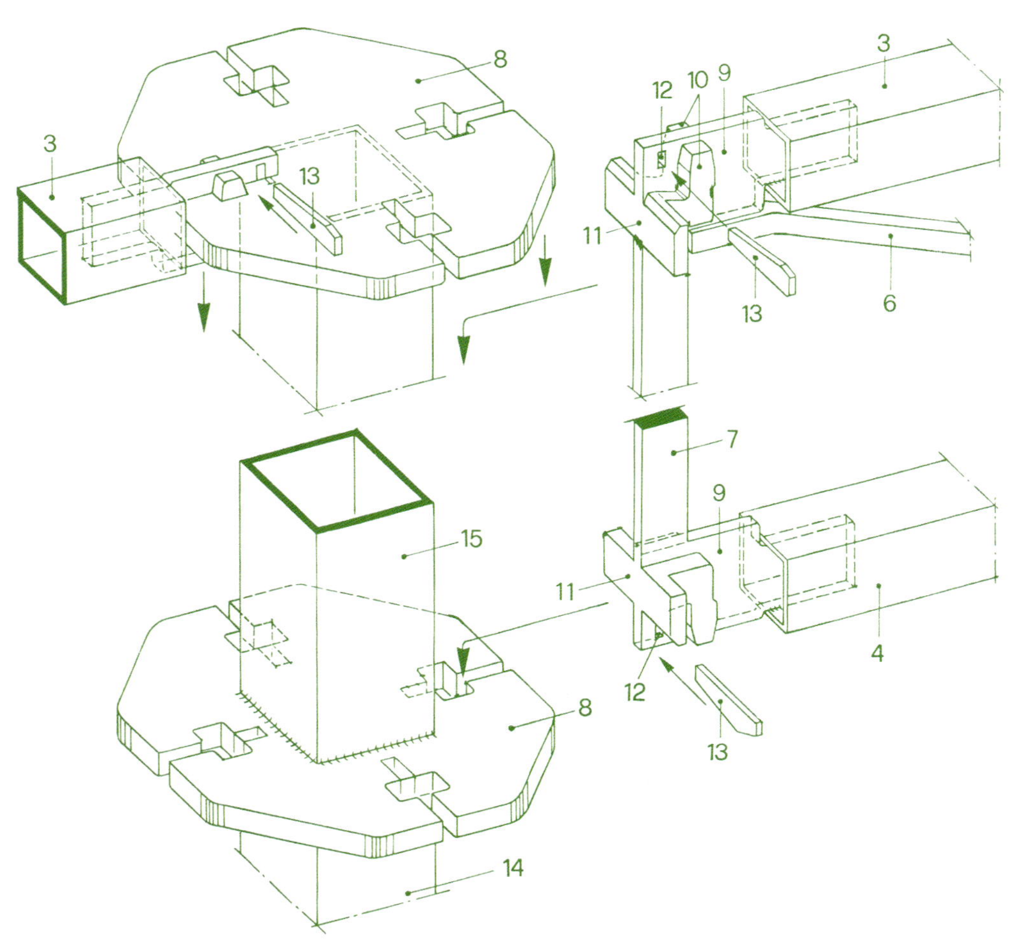

In 1976, the first two prototypes were erected in Saudi Arabia. An additional experimental building was created as Frank Huster's home in the Swabian town of Neckartenzlingen. By the end of 1977, twelve TBS health centers were finally built at the ten airports that existed in Saudi Arabia at the time in order to provide care for the airport personnel and airline passengers.

Above and left: The structural separation of the ceiling and wall elements is visually emphasized by the extended edges of the ceiling elements

Opposite: Floor plans of the upper level (top) and the lower level (bottom)

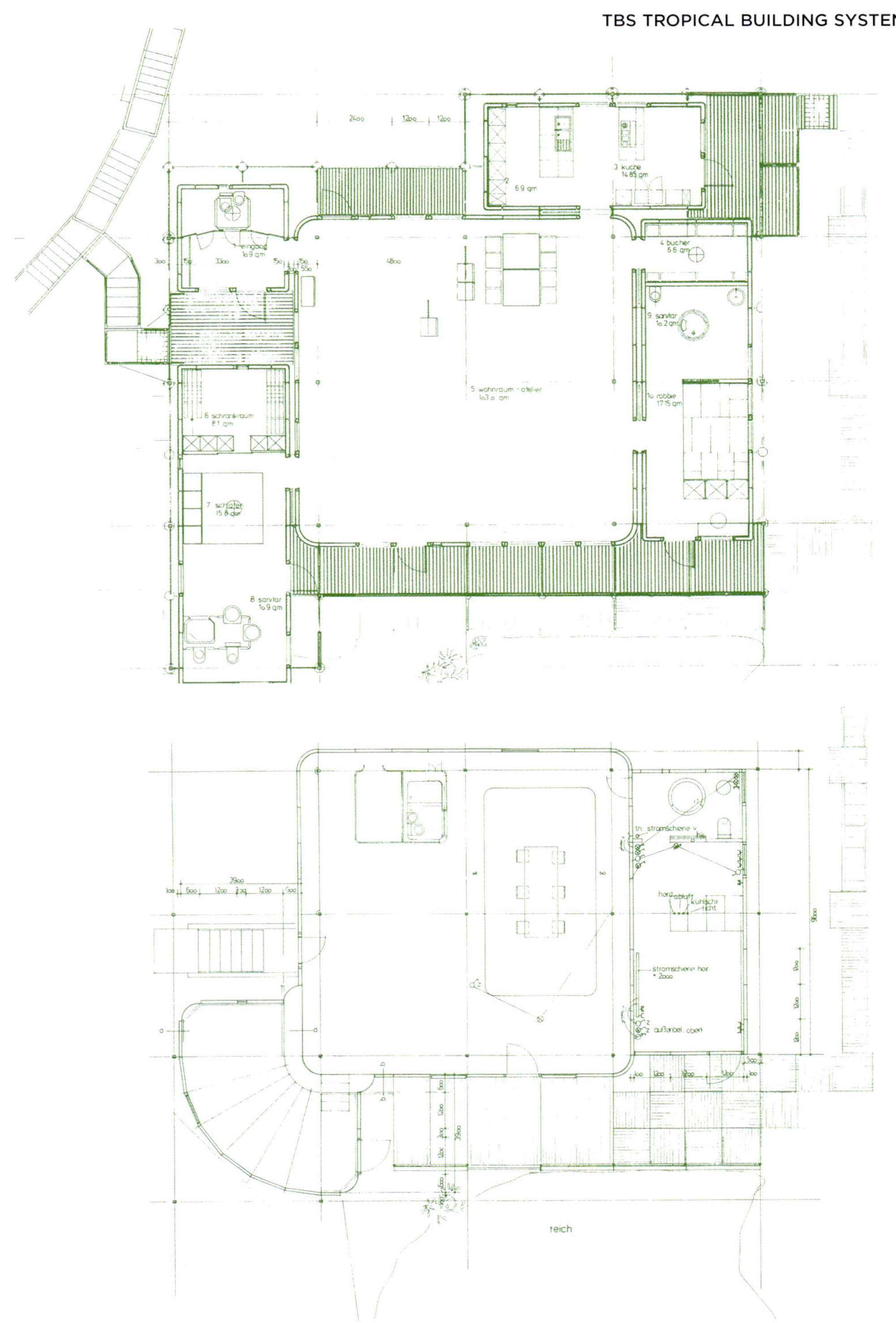

1 eingang
1o 9 qm
3 kuche
14 85 qm
4 bucher
5 6 qm
5 wohnraum - atelier
1o3 o qm
6 schrankraum
8 1 qm
7 schlafen
15 8 qm
8 sanitar
1o 9 qm
9 sanitar
1o 2 qm
1o robbie
17 15 qm
stromschiene v
herd abluft
kuhlschr
stromschiene hor
+ 2ooo
außenbel. oben
teich

BOLWONINGEN

Dries Kreijkamp
’s-Hertogenbosch, Netherlands, 1984

Bolwoningen (Ball houses) is an experimental housing project designed in the late 1970s by the Dutch architect Dries Kreijkamp and completed in 1984 in the city of ’s-Hertogenbosch, which is in the southern Netherlands, near the Belgian border. The project consists of 50 spherical dwellings and represents one of the most distinctive examples of late-20th-century experimental housing in the country.

Kreijkamp was born in 1945 in the Netherlands and trained as an architect during a period marked by strong interest in social reform, alternative living models, and architectural experimentation. His work reflects broader postwar debates about individuality, affordability, and new forms of domestic space.

Each Bolwoning is a spherical concrete structure raised on a cylindrical base. The compact interiors are organized across multiple levels, typically with an entrance and service spaces below and living areas within the sphere above. Prefabricated from glass-fiber-reinforced concrete, the spheres were designed for rapid assembly and low energy use, aligning with wider European efforts toward innovative and sustainable housing solutions in the postwar period. Circular openings admit daylight and frame views, while the curved interior walls challenge conventional ideas of domestic space. The houses were conceived as low-cost rental units, intended for single occupants or couples willing to adapt to nontraditional living conditions. Although Kreijkamp envisioned the design as potentially mobile or floating, the built Bolwoningen remained stationary and have been continuously occupied since their completion. The project was realized within the context of Dutch government-supported experimental housing programs, which encouraged architects to test unconventional forms and construction methods.

Above: A group of houses in a hillside setting and arranged like a stacked tower

Opposite: The spherical form of the structures permitted well ordered geometric arrangements

SCHAKELINGEN OP BASIS VAN DRIEHOEKIGE KAVELS (50 M2 PER KAVEL)

Vijftig bolwoningen - 's-Hertogenbosch

Terug naar de oorspronkelijke ronde woonvorm dankzij nieuw bouwmateriaal

Opdrachtgever	Gemeentelijk Woningbedrijf, 's-Hertogenbosch
Ontwerp	Dries Kreijkamp, 's-Hertogenbosch
Adviseur constructie	Adviesburo voor Bouwkonstrukties Ouwerkerk bv, Leiden
Hoofdaannemer	bv Nederlandse Bouwmaatschappij NBM, 's-Gravenhage
Fabricage bolelementen	Forton Glasbeton bv, 's-Gravenhage/Moerdijk
Foto's	H. J. Stuvel, Leidschendam

De hoofdstad van Noord-Brabant had een onbetwiste primeur op het gebied van de volkshuisvesting toen op 21 juni 1984 de eerste sleutel van een complex van vijftig bolwoningen in het uitbreidingsplan 'Maaspoort' werd uitgereikt. In de wandeling sprak men al gauw van de 'Bossche bollen', gebouwd in opdracht van het Gemeentelijk Woningbedrijf van 's-Hertogenbosch door de Nederlandse Bouwmaatschappij NBM in 's-Gravenhage. Dat is ongetwijfeld een novum in onze Nederlandse wooncultuur, maar toch, bij nadere beschouwing zou men kunnen stellen: terug naar de oorspronkelijke woonvorm van de oermens. Die weg terug is te danken aan een vernuftig ontwerp van Dries Kreijkamp - beeldhouwer en industrieel ontwerper - maar evenzeer aan de toepassingsmogelijkheden van het nieuw ontwikkelde bouwmateriaal (P)GVC, ofwel (Polymeren) Glasvezel Versterkt Cement; Forton Glasbeton bv - een dochteronderneming van het NBM-concern - vervaardigt onder gebruikmaking van dit materiaal in een tijdelijke fabriek op het bouwterrein de feitelijke woonbollen met een doorsnede van 5,50 m.

Kreijkamp is al zo'n twintig jaar bezig met het ontwerpen van bolvormige bouwwerken. Hem inspireren niet alleen de praktische voordelen en mogelijkheden maar ook de mooie natuurlijke vorm. Tot voor kort echter bleek dat alle bedachte bolconstructies onder toepassing van de gebruikelijke bouwmaterialen duurder werden dan traditioneel uitgevoerde en ontworpen woningen. Dankzij (P)GVC slaagde hij in het ontwerpen van een woningtype dat rationeel en betaalbaar geproduceerd kan worden, zo zelfs dat nu in de gesubsidieerde woningbouw een echt alternatief wordt geboden zowel ten aanzien van de woonvorm als van de woonlasten.
Na een gedetailleerd onderzoek door het Bouwcentrum en TNO selecteerde de Stuurgroep Experimenten Volkshuisvesting de bolwoning van Dries Kreijkamp als het enige woningontwerp dat in aanmerking kwam om met subsidie van het Ministerie van Volkshuisvesting te worden gerealiseerd. De prijs is vergelijkbaar met die van de goedkope traditionele stapelbouw.

De bolwoning in 's-Hertogenbosch - het kleinste model dat Kreijkamp heeft ontworpen - heeft een inhoud van

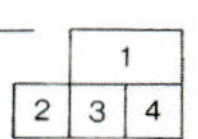

1 - er ontstaat een parkachtige situatie; rechts op de foto de montage van de bolwoningen
2 - de ronde ramen, met een doorsnede van 1,20 m, zijn ten opzichte van de zon in een zo gunstig mogelijke stand geplaatst
3 - de eerste bewoner Paul Slot gaat even een boodschap doen; desgevraagd bevestigt hij nog steeds bijzonder enthousiast te zijn: 'een belevenis!'
4 - op de voorgrond passend parkmeubilair, vervaardigd van beton en wapeningsstaal, in de vorm van grote borstels.

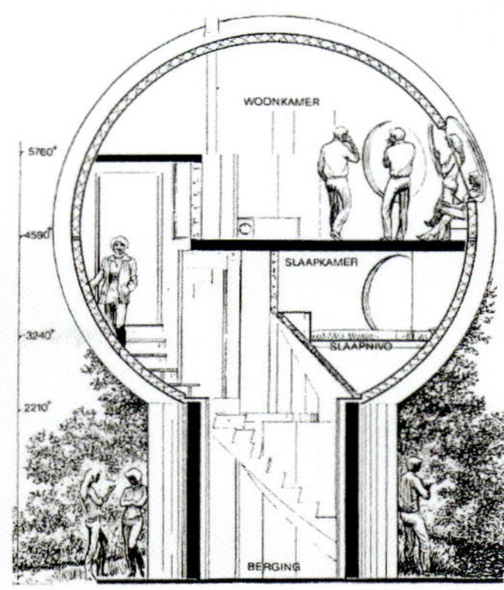

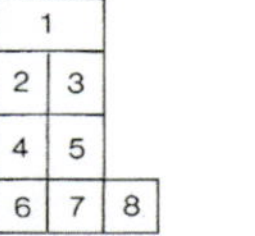

1 - halve bol gereed om te worden gemonteerd
2 - overzicht prefab betonnen cylindervormige voeten
3 - kantelen van de halve onderhelft
4 - geplaatst op de voet
5 - opbouw met prefab elementen
6 - de slaapruimte
7 - woonruimte met ongestoord uitzicht
8 - open keuken in de living.

124 m³ bij een totale vloeroppervlakte van 55 m² en is speciaal bedoeld voor alleenstaanden en kleine gezinnen. In het breedste gedeelte van de bol ligt de woonruimte met open keuken. Om de inhoud optimaal te benutten zijn er vijf niveaus. Op het laagste niveau vindt men de berging, daarboven de laag voor het slapen en enkele treden hoger de douche- en toiletruimte.
Bolwoningen kunnen door hun vorm worden geschakeld tot een woondichtheid die vergelijkbaar is met die van gestapelde wooneenheden.
De bol, die in twee helften wordt gefabriceerd, is een sandwichconstructie, opgevuld met een 10 cm dikke isolerende laag steenwoldeken. De buitenwand, die op zich sterk genoeg is om eigen gewicht, windkracht en sneeuwbelasting te dragen, wordt bevestigd aan een zelfdragende binnenconstructie.
Op deze wijze ontstaat een sterke, duurzame en optimaal geïsoleerde buitenwandconstructie die energie-efficiënt kan worden verwarmd.

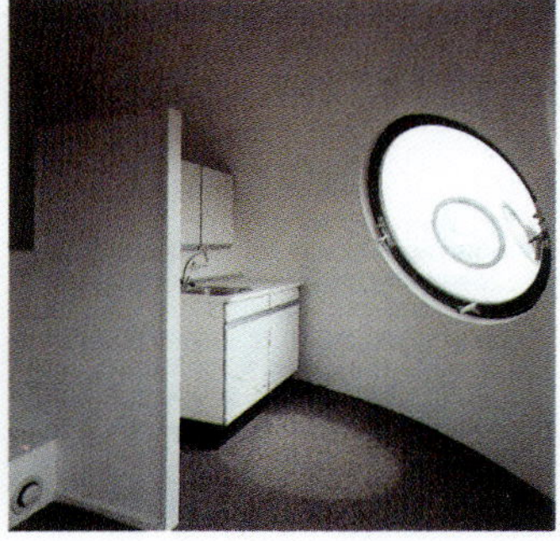

Opposite: Even in a wooded environment, the structures look like something out of science fiction

Above: A group of spheres that give the impression of a well-ordered, industrial lifestyle

Below: An interior view with a kitchen and a typical round window

EASY DOMES

Kári Thomsen, Ole Vanggaard
Easy Domes Ltd.
Tórshavn, Faroe Islands, Denmark, 1992–

Kári Thomsen is presumably the first architect from the Faroe Islands to have his houses slated for construction on the Persian Gulf. The Easy Domes, which he developed along with the Danish engineer Ole Vanggaard, are to be built as a holiday complex in Abu Dhabi.

The first Easy Dome has been standing in Tórshavn, the capital of the Faroe Islands, since 1992: the Greenland Society's House of Culture, with 1,080 sq. ft. of floor space. In subsequent years a number of additional Easy Domes were built on this group of islands, which belong to Denmark. After a number of holiday homes with 269 sq. ft. of floor space had successfully withstood the harsh climate of the North Atlantic for several years, Easy Domes began to be exported throughout the world. They are built in a factory in Denmark. The Easy Dome is somewhat more angular than a football, but built in the same manner: it is a "truncated icosahedron," a regular polygon consisting of pentagonal and hexagonal faces. This form is optimal in terms of volume, weight, materials used, and usable floor space. The polygonal houses from the Faroe Islands are built on foundations of concrete or wood and consist of 21 pinewood elements covered with plywood, 21 plywood or plasterboard elements for the interior cladding, and three elements for the (main) entrance, in addition to thermo energy windows, interior walls, and floors. The assembly can be completed by two to three workers in one day without a crane. The sections are bolted together and the edges are sealed with asphalt paper or rubber.

The holiday homes on the Faroe Islands were also additionally insulated in a traditional manner with a 6 in. layer of peat. The living area is in the lower part of the house with a bedroom for two people above. In 2008 the first residential building of this type was erected in Denmark. With ceilings of over 16 ft., it is a spacious, two-story, low energy house.

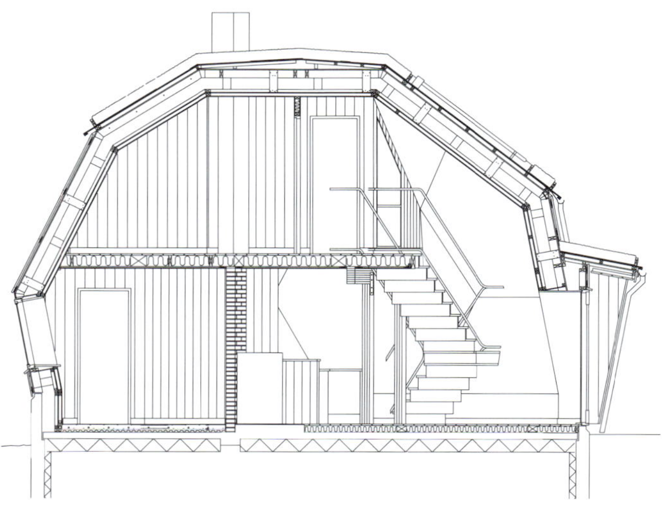

Easy Domes can be built to stand alone or combined within larger units, as in this photograph of a model (opposite)

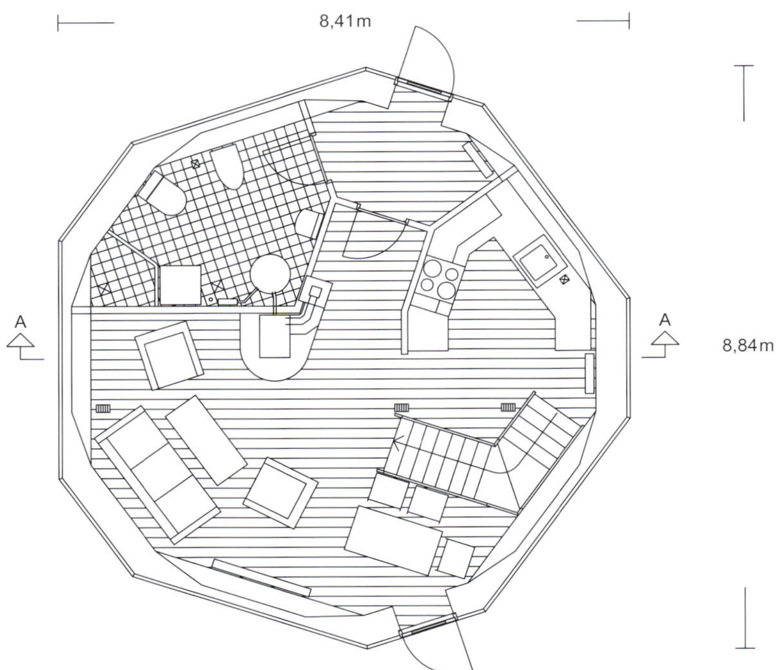
8,41m
8,84m
A
A

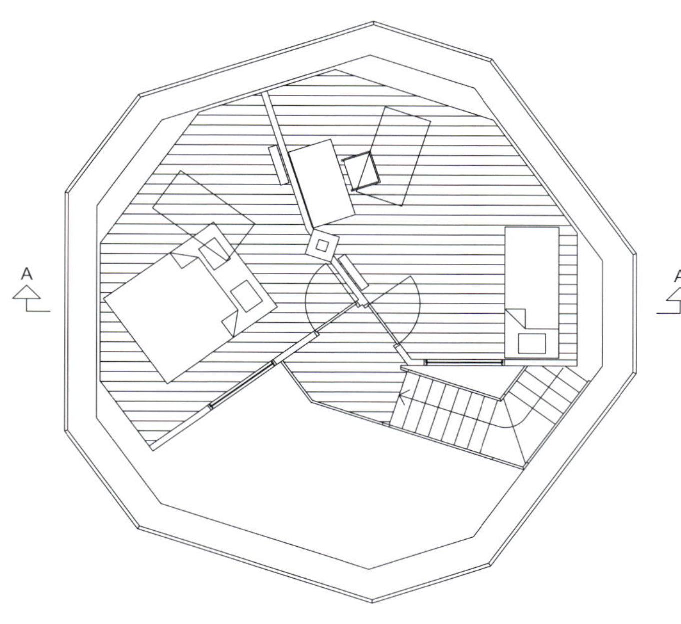

Previous spread and left: Section and floor plans of a house in Denmark with a living room, kitchen and bath on the lower level and two bedrooms on the upper level

Opposite bottom and below: Construction of the house on a concrete foundation

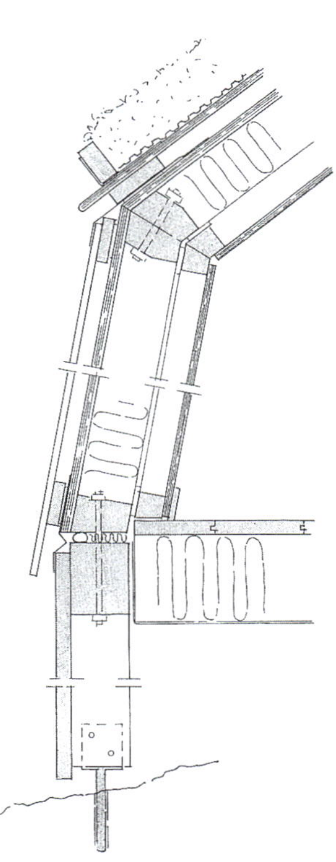

FURNITURE HOUSE

Shigeru Ban
Various locations, 1995–2006

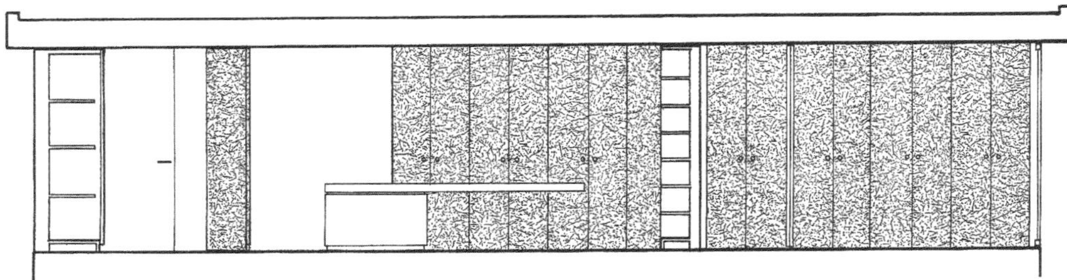

The Furniture House that Shigeru Ban erected in the Japanese city of Yamanakako (Yamanashi prefecture) in 1995 is informed by the architect's experience with earthquakes. In an earthquake, furniture kills people when it falls on them, but it also saves people by supporting collapsed roofs. "So I thought, if furniture is strong enough to kill or save people, why not just make a house out of furniture?"

The Furniture House is constructed entirely of floor-to-ceiling closets and bookshelves that serve both as built-in furniture and as supporting walls. Each of the shelving units, which measure 8 ft. in height and either 18 or 27 in. in depth, weighs roughly 174 lbs. and can be easily assembled by a single person. These modules, which are prefabricated in a furniture factory, are aligned at the building site to form walls, that are connected by means of a wooden beam at the top and then horizontally reinforced with sheets of plywood.

Shigeru Ban's approach to design thrives not least of all from the fact that once he has discovered a system, he always continues to develop upon it. Thus, he built two other Furniture Houses in Japan: a larger one, in 1996, and one made of steel, two years later. For a fourth version, built in China, he discovered a type of indigenous plywood made of woven strips of bamboo, which is usually used for form boards when pouring concrete. A more recent house by the Japanese architect based on prefabricated shelving units is the Sagaponac House, a villa that consists entirely of closets that was built on Long Island in 2006. In designing its floor plan he drew upon the Landhaus in Backstein (Brick Country House), which was designed by Mies van der Rohe (1924), but never built.

Above: The walls either consist of furniture elements or are completely glazed

Opposite: The phases of construction. The furniture is set down on the contiguous ground plate before the roof is set on top of it. In a final step the windows and doors are fit into the remaining openings

Mount Fuji is visible at a distance from the terrace; later, Ban's paper house was built on the slope below

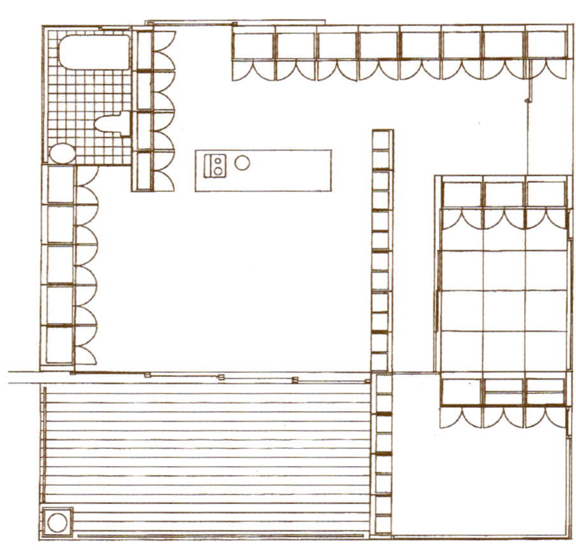

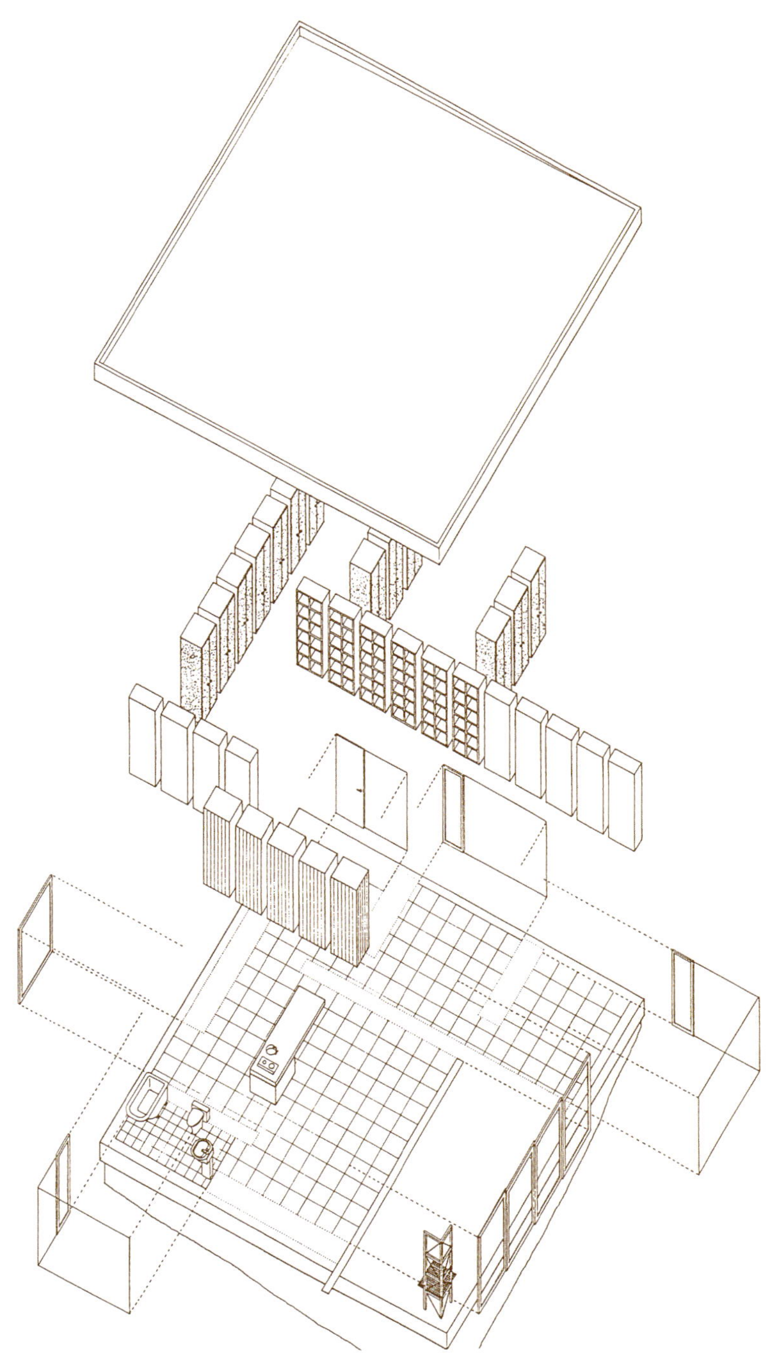

PAPER LOG HOUSE

Shigeru Ban
Various locations, 1995–2022

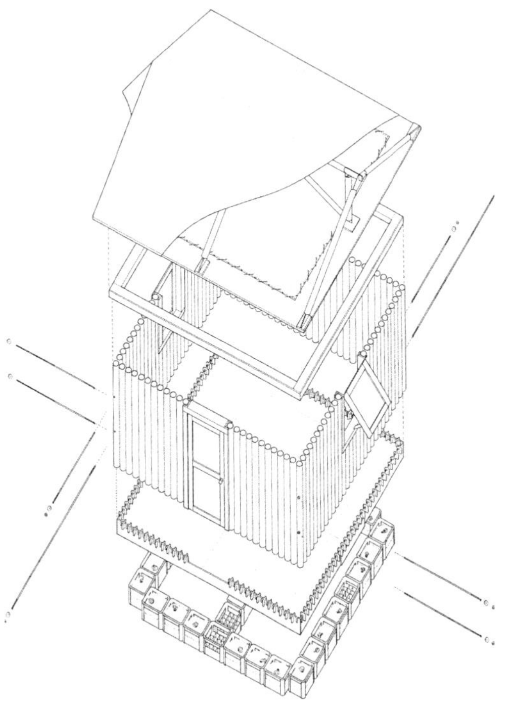

Called Paper Tube Structure 07, this one-story, temporary residence had a total floor area of 172 sq. ft. Designed in May and June of 1995, the year of the Great Hanshin Earthquake in Kobe, this house was inspired by the plight of a group of Vietnamese churchgoers who were still living in plastic-sheet tents months after the January 1995 earthquake. Shigeru Ban asked them why and they explained that government-provided housing was located too far away for easy transport and school registration for their children. He decided to create temporary houses for them. Shigeru Ban explains: "The design criteria called for a cheap structure that could be built by anyone, with reasonable insulated properties that was acceptably attractive in appearance. The solution was a foundation of sand-filled beer cases, walls of paper tubes (diameter 4.25 in., 0.16 in. thick), and with the ceiling and roof made of membrane material. The design was a kind of log-house cabin. The beer cases were rented from the manufacturer and were also used to form steps during the construction process." The simplicity of this process and the fact that the paper tubes could be made on site met all of the criteria for solving difficult living conditions engendered by theearthquake. By the end of the summer of 1995, 27 of these houses had been built for both Vietnamese and Japanese users.

An updated version of the Paper Partition System (PPS) was developed in 2022 for Ukrainian refugees.

Above: An exploded axonometric drawing shows the layered simplicity of the design

Opposite: Even unskilled workers can easily assemble the Paper Log House using the flat-packed elements

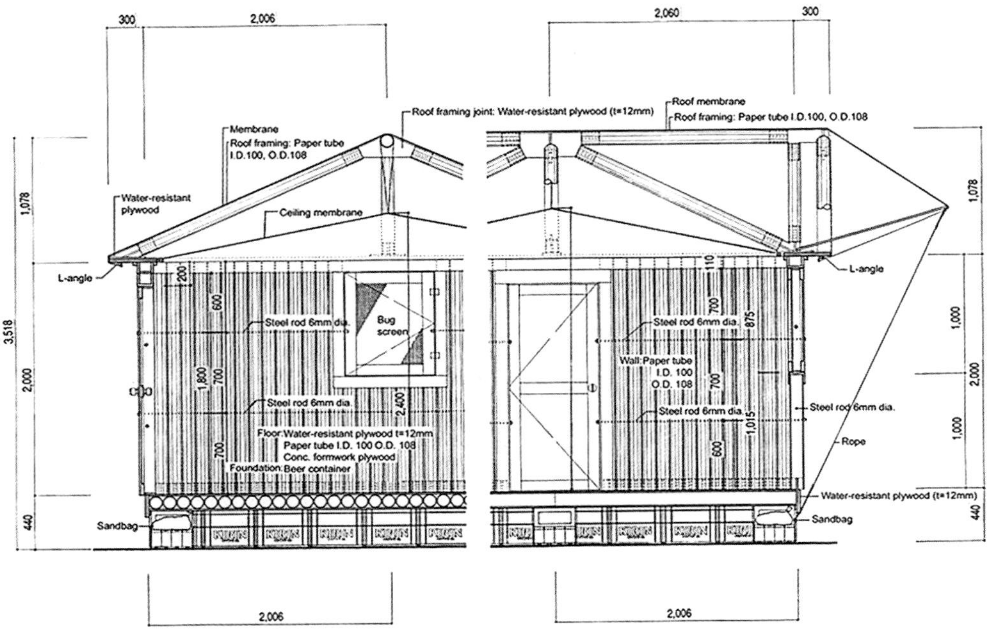

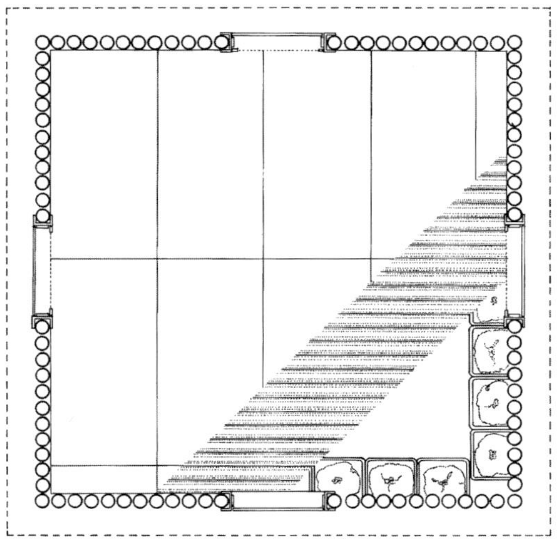

Above and left: Drawings in section and plan explain the design, which is set up on sandbags

Opposite: A completed house is dignified and simple, offering privacy and shelter

Following spread: Grouped together, the houses form a convivial community

キリンビール
キリンビール
キリンビール
キリンビール
キリンビール

LIVING BOX

Thomas Schnyder
Architeam 4
Basel, Switzerland, 1996–2010

The idea of making "as much living space as possible" out of the least amount of material was seminal for the development of the "Living Box," a prefabricated house designed in 1993 by Thomas Schnyder from the Basel architectural office "Architeam 4" for RUWA, a company based in Küblis that specializes in wooden construction; it is an idea he continuously refines, applying the design principles Le Corbusier formulated in his "five points of new architecture" in 1926. The external and internal walls are non-load-bearing. Thus, the floor plans and façades can be freely designed. Pad footings or cellars serve as foundations. Most of the Living Boxes also have a flat roof and ribbon windows.

Schnyder was also inspired by the social Utopian designs of Soviet Constructivists like Moisei Ginzburg. The Living Box is most notable for the fact that it makes it possible to realize smaller living units that can be expanded at will. The basic structure of the Living Box is a supporting skeleton made of prefabricated wooden supports and wood-concrete-composite ceilings on a grid of 8 ft. × 12 ft. = 93 sq. ft. Three pairs of steel cross struts per story provide structural reinforcement. The supporting skeleton can be expanded in every direction. The system is only limited in terms of height, to three stories. This ensures the greatest possible degree of flexibility with regard to its use. Correspondingly, it is

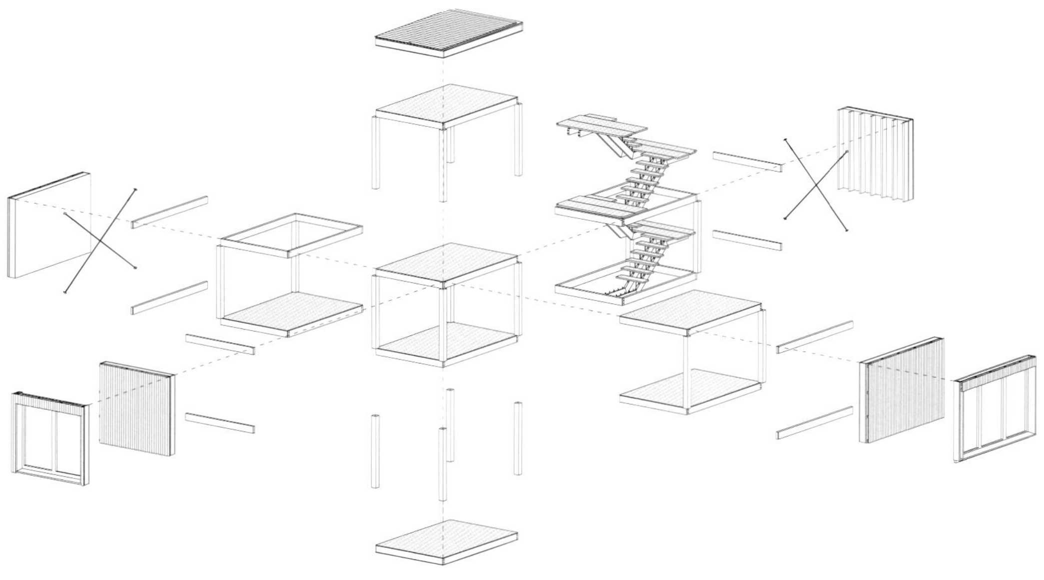

possible to install, and later move, internal walls of wood or glass—by one's self.

Living Boxes are "direct gain houses," which require only a thirtieth of the heating energy of a conventional house in locations with good solar radiation. This is made possible, for one, by the fact that the houses open up towards the south, while the other façades remain for the most part closed: solar radiation is stored in the solid wood-concrete-composite ceilings and gradually dispersed into the ambient air. In addition, the building's skin is airtight and highly insulated by using cellulose from recycled paper and special glass. The ventilation system with heat recovery equipment prevents energy from being exhausted from the building. Residual energy from the exhaust system, solar collectors, and mini heat pumps are used to heat water for domestic use. Solar panels can further reduce energy consumption.

The upgradable installation concept is also innovative: along one of the façades there is a zone for plumbing and utilities; it can be expanded incrementally or used as a closet or a bookcase.

The Living Box Flüeler in Luzein, Switzerland, features an additional pitched roof

The Living Box Wolken in Küblis, Switzerland, 2003

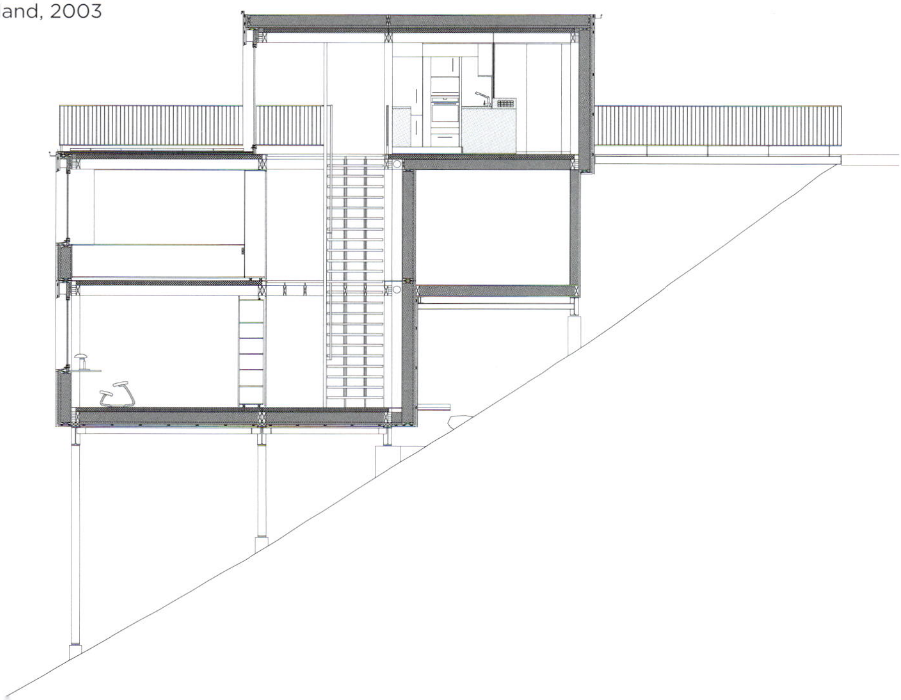

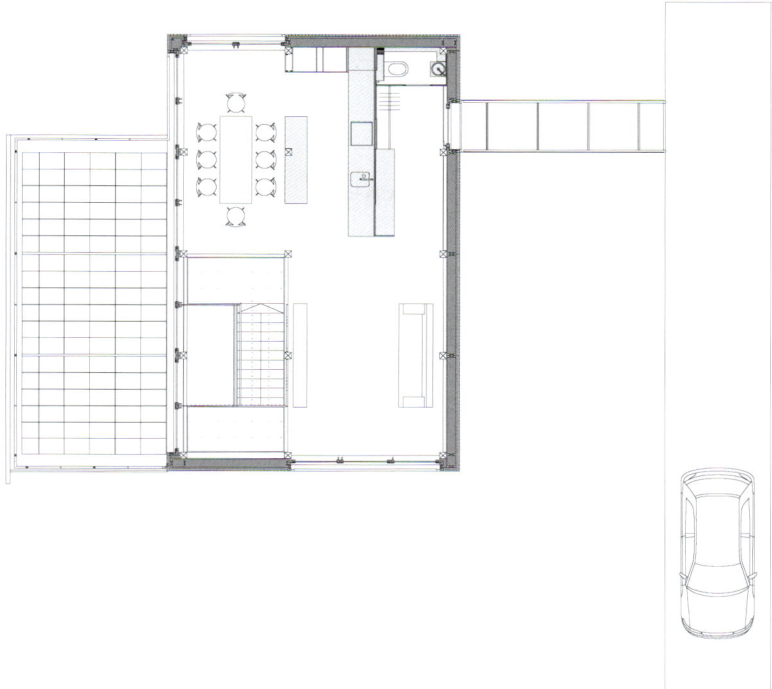

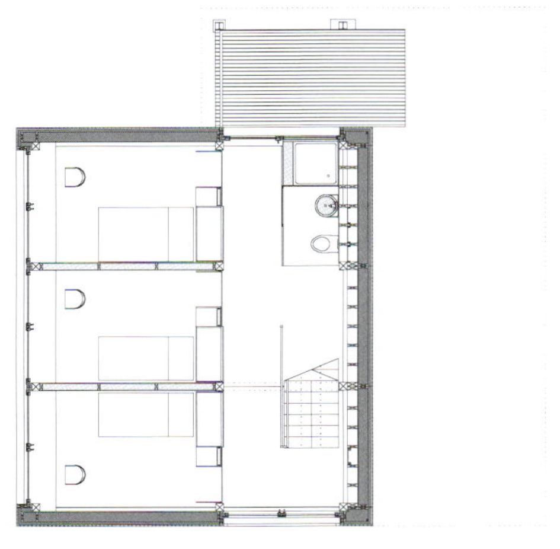

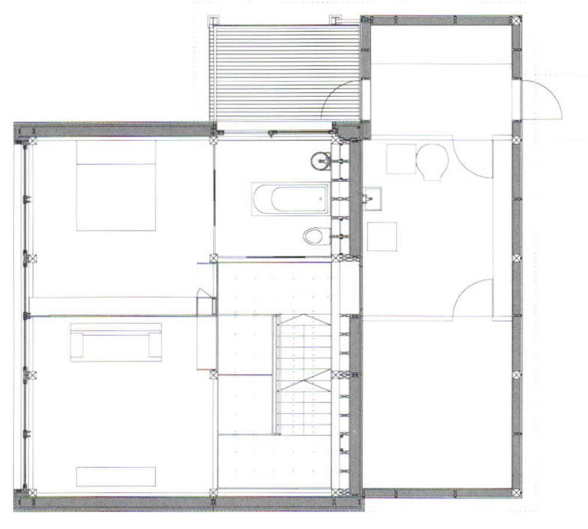

Previous and this spread: Section, floor plans and interior views of the Living Box in Küblis

SU-SI

Oskar Leo Kaufmann, Johannes Kaufmann
KFN Kaufmann Product GmbH
Dornbirn, Austria, 1998–

The Kaufmanns are a family from the Vorarlberg region that has been involved in carpentry for generations. The son of this dynasty, the architect Oskar Leo Kaufmann, established the company KFN Products along with his cousin, the carpenter Johannes Kaufmann. Just a year later, they were already enjoying tremendous success: a prefabricated house that he had originally designed for his sister Susanne became a big seller. In each of the following two years, roughly twenty of these houses were sold under the name SU-SI house (in honor of his sister). The house was low in cost: very few of the buyers paid more than €80,000 for their building kits.

The components are delivered by truck and the house can be erected on site within a few days. The sanitary fixtures and heating are preinstalled. The SU-SI can even be built on stilts in order to create a carport; otherwise the box rests on a concrete foundation.

The flat-roofed house is supported by a post-and-beam structure. On the long side, which features floor-to-ceiling glazing, the supporting structure simultaneously serves as a continuous shelving unit. The entire structure consists of wood, the ceiling and floors are made of solid spruce, and the walls of laminated wooden panels. Other materials can be also be selected for the outer skin, the interior cladding, and the floors.

The standard house, which is 10 ft. high, can be delivered in various sizes with lengths ranging from 10 to 13 ft. and widths from 33 to 46 ft., resulting in 323 to 538 sq. ft. of living space.

The first Su-Si had only 452 sq. ft. of floor space, yet still seemed spacious

The bar-shaped structure is delineated on either of the narrow sides by the kitchen and the bathroom

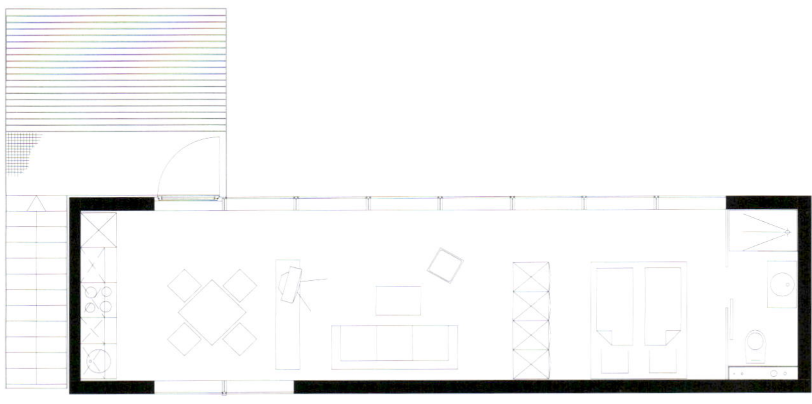

SMALLHOUSE / WEBERHAUS OPTION

Bauart Architekten
WeberHaus GmbH & Co. KG
Rheinau-Linx, Germany, 1999–

The Swiss architectural group Bauart, centered around Marco Ryter, has specialized in solutions involving wooden construction since 1987, when the company was established, and built various municipal facilities in Switzerland such as schools and kindergartens. The architects were also seeking to develop a prefabricated house out of wood that, despite a relatively limited floor space of roughly 750 sq. ft., would overshadow many larger conventional single-family houses in its spaciousness and elegance. Bauart presented the smallhouse in 1999 for the first time, it was built as a modular wooden structure.

The two-story residential cube has a footprint of 38 × 15 ft. and no corridors; each of the floors is divided only by either the open kitchen or the bathroom. Thus, four rooms—or, more precisely, functional areas—are created in a rather matter-of-fact manner; there are no other internal divisions. Yet the houses do not seem confined, not least of all due to the open stairs and large windows, which can fill the entire back wall of the one or the other floor, thereby providing plenty of natural light. The smallhouse does not present itself as a hermetic box, but rather as a flowing continuum.

In the meantime, the prototype presented in 1999 has been developed further in conjunction with the German company WeberHaus. Under the name WeberHaus Option it has since been introduced onto the market. The prefabricated elements are assembled on a floor slab cast on site. The flat-roofed house, with its neutral, reduced design vocabulary, is suited for use in the most diverse locations: as an extension of an already existing building, as a residential unit for one or two people, as a holiday home, or as a studio. Fully equipped bathrooms (with bathtubs) are offered, as well as fireplaces. It is possible to arrange a number of cubes alongside each other; the modular concept also allows for floor plans in the form of an L or a U.

The photograph of the model (opposite left) shows the back of the house, the photograph of the house (below) shows the completed front

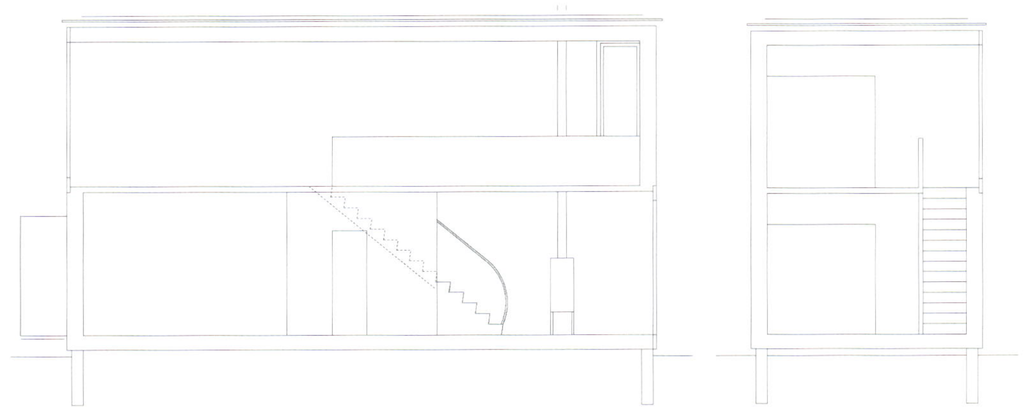

The appearance of the interior can be varied by using different materials for the floor, walls, and ceilings

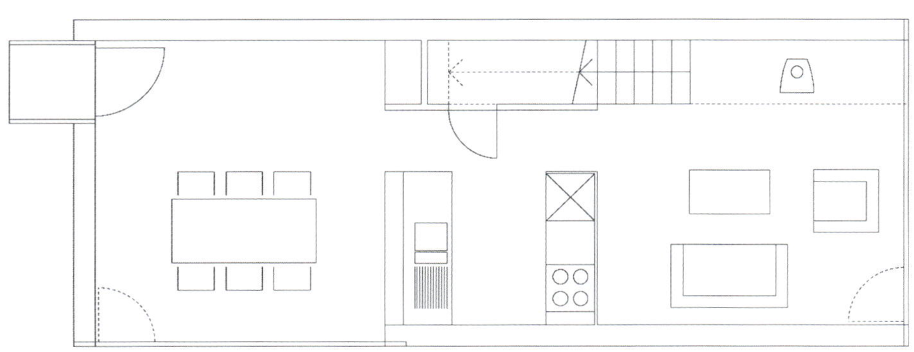

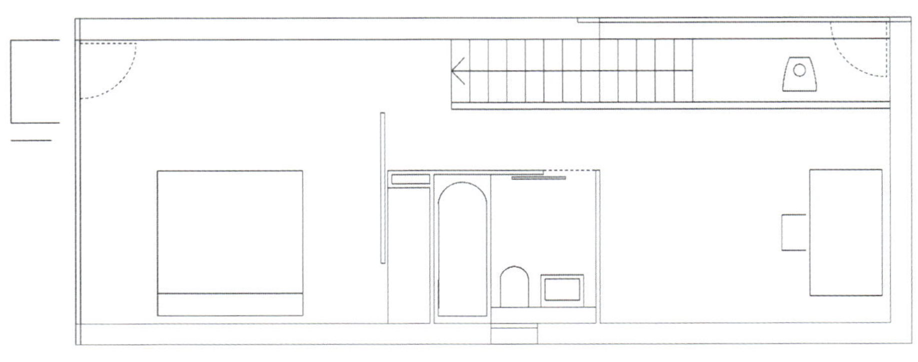

LV HOME

Rocio Romero
St. Louis, Missouri, USA, 2000–2018

The Chilean-American architect and Berkeley graduate Rocio Romero originally designed the LV prefabricated house as a weekend house for her parents to use in Laguna Verde, a small town south of Valparaiso in Chile, hence the name. It offered a little over 1,000 sq. ft. of living space and was built directly on a hill overlooking the Pacific Coast. The view of the ocean and the landscape was intended to be part of the living experience. Low cost, weather resistance, and energy efficiency were the most important considerations informing the design.

The weekend house then became the prototype for the LV Home, which is a wood and metal frame structure on concrete supports. The outer skin consists mainly of corrugated sheet zinc aluminum, aluminum, and laminated glass, while the interiors are executed in laminated wood. Romero also designed furniture made of rust-free steel and a built-in kitchen for the house. With its elongated floor plan and 9 ft. ceilings, the house contains a living room, two bathrooms, two bedrooms, and a kitchen area. On one side there are sliding glass doors that can

LV Homes in Elliott, Maine (opposite) and Perryville, Missouri (above)

be opened completely, thus making for a nearly seamless transition between the living area and the surrounding landscape.

All of the LV Series prefabricated homes have a standard width of about 25 ft., but they vary in size due to differences in the length; the smallest, the LVM, is about 25 ft. long and the largest, the LVL, is 59 ft. 6 in. long. The standard siding on the LV Series Home is galvanized steel coated with silver metallic Kynar 500. LV Homes were available starting at roughly $37,000. However, with expenditures for construction and the interior finish, the total reached an average $138,000 to $224,000. The standardized panel building kit was produced in a factory in Perryville, Missouri, which is about an hour away from St. Louis. Since the completion of the prototype in 2000, Romero had introduced her LV onto the market in various sizes and versions suited for mass production.

Plan of a house built with a cellar

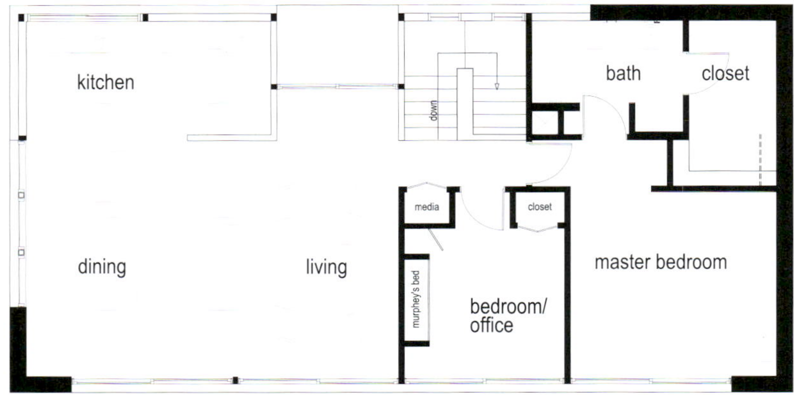

Above: Plan of a house built on one level

Opposite: A narrow band of windows on the side opposite the terrace facilitates cross-ventilation

GLIDEHOUSE

Michelle Kaufmann
Blu Homes, Inc.
Waltham, Massachusetts, USA, 2003–2009

After six months of fruitlessly searching for an affordable single-family home, Michelle Kaufmann lost her patience. The architect, a former employee in Frank O. Gehry's office, decided to build the home she envisioned for herself: a modern house, based on principles of sustainability, at the lowest possible cost. During the design process, friends and colleagues already began asking her if she could also build them one.

Hence, Michelle Kaufmann established her own office, mkd, in 2002. While designing her own home, she also created a model for the first of her houses to be built in series, the Glidehouse, which was an immediate success. In the meantime, six additional models were added. They came completely assembled and are set down on a solid foundation on site. Smaller houses were built as a single module, larger houses consist of a number of modules, which were joined together on site. They were delivered by truck, and this limits their size: as a rule they have been 15 ½ ft. wide and just as tall. The reference costs were $250 to $300 per square foot (incl. transport and assembly).

Kaufmann saw her "pre-designed" houses explicitly as "products" that were available in different versions. In addition to the houses produced in series, Kaufmann and her team were also willing to develop individual designs, which then would have been built in a factory.

With their clear lines, Kaufmann's houses stand in the tradition of classic Modernism. They came also energy efficient and made of sustainable materials. There were two versions, one for

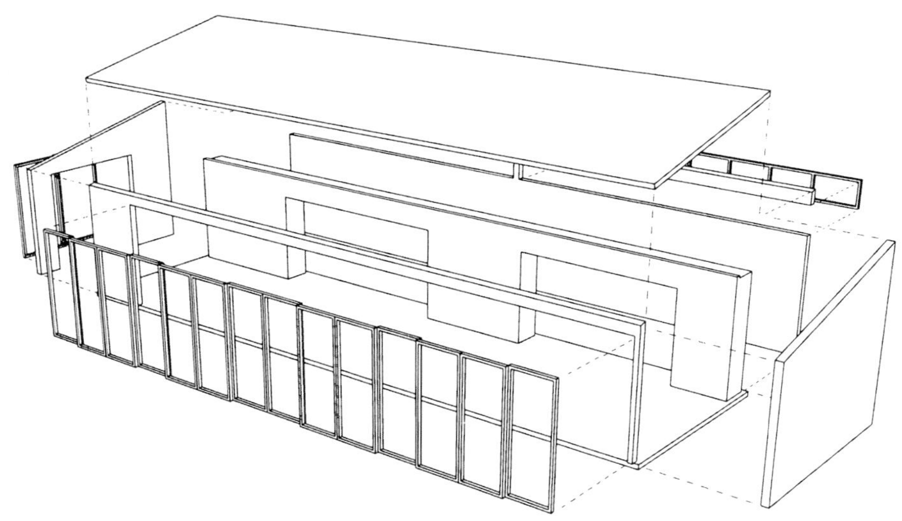

Opposite: Drawing of elements preinstalled in the factory

Above and below: The mono-pitched roofs arranged opposite each other define the external and internal spaces

Above: The external sliding solar protection elements prevent the interior from becoming too hot

Opposite: The Glidehouse G3 contains three bedrooms on 1,568 sq. ft. of floor space

the snowy regions in the north, and the other one for the milder climate of California. Large glass windows with sliding doors open the house up towards the south, the other external walls were made of weatherproof Cor-ten steel. The roofs had been covered with heat resistant galvanized sheet metal and allowed for the easy installation of photovoltaic cells.

The architect described the inclusion of a large wall of cabinets with abundant storage space as a design characteristic—meant to ensure that the living space remains free of clutter.

The Glidehouse, Michelle Kaufmann's first and most successful model, was available in five different sizes: they range from the 672 sq. ft. "studio" (with a separate bedroom and bathroom) to the large Glidehouse, with a courtyard and an H-shaped floor plan made up of four modules totaling 2,240 sq. ft. of floor space. The center of this house was a large living and dining area with a kitchen. The four bedrooms and three bathrooms, as well as a "library," were in the wings.

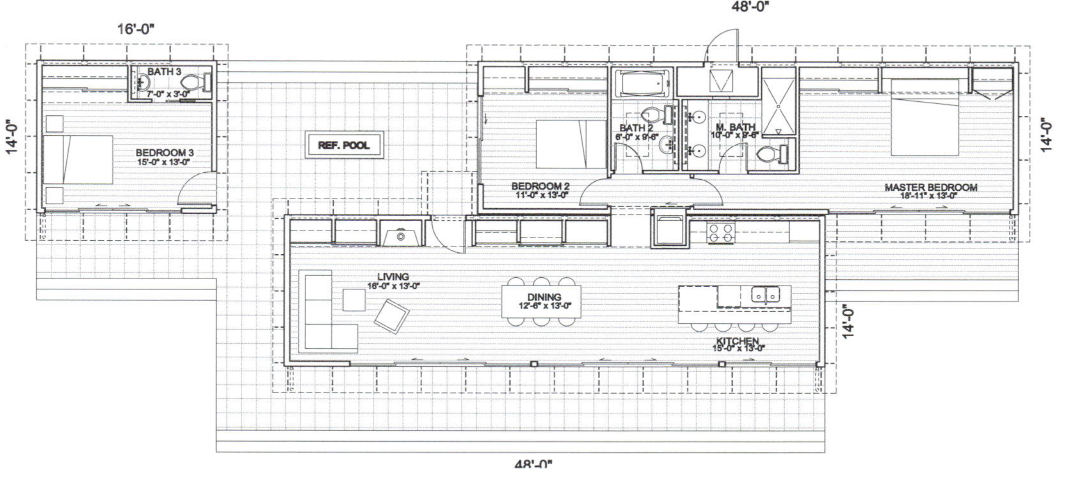
48'-0"
16'-0"
BATH 3
7'-0" x 3'-0"
14'-0"
BEDROOM 3
15'-0" x 13'-0"
REF. POOL
BATH 2
6'-0" x 9'-6"
M. BATH
10'-0" x 9'-6"
14'-0"
BEDROOM 2
11'-0" x 13'-0"
MASTER BEDROOM
18'-11" x 13'-0"
LIVING
16'-0" x 13'-0"
DINING
12'-6" x 13'-0"
14'-0"
KITCHEN
15'-0" x 13'-0"

WEEHOUSE

Alchemy Architects
St. Paul, Minnesota, USA, 2003–

The weeHouses designed by Alchemy Architects prove that it is possible to do a lot with a small space. The architectural office, founded by Geoffrey Warner in 1992, originally designed a small vacation home for the violinist Stephanie Arade in 1992. The wood and steel structure was completely assembled in a factory and then installed on Lake Pepin, Wisconsin, in 2003. The 336-sq. ft. house, which is indeed "wee," was photogenically located on a slope, where it attracted considerable attention from architectural journals and brought the "workshop of alchemists" numerous subsequent commissions. This marked the birth of the prefabricated house line called weeHouses. In the meantime, the architects have already built over forty prefabricated houses in the United States and Canada, most of them as vacation homes. "People are more inclined to experiment in this sector and, besides, they want everything to be built very fast," says Geoffrey Warner.

The basic weeHouse module is a 14 ft.-wide and 8 ft.-high box, which is available in three lengths: 26 ft. (for either the one-room "studio" or the "weeHouse small" with a separate bathroom), 48 ft., and 58 ft. The "weeHouse large" measures 812 sq. ft. and has a living and dining area with a kitchen unit, two bedrooms, and a

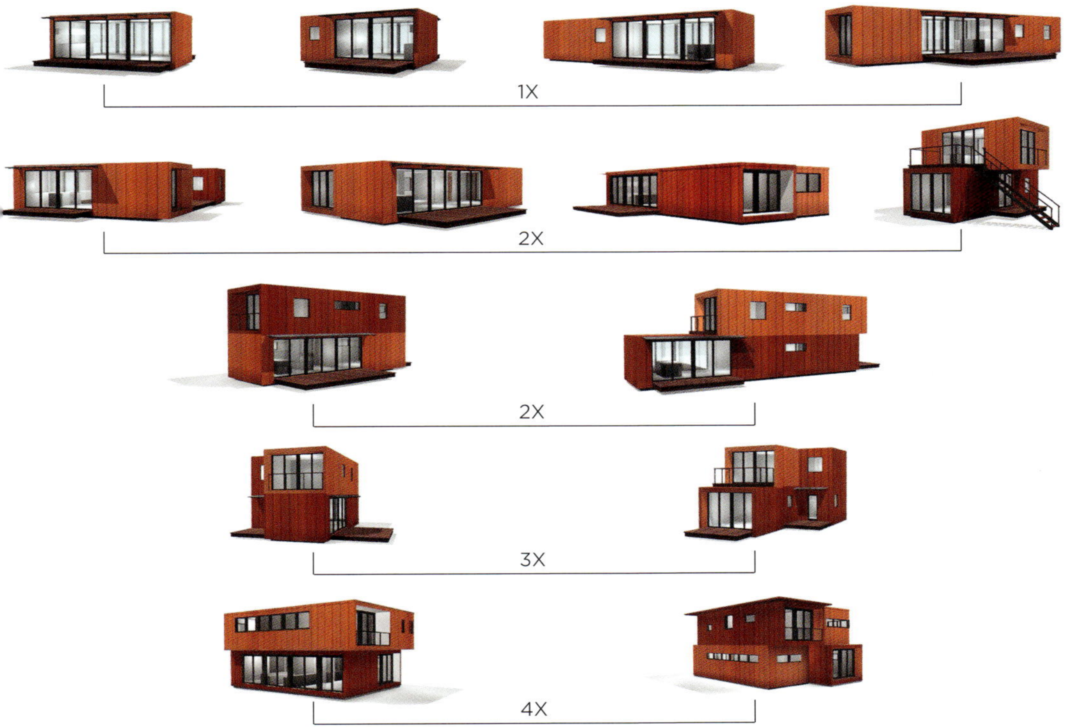

bathroom. By stacking the basic modules, or by placing them alongside each other, five other variations can be created—including a two-story, 1,372 sq. ft. "tall pair large," which has a living and dining room with a kitchen area, along with a bedroom and a bathroom, on the ground floor, as well as two bedrooms, a bathroom, and a roof terrace on the upper floor.

Once the client has decided upon the size, he has only a limited number of alternatives with regard to the foundation, roof, external walls, and interior design. Hence, all of the "weeHouses" that have been built to date clearly reveal the same handwriting: clean, simple lines and high quality materials. They are also quite reasonably priced: the reference price is currently $200–650 per square foot. The houses are completely built in the factory and then delivered by truck either as a single module or in two parts, depending on the size, and then installed on the site.

The prototype of the weeHouse in Pepin, Wisconsin, 2003. The exterior (following spread) is clad in cementitious siding painted with an oxidizing paint

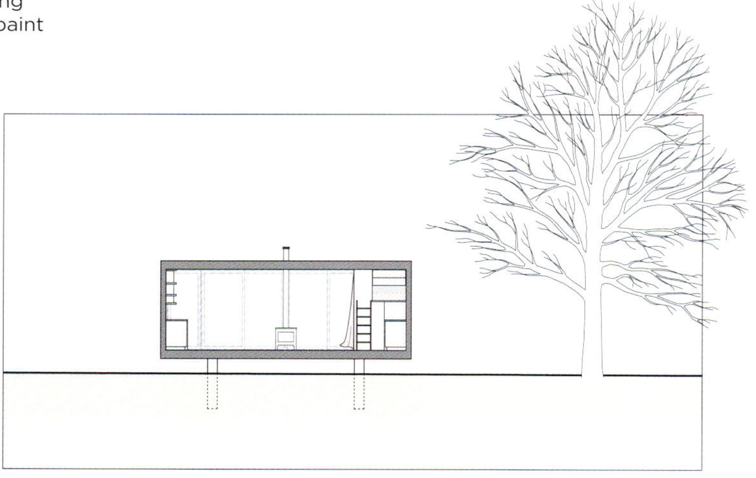

The interior is completely wrapped in Douglas fir. Section and plan (opposite top and below) show the simpler layout

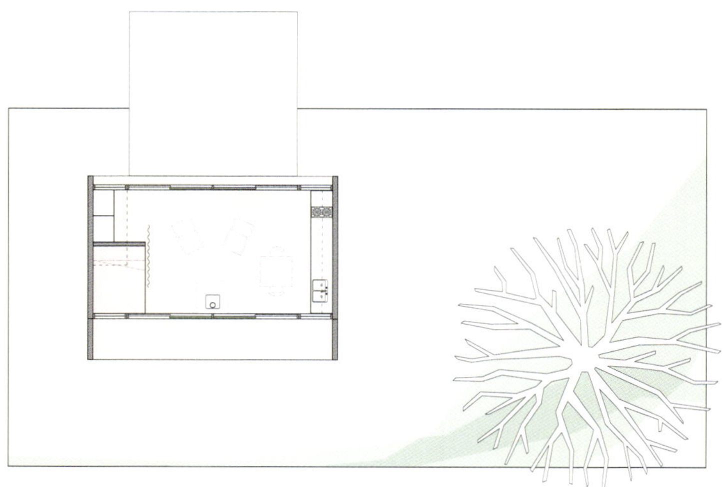

A weeHouse in Marfa, Texas, outside of a small artists' colony in West Texas

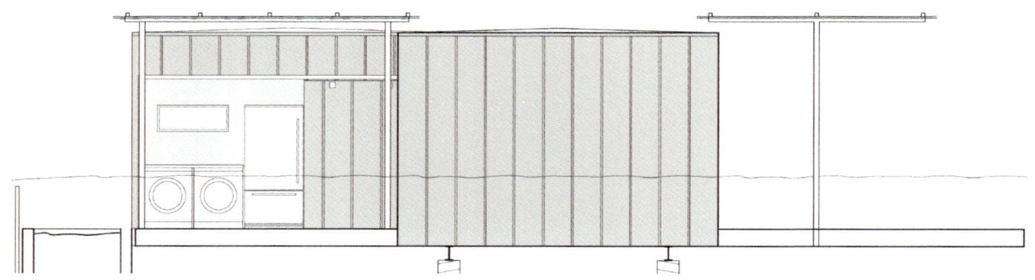

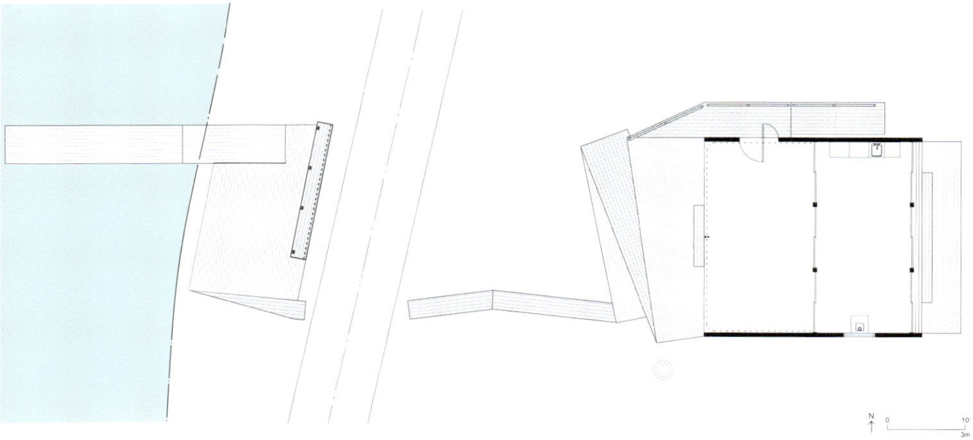

N 0 10' 3m

SITE PLAN

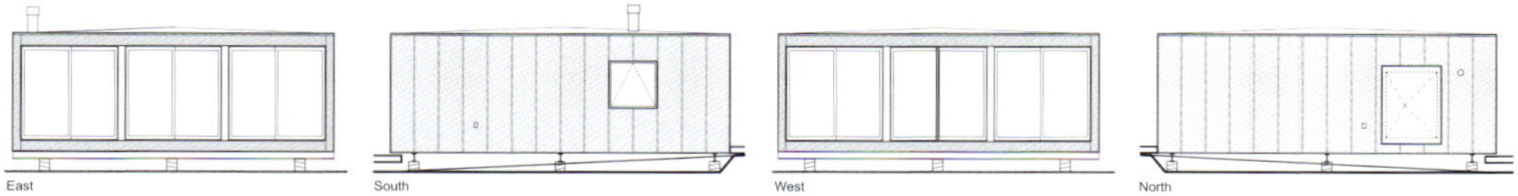

East

South

West

North

ELEVATIONS

Opposite: A weeHouse in Burlington, Wisconsin, a 28 x 28 ft., two-module house with an open porch, blue and yellow container siding, ipe floors, and eucalyptus cabinets

Below: A weeHouse in Honesdale, Pennsylvania, with three bedrooms on a total of 2,200 sq. ft. of floor space. This retreat home consists of a larger main unit accommodating most daily activities and a smaller sleeping tower. Both units are connected by an elevated patio bridge component

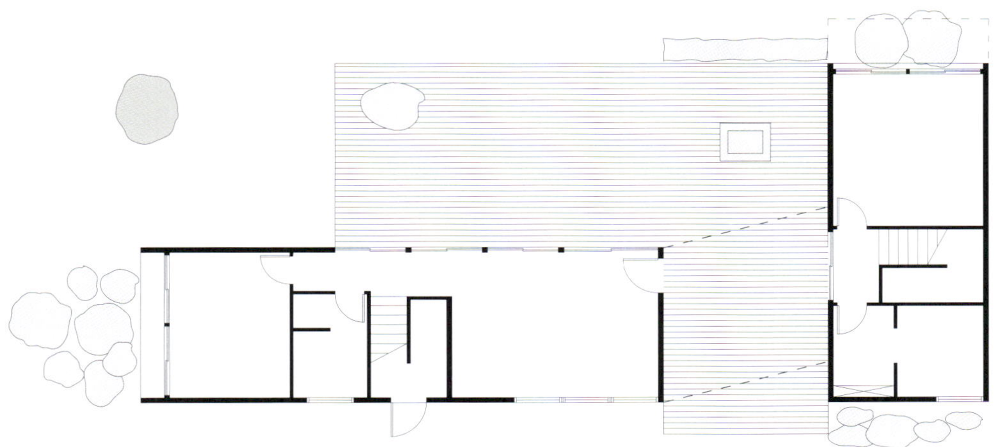

MODERN MODULAR

Resolution: 4 Architecture
New York, USA, 2003–

A team of New York architects, Joseph Tanney and Robert Luntz, established Resolution: 4 Architecture in 1990. The office developed factory finished modules on the basis of wood frame construction. By applying this principle, which the two architects call "Modern Modular," it is possible to build prefabricated houses with diverse floor plans and sizes and respond to individual client wishes on the most diverse building sites. The company offers 20 different models. The prefabricated modules are produced by different companies and delivered to the building site by truck.

In 2003 the office won the prestigious competition staged by *Dwell* magazine for their modern modular principle. In the meantime, a number of houses have been built according to the modern modular principle, including the "Dwell Home" and the "Mountain Retreat." The houses are produced and equipped according to state-of-the-art ecological criteria. They have a solar power system, geothermal heating and cooling, aluminum-clad low energy windows and doors, and much more.

The Dwell Home (which is named for the magazine that awarded the prize) was produced by Carolina Building Solutions, a prefabricated housing company in Pittsboro, North Carolina. The five modules arranged as a two-story structure consists of two interlocking rectangular

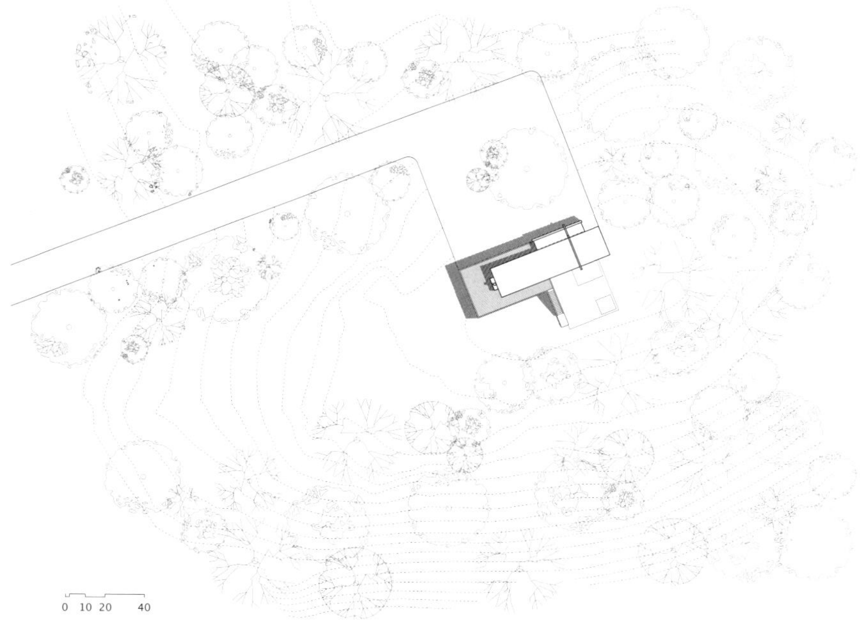

volumes that provide 2,042 sq. ft. of living space. The living, dining, and kitchen area is located on the ground floor and opens onto the spacious deck. The private part of the house, with three bedrooms and two bathrooms, is located in the rectangular volume that stands at a right angle.

The Mountain Retreat, which was built in 2005 by the prefabricated housing company Apex Homes, is somewhat smaller with its 1,800 sq. ft. of floor space. A large part of the building's volume rests on slender concrete columns. Thus, a carport is created on the ground level in addition to a separately accessed residential unit. The actual residential levels are located above it, creating the impression of a tree house suspended in the crowns of the surrounding trees. The loft-like living space contains the kitchen and dining area and is surrounded by a cedar veranda on all three of its nearly fully glazed sides. The gray exterior of the cubic stairway stands in contrast to the horizontal lines of the cedar-clad façade. Inside, this alternation between light and dark is repeated in the interplay between the white-washed bamboo floors and the dark countertops in the kitchen and the bathroom. A special feature of the design is the butterfly roof, the slant of which is echoed by trapezoidal windows just underneath it, which provide additional light. The architects even designed waterspouts that channel rainwater off the roof in decorative cascades.

Opposite: Floor plans of the ground floor (top) and the upper floor (center)

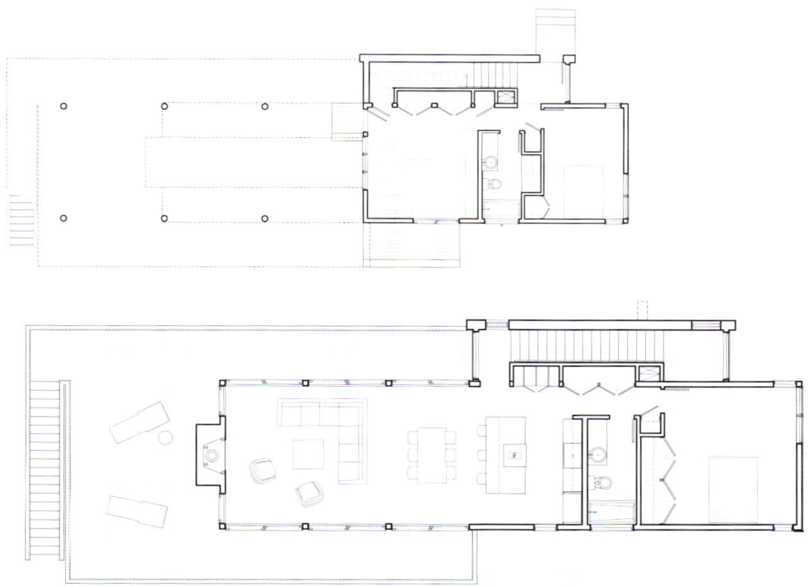

The original Dwell Home was the winning design of the Dwell Home Design Invitational. Sixteen architecture firms from the U.S. and abroad were selected to submit design entries

GANDO TEACHERS' HOUSING

Francis Kéré
Gando, Burkina Faso, 2004

Local women prepare the base of one of the structures

The Gando Teachers' Housing project was completed in 2004 by the architect Francis Kéré. Conceived as part of a broader effort to improve educational infrastructure in Kéré's home village of Gando in eastern Burkina Faso, the project provides dignified, climate-responsive housing for teachers, addressing a challenge in local rural education: the attraction and retention of qualified staff. Francis Kéré was born in 1965 and is internationally recognized for his socially engaged approach to architecture; he was awarded the Pritzker Architecture Prize in 2022.

The Gando Teachers' Housing can be described as prefabricated because many of its building components were produced in advance in a controlled and repeatable manner before assembly on site, even though they were made locally rather than in an industrial factory. The stabilized earth blocks used for the walls were compressed in molds, allowing units of consistent size and quality to be fabricated ahead of construction and then assembled systematically. Roof elements and structural details followed standardized dimensions that could be repeated

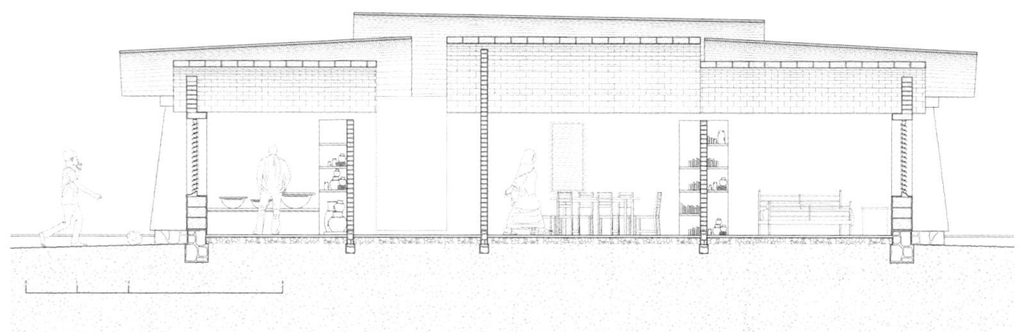

Long and short elevation drawings of the design

across housing units, enabling efficient construction, reduced material waste, and long-term ease of repair and replacement.

The Teachers' Housing follows principles first developed in Kéré's 2001 Gando Primary School project. Built primarily with locally sourced materials, the housing responds to the region's hot climate through passive design strategies rather than mechanical systems. Thick earthen walls provide thermal mass, while carefully positioned openings promote cross-ventilation and natural cooling. Deep overhangs and shaded outdoor spaces protect interiors from intense sunlight and seasonal rains. The housing consists of modest, clearly organized units arranged to support both privacy and community interaction. Construction relied heavily on local labor, with villagers trained in improved building techniques, reinforcing skills transfer and local ownership of the project. This participatory process is central to Kéré's philosophy, which views architecture as a collective, socially rooted endeavor rather than an imposed object.

Opposite: The houses align to form elegant, modern forms

Right: An axonometric drawing showing the exploded design

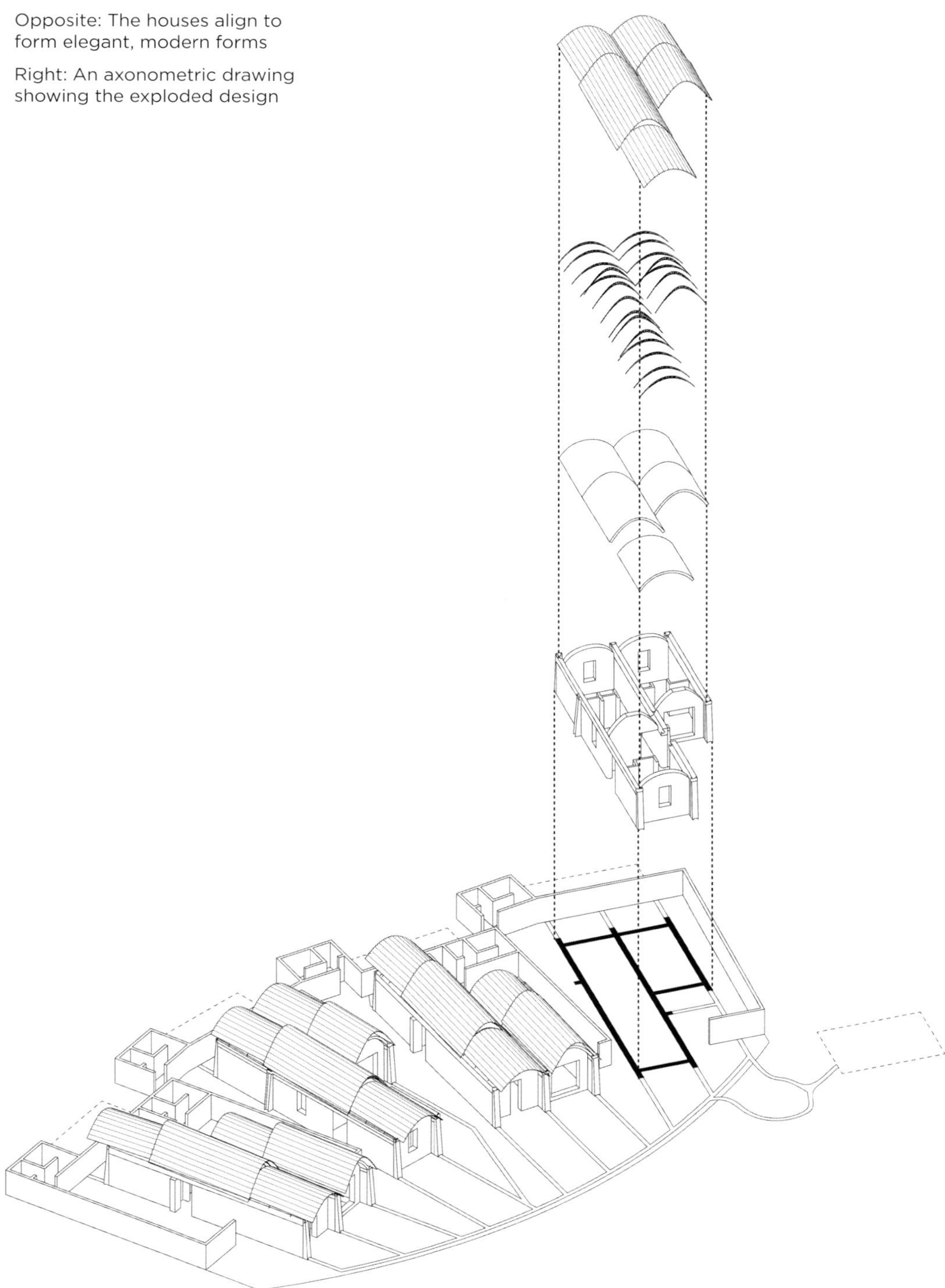

FLATPAK HOUSE

Charlie Lazor
Minneapolis, Minnesota, USA, 2004–

The reviews of the first FlatPak house by Charlie Lazor in Minneapolis were euphoric. *Newsweek* described the FlatPak system as "the first revolution in American housing in decades." *Dwell* wrote, "FlatPak just might be the project that revolutionizes the prefab industry."

What made the system developed by Charlie Lazor and his Lazor Office so special was the flexibility it afforded builders. Every FlatPak house is developed on the basis of 8 ft.-wide wall elements, which can be combined at will. The step-by-step instructions on the Internet promise, "Every 8′, you, along with your FlatPak designer make a decision: all glass, no glass, some glass, high glass, low glass, frosted glass, glass that opens, glass that doesn't." Wall elements made of wood, glass, concrete, and stone are available. A FlatPak house can be up to four stories high and, on steep slopes, it can be built on stilts. The design calls for a roof at a slight angle.

In arranging the rooms, the builder can choose one of a number of standard floor plans or design an individual floor plan within a 2 ft. grid. In designing the interior, the builder can choose from a variety of fittings offered by FlatPak. They can also be freely combined and installed. It doesn't matter whether you choose one, two, three, or four bathrooms.

Design variations

concrete
wood
cement board
metal
glass

The individual parts are produced in a factory in Wisconsin, delivered by truck, boat, or helicopter, and assembled within a few days by a FlatPak fulfillment team. The prices depend upon the materials chosen and can be expected to range between $350 and $750 per square foot.

The man behind the idea, Charlie Lazor, studied architecture at Yale University, then opened an office for furniture design with two partners. He established the Lazor Office in 2003, in order to design architecture and consumer products. He built the first FlatPak house for his family in Minneapolis in 2004.

Below and opposite bottom: The prototype in Minneapolis, Minnesota

Opposite top: FlatPak house in Woodstock, New York

FlatPak houses in Woodstock, New York (living room), Aspen, Colorado (bathroom), and in the Catskill Mountains, New York (exterior)

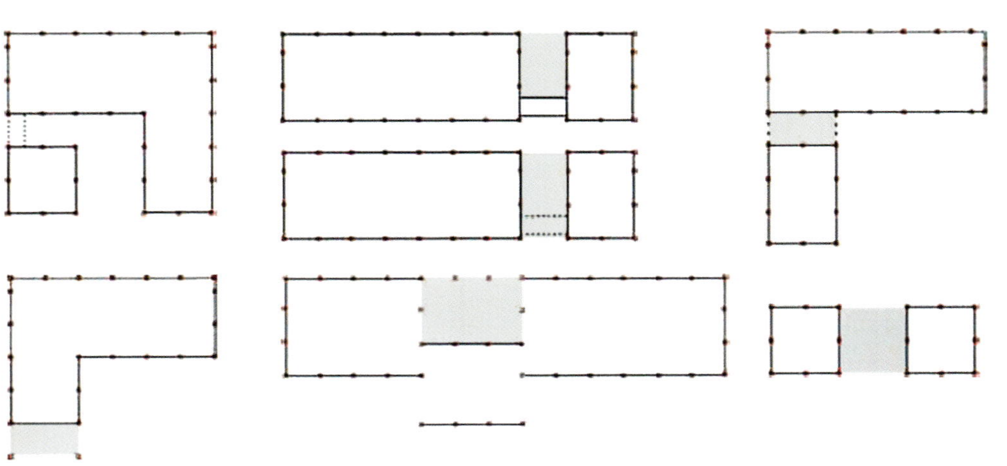

ROTORHAUS

Luigi Colani
Hanse-Haus GmbH
Oberleichtersbach, Germany, 2004

Luigi Colani was always good for a surprise. On the occasion of the 75th anniversary of Hanse-Haus, he created something very special: a compact prefabricated house on a floor plan measuring only 20 ft. × 20 ft., which nevertheless seems spacious. A fully functional model of this "residential study for the future" has been on exhibition at the Hanse-Haus Visitors' Center in Oberleichtersbach, south of the city of Fulda, since 2004.

The goal in designing the house was to create maximum living space on the basis of minimum dimensions. Colani succeed in doing so by installing a sort of rotating stage in one of the corners, an innovation he refers to as a "rotor." It contains three different "functional areas": "sleeping," "cooking," and "bathing." When a button is pressed, the specially developed, silent "RotActions Module" is set in motion, turning the desired functional area towards the living space,

Opposite: Luigi Colani at the presentation of the prototype

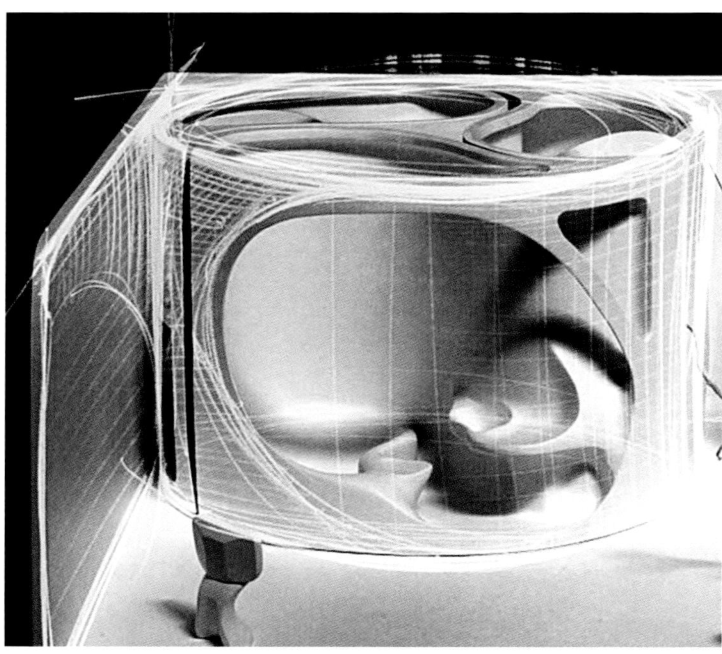

Despite its small size, the little house has a hallway from which the toilet is accessed

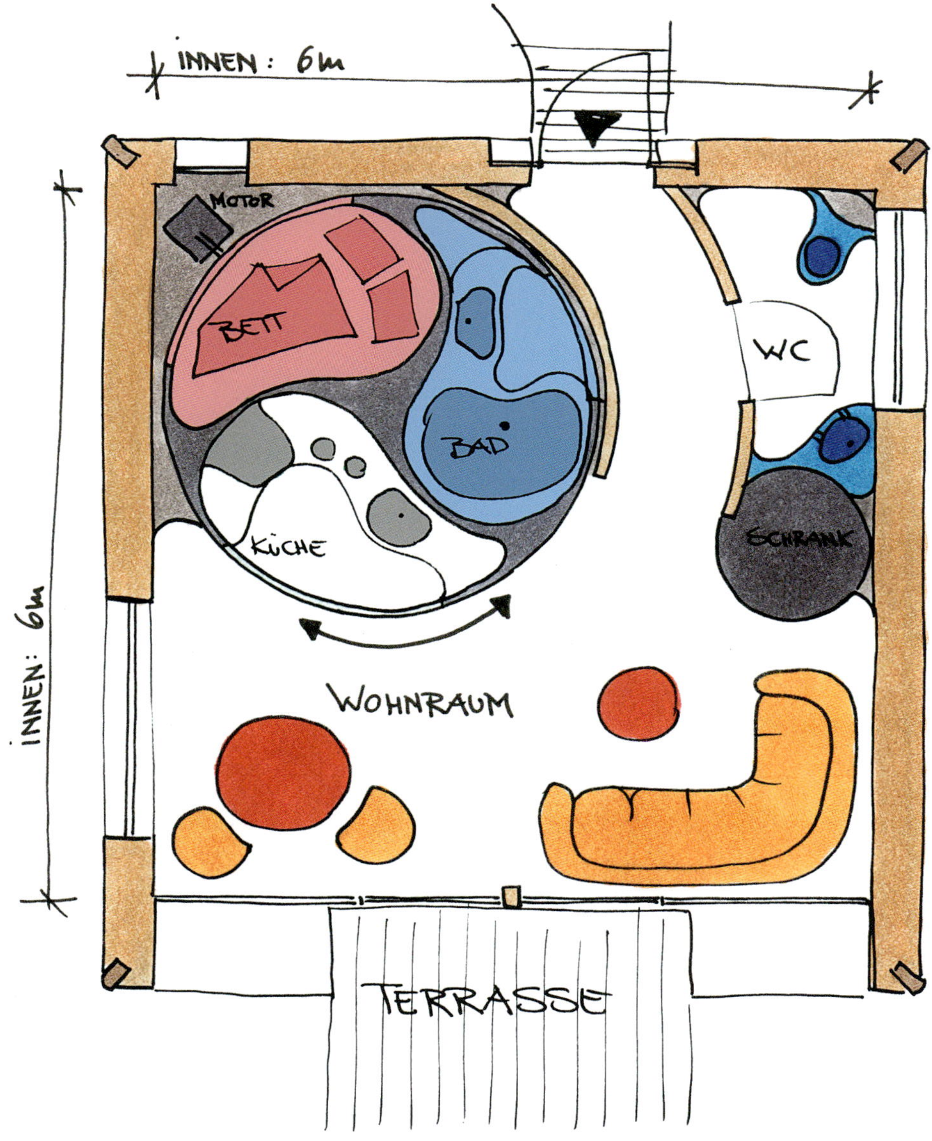

thus making it a spacious kitchen, bedroom, or equally spacious bathroom. Each of the cells in the rotor measures 32 sq. ft., the living space itself measures 215 sq. ft., it is augmented by a small hallway, a toilet, and a built-in closet.

The model house is shaped like a simple box, but nevertheless seems just as dynamic as it does "organic" (Colani) due to the slight curve of the external walls and its rounded openings for the windows and the door. From the living room there is a clear view of the garden and terrace through floor-to-ceiling windows that include a sliding door. The interior is also dominated by the soft lines so typical of Colani. The building's outer shell is constructed in a manner that allows it to be stacked, if necessary. Like all of the Hanse Houses, the Rotor House is based on a wooden frame, which is glued together instead of being nailed. The interior is clad entirely in white plastic.

Size and shape of the rotor opening varies with its uses: the "bedroom" broadly resembles a cave shape

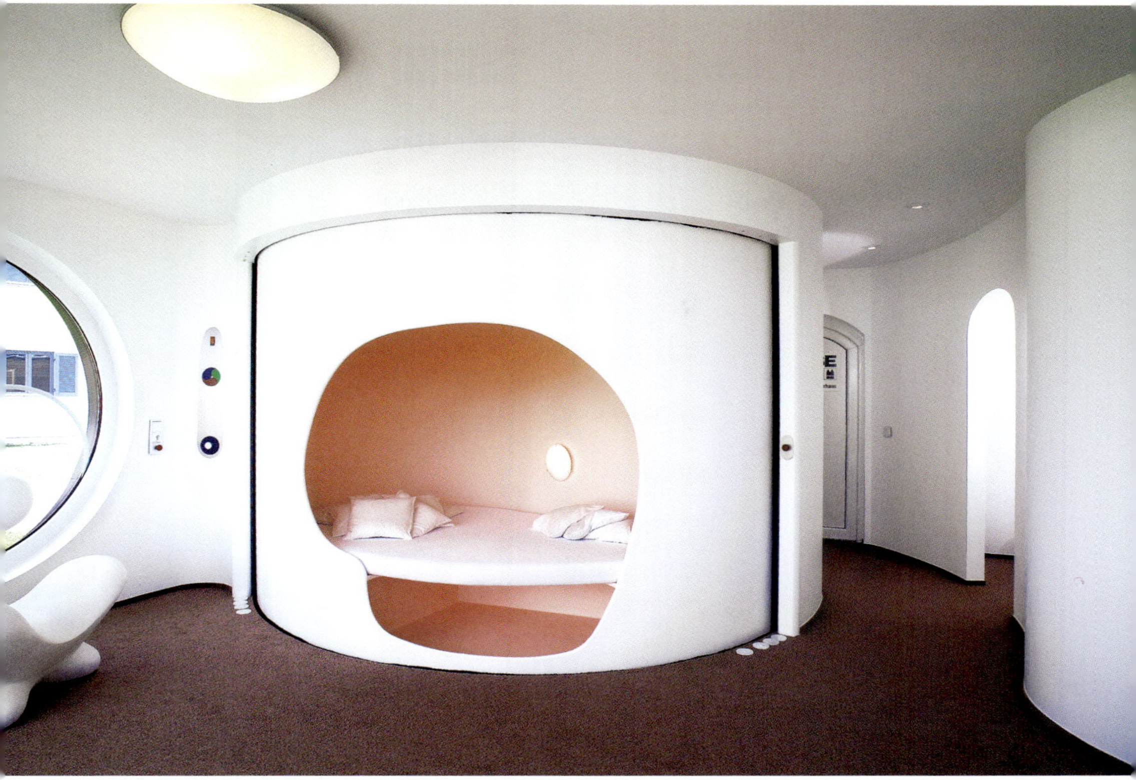

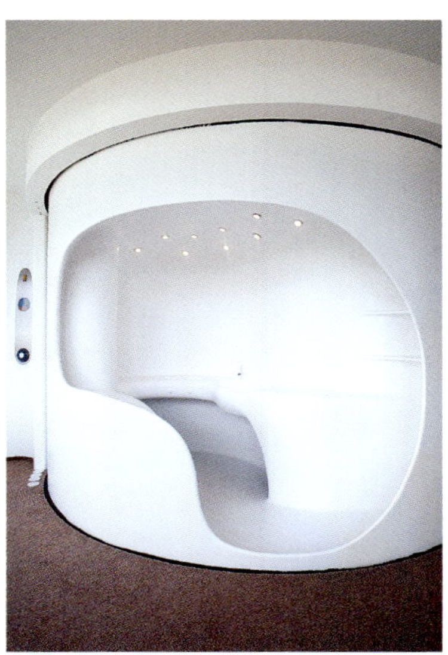

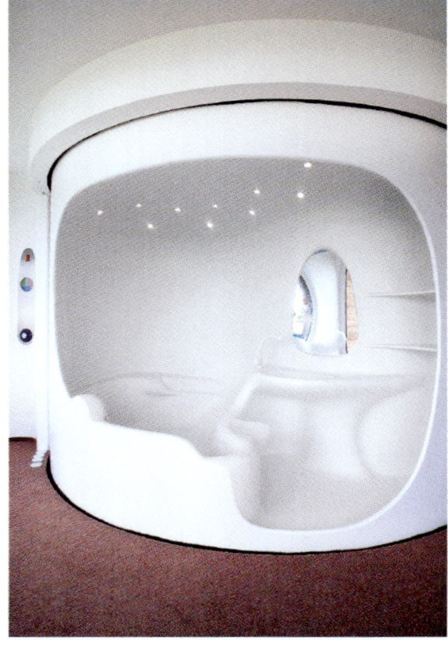

The round window with its virtual mullions repeats the rotary motif of the floor plan

ESPACE MOBILE

sps-architekten
Meiberger Holzbau
Lofer, Austria, 2004–2009

Imagine being required to move to a different city for a year for professional reasons and then subsequently taking the following year off in order to spend it in the mountains or near the ocean. How comfortable it would be, if it were possible to take your own house with you! There is a solution in cases like this: Espace mobile (mobile space)—the house you can take with you. You only need to buy a house once and then rent or buy a new piece of land whenever you need a place to put it.

The Espace mobile is a module that is produced in a factory, delivered by truck, and set down on the site by crane. The interior of the 53 ft. long, 15 ft.-wide and 10 ft.-high cube can be divided flexibly and thus be used for a variety of purposes: as an independent residence, as an extension to an existing house, as a temporary office, for example on a building site, as a classroom, an information stand, or a café. Once it has fulfilled its purpose, a crane and truck can come to transport it to another location. The building site that is left behind can then be used for a different purpose.

The Espace mobile is a wooden structure that adheres to low-energy standards. The model house, complete with its façade, windows, doors, flooring, plumbing, electrical installations, and an open fireplace, was prefabricated within twelve days and made ready for occupancy on site within two—including all of the connections to public utilities. By 2009 it was available as a module in four different lengths at prices between €80,000 and €140,000. The model house was €95,000.

It is bright inside due to a large glazed wall on one of the long sides. The model house, located on a slope, can be reached over a catwalk. Painted red, with a terrace in front, it makes a very attractive impression. As a result of its subdued, unadorned design, it is predestined to fit into a wide variety of environments.

This "mobile space" was developed by Simon Speigner and his office sps-architekten in Thalgau near Salzburg. Ultimately, it was never produced in series, and its purported mobility has yet to be put to the test. The model house developed for the Punto ese Project Development Company in Mondsee, Austria, is not only the sole example to date, it is also still in its original location.

Above: This concept displays the frame with a completely glazed front

Opposite: The structure, up on stilts, can only be accessed via a bridge

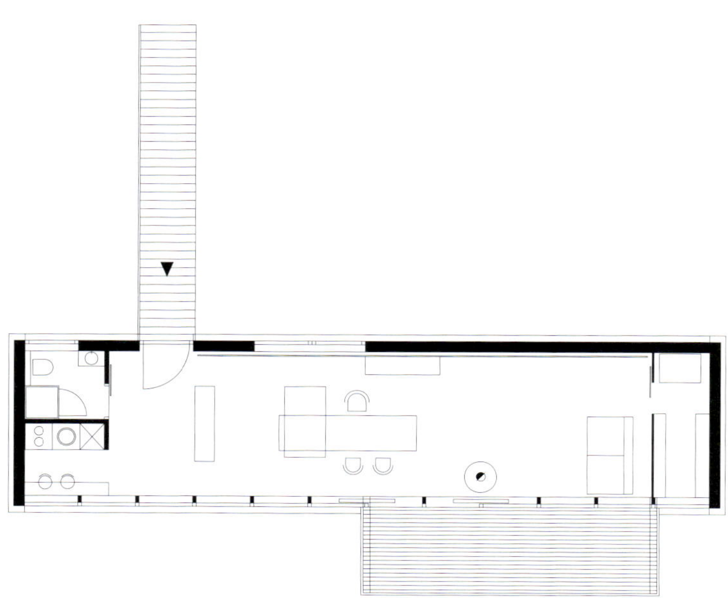

MUJI HOUSE

Kazuhiko Namba
MUJI.net Co., Ltd.
Tokyo, Japan, 2004–

Kazuhiko Namba's Muji House is the first prefabricated house developed by the architect in cooperation with the Japanese multistore Muji. The company had been previously known for its spectrum of products ranging from office articles to home furnishings to a line of fashions. Namba, who specializes in modular buildings, designed a simple residential cube with an open floor plan on a reinforced concrete slab base; it is particularly well suited to fit into dense urban contexts. While there is a small courtyard in front of the entry area on the street side of the house, the back of the extensively glazed house, clad in galvanized steel panels, faces a small garden area. Inside, a U-shaped gallery which provides space for sleeping and working, overlooks the two-story living and kitchen area.

With its various storage areas and a floor plan that corresponds exactly to the available furniture at the store, today's "Wood House", which is currently only available in Japan and typically costs $150,000–$200,000, is essentially the perfect home for the company's wide range of products, from soap dispensers to bed frames. The label is continuing to expand its involvement in the prefab segment: Kengo Kuma designed "Window house" (2008); Sou Fujimoto, Shigeru Ban and Toyo Ito also developed concepts (2010s).

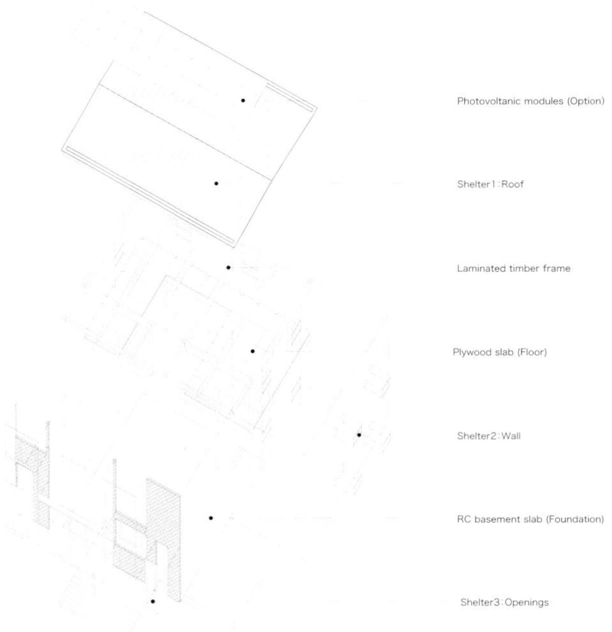

Opposite: Axonometric drawing

Below: The open front of the house on a crowded building site

Above: An extension of the roof over the balcony and the terrace

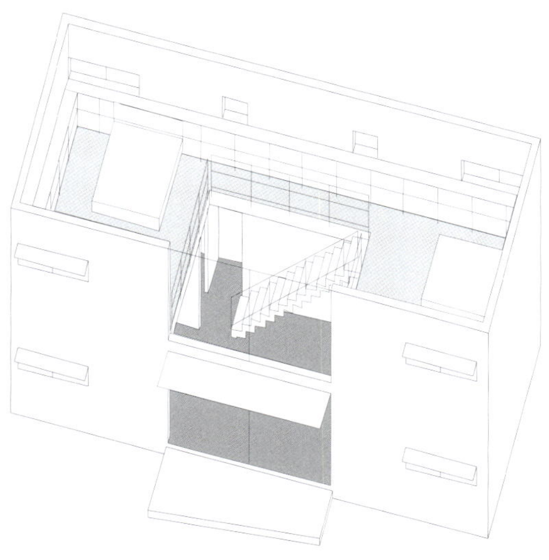

Opposite and above:
The interior views illustrate the concept of a large, open space

Right: Plans of the upper level (center) and ground floor (bottom)

MICRO-COMPACT HOME

Horden Cherry Lee Architects, Haack + Höpfner.Architekten
micro compact home production gmbh
Uttendorf, Austria, 2005–

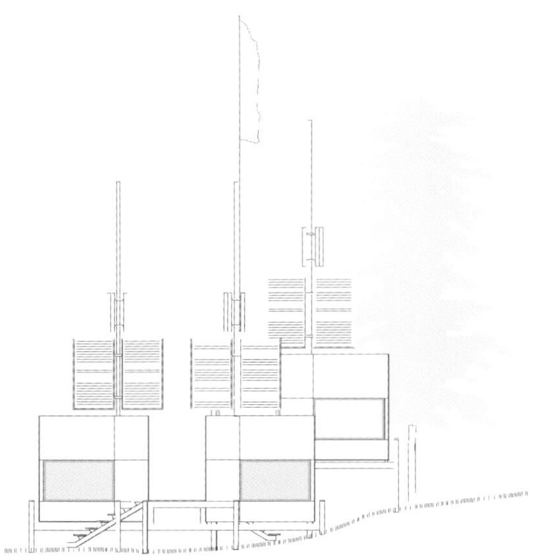

Munich, world famous as an Eldorado among bier lovers, is not exactly a paradise for students in search of housing. There is not enough and it is expensive. It was against this background that architecture students were given the task in a seminar to develop a spatial concept for a minimal residential cell. It resulted in the design of a cubic micro house called "i-home," and it was so remarkable that it was even featured in national media.

Now sponsors were eager to support the idea, including the mobile telephone company O2. After the cube was further developed by the architectural office Haack + Höpfner, in cooperation with Richard Horden, and then named micro-compact home (m-ch), the first seven were erected in the "O2 Village," within the students' village in the Munich district of Freimann, at the beginning of the winter semester 2005. There they not only attracted attention, but also great recognition: the Federation of German Architects awarded the m-ch its prize for residential construction in 2006. In 2007 it had the honor of being presented within the context of the MoMA exhibition *Home Delivery: Fabricating the Modern Dwelling* as a commissioned project.

This residential cube measuring nearly 8 ft. 9 in. on the edges, and with only 76 sq. ft. of floor space, features cutting-edge technology and combines all of the functional areas of a conventional house by making use of the full height of the room. The wooden skeleton structure is clad on the outside in flat anodized aluminum panels and on the inside in PVC. The flooring material is based on an epoxy compound, and the windows are double-glazed. In order to achieve good thermal performance, a special vacuum insulation was chosen. The unit, which cost between €25,000 and €38,000 and produced by Gatterbauer in Austria, weighs 2.2 tons and can be delivered by truck or even on a trailer pulled by a car.

Not a square inch of the m-ch is wasted space. After stepping into the house through the first sliding door, the visitor finds himself in an entryway that also serves as a shower, the doormat is in the shower basin. One only needs to turn to the right to reach the toilet. The actual living space is entered by going through

Below left: Design for a houseboat based on a living cube. It was to be clad in gold anodized aluminum and moored in the Venetian Lagoon—as a refuge for honeymooners

Below right: Design for a Tree Village, a student dormitory with 30 cubes stacked up to a height of just over 49 ft. around a central open stairway

a second sliding door, on the right is a kitchen unit with the most modern appliances, on the left is a bed suited for a student who has no desire to make one—it simply folds up against the wall. The house includes other features to make studying easier: people who get great ideas in their sleep can slip right down from their beds and capture their inspiring thoughts on paper or type them into a computer at the desk located next to it—thus gliding from the sphere of dreams into sphere of work. The micro house, despite its small size, strictly separates the sleeping and living areas. However, in order to ensure that this cell for students does not seem too much like a monk's cell, the bed is big enough for two; there is also enough room and places to sit at the desk to allow time to be spent with friends over chips and beer—and if things escalate to a bacchanal, the seat can be turned into a guest bed. In order to prevent attacks of claustrophobia, the residential cube has big windows that connect the interior with the exterior.

Below: Latitudinal and cross section

Opposite: A cube being delivered by a building crane

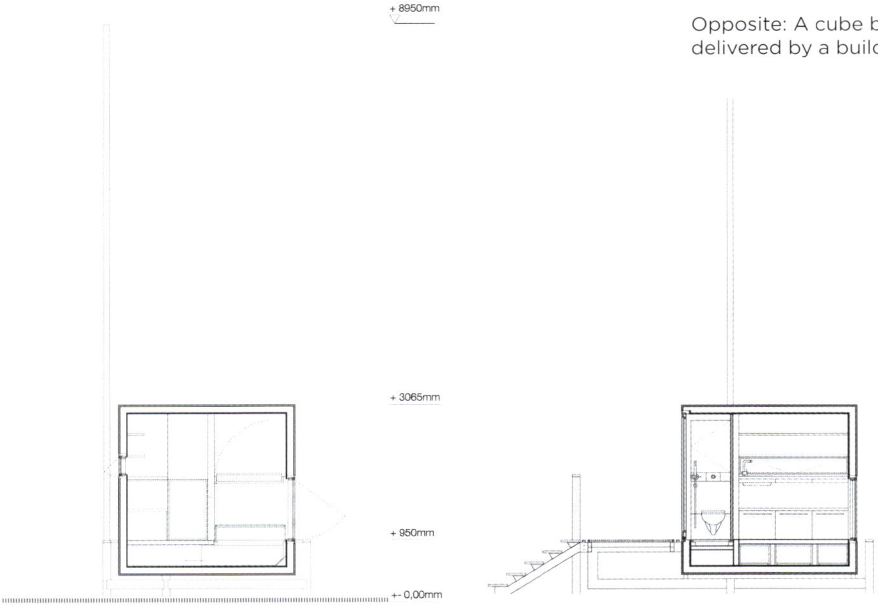

can jump

Above and opposite:
Views of the student village
at Munich-Freimann

Below: An inhabited
student cube

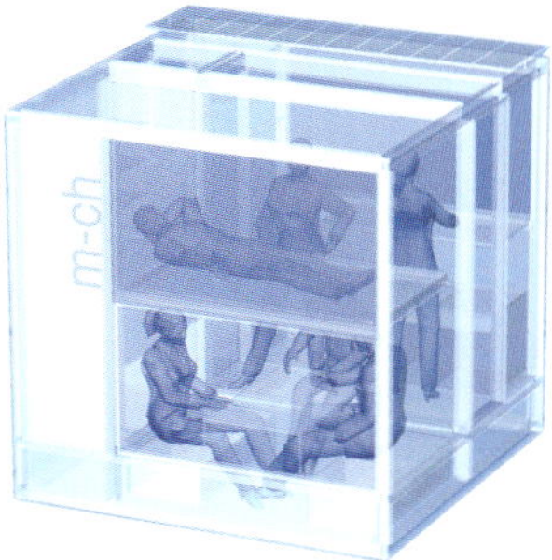

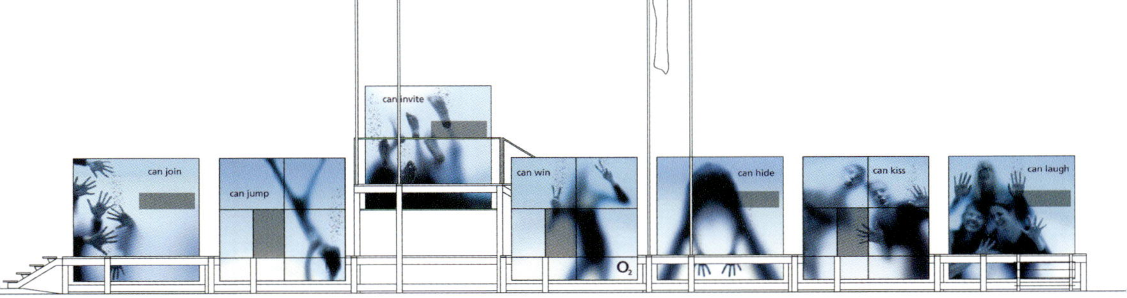

BLACK BARN

Pinc House AB
Ittur Group
Stockholm, Sweden, 2005–mid 2010s

Pinc House of Stockholm ranked among the architectural offices noteworthy for having brought prefabricated houses onto the market that combine quality design with high standards in terms of building ecology and energy efficiency. Together with the Ittur Group, which absorbed them in the late 2010s, they offered three models in four different sizes. For Black Barn, introduced in 2005 they won the prestigious Red Dot Design Award that same year.

With its black-tarred wooden roof, elongated central space, and visible interior roof beams, the Black Barn, designed by Maria Rutensköld, Johan Lionell, and Jan Rutensköld, is a modern interpretation of the indigenous long house which has a tradition dating back to the Vikings. Unlike traditional longhouses, the black-washed pine mass of the building's exterior is perforated by numerous windows. Inside, black and white are the predominant colors.

The largest of the four Black Barn models has nearly 2,600 sq. ft. of floor space and a loft-like open floor plan, with two bathrooms and two bedrooms on the ground floor, while a master suite and a large multifunctional space, along with a sauna and a laundry, are on the top floor.

There was also a version of the Black Barn for terraced housing developments. Each of the houses has its own garage. The open living area is on the lower level, but has a high ceiling that extends its height to that of the upper level. The bedrooms are on the upper level.

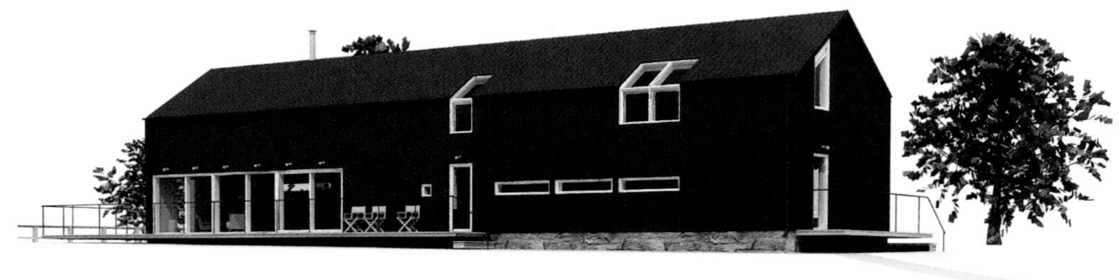

© 2005 Pinc/Pinc House

With its distinctive pitched roof and elongated design, Black Barn is a modern adaptation of the Viking longhouse

The sculptural mass of the black-washed wood exterior contrasts with the lightness of its interior, which features walls and pine floors painted white (following spread)

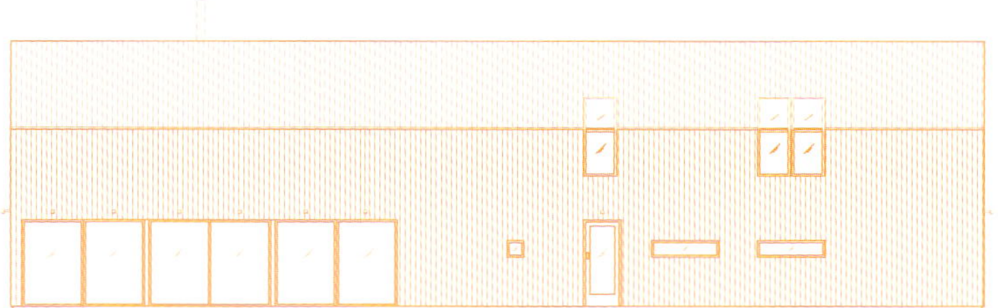

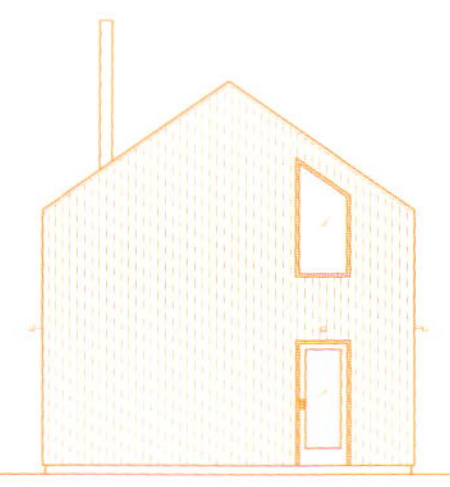

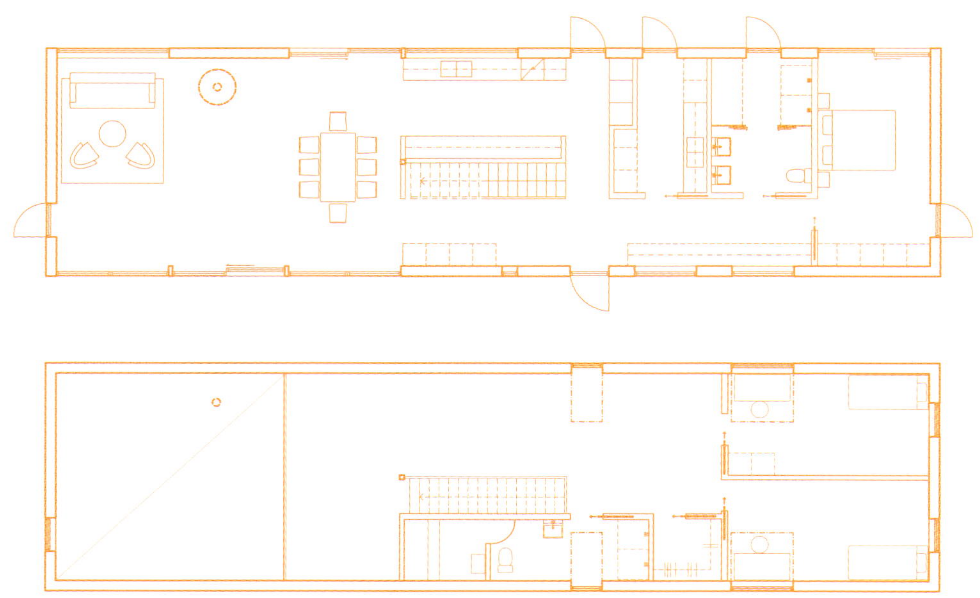

Opposite: Floor plans of the ground floor (top) and the upper level (center)

ZENKAYA

Eric Bigot
ZenKaya Ecohomes
Pretoria, South Africa, 2005–mid 2010s

"Imagine a place where your soul is at peace. This place already exists. ZenKaya, for your peace of mind." It is no coincidence that Eric Bigot called his architectural office ZenKaya: this Japanese-South African linguistic creation means "Zen house." His ecohomes are very straightforward in terms of form and function, low in cost, built, delivered, and installed within a few weeks. They are also easy to purchase: since Bigot argues that the purchase of a house should be no more complicated than the purchase of an car. This French architect, who has worked in New York, Japan, and many African countries, now lives in South Africa.

ZenKaya houses were available in various sizes "from S to XL." They were completely prefabricated and delivered to the building site by truck. Thus, their width is standardized at 11 ft.; the ceiling height is 8 ft. They vary only in terms of their length: the smallest version, the "ZenKaya Studio" is 20 ft. in length (67 sq. ft.) and has an all-purpose space—a kitchenette if desired—and a separate bathroom. The largest model is the 60 ft. "ZenKaya two bedrooms" with a living room, dining room, kitchen, two bedrooms, and a bathroom (610 sq. ft.).

Below: Not only were there two types of wall construction using different types of insulation, but there were also numerous surfaces to choose from

The ZenKaya House earned the praise of architectural critics as a result of its both simple and dynamic appearance: the ceiling and floor are connected on one end of the house, forming a continuous band of white that encompasses it like a U flipped over on one side. The main façade is determined by the internal division of space: the façade in front of the bathroom is paneled in wood, while the façade in front of the main room is not only fully glazed, but can also be completely opened, letting the outside in. A veranda is located on the other end of the house and enclosed within its cubic form by virtue of the overhanging roof and extended floor structure. The main room and the veranda are only separated by a sliding-glass door that can also be completely opened. Bigot describes this as "responsible design." "When a designer is forced to meet all the program requirements on a defined space, the result is often a pure and logical design, leaving unnecessary bells and whistles behind." However, if the client wished to do so, he was able to choose a different fit out for the kitchen and bath, walls, and floors.

ZENKAYA.com

The drawings show the ZenKaya loft layout and one bedroom and studio layout

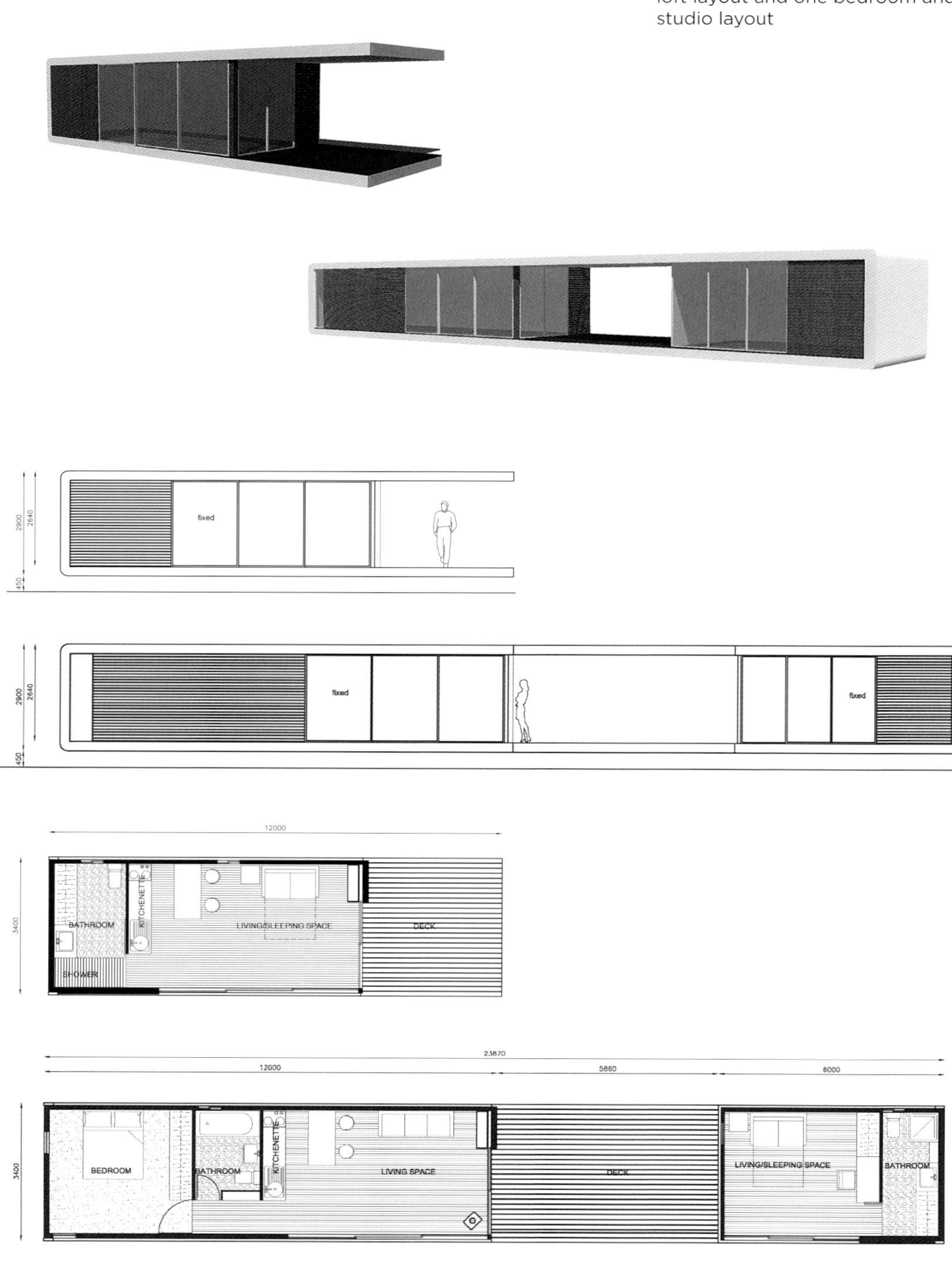

FREEDOM HOUSE

Prebuilt Pty Ltd.
Kilsyth, Victoria, Australia, 2005–

The Freedom House has been produced in series since 2005 and sold in multiple locations across Australia. The house is a wooden skeleton structure clad in corrugated sheet metal, which, as a material that has traditionally been popular in Australia because of its flexibility and weather resistance, is a central element of its design. The mass of the building is set on low footings of steel or wood and can therefore be just as easily built on a slope as on flat building sites.

The Freedom House offers enough space for a family and is delivered in five different sizes, each with a fully equipped kitchen and bathroom. At a cost of between AU$165,000 and AU$266,000, the most spacious luxury version offers three bedrooms, two bathrooms, and a study in addition to the living area. The open floor plan creates a loft-like atmosphere, the hardwood floors feature radiant heating, and the windows have thermal glazing. Prebuilt specifically constructed the building components of the house so that they could be completely delivered in one truckload. Unlike the usual, often boxy prefabricated houses, the Freedom House with its monopitch roofs at opposing angles emits a sculptural quality all its own.

Below: Elevations of the house; decks could be added as desired

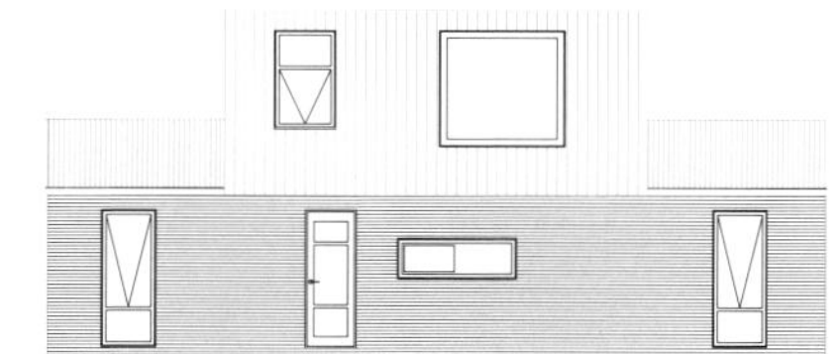

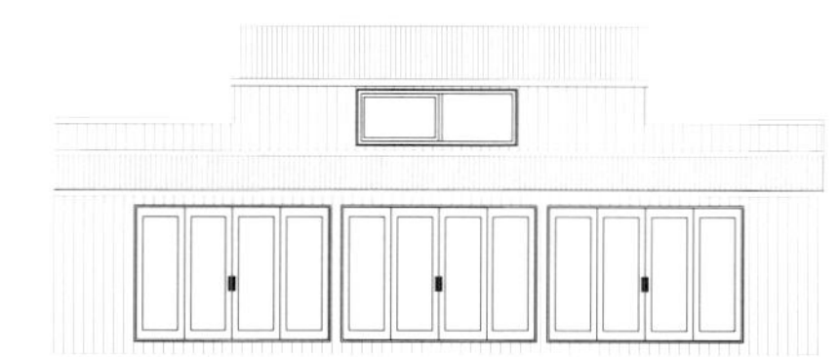

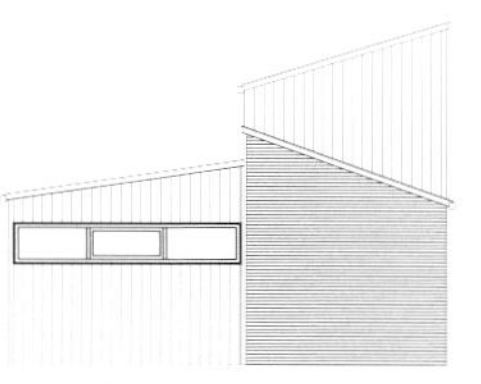

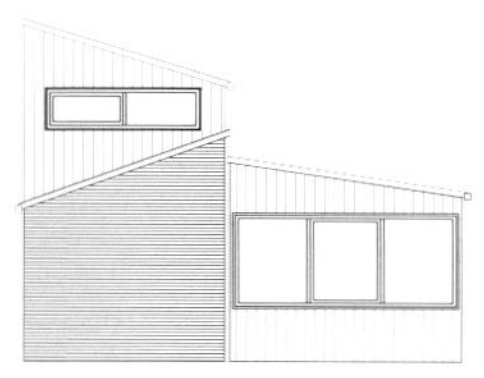

Following spread: Three-bedroom, two-bath model with 1,200 sq. ft. of floor space in a rural setting

12000
9765
6765
3000
UP

The house was delivered with built-in closets and kitchen cabinets—they are practical because they make the best use of space

MOD HOUSE

Pleysier Perkins
Prebuilt Pty Ltd.
Kilsyth, Victoria, Australia, 2005–

"The Prebuilt Mod House Range is for those who like their homes clean and crisp with a modernist edge." Thus the characterization of the Mod House, which Prebuilt offers as one of six prefabricated houses designed by various architects for this company located in a Melbourne suburb. The Mod House was designed by the Melbourne architectural office of Pleysier Perkins.

The Mod House is based on a highly flexible system of pavilion modules, which can be as large as 52 ½ ft. × 18 ft.—transporting anything larger by truck is prohibited in Australia. The individual modules can be combined at will: in the form of an I, an L, or a U, and as one-, two-, or three-story dwellings; the client can also determine the location of the doors and windows. Houses ranging in size from a three-bedroom for AU$703,000 to a four bedrooms and two living rooms for AU$953,000. The one-bedroom model is no longer available

Hence, the Mod Houses that have been built are highly divergent in terms of their floor plans, exteriors, the way they extend into their surroundings, i.e., by means of pergolas or terraces, and whether they stand on or off the ground. A characteristic feature of the Mod Houses is a flat roof, the lateral orientation of the overall layout and the individual parts, and the clear modern lines and austerity of the external view.

The Mod Houses are, like all of the houses by Prebuilt, wood-frame structures. They are produced entirely in a factory, delivered by truck,

and set down on a foundation made of steel or on wooden footings—on ground level or as high as about 20 ft. off the ground. The assembly and installation of a house takes only a few hours. They use solar energy and have a water recycling system.

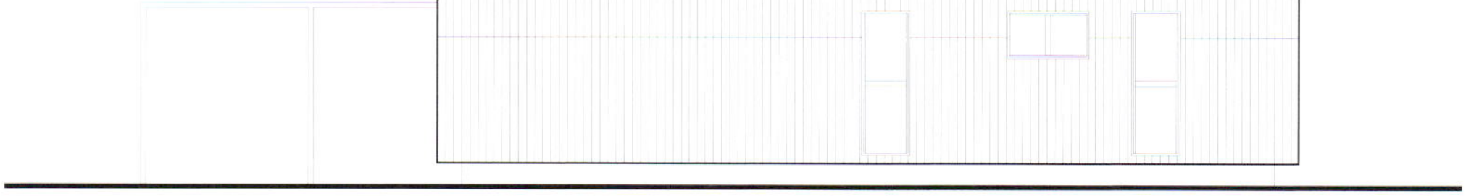

Above and opposite bottom: Mod House comes with different finishes

Below and opposite top: Similar modules make different floor plans

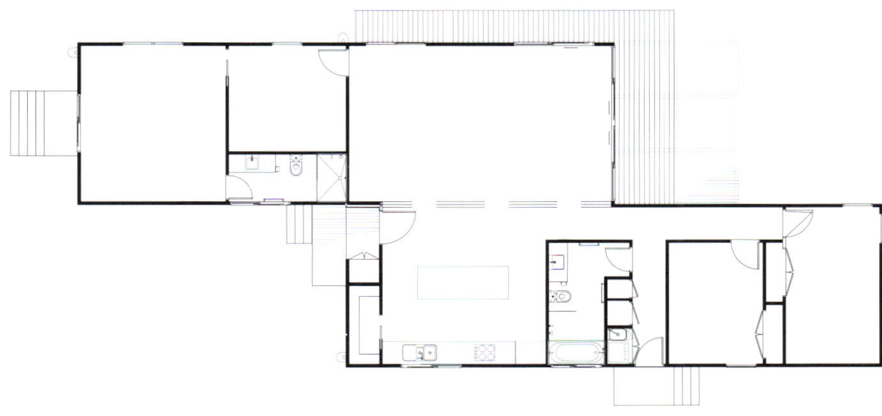

HIVE MODULAR B-LINE

Marc Asmus, Bryan Meyer, Paul Stankey
Hive Modular LLC
Minneapolis, Minnesota, USA, 2005–2014

In 2004, the architects Marc Asmus and Bryan Meyer founded Hive Modular LLC along with the interior decorator Paul Stankey in order to develop "cool" prefabricated houses. In professional practice, all three of the partners had frequently encountered the discrepancy between their concept of good architecture, on the one hand, and the constrained financial means of most clients, on the other. In 2005, the first prototype of the Hive Modular House was erected in Minneapolis; in the meantime, the office offers an extensive assortment of designs and styles. The original B-Line is now followed up by two Casita models with 646 sq. ft. of floor space and larger custom-build options. The only limits to size are set by the Department of Transportation's regulations for highway load sizes. The width of the modules is limited to 16 ft. and the length to 62 ft. The standard house models of the B-Line had 9 ft. ceilings; however, one module could be stacked on top of another for a 20 ft. ceiling.

Hive Modular houses are wood frame structures with fiberglass insulation in the walls. The basic shape of the "B-Line" was a simple single-story "bar," thus the B in the name, which could have been expanded as needed. The client chose between three sizes, determined the arrangement of the windows and doors, opted for a flat or a pitched roof, as well as various packages for the interior design, and had to decide how the exterior should look. The external walls were made of fiber cement. They were produced in various colors or painted later. External wall modules clad in metal or wooden shingles were also available.

The two-story versions B-Line Medium 001 (opposite top) and B-Line Medium 003 (left) were particularly well suited for urban building sites

Since the pitched roof could be replaced by a mono-pitched roof, the building was able to adapted to different building codes and personal tastes

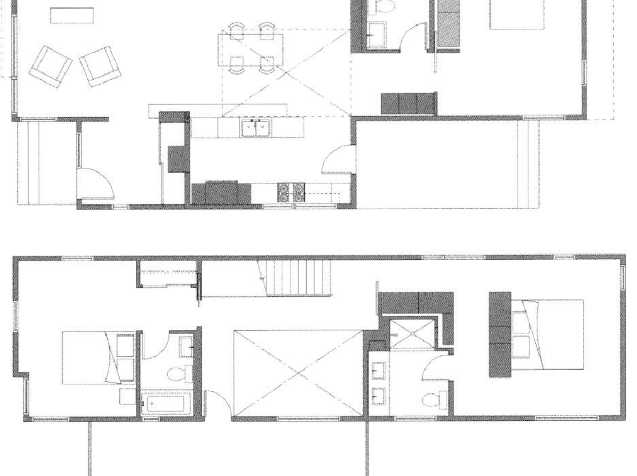

Opposite: The living room in the B-Line Medium 003 (top) and in the B-Line Medium 002 (bottom) in comparison

Above: Floor plans of the B-Line Medium 001 with 1,780 sq. ft. of floor space

Right: Floor plans of the B-Line Medium 003 with 2,000 sq. ft.

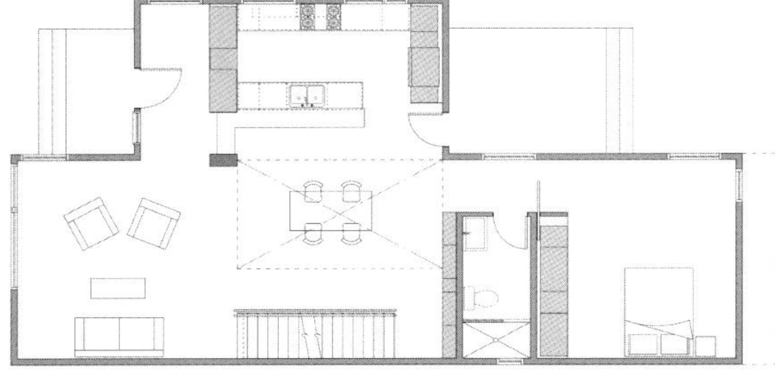

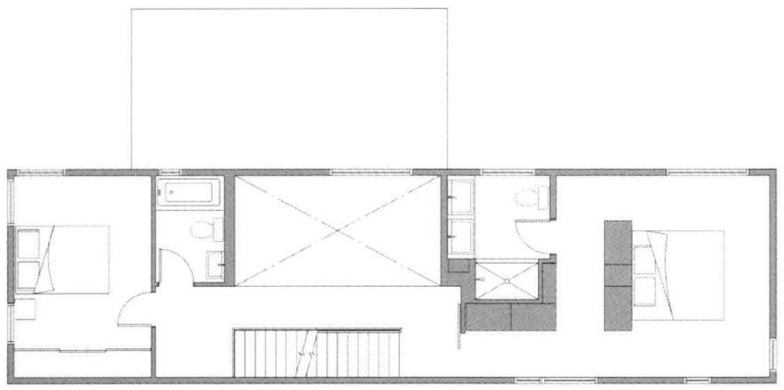

The small version was designed mainly as a second or weekend home. With 990 sq. ft. of floor space, it offered an open living space, two bedrooms, and one bathroom. In the B-Line Medium there was an upper story, a central room with a metal stairway, and a separate bathroom for each bedroom. Additional features were found in the B-Line Large, which offered 2,400 sq. ft. of floor space, included a master bedroom on the ground floor, three bedrooms upstairs, a foyer, and small functional rooms.

MARMOL RADZINER PREFAB

Marmol Radziner + Associates
Los Angeles, California, USA, 2005–

The architectural office of Marmol Radziner + Associates, which employs a staff of over 100 in Los Angeles, originally gained experience with the use of prefabricated modules in office buildings. In 1996, the Californians built the first office building using prefabricated steel-frame structures, then, in 2005, the first residential building made of prefabricated modules: the Desert House is located outside of Palm Springs; it belongs to the head of the company Leo Marmol and served as a model for a continually increasing range of prefabricated houses by the company.

In the Desert House there is no longer a clear separation between indoors and outdoors. The house is not defined by its exterior walls, but instead by the span of the roof landscape into which large areas beyond the walls of glass and wood are integrated. Rooms are thus formed that one is inclined to furnish with chairs or a dining table, and which are protected from the sun and heat by the continuous roof, although not necessary by walls on all sides. These open areas, under the roof, connect the main volume of the building to a second wing, in which a guest apartment and a studio are located. The slightly staggered L shape of the overall complex creates a sort of interior courtyard with a swimming pool and a fire pit.

The Desert House is a steel frame structure, i.e., the frames of the floors and ceilings and the supports are made of steel. Metal plates covered

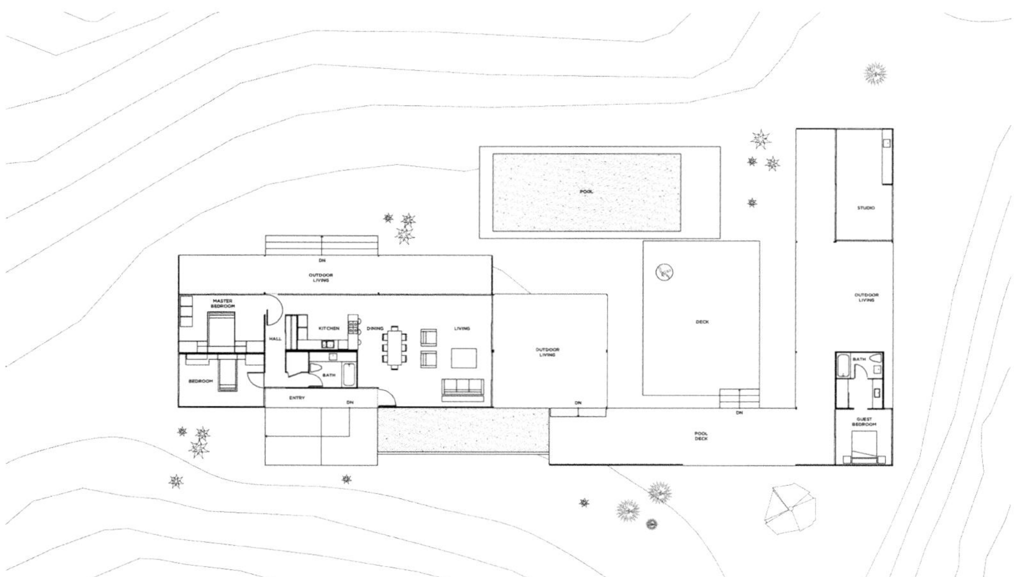

with a layer of concrete are fitted into the floor frames—in the cooler months they store heat. The edges of the roof are designed to provide protection against sun from the south and the west. All of the energy required in the house is produced by solar panels.

In the meantime, Marmol Radziner has built at least a dozen prefabricated residential buildings. Another model project is the two-story Palms House, which consists of 14 modules; it includes three bedrooms and two bathrooms on 2,800 sq. ft. of floor space. The standard ceiling height of all of Marmol Radziner houses is 9 ft.; but it can be increased to 14 ft. by adding a hat module.

The Desert House consists of four house and six roof modules, the room within the walls measures roughly 2,000 sq. ft.

KIP HOUSE

Kim Herforth Nielsen, 3XN
M2 A/S
Aarhus, Denmark, 2005–2010

"The same boring prefabricated houses have ruined our cities," says Kim Herforth Nielsen, artistic director of the architectural office 3XN. "We have attractive inner cities in Denmark, but all around them it always looks the same." Hence, he did not hesitate when the prefabricated house company M2 asked him to design a house. A number of other famous offices in Denmark also agreed, and thus began M2's campaign to "revolutionize" the Danish domestic prefabricated housing market: with unusual houses, designed by the most interesting architects in the country, offered at the same prices as "traditional" prefabricated houses—that means square foot prices of roughly €158 for standard versions. M2 offered 16 houses in 2009—in different versions that could be individually finished according to the clients' choices of materials and interior design. Equipped with features such as Boform kitchens, Philippe Starck fittings, and sound systems from Bang & Olufsen, highest quality design was guaranteed. A house designed by a star architect, ready for occupation for a guaranteed price was an attractive offer: roughly 50 of the 3XN Kip houses alone had been built.

3XN designed a total of four residential and holiday home models for M2, a welcome reprieve from the large projects all over the world with which the 160 employees in Aarhus and Copenhagen used to be engaged at this point. In 1986, three architects by the name of Nielsen joined forces, hence the name of the office. Now only one of them is still there; Kim Herforth Nielsen, who is the "head architect" within a team of five partners.

The Kip House is a minimalistic design that gives rise to exciting views and spatial effects through simple means. It is basically a single-story house with a rectangular floor plan and a pitched roof. However, the middle axis of the rectangle is shifted to one side, thereby creating an arrow-shaped layout. At the same time, the pitched roof also soars to a dramatic height at the tip of the arrow. The exterior walls are clad in blackened wood or completely glazed, the roof is covered with black roofing paper.

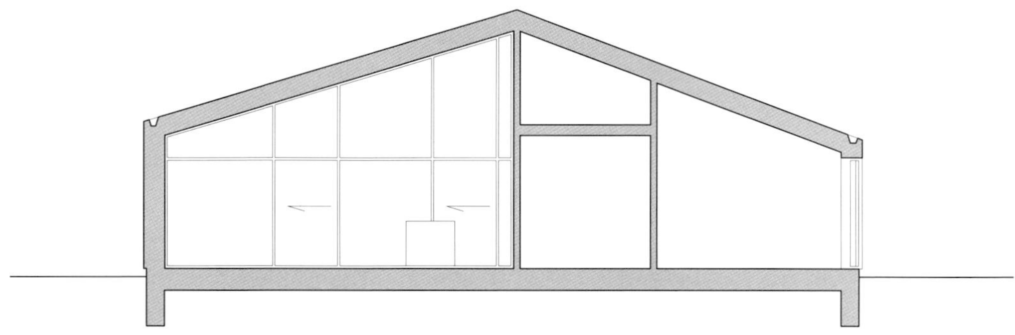

The basic idea behind the arrangement of the rooms was the separation between "active" and "passive" areas, with three or four bedrooms located in the latter (depending on the client's wishes). The two parts are separated by the kitchen area—which is part of the living and dining area—and by two bathrooms, as well as three "bridges" that connect the two parts of the house. There is no continuous hallway.

The bedrooms receive light through floor-to-ceiling windows, the dining and living area is illuminated through a glass wall on one side and an additional triangular window on the other. The back section can be separated as an office area, if needed. All of the interior walls are painted white. The house was available in four variations, with living spaces of either 1,668 or 1,873 sq. ft., half of which could have been built with a cellar, if desired.

In the M2 turn-key villa development program 3XN designed not only the Kip House, but also the Flower House, the X House, the Twist House and the Basic House, as well as the KipUp House and Trapez House summer cottages

View of the neighboring Flower House from the living area (opposite bottom) and floor plan (right)

FACADE 1
Mulighed for isoleret parti (Tilkøb)
Mulighed for isoleret parti (Tilkøb)
FACADE 2
08 SOVEVÆRELSE 15,5 m²
06 VÆRELSE 10 m²
03 VÆRELSE 10 m²
09 VÆRELSE 7,5 m²
Udvendig spulehane
07 BAD/TOILET 7 m²
05 BAD/TOILET 4 m²
02 BRYGGERS 5 m²
TT
VM
Teknik
01 ENTRE 4 m²
Indgang
Skydedør til entré (Tilkøb)
OPV
04 OPHOLD/KØKKEN 91 m²
13254
Terrasse (Tilkøb)
FACADE 3
16640

KATRINA COTTAGES

Marianne Cusato
New York, USA, 2006–2011

In August 2005 Hurricane Katrina ravaged the Gulf Coast of the United States causing extensive damage in Florida, Louisiana, Mississippi, Alabama, and Georgia. In New Orleans nearly 80% of the city was submerged under up to 15ft. of water after two levees burst. At the time, the idea of abandoning the city altogether was even considered. Only a few days after this natural catastrophe, however, the movement for Katrina Cottages formed around the architect and city planner Andres Duany with the goal of rebuilding the destroyed areas while preserving the Old Southern settlement patterns.

Hence, the Katrina Cottages were executed in the historical cottage style: with pitched roofs, a veranda out front and traditional decorative elements. And since they were prefabricated, they were built within a few days at low cost. Thus, they served as an alternative to the anonymous emergency trailers that lined the streets in the affected areas and became so loathsome to the inhabitants over time. The Katrina Cottages were sold in a growing number of variations produced by diverse manufacturers. Thus, the home improvement store Lowe's offered 19 different Katrina Cottages in sizes ranging between 308 and 1,807sq.ft., based on designs by Marianne Cusato, Andres Duany, W.A. Lawrence, Eric Moser, and Geoffrey Mouen.

One of the first cottages was designed by the New York architect Marianne Cusato. She presented her KC 308 at the *International Builders' Show* in Orlando in January 2006. With a footprint of 308sq.ft., it was so small that it can be assembled elsewhere and delivered to its destination by truck. The KC 308 was a simple wood frame structure with a corrugated metal roof and foam-filled two-layer cladding. The larger model, KC 544 with 544sq.ft. of floor space, was also designed by Cusato and encompasses two bedrooms and a bathroom. The steel frame structure uses prefabricated panels that are attached on site. Other cottages are erected directly on the building site. Although the commercial kit ended around 2011, the architectural plans can still be purchased on Marianne Cusato's homepage for construction with a contractor.

The houses designed by the Katrina Cottage Architects are, in the meantime, so popular, that they are even bought by people in other areas for use as first or second homes. This is partly due to the fact that they take account of an important lesson taught by the catastrophe, one that is also of importance beyond the Gulf Coast: they are designed to withstand gusts of up to 125 miles per hour.

Cottage Square in Ocean Springs, Mississippi. The cottages in this photo are KC 308 and KC 544, with a cottage by Eric Moser in between

Exterior, elevations, floor plan and living room of the Katrina Cottage 910/1185

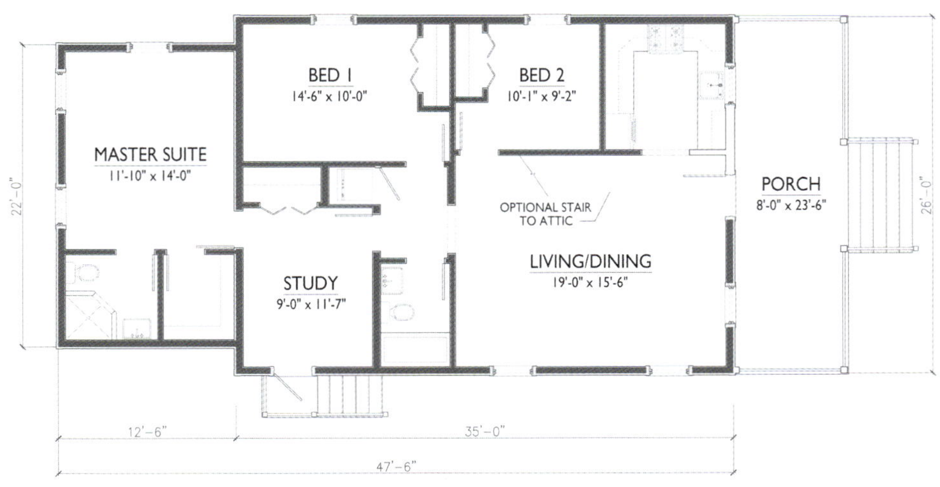
BED 1
14'-6" x 10'-0"
BED 2
10'-1" x 9'-2"
MASTER SUITE
11'-10" x 14'-0"
OPTIONAL STAIR
TO ATTIC
PORCH
8'-0" x 23'-6"
STUDY
9'-0" x 11'-7"
LIVING/DINING
19'-0" x 15'-6"
22'-0"
26'-0"
12'-6"
35'-0"
47'-6"

The Katrina Cottage 308 at Cottage Square in Ocean Springs, Mississippi, floor plan and elevations

The Katrina Cottage 544, a two-bedroom house, in Ocean Springs, Mississippi, floor plan and elevations

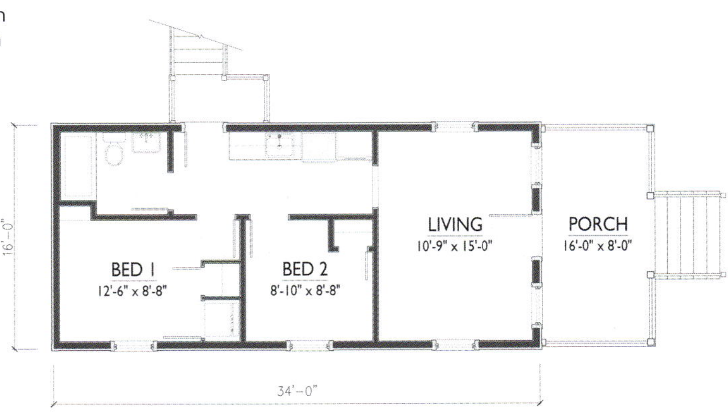

LIVINGHOME RK1

Ray Kappe
LivingHomes / Plant Prefab
Los Angeles, California, USA, 2006–

It comes as no surprise that the LivingHome RK1 was developed by an architect who has long been considering the problem of site-specific design: tower-like modules produced on the basis of steel structures provide the basic framework and ensure that the buildings withstand earthquakes. The horizontal elements suspended within this framework forge connections while remaining as open as possible. This principle, originally conceived for student dormitories, has now been applied to a prefabricated house. It consists of eleven modules and has 2,500 sq. ft. of living space. The initial prototype was erected in Santa Monica with the help of a mobile crane within a period of eight hours; notable characteristics of the house are the two-story living room, onto which galleries open, extensive floor-to-ceiling glazing, and terraces on various levels. Closets serve as room dividers and allow for a great degree of flexibility in terms of interior decorating.

The LivingHome RK1 was the first house to receive the Leadership in Energy and Environmental Design (LEED) Award. This award for energy efficient and ecological buildings has been awarded in the United States since 1998. The LivingHome RK1 earned the LEED award by including a number of features: rainwater

The modular concept

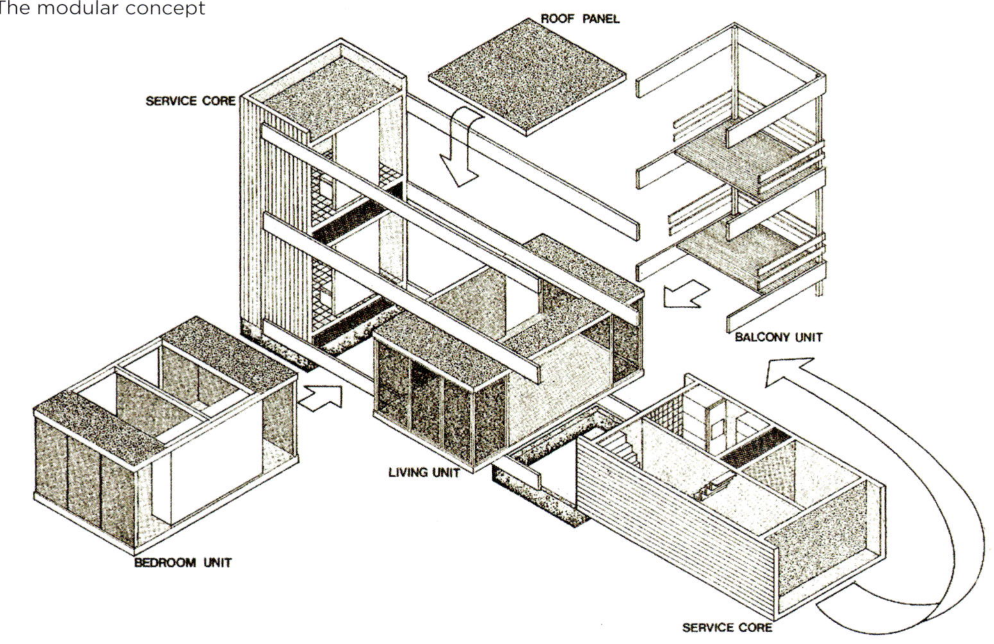

collection for use in the garden, photovoltaic cells to improve the energy balance, some polycarbonate glazing, and even optimal ventilation of the bathrooms. An essential part of the concept is the greening of the interior, since plants help to improve the indoor air and climate. Yet what is most remarkable is the fact that, despite all of these measures, the house still remains elegant and residents do not feel constrained by dogmatic building theories.

A special highlight is the gallery over the living room

Plan of the ground floor

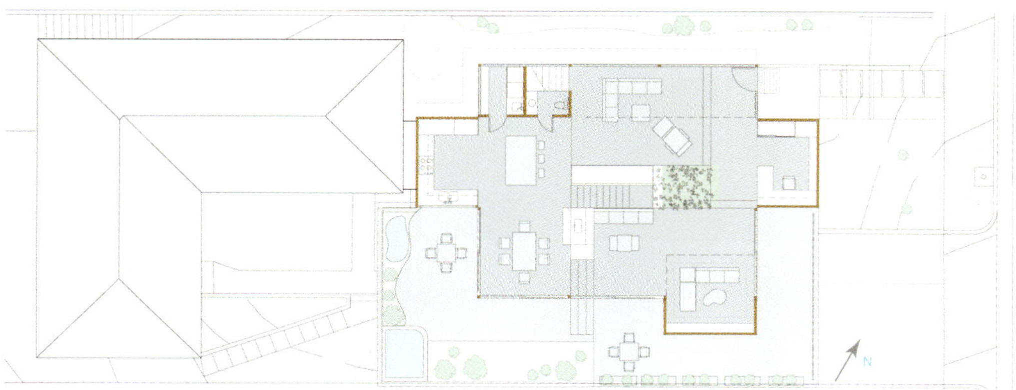

The spacious living room is divided into various functional areas

Left: The glass ceiling of the bathroom opens the small room in an unexpected manner

Below: Closets serve as room dividers and ensure flexibility in interior decorating

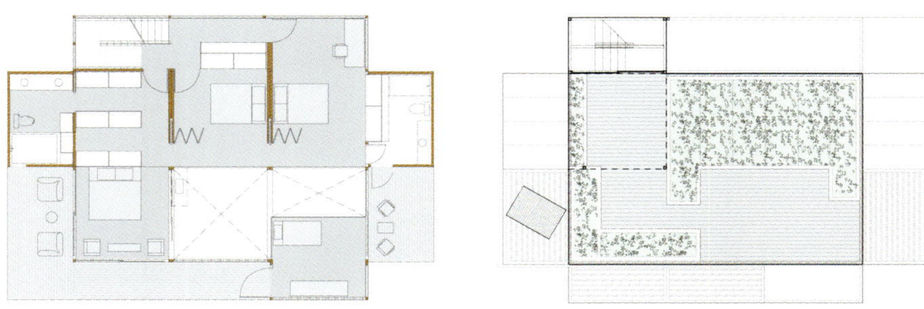

Plans of the upper level
and top level

LOFTCUBE

Studio Aisslinger
Loftcube GmbH
Munich, Germany, 2007–

Above and opposite bottom: Decorating suggestions for the house that was presented. Notable in this context is the use of thick, light-colored carpet

Following spread: Installation within the context of the Berlin *Designmai* exhibition in 2003 on the roof of a former cold storage warehouse on the banks of the Spree River

The basic idea behind the Loftcube designed by Werner Aisslinger was the development of a living capsule that could be set down on the flat roofs of typical postwar urban buildings. For him, an important source of inspiration was the roof landscape on Le Corbusier's Unité d'habitation in Marseille.

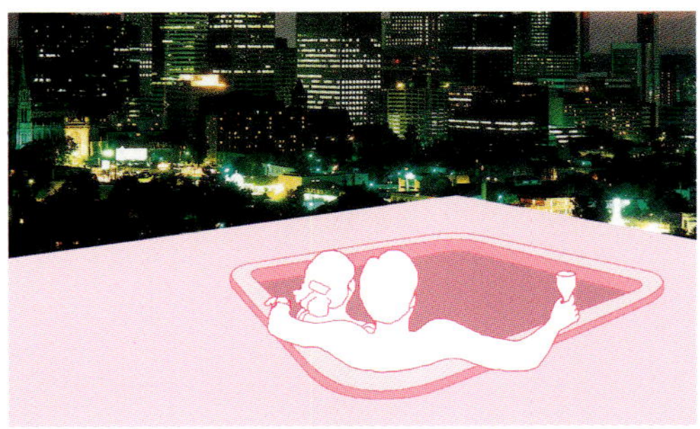

The Loftcube, which rests on four stilts measuring nearly 5 ft. in height, is available in two sizes: 420 and 600 sq. ft. Both versions can be connected by gangways to form larger residential landscapes. The outer skin of the cube, which can be assembled in two to three days, is made of white glass-fiber reinforced plastic panels, reminiscent of a 1970s design. Wooden louvers in front of the windows provide protection both against the sun as well as observation by potential neighbors. Access to the interior is gained via a gangway made of powder-coated steel with hardwood steps. Most of the interior is made of highly flexible acrylic polymer elements that can be adapted to the needs of the inhabitants. It also features sliding partitions. The wall panel between the kitchen area and the bathroom includes a water faucet that swivels in either direction, so that it can be used both for the kitchen sink and the washbasin. The bathroom floors are made of white, washed pebbles for a feeling similar to standing on a beach. The mobile house draws water and electricity from the building that supports it. "It is parasitic architecture," according to Aisslinger, "a smaller object that is docked onto a larger one." Since 2007, the Loftcube has been produced in series with a complete interior program. One can imagine the capsule not only on the wasteland of unused flat roofs, but also as a futuristic weekend house on a lake.

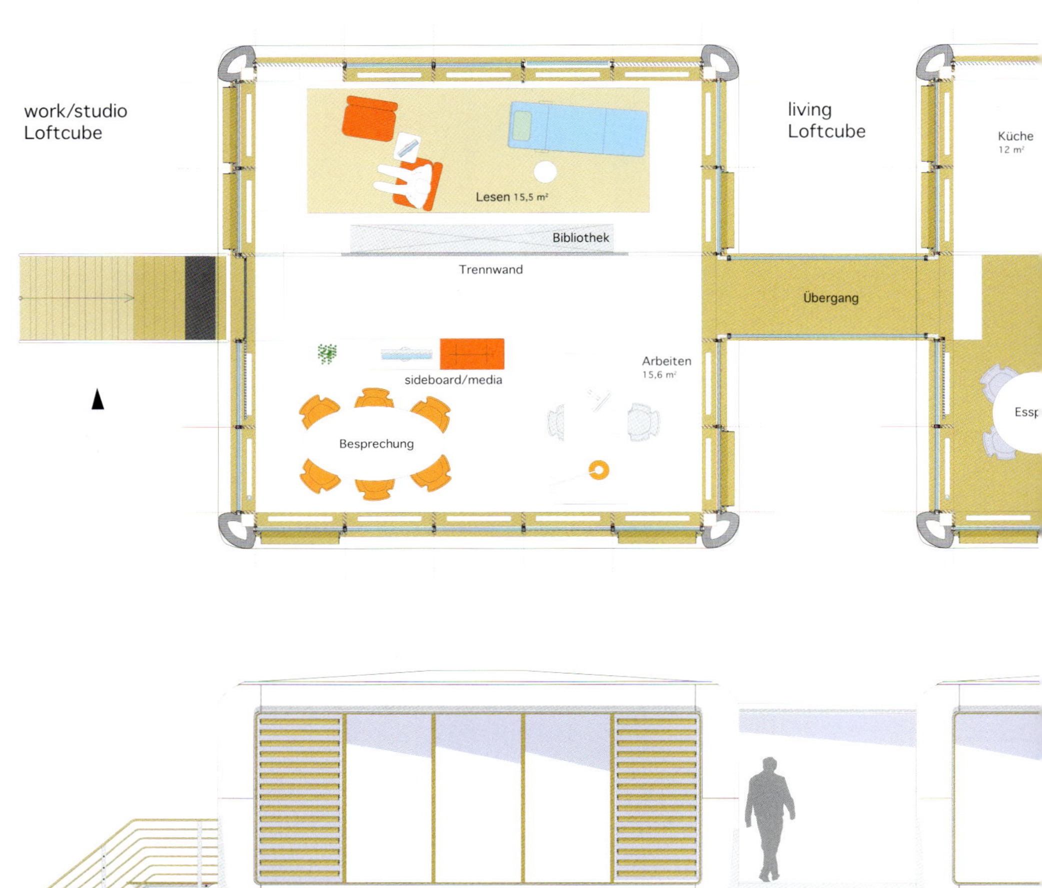

Sketch of a group of Loftcubes for combined studio and residential use

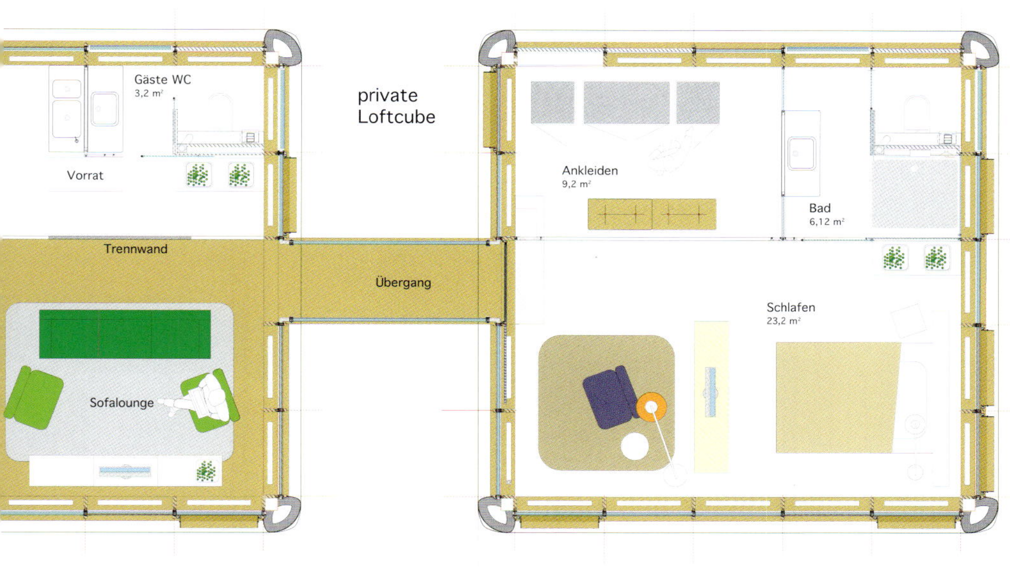
Gäste WC
3,2 m²
Vorrat
private
Loftcube
Ankleiden
9,2 m²
Bad
6,12 m²
Trennwand
Übergang
Schlafen
23,2 m²
Sofalounge

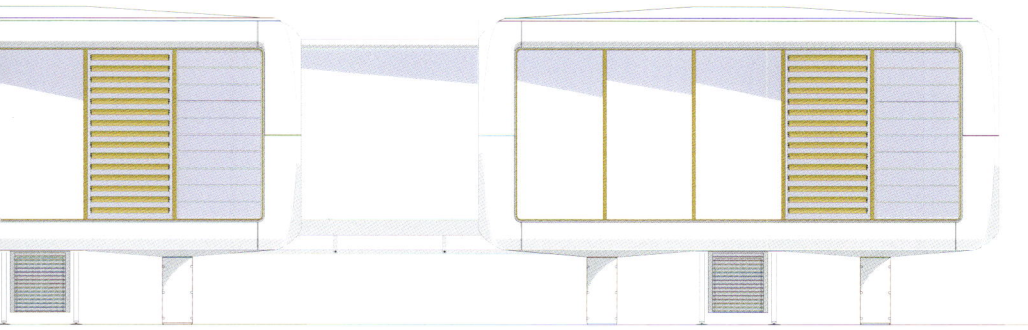

Above: A photomontage featuring a Norwegian landscape

Opposite: Illustration of a design with a pool on the roof

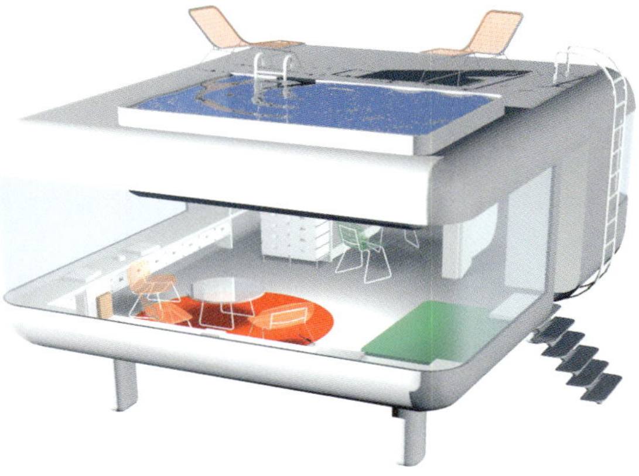

BOXHOME

Rintala Eggertsson Architects
Oslo, Norway, 2007

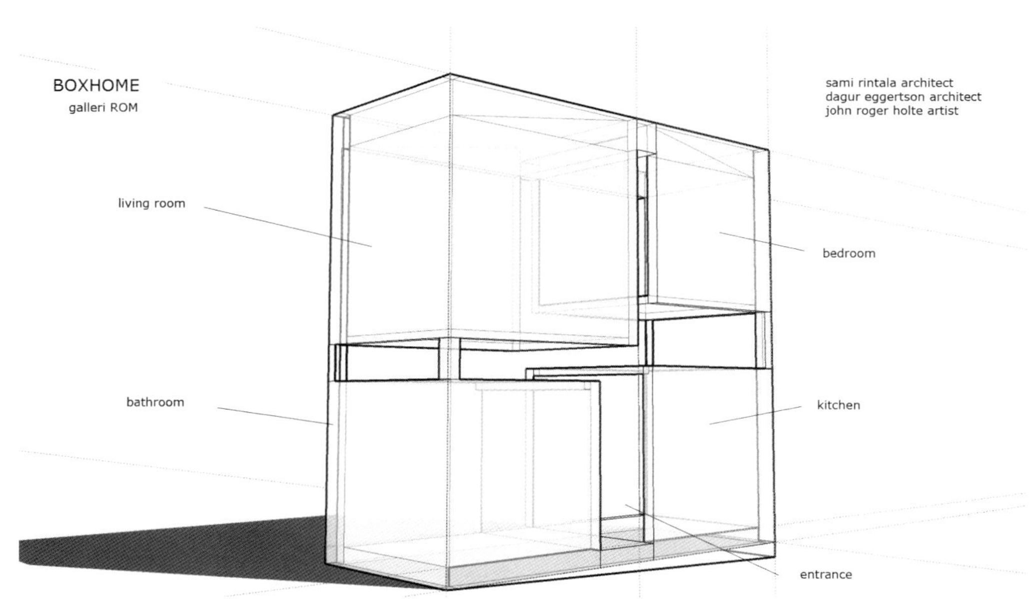

This is as small as it gets: this experimental house built in 2007 by the architectural office Rintala Eggertsson, which operates in Oslo and Bodö, is only 18 ft. long, 7½ ft. wide, and 19 ft. high. Yet the architects have still succeeded in combining four different living areas on 205 sq. ft. of living space: the kitchen, which includes a dining table, and the bathroom are on the lower level, the living room and the bedroom are on the upper level, which is reached by climbing a ladder. All of the interior areas and the built-in furniture are made of different kinds of wood, which, in turn, define the various zones of the house: pine and birch in the kitchen, spruce in the bathroom, oak in the living room, and walnut in the bedroom.

Sami Rintala and Dagur Eggertsson believe their building expresses an attitude that should also be applied to larger single-family houses: the reduction to the most essential does not mean forfeiting sensuality.

The Finnish-Icelandic architectural duo provides four arguments underlining the need for such a house: first of all because it makes economic and ecological sense to build small houses that use fewer resources and less energy, and which can also be completed in a shorter period of time, since the climatic conditions in Northern Europe require heating for more than half of the year, while construction now accounts for a third of the world's energy consumption. Secondly, housing construction should no longer

be entrusted to "an uncontrolled group of actors interested only in maximizing income"—but that people should instead take charge of building their own homes. Thirdly, in Western society we should be clear about the consequences of our consumer culture. The most important goal, however, is the fourth one: "to create a peaceful, little home, a kind of urban cave, into which a person can withdraw when they need to forget the intensity of the surrounding city for a while."

The Boxhome is a wooden cube characterized by extreme formal reduction with windows cut into its façade clad in sheet aluminum

Construction of the model house in Oslo

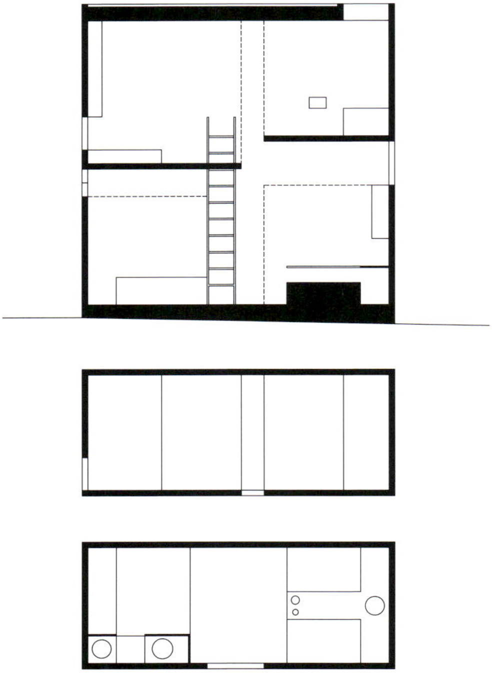

Interior views, section and floor plans

PLUS HOUSE

Claesson Koivisto Rune
Arkitekthus
Stockholm, Sweden, 2007–mid-2010s

In Sweden, where prefabricated houses are quite popular, architecturally successful and affordable alternatives to the standard catalog models have been available for a number of years now. One of the leaders in this context is the Stockholm company Arkitekthus. The supporting walls, floors, and roofs of their houses are prefabricated, all the other elements—the inner workings and the external walls—are built on a concrete foundation on site. Arkitekthus cooperates with four prestigious architectural offices in Sweden, two of their prefabricated house models were designed by Claesson Koivisto Rune.

The Plus House, designated as AH#001 in the Arkitekthus catalog, was created in 2007, the reference model is located in Tyresö, southeast of Stockholm. The two-story wooden building is a modern variation developed on the basis of the classic Swedish country house. In this case, the house has no windows in the usual sense—instead, some of the walls are entirely glazed: the two long sides on the ground floor, and the gable ends of the upper story under the pitched roof. The two visual axes that result intersect each other, forming a plus sign, thus the name of the house. The glass walls are slightly retracted and divided into smaller fields by mullions and transoms. The other external walls are austerely clad in vertical wooden boards. The pitched roof is covered with zinc sheeting. The glass walls not only allow ample daylight into the house, they also integrate it into the natural surroundings—an effect that is enhanced by the terraces located in front of it.

The Plus House was available in two sizes, with either 1,800 sq. ft. or 2,000 sq. ft. of living space. The height of the larger version was 26 ft., and the height of the smaller one was 24 ft. The ground floor was a continuum of space from which only two small rooms, the toilet and a utili-

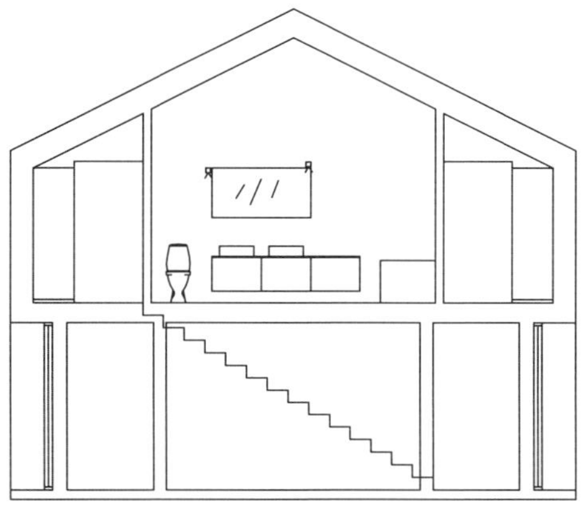

ty room, are separated. In the larger version they were located in the middle of the house next to the stairway, and thus divide the remaining space into a living room and a dining room with a kitchen. In the smaller version the two smaller rooms were located on the narrow side, the remaining space is only divided into two areas by a stairway leading straight upstairs. On the upper floor, where the rooms in the larger version were nearly 9 ft. high, three separate bedrooms and one bathroom are provided. The larger variation was offered for roughly €415,000, the smaller one for €385,000.

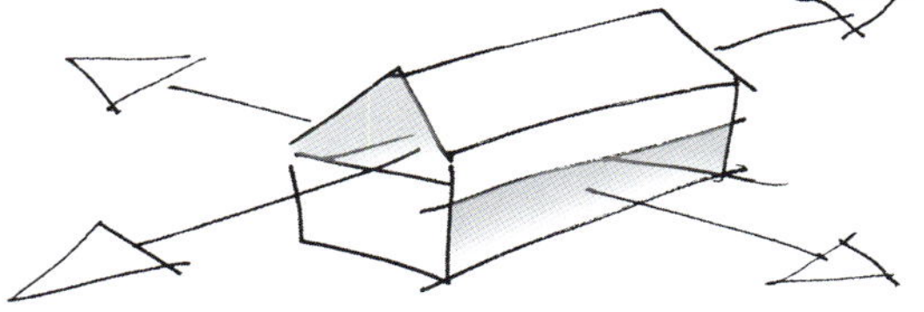

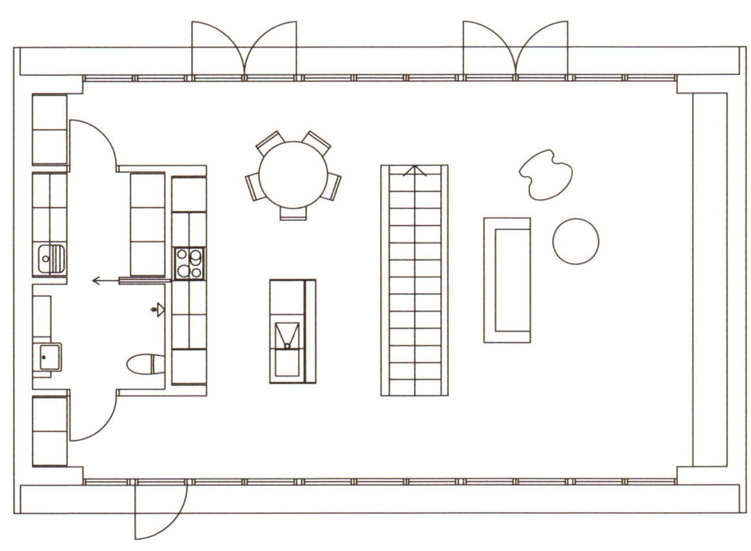

The glass walls are each slightly recessed, so that a narrow balcony is created on the upper level

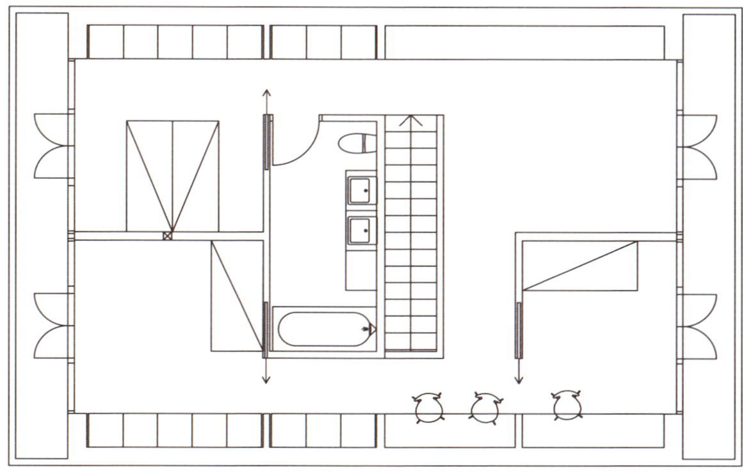

FOLDED ROOF HOUSE

Claesson Koivisto Rune
Arkitekthus
Stockholm, Sweden, 2008–2013

A year after the development of the Plus House, Claesson Koivisto Rune created a second design for the prefabricated house company Arkitekthus: the Folded Roof House (AH#002), which was first built on Muskö, an island south of Stockholm, in 2008. It is a one-story wooden house with an asymmetrically folded butterfly roof made of rust-free steel.

The entrance to the house is located on one of the long sides, which creates the impression of a closed block, due to the fact that it has no windows and is clad in vertical wooden boards. Hence, the visitor is all the more surprised by the brightness and openness of the house. As was already the case with the Plus House, large wall areas are executed entirely in glass. A large living and a dining room with a kitchen form the center of the house, with three bedrooms and two bathrooms on the two narrow sides. The two narrow sides and one entire side of the main room are completely glazed—and provide a view of the sea surrounding the island of Muskö. The glass walls are set back slightly into the cubic volume of the house, thus the terraces in front of them are partially protected by overhanging roofs; this enhances the correspondence between the interior and the exterior spaces.

The house with 1,500 sq. ft. of living space cost roughly €340,000, and a smaller version with 1,200 sq. ft. of space cost €300,000. The house on Muskö has two separate additions, a guest house and a sauna, which were not included in the standard model.

Arkitekthus clients were able to make a number of particularly interesting choices. People interested in the house were asked, "Are you more the modern or the classic type?" with a familiarity similar to the tone adopted by IKEA. Every house was available in two interior variations, which were then completely styled by the architect involved—ensuring that the final product took a more coherent appearance. According to the company, the designs in the "classic" line used oak to evoke a "warm" character, while in the "modern" line contrasts between light-colored wood and dark stone were characteristic. However, even the classic version was more modern than conservative. In this context the conviction that architects have complete control over their designs is alive and well. Arkitekthus also emphasizes the ample storage space in all of their houses indicating that their ambitious prefabricated houses from Sweden are geared towards people's practical needs.

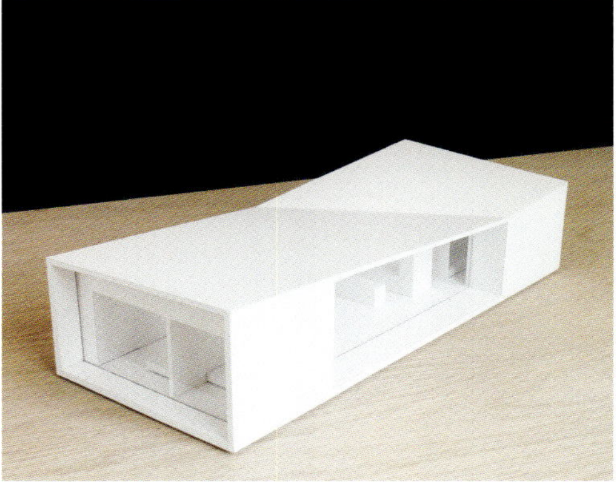

The living room, kitchen, and hallway have been combined to form one large room from which the bathroom and the bedrooms can be reached

The terrace in front of the sauna

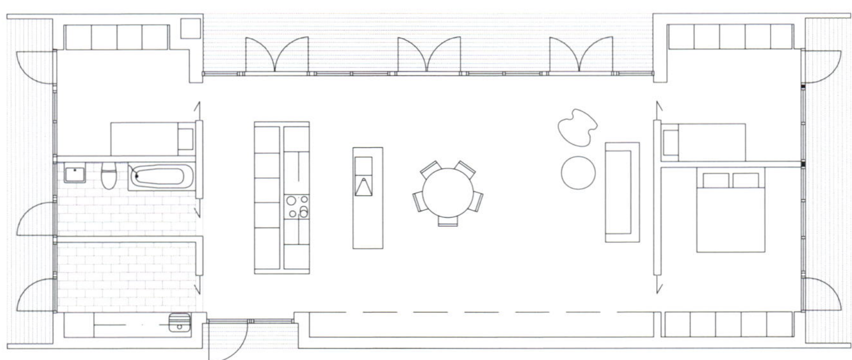

DHAN SERIES HOUSE

Brian Donovan, Timothy Hill
Happy Haus
Fortitude Valley, Queensland, Australia, 2008–mid 2010s

The name of these houses was not "Happy House," but instead, in perfect Denglish, "Happy *Haus*." Yet, they camr from Australia—more precisely from Brisbane, Queensland. They were produced in individual modules in a factory in South Queensland and assembled on site.

The company offered two models: the "White Series" by the Brisbane architectural office of Owen and Vokes and the "DHAN Series," which was developed by Brian Donovan and Timothy Hill operated one of the most successful architectural offices in Australia before merging into BVN in 2012. Donovan and Hill's express intention was to develop a type of house that would be relevant for Australians. They cited "open-plan living and connectivity" as their design principles; and it was indeed a characteristic of their houses.

The DHAN series consisted of three building elements: the "base," the "expander," and the "shed." The "base" is an elongated rectangular module, which was available in four different floor plans. It encompasses a kitchen, a bathroom, and a living room, which can be divided into a living room and bedroom by a wardrobe unit. This base can stand alone or be augmented by an "expander" module. They were available in sizes ranging from one to three bedrooms. A "studio"—an independent living unit with a

bedroom, bathroom, kitchen, and living area—was also available. The third building element is the "shed" module: a shelter open on two sides, which will mainly be used as a garage.

Using these three modules, the house could be configured and expanded at will. However, the extensions are not directly docked onto the base—each element stands alone and is connected to others via a common roof that spans the space in between them. The houses are raised slightly off the ground. Asymmetrical butterfly roofs and solar protection elements on the windows are characteristic for the houses of the DHAN series.

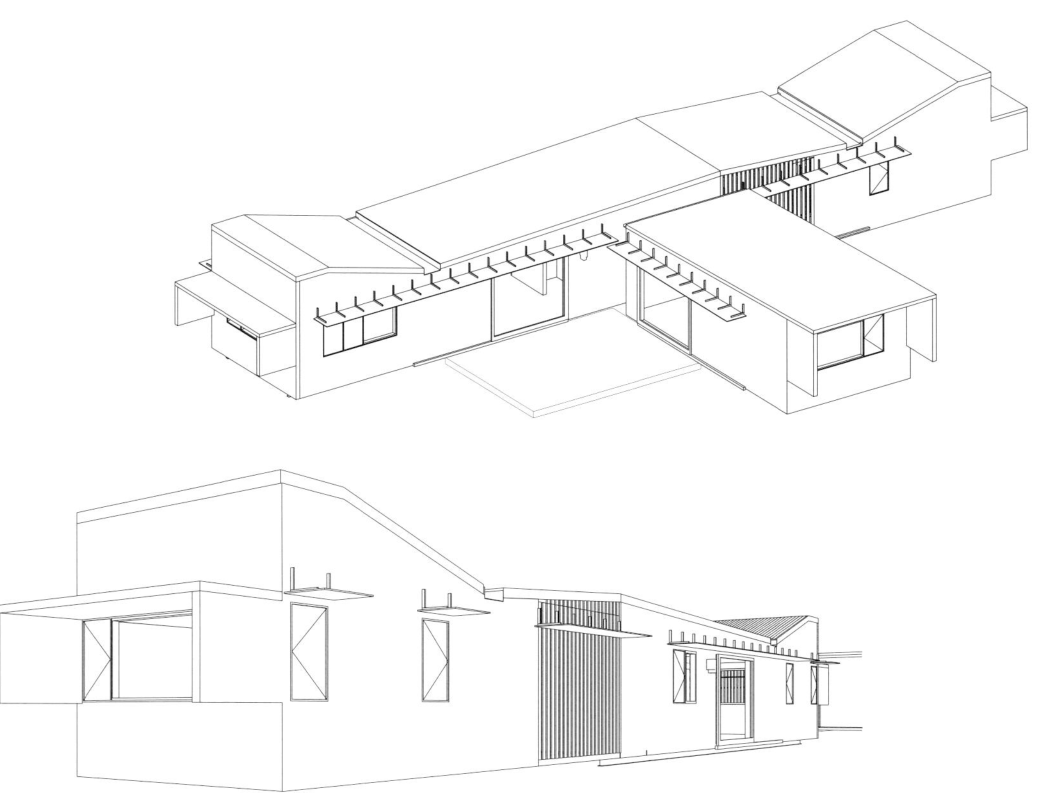

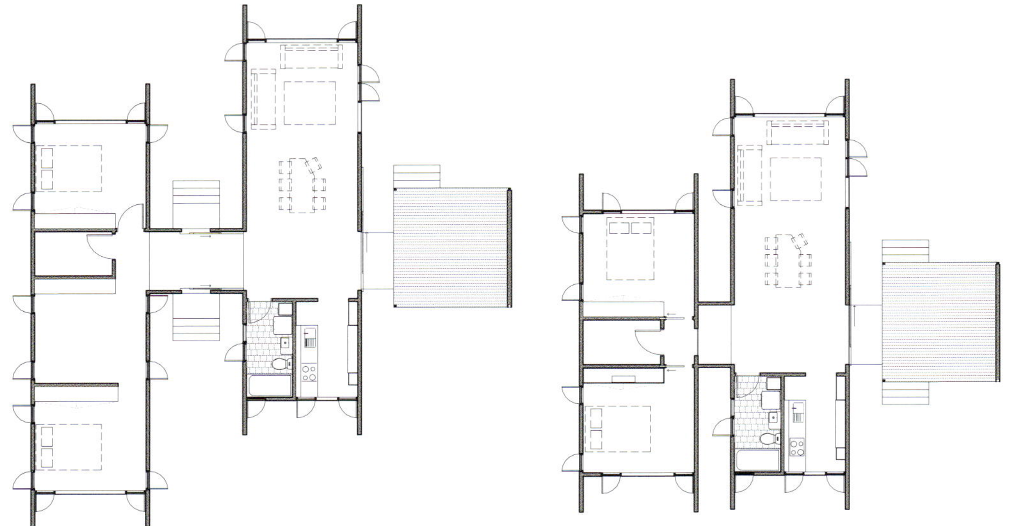

Above and opposite bottom: Floor plans of three variations with two or tree bedrooms

Below: Characteristic of the interior decoration is the contrast between the walls, which are painted white, and the natural wood of the windows, doors, and moldings under the ceilings. Lighting is installed in the molding, which also serves to hang pictures

Above: The external walls are made of plywood and can be chosen in various colors

SYSTEM 3

Oskar Leo Kaufmann, Albert Rüf
Dornbirn, Austria, 2008

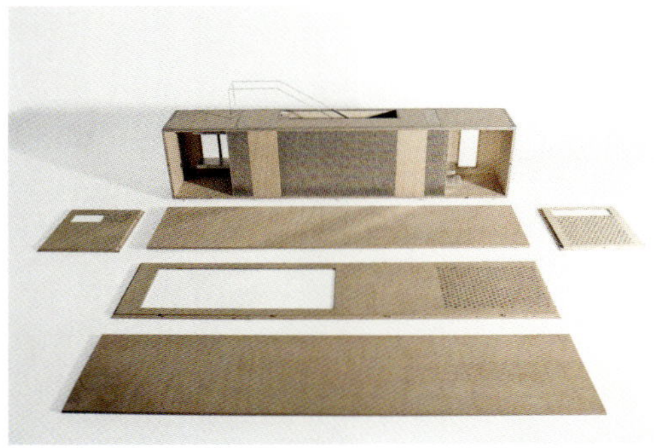

In 2008, the Museum of Modern Art in New York staged an exhibition on prefabricated architecture and invited five architectural offices to present a project on site. Among those invited were Oskar Leo Kaufmann and Albert Rüf from Vorarlberg, who impressively demonstrated how quickly a prefabricated house could be assembled. One morning a truck with a shipping container rolled into the courtyard of the MoMA. First the "serving unit" was unloaded. An hour later the building crew began to assemble the wall, floor, and roof elements of the "naked space." After four and a half hours the 722-sq. ft. house, complete with furniture, was ready for the inhabitants to move in. In the meantime, the prototype had been developed further and was suited for mass production.

The ingenious idea behind "System 3" is basically a very simple one that was developed on the basis of previous projects; in terms of building technology, the house is divided into two separate areas. All of the complex building elements and installations are combined in the "serving space," which includes the kitchen, bathroom, electrical installations, heating, ventilation, Internet connection, and a stairway leading up to the flat roof. This segment is completely prefabricated. The dining room, living room, and bedrooms are docked onto this functional core, requiring only wall, floor, and ceiling elements. This is the "naked space," which only becomes living space through individual furnishings.

Through processes controlled by computers, it is possible to create openings anywhere in the wall elements and in any shape desired to accommodate large windows, doors, or a number of small oculi, as Kaufmann and Rüf demonstrated on the example of the prototype in New York. In order to ensure problem-free transport, the maximum size of the service unit corresponds with international container standards, and the elements used to construct the naked space are also oriented on these dimensions. In the case of the New York prototype, the functional core and all of the other building components fit into a single container.

The size, features, and configuration of the service unit can be individually determined by the client, however there are also maximum dimensions for the wall, floor, and ceiling elements: 9.5 × 38 ft. These wall elements are nearly 5 in. thick and made of plywood. They are fitted out with prefabricated windows and doors on site. In New York, the external walls were protected by marine varnish, but alternative "skins" can also be chosen. It is also possible to install solar cells. The architects offered metal furniture for the interior, lighting can be installed by means of cables and hooks anyplace that it is required. The internal walls can be painted in any color chosen by the client.

This system, which is both simple and—due to its production method—cost-effective, is also extremely flexible. Every service unit can be augmented on either of the long sides by naked spaces or additional service units as desired. Multi-story buildings are also possible.

The exhibit was dismantled in New York, transported back to Austria, and reassembled in Dornbirn in the park of the inatura Museum.

Opposite: The "System 3" skin is like a jacket. It can be removed, changed, and washed. The skin is made of different membranes and foils and includes thermal insulation, waterproofing, and a vapor barrier

Following spread: The presentation of the house in New York City, 2008

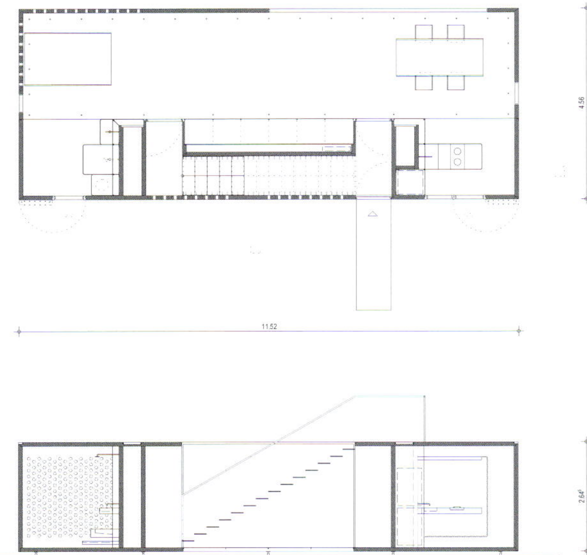

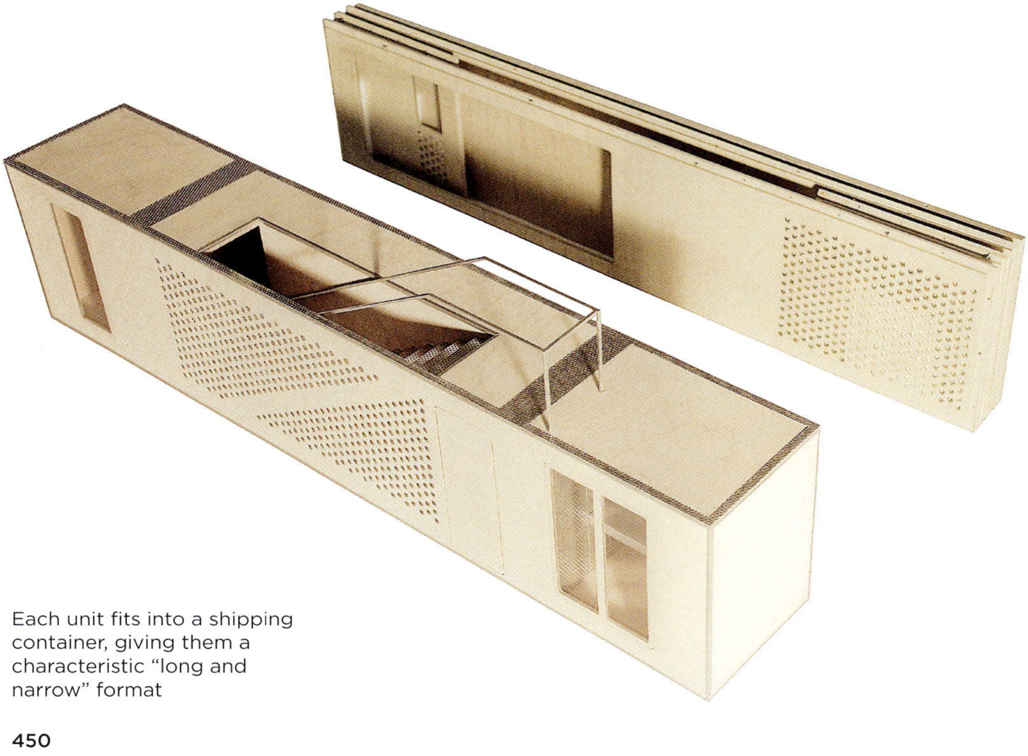

Each unit fits into a shipping container, giving them a characteristic "long and narrow" format

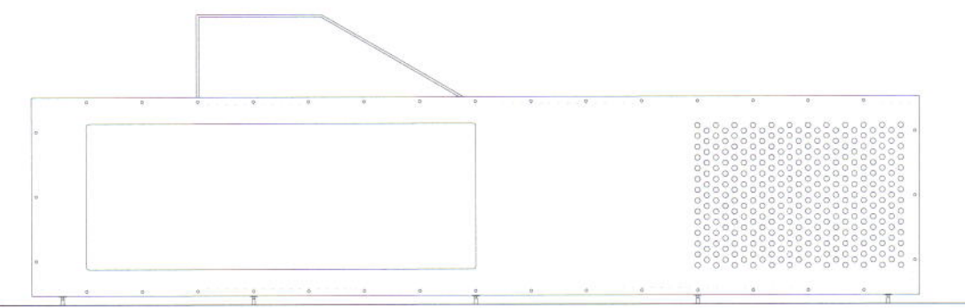

MoMA
WWW.MOMA.ORG

The furniture and all of the interior elements are made of blank metal. Shelves, lockers, and hooks can be fastened to the wood panels with screws, without worrying about electric cables

SOE KER TIE HOUSE

TYIN Tegnestue Architects
Noh Bo Tak, Thailand, 2008–2009

Should architects from the West provide developmental aid to Third World countries by building houses there? There are many reasons for not doing so, according to the home page of the architects from the Norwegian TYIN Tegnestue (which means drafting room)—but there are even more reasons for doing so. The non-profit organization, which was operated by five architectural students from the University of Trondheim and sponsored by over 60 Norwegian companies and private donors, embraced the task of building houses for and with people in the Third World: at low cost, adapted to local structures and traditions, and with the goal of training people to build better houses on their own in the future. The express interest of the Norwegians in this context was that the participants learn from each other. TYIN Tegnestue decided to close the practice 2019.

In August of 2008, three of the Norwegian architecture students traveled to Noh Bo, a little village near the border between Thailand and Burma, mainly populated by Karen, who are refugees escaping ethnic oppression in Burma. Since 2006, a Norwegian named Ole Jørgen Edna has been running an orphanage in this

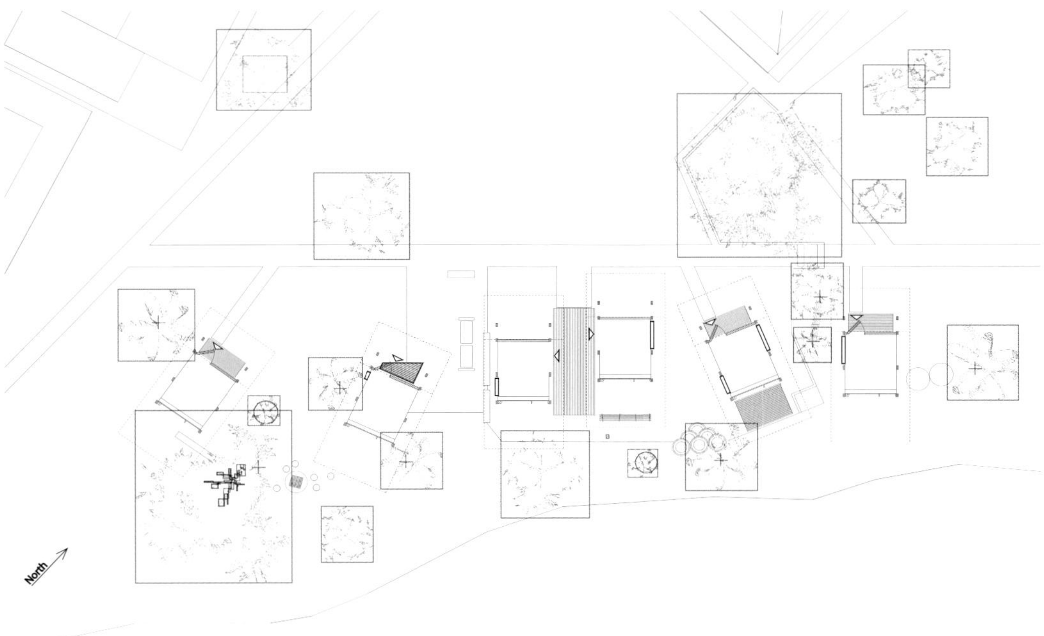

village, which he was desperately seeking to expand. The students from Trondheim designed and built six dormitories for 24 children in three months in collaboration with local laborers. The basic idea was "to create an atmosphere similar to what the children would have experienced in a more normal situation." Every child was to be ensured their own private sphere, a house, and neighbors to play with. The six sleeping places per house were distributed over three levels arranged in alternation.

The local laborers referred to the designs as *Soe Ker Tie Hias*, butterfly houses. The side and back façades are made of woven bamboo—a technique typical of the region. The form of the roof facilitates both natural ventilation and the collection of rainwater. The individual elements of the ironwood structure were prefabricated and connected to each other on site using bolts in order to achieve greater stability. The building is raised slightly off the ground and the four corner footings stand on old tires in order to protect the houses and the footings from dampness.

"After six months of learning from each other in Noh Bo, we hope that we have left something useful behind: important principles such as diagonal bracing, the economical use of building materials, and protection against dampness, will hopefully lead to more sustainable building practices in the future."

Above: Site plan

Following spread: The arrangement of the houses makes it possible for children to maintain social contacts in the neighborhood, while at the same time offering them an opportunity to spend time alone

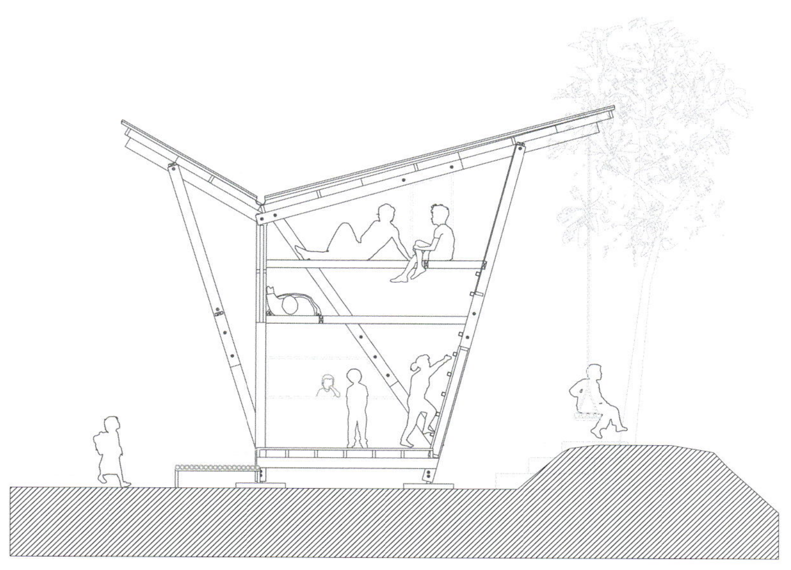

The use of bamboo has a long tradition in the region

Various types of walls create an exciting interplay of light and shadow

UNIVERSAL WORLD HOUSE

Prof. Dirk Donath, Bauhaus-Universität Weimar
Consido AG
Schaffhausen, Switzerland, 2009–

One of the most basic motivations for erecting buildings out of prefabricated elements is the goal of finding quick, low-cost solutions to alleviate an existing shortage of housing. Thus it comes as no great surprise that, in a world increasingly given to thinking in globalized categories, prefabrication is now being employed to create more dignified living conditions in the Third World. And it is against this background that the Consido AG developed the Universal World House, which is intended to replace the sheet metal huts found in the slums of developing countries.

The house was designed between 2007 and 2008 by a professor for architecture at the Bauhaus University in Weimar, Dirk Donath. It has nearly 390 sq. ft. of floor space and costs roughly €3,600 with basic furnishings. These basic furnishings include integrated single and double beds, a simply equipped kitchen, some built-in furnishings, a veranda with a shower, toilet, and a wash basin for a large family in a separate segment. The wall to the living area can be flipped up in order to both open up the house and provide additional shade.

The cost of the house was so low because of the material used. It consists of honeycomb-core panels made of a substance that, up until now, was hardly considered exemplary for its water resistance, resilience, or even stability: paper. However, when formed in a honeycomb-like structure, it becomes the stable core of a modular building system. Because of their light weight and their high tensile strength, honey-comb structures are used in the construction of airplanes and yachts. But instead of using aluminum, or some other material that is costly and energy intensive in its production, as is done in such cases, cellulose soaked in polyurethane resin is used in Consido AG's innovative SwissCell® panels, which are transformed into extremely stable, lightweight and water-resistant structures with a thickness of 2 in. through a special process using high pressure and temperatures. The homogenous bond between the outer layer and cell layers ensures a high level of tensile strength, while the combination of materials ensures that the composite is weather resistant.

The intention of this development project was to help people help themselves. This would have meant not only that the house would be assembled on-site, as is customary in prefabricated construction, but also that the components would have been manufactured on-site. To minimize transportation costs and create new jobs locally, Consido would have supplied only the raw materials and the necessary production line in the form of a mobile production unit. A prototype plant was built in the German city of Kiel to manufacture the required machinery.

A number of countries from Africa, Asia, South America and Russia have expressed interest. In addition, intensive contact has been established with potential customers, including many international NGOs such as World Vision, Misereor, and UN organisations.

Right: The innovative SwissCell® Panels have a honeycomb core made of cellulose soaked in polyurethane resin

Below: The numerous variations of the house make it suited for diverse uses and family structures

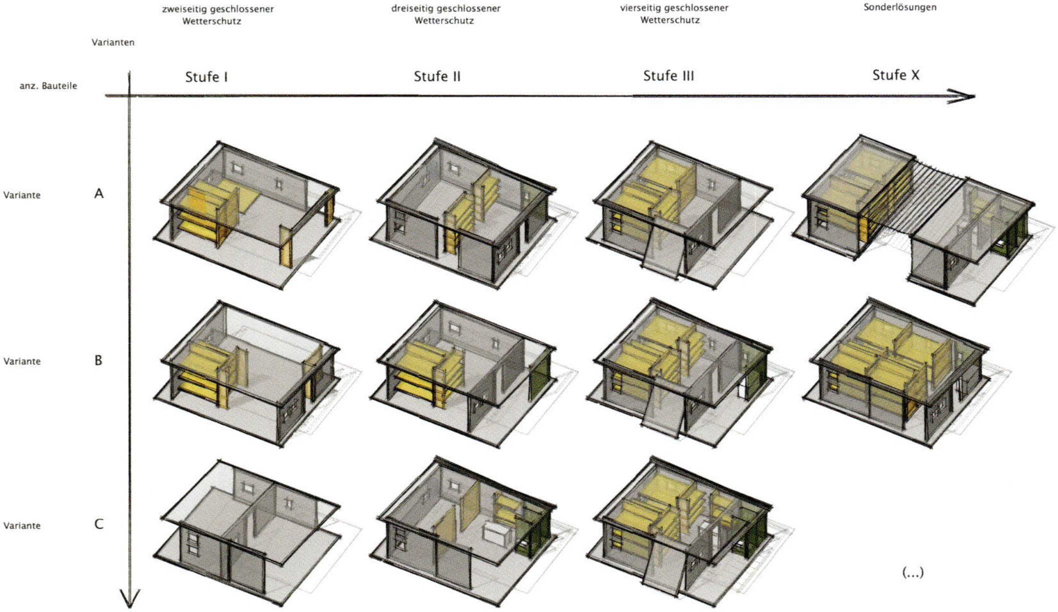

	Varianten	zweiseitig geschlossener Wetterschutz	dreiseitig geschlossener Wetterschutz	vierseitig geschlossener Wetterschutz	Sonderlösungen
anz. Bauteile		Stufe I	Stufe II	Stufe III	Stufe X
Variante	A				
Variante	B				
Variante	C				(...)

Material from a single tree suffices for the production of a Universal World House. It has an expected life of 50 years and can be completely recycled

Below: The outer wall can be flipped up to both provide solar protection and to overcome the separation between interior and exterior space

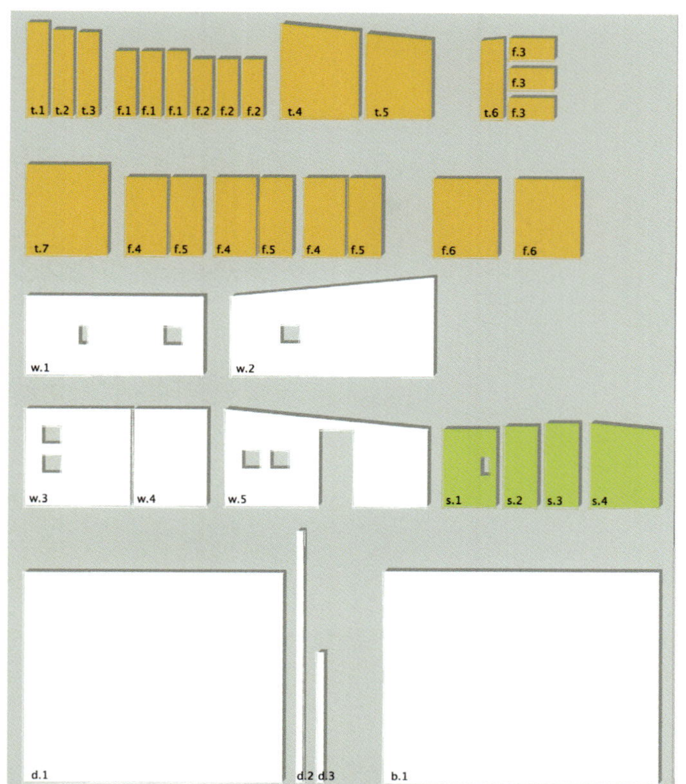

Regalplatten

Betten (bzw. Regale)

Aussenwände

Aussenwände / Sanitäreinheit

Boden- und Dachfläche, Dachzubehör

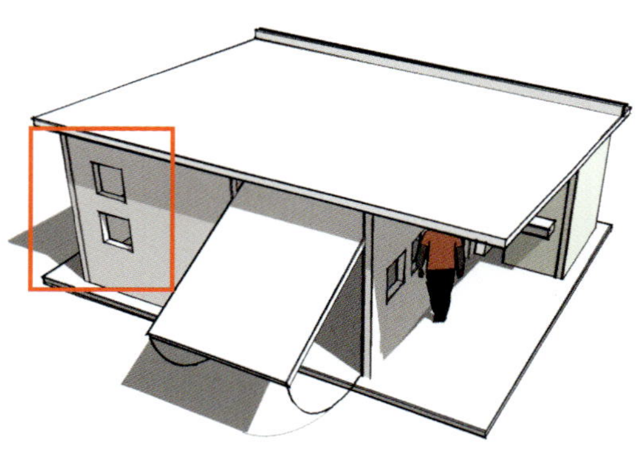

geschlossen

geöffnet

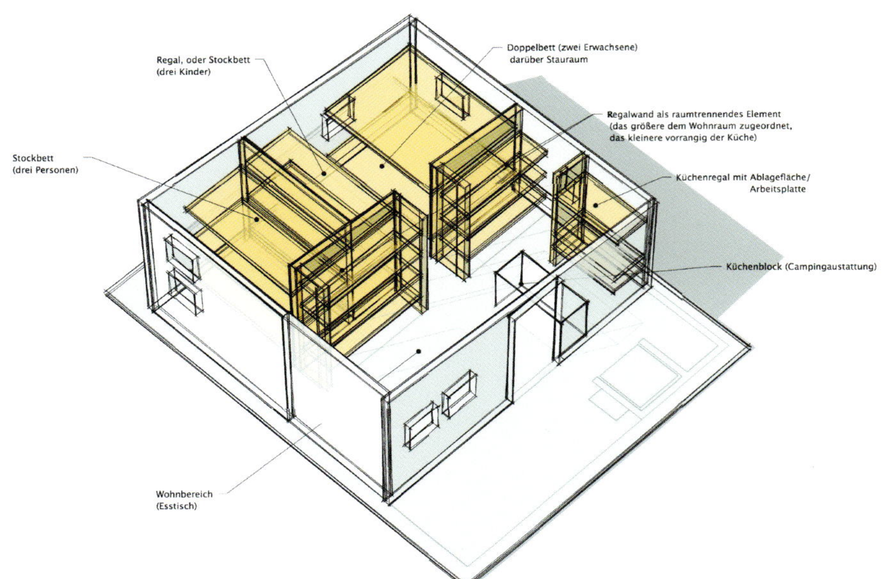

Regal, oder Stockbett
(drei Kinder)
Doppelbett (zwei Erwachsene)
darüber Stauraum
Regalwand als raumtrennendes Element
(das größere dem Wohnraum zugeordnet,
das kleinere vorrangig der Küche)
Stockbett
(drei Personen)
Küchenregal mit Ablagefläche/
Arbeitsplatte
Küchenblock (Campingaustattung)
Wohnbereich
(Esstisch)

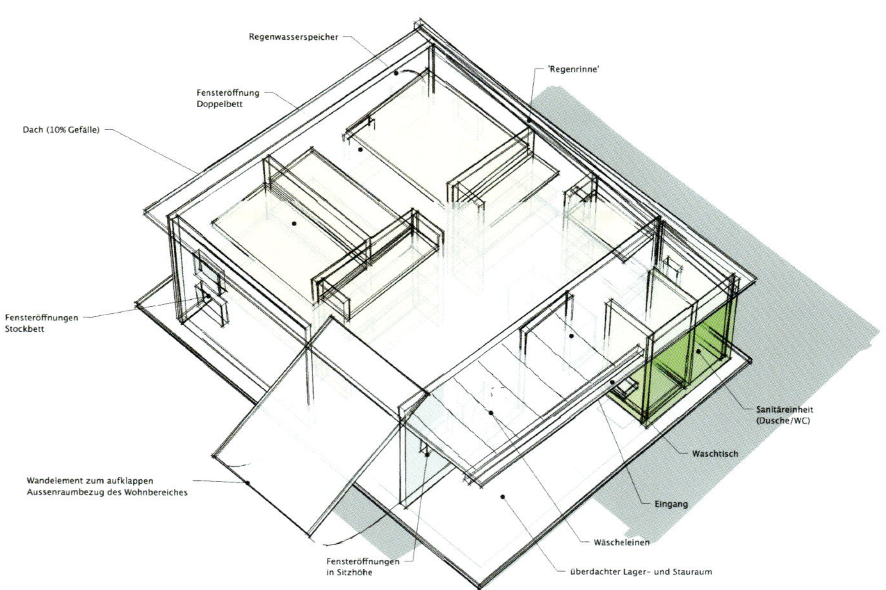
Regenwasserspeicher
'Regenrinne'
Fensteröffnung
Doppelbett
Dach (10% Gefälle)
Fensteröffnungen
Stockbett
Sanitäreinheit
(Dusche/WC)
Waschtisch
Wandelement zum aufklappen
Aussenraumbezug des Wohnbereiches
Eingang
Wäscheleinen
Fensteröffnungen
in Sitzhöhe
überdachter Lager- und Stauraum

BETTER SHELTER

IKEA, UNHCR
Various locations, 2009–

Better Shelter is a humanitarian housing initiative launched in 2009 through a collaboration between the Swedish furniture designer IKEA and UNHCR, the United Nations agency mandated to protect refugees, forcibly displaced communities, and to assist in providing safety, shelter, and long-term solutions. Conceived in response to the limitations of conventional emergency tents, the project aims to provide safer, more durable, and more dignified temporary housing in times of crisis around the world.

The Better Shelter unit is a flat-packed, modular shelter system, designed to be easily transported, assembled, and adapted on site. Drawing on IKEA's expertise in industrial design, logistics, and mass production, the shelters can typically be assembled by a small team without specialized tools. A lightweight steel frame supports rigid injection-molded plastic panel walls, while integrated solar panels provide basic interior lighting and charging capacity, improving safety and functionality for occupants.

Developed through extensive field testing and consultation with humanitarian organizations and refugees, the shelters were designed to last several years, significantly longer than standard emergency tents. They offer improved protection from weather, greater privacy, lockable doors, and better thermal performance, addressing both physical needs and psychological well-being. The standardized yet adaptable design allows the shelters to be deployed in a wide range of climates and geographic contexts.

This system reflects a shift in humanitarian thinking toward longer-term emergency responses, acknowledging that displacement often lasts for years rather than months. By applying principles of prefabrication, modularity, and user-centered design, the project connects industrial manufacturing and humanitarian aid. Since its introduction, Better Shelter units have been deployed in numerous refugee camps and crisis zones worldwide, becoming a widely recognized example of how global design and production systems can be mobilized to address urgent social needs. Since 2015 more than 100,000 Better Shelter units were delivered to over 80 countries.

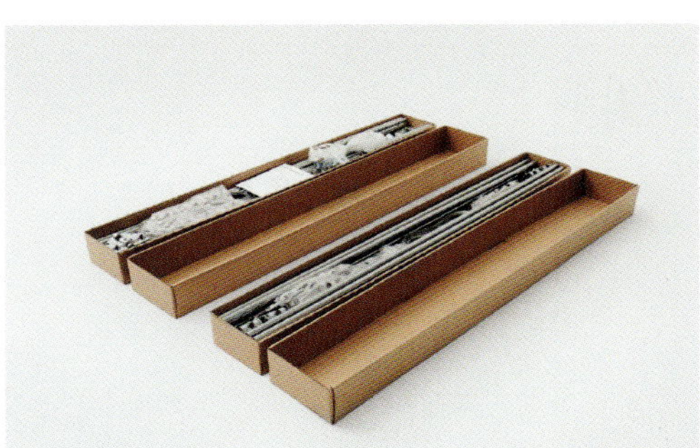

Below: Drawings show the different ways the shelters can be covered, depending on the circumstances and available materials

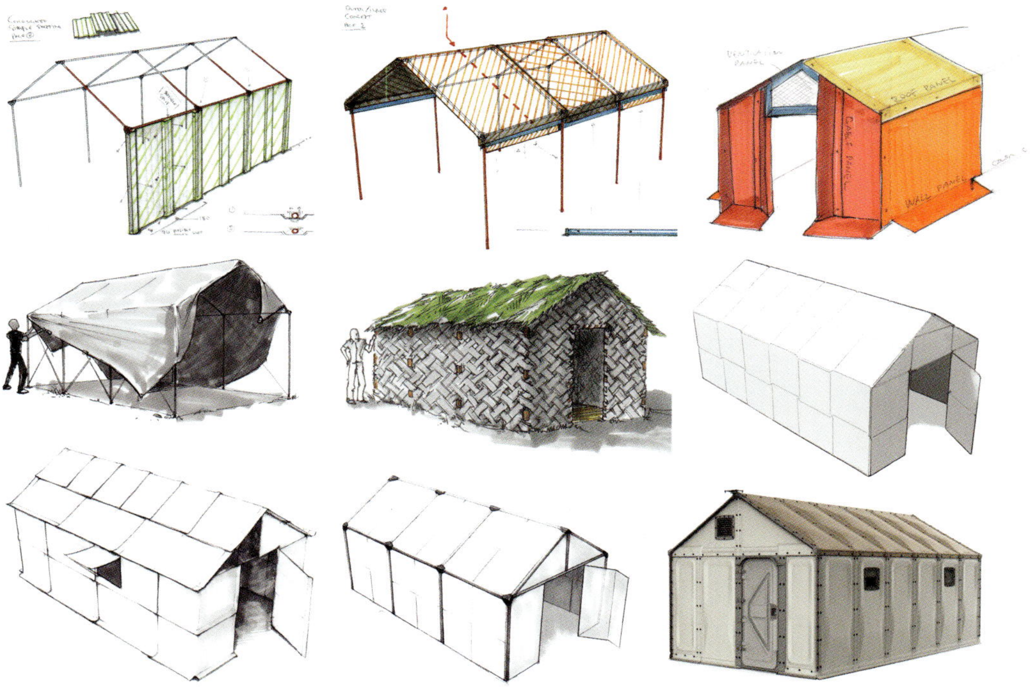

Opposite and left: Ease of shipping and assembly are emphasized in these images

Below: In a metal-clad unit, a pattern of local decorations alleviates the structure's industrial harshness

Opposite: The interiors provide dignified shelter and space for personal belongings

DIOGENE HOUSE

Renzo Piano Building Workshop
Vitra AG
Weil am Rhein, Germany, 2011–2013

Diogene House is a 81 sq. ft., self-contained dwelling designed by Renzo Piano (RPBW, Renzo Piano Building Workshop). The project explores minimal living reduced to its essential elements. Named after the Greek philosopher Diogenes (c. 404–323 BC), who advocated a life of simplicity and independence, the house reflects ideas of autonomy, restraint, and freedom rather than proposing a prototype for mass housing. Despite its small footprint, it contains all the basic functions of a dwelling: sleeping, working, cooking, washing, and sanitation.

Diogene House is designed to operate off grid. Photovoltaic panels mounted on the roof generate electricity, rainwater is collected and filtered for domestic use, and wastewater is treated on site, while natural ventilation replaces mechanical climate control. The structure is built primarily from lightweight aluminum panels, ensuring durability, transportability, and a high degree of precision in construction. Diogene House can be described as prefabricated because it was manufactured off site as a self-contained unit and then transported and installed on the Vitra Campus. Like Le Corbusier's Cabanon (Roquebrune-Cap-Martin, France, 1951), the project explores extreme minimal living, but contrasts handcrafted, on-site construction with a technically autonomous, fully prefabricated micro-dwelling produced through contemporary industrial methods.

Large openings frame carefully controlled views of the surrounding landscape, blurring the boundary between interior and exterior. The interior is deliberately austere, with built-in furnishings and minimal finishes that emphasize function over comfort and avoid excess. Rather than proposing a universal solution, Diogene House serves as a conceptual experiment, inviting visitors to reconsider how much space, energy, and material are truly necessary to live well.

Opposite: A model displays the foundation and roof design of the house

Right: A drawing of the technical building equipment of the structure

Below: An exploded axonometric with the different structural elements visible

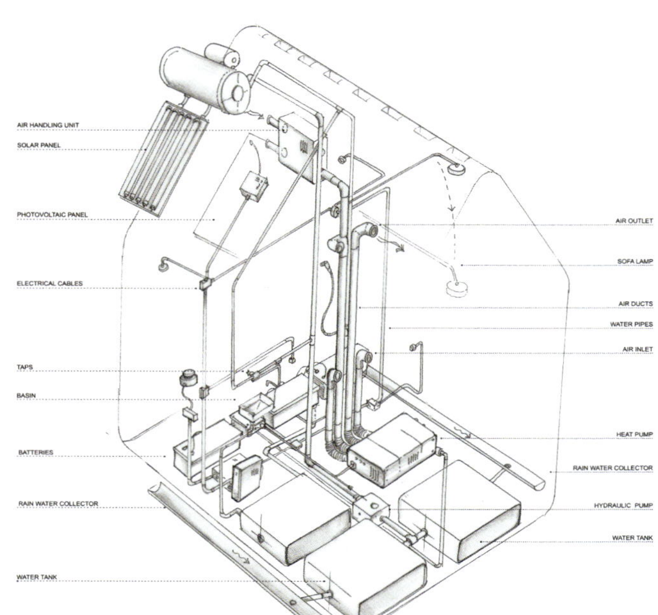

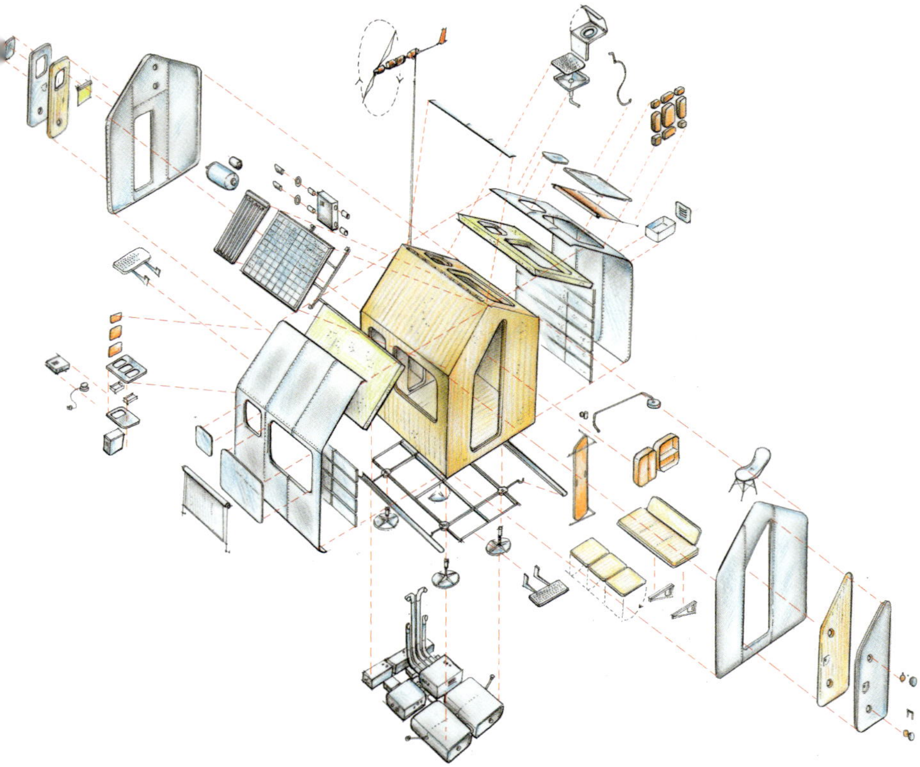

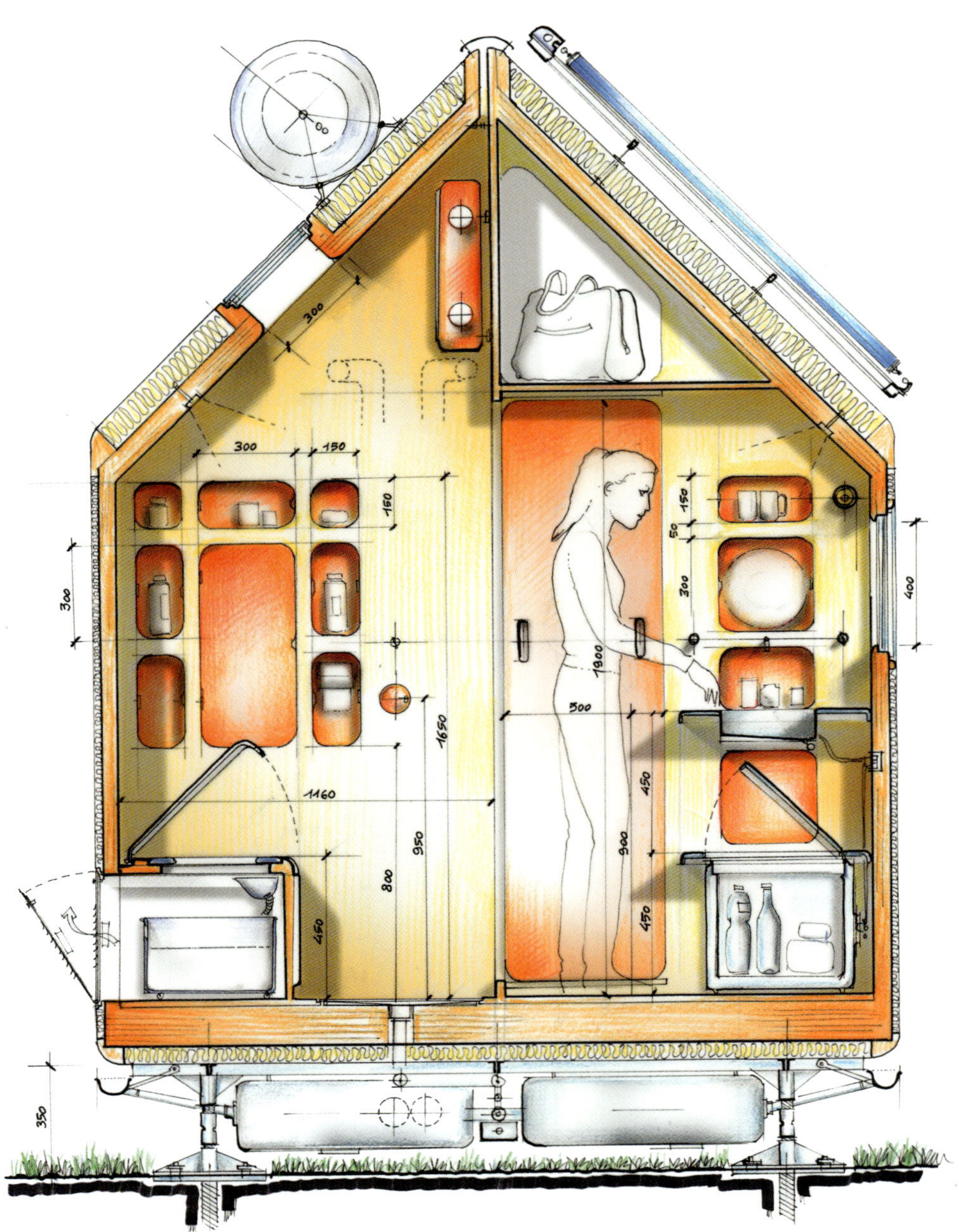

Every detail has been considered to provide everything necessary for living in the most minimal space possible

Elements such can be folded up to create different configurations or to provide slightly more space.

Above and right: Although the camera lens makes the space look more ample than it is, natural daylight makes the interior pleasant

Opposite: Set up off the ground the autonomous house can readily be moved without causing any damage to the site

JYUBAKO

Kengo Kuma & Associates
Snow Peak
Japan, 2015–

Jyubako (Living Box) is a mobile home developed and produced by Kengo Kuma and the Japanese outdoor goods manufacturer Snow Peak. Designed to be moved as a trailer, the house naturally had to conform to a number of regulatory requirements, in particular for its size and weight. In order to give a spacious feeling to the living space, the architect designed the entire structure with raw plywood panels, some of which can be opened, creating awnings, a table, and a deck, when the house is in use. Jyubako is sold completely bare inside so that clients can adapt it to their own preferences and use. It is, as Kengo Kuma says, "a proposal for another kind of nomadic lifestyle." Kuma took a personal interest in this project, as he explains: "In my second year of graduate school I traveled through the Sahara by car in order to learn about the architecture of Africa. When I was tired, I went to sleep on the roof of the car. The starlit desert sky is more beautiful than can be imagined. I thought of life as a kind of diaspora, living while moving far from my home. Based on that experience I wrote my Master's thesis, so my starting point as an architect is a journey. Designing this mobile house was very rewarding, because I felt that I could return to the origins of my work for the first time in decades."

Opposite and above: In the context of a modest mobile home, the architect uses wood to create simple, bright spaces that can be inhabited by the owners in a very flexible fashion

Below: Elevation drawings show the volume with its wheels beneath

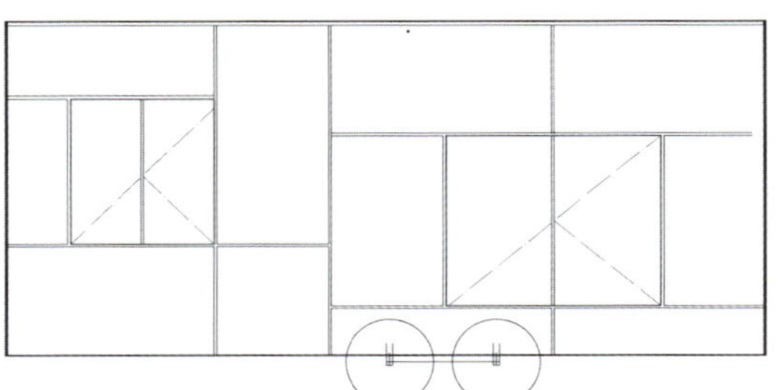

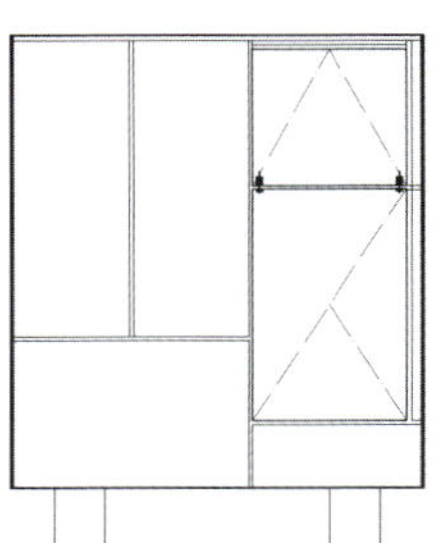

snow peak
outdoor lifestyle creator
since1958

CURUCACA MINIMOD

MAPA
Santa Catarina, Brazil, 2017

The Minimod designs of MAPA are intended as "primitive retreats with a contemporary reinterpretation." They are prefabricated, compact, and energy efficient. The Curucaca Valley is in the mountains of southern Brazil in the state of Santa Catarina. The architects explain that "Brazil's CLT wood technology combines the efficiency of industrialized products with new technologies focused on sustainability with the sensitivity of natural material par excellence." They compare this design to PnP (plug-and-play) devices or computers that can be used directly, without user intervention. "As such," they say, "the necessary steps to install and enjoy a Minimod must be simple and fast. From the factory to the landscape." This structure was built with cross-laminated timber, black corrugated metal cladding, and glass. It has a green roof and is lifted off the ground on low pilotis. It has two bedrooms with bathrooms at either end and a central living and dining area. Indoors, a wood-burning stove generates heat, and sliding glass walls can be opened to the outdoor deck when weather permits.

The rectangular house sits lightly on the ground and is entirely surrounded by its green environment—even the roof is green

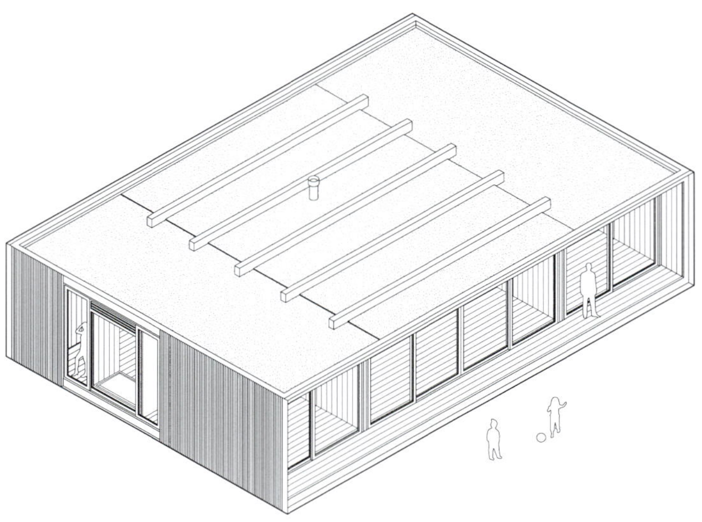

Above: Sliding glass doors and an outdoor terrace connect the interior to the outdoors and the forest. Furnishing is simple, as befits the house and its site

Below: A section drawing

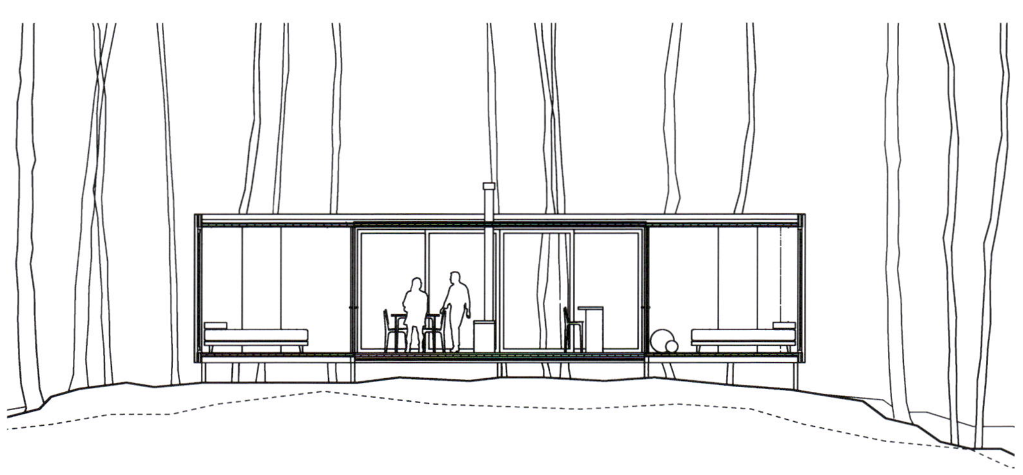

Above: Existing trees on the site were almost entirely preserved—the large opening again connects residents to their environment

Below: A small wood-burning stove provides heat. The entire interior—ceiling, floor, and walls—is clad in wood

ESSENTIAL HOMES

Norman Foster Foundation
Holcim
Various locations, 2022–

The Essential Homes Research Project is a project undertaken by Norman Foster through his Norman Foster Foundation (NFF) together with Holcim. It was first presented in 2023 in the Giardini Marineressa and the Palazzo Mora in Venice. Foster focuses here on the fact that in recent times, refugee camps have tended to become relatively permanent, rendering tents and other light structures inadequate. Here, he proposes to use low carbon, rollable concrete sheets, energy-efficient insulation systems, and permeable concrete pathways to create homes that can be readily constructed and reused or recycled. The stated goal is to be able to "create communities instead of camps" With the support of the concrete firm Holcim, "a global leader in innovative and sustainable building solutions," NFF has mobilized the technical and industrial capacity to make a real difference in an area of world-wide concern. The Giardini prototype measured approximately 582 sq. ft. in built space, with a further "minimal version" described as having an area of 194 sq. ft. The project emphasizes prefabrication, rapid assembly, and lightweight construction, alongside innovative low-carbon materials, to enable scalable deployment in contexts of humanitarian need, urban density, and post-disaster reconstruction. Essential Homes positions architecture as a practical tool for social equity, combining technological innovation with a clear ethical ambition: to provide dignified housing using the least possible resources.

Opposite and above: Made with low-carbon, recyclable, rollable concrete the roof of the shelters creates a 388 sq. ft. space. It will be sold for about $19,000

Right: Location of the structure in the Giardini della Marinaressa during the 2022 *Architecture Biennale*

Following spread: The structure in its Venice setting

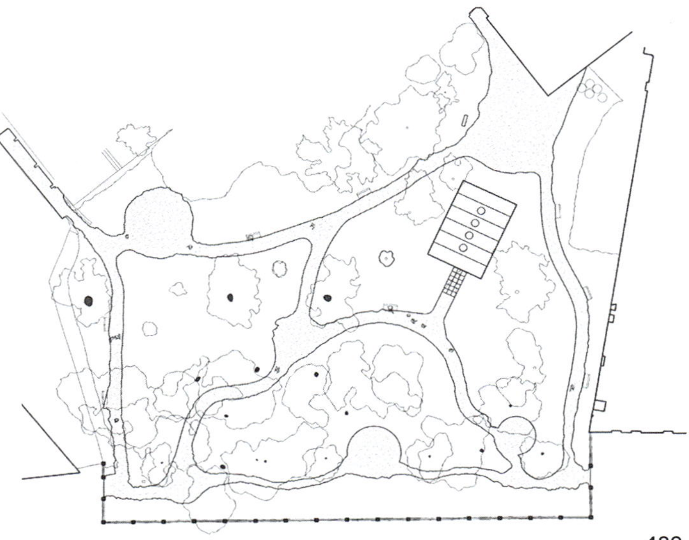

Above: The interior of the prototype house, with its simple, light design

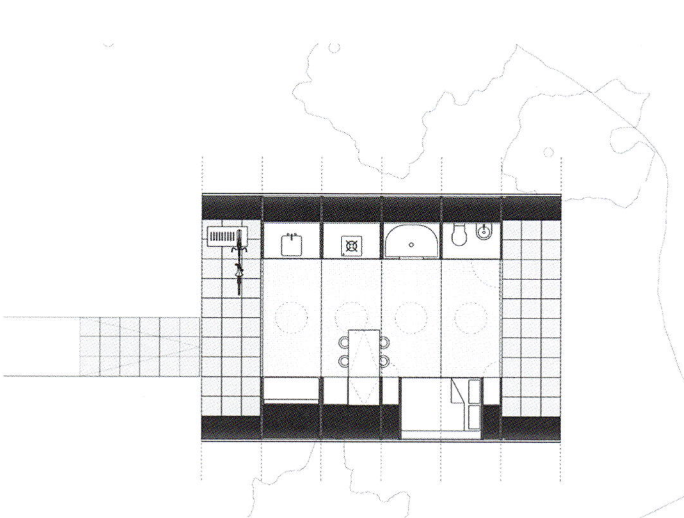

Left: A minimal floor plan

Opposite top: Short and long sections of the building showing its arched design (top) and basic rectangular form (center)

Opposite bottom: Interior view with sleeping and eating areas

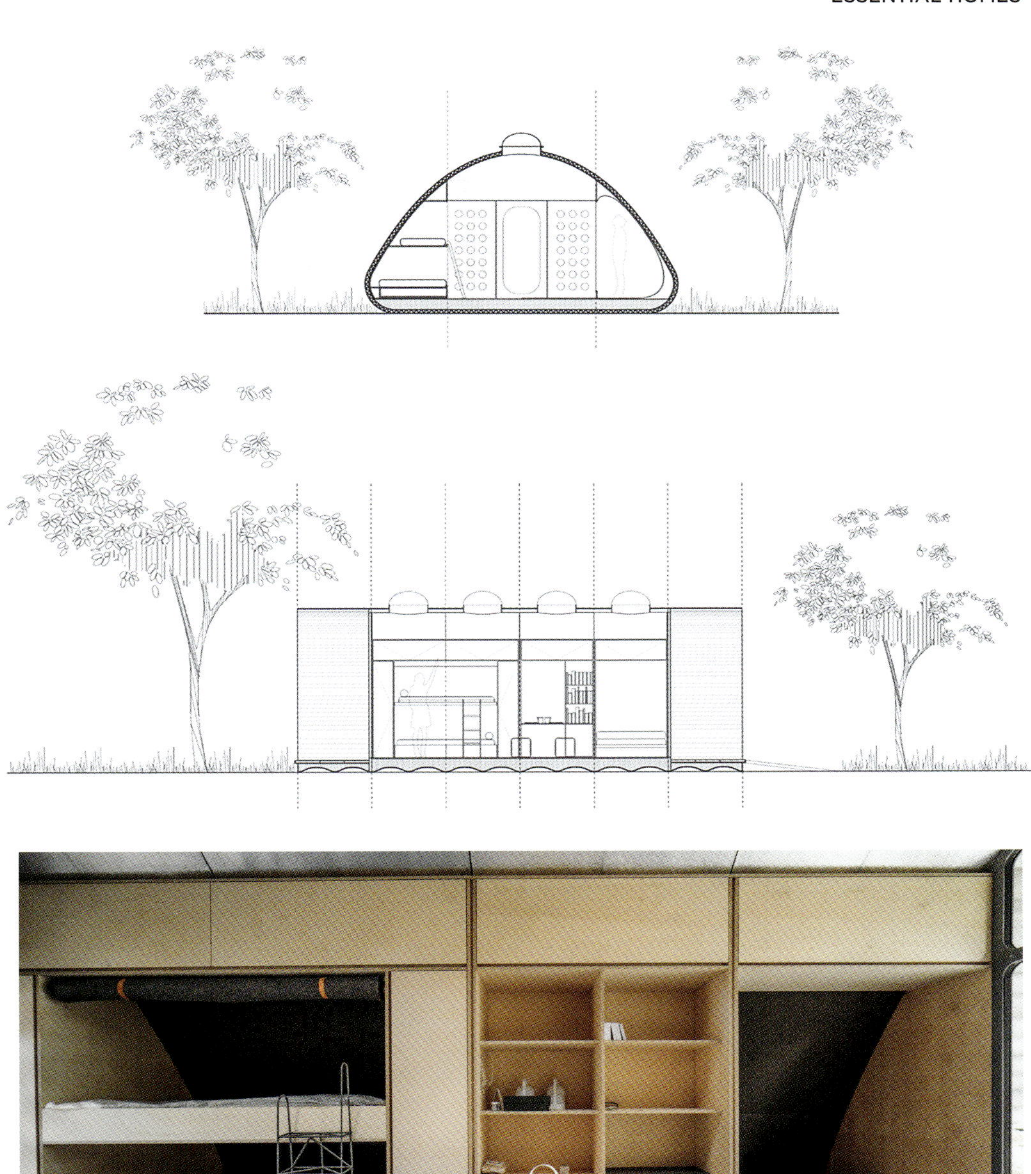

Opposite top: Essential Home volumes can be arranged into village-like structures.

Opposite bottom: The structures require no foundations and can readily be be lifted from humid ground

Below: The volumes can be grouped together to create longer buildings and assembled into larger communities.

RE:UKRAINE

Balbek Bureau
Ukraine, 2022–

RE:Ukraine is an architectural and humanitarian initiative launched by the Kyiv design studio Balbek Bureau in response to the large-scale displacement caused by the Russian invasion of Ukraine. Conceived during the early months of the war, the project addresses an urgent need for rapidly deployable, dignified housing for people forced to flee their homes, both within Ukraine and across its borders. A pilot settlement outside Lutsk, in the village of Zhydychyn near the Polish border, opened its first residential section in autumn 2023. This built settlement forms part of the RE:Ukraine temporary housing system for internally displaced persons (IDPs), demonstrating the project's feasibility under real conditions.

Rather than proposing a single building type, RE:Ukraine operates as a system of adaptable, modular living units designed for emergency accommodation, temporary settlements, and longer-term transitional housing. The project prioritizes speed of construction, affordability, and flexibility, allowing housing to be deployed in small clusters or expanded into larger communities as needs evolve. Individual housing units take the form of standardized modular boxes measuring approximately 21.65 × 10.83 ft. These boxes serve as the basic building blocks of a settlement. Units can serve multiple roles—private living spaces, communal kitchens, sanitary modules, or public facilities—depending on how they are fitted out and grouped. Each residential module typically accommodates a single household and is supported in the neighborhood by shared amenities, green areas, and community infrastructure.

The units are explicitly designed as prefabricated architecture. They are manufactured off site, transported easily, and rapidly assembled on location. Construction is based on a timber-frame structural system, combined with timber panels, plywood or OSB boards for walls, floors, and roofs. Thermal insulation—typically mineral wool—is integrated into wall and roof cavities, while exterior cladding panels provide weather protection. Interiors are finished with simple plywood panels, complemented by standard off-the-shelf windows and doors, and connected using metal fasteners that allow for assembly, disassembly, and reuse. This consistent material strategy improves construction speed, quality control, and cost efficiency. Beyond technical performance, RE:Ukraine emphasizes human dignity and psychological well-being. By combining prefabrication, modest materials, and careful spatial design, the project enables displaced residents to move from emergency shelters to stable temporary homes within months.

An exploded axonometric drawing reveals the complete rectangular design and the construction materials

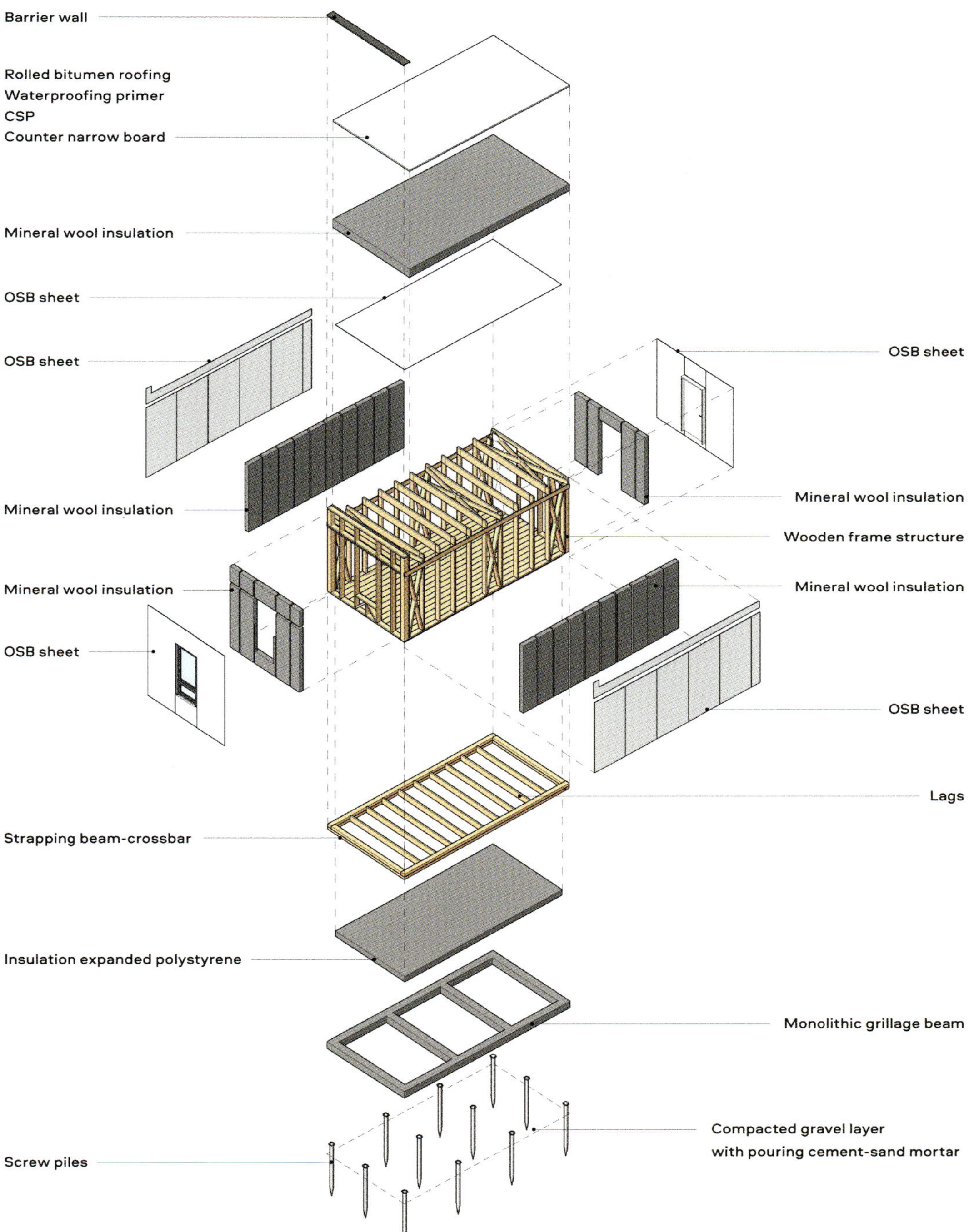
Barrier wall
Rolled bitumen roofing
Waterproofing primer
CSP
Counter narrow board
Mineral wool insulation
OSB sheet
OSB sheet
OSB sheet
Mineral wool insulation
Mineral wool insulation
Wooden frame structure
Mineral wool insulation
Mineral wool insulation
OSB sheet
OSB sheet
Lags
Strapping beam-crossbar
Insulation expanded polystyrene
Monolithic grillage beam
Compacted gravel layer
with pouring cement-sand mortar
Screw piles

Above: The rectangular designs can readily be grouped into communities

Below: Axonometric drawings display a number of the available spatial options inside the volumes

Opposite: Both low and light in their appearance, the buildings make for humane, convivial neighborhoods

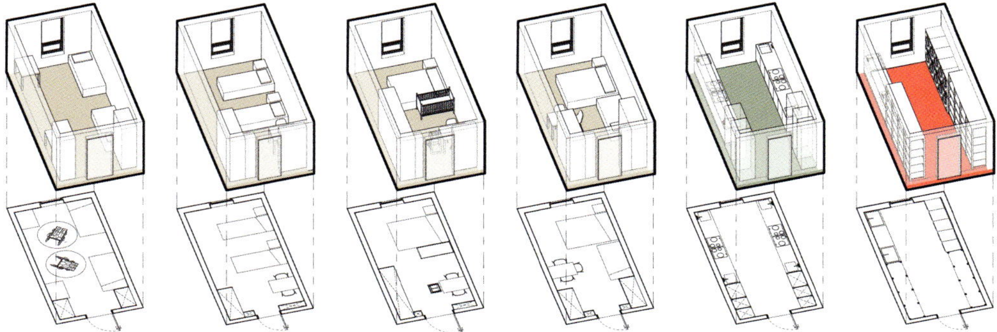

6600
3300
3300
3300
3300
3300
3300
26400

6550 3300 3300 3300 3300 3300 6550
29600

Opposite top: A plan for a community of houses showing different interior layouts

Opposite below, above and below: Interior living spaces are entirely flexible, as shown in these renderings

DESERTA ECOFOLIE

Pedro Alonso, Pamela Prado
Venice, Italy, 2025

Deserta Ecofolie is an experimental architectural installation presented in 2025 at the *Venice Architecture Biennale* conceived by Chilean architects Pedro Ignacio Alonso and Pamela Prado. The project was included in the *Biennale's* main exhibition *Intelligens. Natural. Artificial. Collective.*, curated by Carlo Ratti, and was constructed in the garden area adjacent to the Arsenale.

Deserta Ecofolie explores architecture as a lightweight, reversible, prefabricated environmental system rather than a permanent building. The installation is composed of pre-cut, factory-made components—including reflective and translucent polymer foils, flexible technical fabrics, and light metal elements such as aluminum profiles, cables, and fixings—which are transported compactly and assembled on site with minimal infrastructure. This prefabricated approach enables rapid installation, precise material control, and full disassembly for reuse.

Installed as a full-scale prototype, the project occupied a footprint of approximately 323 sq. ft., forming a walk-in, inhabitable field that modulates sunlight, heat, and airflow to create shaded microclimates. Rather than enclosing space, the thin membrane envelope operated as an adaptive surface, demonstrating how prefabrication can support climatic responsiveness with extremely low material mass. Deserta Ecofolie functions as a speculative model for temporary habitation, with potential applications for

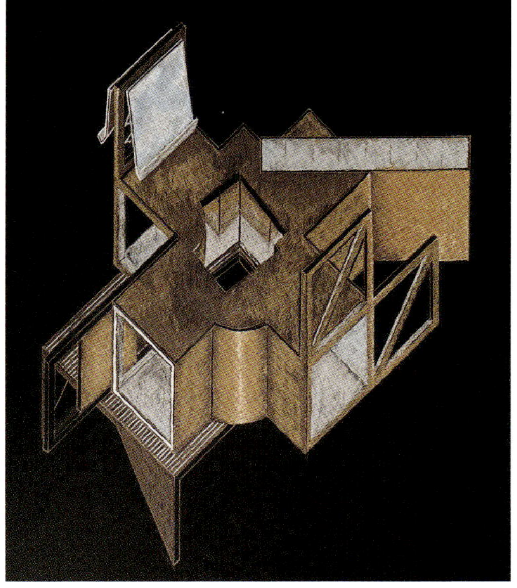

displaced populations and emergency shelter in extreme climates. Its prefabricated, transportable system suggests how lightweight architectural envelopes could be rapidly deployed to provide shade, thermal relief, and dignified communal space for people affected by displacement, while minimizing environmental impact and material permanence.

Opposite: Drawings show the unusual flexibility of the building system, which allows for architectural variety beyond what prefabrication usually supposes

Above and left: Easily transported and assembled materials are an essential feature of the project which may be best suited to a warm climate

Previous spread: Standing alone in a garden environment, the house has an almost organic presence, suited to its eco-friendly concept

Below: The use of light-colored plywood interior surfaces together with generous glazing opens the structure to its environment in an agreeable way

Opposite: Though decidedly modern in its conception and design, the installed project gives a clear sense of impermanence and modesty

BIBLIOGRAPHY

Arieff, Allison: *Prefab.* Layton, Utah: Gibbs Smith, 2002

Bancilhon, Philippe: *Jean Benjamin Maneval. La Bulle Six Coques.* Paris: Jousse entreprise éditions, 2004

Bemis, Albert Farwel: *The Evolving House.* Cambridge, Mass: MIT, 1936

Broadhurst, Ron (ed.): *Home delivery. Fabricating the modern dwelling* [exhibition at The Museum of Modern Art, New York]. Basel / Boston / Berlin: Birkhäuser, 2008

Cherner, Norman: *Fabricating Houses from Component Parts. How to build a house for $6,000.* New York, New York: Reinhold Publishing, 1957

Cinqualbre, Olivier / Pacquement, Alfred / Rubin, Robert M.: *Jean Prouvé: La maison tropicale / The Tropical House.* Paris: Centre Pompidou, 2009

Cooke, Amanda / Friedman, Avi: *Ahead of Their Time. The Sears Catalogue Prefabricated Houses, in: Journal of Design History, 14/1, 2001*, pp. 53–70

Davies, Colin: *The Prefabricated Home.* London: Reaktion Books, 2005

Decker, Julie / Chiei, Chris: *Quonset Hut. Metal Living for a Modern Age.* New York: Princeton Architectural Press, 2005

Ebong, Ima: *Kit Homes Modern.* New York: Collins Design, 2005

Enjolras, Christian: *Jean Prouvé. Les maisons de Meudon 1949–1999.* Paris: Editions de la Villetta, 2003

Fetters, Thomas L.: *The Lustron Home. The History of a Postwar Prefabricated Housing Experiment.* Jefferson, N.C.: McFarland, 2002

Fuller, Richard Buckminster: *Critical Path.* New York: St. Martin's Griffin, 1982

Genzel, Elke / Voigt, Pamela: *Kunststoffbauten. Teil 1: Die Pioniere.* Weimar: Verlag der Bauhaus-Universität, 2005

Gloag, John / Wornum, Grey: *House out of Factory.* London: George Allen & Unwin, 1946

Graff, Raymond / Matern, Rudolph A. / Williams, Henry Lionel: *The Prefabricated House. A Practical Guide for the Prospective Buyer.* Garden City, N.Y.: Doubleday & Co., 1947

Hays, K. Michael / Miller, Dana: *Buckminster Fuller. Starting with the Universe.* New York: Yale University Press, 2008

Herbers, Jill: *Prefab Modern.* New York: Harper Design International, 2004

Herbert, Gilbert: *Pioneers of Prefabrication. The British Contribution in the 19th Century.* Baltimore: Johns Hopkins University Press, 1978

Herbert, Gilbert: *The Dream of the Factory-Made House. Walter Gropius and Konrad Wachsmann.* Cambridge, Mass.: Harvard UP, 1984

Home, Marko / Taanila, Mika: *Futuro. Tomorrow's House from Yesterday.* Helsinki: Desura, 2002

Institut für das Bauen mit Kunststoffen: *Untersuchung über die Wohn- und Konstruktionsformen von Kunststoffhäusern und Raumzellen in Abhängigkeit von der Rentabilitätsschwelle*, in: *Plasticonstruction*, 5, 1973, pp. 245–257

Jandl, H. Ward, et alii: *Yesterday's Houses of Tomorrow. Innovative American Homes 1850 to 1950.* Washington D.C.: The Preservation Press, 1991

Junghanns, Kurt: *Das Haus für alle. Zur Geschichte der Vorfertigung in Deutschland.* Berlin: Ernst & Sohn, 1994

Koch, Carl / Lewis, Andy: *At Home With Tomorrow.* New York / Toronto: Rinehart & Co., 1958

Krausse, Joachim / Lichtenstein, Claude (eds.): *Your Private Sky. R. Buckminster Fuller: The Art of Design Science.* Baden (AG): Lars Müller, 1999

Meyer-Bohe, Walter: *Vorgefertigte Wohnhäuser.* Munich: Callwey, 1959

Nerdinger, Winfried: *The Architect Walter Gropius: Drawings, Prints, and Photographs from Busch-Reisinger Museum.* Harvard University Art Museums Cambridge, Mass., and Bauhaus-Archiv Berlin (eds.), Berlin: Mann, 1985

Peters, Nils: *Jean Prouvé. The Dynamics of Creation.* Cologne: Taschen, 2006

Pfeiffer, Bruce Brooks: *Frank Lloyd Wright. The Complete Works 1943–1959.* Cologne: Taschen, 2009

Rosa, Joseph: *Albert Frey, Architect.* New York: Rizzoli International, 1990

Rubin, Robert M.: *Jean Prouvé: A Tropical House.* February 14–May 6, 2005, Yale School of Architecture Gallery, New Haven: Yale School of Architecture, 2005

Smith, Elizabeth (ed.): *Blueprints for Modern Living. History and Legacy of the Case Study Houses.* Cambridge, Mass.: MIT Press, 1989

Sprague, Paul E.: *The Origin of Balloon Framing*, in: *Journal of the Society of Architectural Historians*, 40, 1981, pp. 311–319

Strauch, Dietmar: *Einstein in Caputh. Die Geschichte eines Sommerhauses.* Berlin: Anton Hain Verlag, 2001

Trulove, James Grayson / Cha, Ray: *Prefab Now.* New York: Collins Design, 2007

Touchaleaume, Éric: *Jean Prouvé. Les Maisons Tropicales.* Paris: Galerie 54, 2006

von Vegesack, Alexander (ed.): *Jean Prouvé. Die Poetik des technischen Objekts.* Weil am Rhein: Vitra Design Museum, 2005

PHOTO CREDITS

Courtesy of 3XN architects: 400, 403 top; Photo Adam Mørk: 401, 402 both, 403 bottom,

© Pasi Aalto, Trondheim: 456, 458/459, 460 top, 461, 462 all, 463

Aedes, International Institute of Social History: 273 bottom

Akademie der Künste, Berlin, Konrad-Wachsmann-Archiv: 54, 60–61, 102, 103 both, 104/105, 106 top, 107 both, 108; Photo: Dick Whittington: 106 bottom; Photo Anna Wachsmann: 103 top, 109

akg-images © Walter Müller: 35

Courtesy of Alchemy LLC, St. Paul, MN: 322, 323, 324 both, 325 both, 326/327 top, 327 bottom, 328 all 329 both

Price Collection, Alexander Turnbull Library: 9

© Pedro Ignacio Alonso: 502

Courtesy of Architeam 4, Basel: 294, 296 bottom, 297 top, 298 top

Architectural Forum, F. J. Wilder: 91, 94

architecture, No. 11 / 12, 1954: 154

L'Architecture d'Aujourd' hui, No. 4, 1946: 140

L'Architecture d'Aujourd' hui, No. 131, 1967: 190, 191, 192 bottom, 193 bottom both, 194 both

Courtesy of Arkitekthus, Stockholm: 432, 434 bottom, 437 top, 438 bottom, 443 bottom

Arkitekturmuseet, Stockholm: 24/25

The Art Institute of Chicago: 90; Ryerson and Burnham Archives, Kaufmann and Fabry Co.: 23; Ryerson and Burnham Archives 87, 92, 93 both, 94 bottom, 95

© ArtWorks: 503 top right, 503 bottom

Avery Architectural and Fine Arts Library, Columbia University: 88/89

© Hans Bach, Potsdam: 55 top, 56, 57 top, 58 top both, 59

© balbek bureau: 497–501

Courtesy of Shigeru Ban Architects, Tokyo: 280, 281, 283 bottom, 284

Courtesy of Bauart Architekten: 304 right, 306 top, 308 bottom, 309 bottom; Photo Bern Gempeler: 304 left; Photo Andi Greber: 306 bottom, 307, 308 top, 309 top

Bauhaus-Archiv Berlin: 21, 80 top, 81 top; Photo Lucia Moholy: 18, 19

© Chiara Becattini, Celestia Studio: 488, 489 top, 490/491, 492 top, 493 bottom, back cover

© Adolf Bereuter: 449, 451 top, 452/453, 454/455

© 2010 CJ Berg Photographics/Sunshine Divis Photography: 414 top, 415 both, 416 both, 417

© Better Shelter: 471 top

© Better Shelter/Frida Ström: 470 both, 471 bottom

© Better Shelter/Ali Haj Suleiman: 472

© Better Shelter/Björn Wallander: 473

© Louise Billgert, Stockholm: 439 top,440/441, 442 both, 443 top

© Blaich, Mary DiBiase: 166

BluHomes' mkDesigns: 316, 317 all, 321 top

© Reiner Blunck, Tübingen: 230 top left, 230 bottom, 231 top, 232, 233, 234, 235, 237 bottom both

Courtesy of BoKlok AB: 39

© Tom Bonner, Santa Monica, CA: 411 top, 412, 413

© Ivan Brodey, Oslo: 427, 428 bottom both, 429

© Are Carlsen, Oslo: 428 top, 430 bottom

© Centre National d'Art et de Culture Georges Pompidou – Bibliothèque Kandinsky, Paris: 143, 146/147, 150 bottom, 152/153, 174 top, 175

© Benny Chan, Los Angeles, CA: 397

Courtesy of Benjamin Cherner, New York: 178 top, 179 both, 180 top

Cherner, Norman: *Fabricating Houses from Component Parts. How to build a house for $6000.* New York, New York: Reinhold Publishing, 1957: 176, 177, 178 bottom, 180 bottom, 181 both

CINARK – Center for Industrialised Architecture, Royal Danish Academy: 503 top left

Courtesy of Claesson Koivisto Rune, Stockholm: 433 bottom, 438 top, 439 bottom

Clarke Historical Library, Central Michigan University: 15

Special Collections, John D. Rockefeller, Jr. Library, The Colonial Williamsburg Foundations: 62 both, 66 top both, 68, 70, 71 both, 72/73

© Bettmann/CORBIS: front cover, 207

Courtesy of *Cottage Living Magazine*: 406 top, 407 bottom; Photo Ralph Crane: 36, 37

Courtesy of Marianne Cusato, New York, NY: 406 bottom, 407 top, 408 bottom both, 409 bottom both; © Richard Chenoweth: 404; Photo Bruce Tolar: 405; Photo Josh Gibson: 408 top; Photo Jeffrey K. Bounds: 409 top

© Michel Denancé, Paris: 169, 170/171, 172, 173

Designmuseo Helsinki, Photo Simo Rista: 188

dookphoto.com: 376, 377 both, 378/379, 381

© Hubert Dorfstetter, Thaur: 355 both,356 top, 357

Courtesy of Easy Domes Ltd., Tórshavn: 274, 275 both, 276 all, 277 all, 278/279

Erfgoed 's-Hertogenbosch/Collectie Beeld en Geluid/Felix Janssens: 273 top

Courtesy of Wolfgang Feierbach, Altenstadt: 212, 213, 214, 215 both, 216, 220/221, 222; Photo Klaus Meier-Ude: 217, 218, 219, 223 both, 224, 225, 226/227

© Floto + Warner, New York, NY: 331, 332 both, 333 bottom

© Renee Flugge: 444 bottom

Fonds Candilis, Georges/ SIAF/Cité de l'architecture et du patrimoine/Archives d'architecture contemporaine/photos © Drina Candilis-Huisman: 246–255

© Tristan Fopma: 272

Norman Foster Foundation: 489 bottom, 492 bottom, 493 top

Norman Foster Foundation/Dbox: 494 both, 495

Photo Lionel Freedman: 162/163

Courtesy, The Estate of R. Buckminster Fuller: 6/7, 96, 97, 100/101, 110, 111 bottom, 112/113, 114/115, 116, 117 both, 118/119

Photo Avalon/Hulton Archive/Getty Images: 2/3

Photo © Arnold Newman/ Getty Images: front and back endpapers, 132/133

© J. Paul Getty Trust. Used with permission. Julius Shulman Photography Archive, Research Library at the Getty Research Institute: 32/33, 122 both, 123 top, 124/125

© Steve Gleason, Warren, MA: 46, 52 both, 53 both

© David Glomb, Rancho Mirage, CA: 398, 399 both

© Peter Gössel, Bremen: 375 466 all, 468 bottom, 469 bottom

© John Gollings, St. Kilda: 386 bottom 388, 389 top, 390 top, 391 bottom

© Pedro Guerrero, Tucson, AZ: 165, 167

Haack + Höpfner, Munich, Horden Cherry Lee Architects, London: 366 top both, 367, 369 middle, 369 bottom

Courtesy of Hanse-Haus GmbH, Oberleichtersbach: 346, 347, 348, 349, 350, 351 all, 352, 353

Courtesy of Happy Haus, Fortitude Valley, Queensland: 444 top, 445 both, 446 top, 447 bottom

Special Collections, Frances Loeb Library, Graduate School of Design, Harvard University: 120, 121, 123 bottom; Photo Julius Shulman: 126, 127

Courtesy of Architekturbüro Hellmuth: 230 top right, 231 bottom, 236, 237 top, 228, 229 both

© Hiroyuki Hirai, Tokyo: 282 both, 283 top, 285, 289

Courtesy of Hive Moduar LLC, Minneapolis, MN: 392, 393 all, 394 all, 395 bottom; Photo T. J. Thoraldson 395 top

© Rasmus Hjortshøj: 504/505, 506, 507

E. F. Hodgson Co.: *Hodgson portable houses*, Boston, Massachusetts, 1908: 47 top, 50, 51

E. F. Hodgson Co.: *Hodgson portable houses, poultry and pet stock*, Boston, Massachusetts, 1920: 16/17, 48/49

Horden Cherry Lee Architects, London: 364, 365 both

© Ariel Huber: 474

Courtesy of Huf Haus GmbH & Co. KG, Hartenfels: 256 both, 257, 258/259

© Frank Huster/ Robert Hipp-Huster, Neckartenzlingen: 262, 263, 264 both, 265 both

Interior Design, November, 1968: 202 top

© Steffen Jänicke, Berlin: 419 bottom both, 420/421

Courtesy of Ray Kappe, Pacific Palisades, CA: 410

Courtesy of Oskar Leo Kaufmann, Dornbirn: 300, 301 bottom, 302 top, 448, 450 both, 451 bottom,

© Tom Kawara, Zurich: 296 top, 297 bottom, 299 top, 295, 298 bottom, 299 bottom

© Kéré Architecture: 337, 339

© Sascha Kletzsch, Munich: 366 bottom, 368 all, 369 top

Courtesy of Andreas Knitz, Berg / Ravensburg: 191 top, 195 top

Koch, Carl/Lewis, Andy: *At Home With Tomorrow*. New York/Toronto: Rinehart & Co., 1958: 156, 159 both, 161 top

© Julien Lanoo: 478 both, 479

Courtesy of Lazor Office LLS, Minneapolis, MN: 340 both, 341, 342, 343 bottom, 344 bottom, 345 bottom,; Photo Tomm Brown: 345 top; Photo Randy O'Rourke: 343 top, 344 top

Courtesy of the Library of Congress, Prints and Photographs Division: 34; Farm Security Administration/Office of War Information Photograph Collection: 30, 31, 47 bottom; Historic American Buildings Survey: 26, Photo Jack E. Boucher: 138 bottom

Photo John Phillips/LIFE Magazine/© Time Inc.: 99

Photo John G. Zimmerman/LIFE Magazine/ © Time Inc.: 198, 199, 200/201, 202 bottom, 203

© Åke E:son Lindman, Bromma: 433 top, 434 top, 435, 436, 437 bottom

© Jon Linkins, Enoggera, Queensland: 447 top, 446 bottom

Courtesy of LivingHomes, Los Angeles, CA: 411 bottom, 414 bottom, 417 bottom both

Courtesy of LoftCube GmbH, Munich: 419 top, 422/423, 424/425 top, 425 bottom

Lustron Home Erection Manual: 130 bottom, 131, 134 top

© Ignacio Martinez, Navia: 301 top, 302 bottom, 303

mauritius images/Picture Partners/Alamy Stock Photos: 270/271

MUJI.net Co., Ltd.: 360

Courtesy of Jerry Murbach: 1

Museum Eberswalde: 74, 75, 76, 77, 78, 79 top, 84, 85, 86, 87

Museum of Finnish Architecture, Helsinki: 182, 183, 184/185, 186 both, 187, 189, 209 top, 210/211; Photo Carl Gustav Hagström: 209 bottom

Courtesy of Kazuhiko Namba + Kai-Workshop, Tokyo: 358, 361 bottom, 363 bottom both

Robert Carrick/National Library of Australia: 8

Frank Hurley/National Library of Australia: 28

Damian McDonald/National Library of Australia: 44/45

National Trust of Australia (Vic): 42

National Trust for Historic Preservation: 130 top. 136 bottom, 137 both

Nieuwe Instituut, Library Collection: 266, 267

Nivag Review, September 1984: 268, 269

Ohio Historical Society: 134, 128, 129, 134 bottom, 135 top, 136, 138 top, 139

© Erik-Jan Ouwekerk: 336, 338

picture-alliance/dpa: Photo Ensio Ilmonen/ Lehtikuva: 243; Photo Lehtikuva: 242, 240/241, 244, 245; Photo Wilhelm Bertram: 193 top, 196/197, 206; Photo Scanpix Gunnar Källström: 205

Courtesy of Pinc House AB, Stockholm: 370, 372 bottom, 374 top both; Photo Charlie Drevstam: 371 bottom, 371 top 372 top, 373, 375, 374 bottom

Popular Mechanics, August 1931: 67

Popular Science, March 1946: 4

Courtesy of Prebuilt Pty Ltd., Kilsyth: 382 all, 383, 384/385, 386 both, 387 both, 389 bottom, 390 bottom, 391 top

Family Prouvé: 141, 142 both, 144/145, 150 top, 151, 168, 174 bottom

Courtesy of Quik Build LLC: 38 both

Courtesy of Marmol Radziner + Associates, Los Angeles, CA: 396

Courtesy of Resolution: 4 Architecture, New York, NY: 320, 333 top both, 334 bottom both; Photo Roger Davies: 334 top, 335 both

Revue de l'Aluminium, no. 185, 1952, page 58: 148, 149, 155

Renzo Piano Building Workshop – Architect © Politecnico di Milano: 475 both, 476, 477

Courtesy of Rintala Eggertsson Architects, Oslo: 426, 430 top right; Photo Sami Rintala: 430 top left, 431

Courtesy of Rocio Romero LLC, St. Louis, MO: 312 top, 314 bottom; Photo Ethan: 311; Photo Karl Petzke: 312 bottom; Photo Frank Di Piazza: 314 top left; Photo Traci Roloff: 310, 314 top right, 315; Photo Jennifer Watson: 313

© Douglas Royalty/Connecticut College: 86

© Hiro Sakaguchi, Tokyo: 359, 361 top, 362, 363 top,

Digital image © 2026, The Museum of Modern Art/ Scala, Florence: 22

Sears Archives: 11

Sears, Roebuck and Co.: *Modern Homes*. Chicago, Illinois: 1913: 12/13

Snow Peak USA: 491

Courtesy of sps-architekten, Thalgau: 354, 356 bottom

La Trobe Collection, State Library of Victoria: 43 top

South Australian Record, 27 November 1837: 43 bottom

S. P. Luftbild GmbH, Dattenberg: 260/261

Courtesy of Matti Suuronen, Espoo: 204, 438 both

© John Swain, Sacramento, CA: 318/319, 320, 321 bottom

Courtesy of Mikko Tuovinen: 238, 239

Courtesy of TYIN tegnestue, Trondheim: 457, 460 bottom

United States Patent and Trademark Office: 10, 98 both, 111 top

Albert Frey Collection, Architecture & Design Collection, University Art Museum, University of California, Santa Barbara: 63, 64/65, 66 bottom, 69

© Voluntary Architects' Network: 286, 288 both, 292/293

Wachsmann, Konrad: *Holzhausbau – Technik und Gestaltung*. Ernst Wasmuth Verlag, Berlin, 1930: 55 bottom, 57 bottom, 58 bottom

Wagner, Martin: *Das wachsende Haus*. Berlin, 1932: 79 bottom, 80 bottom, 81 bottom

Courtesy of The Wall AG, Schaffhausen: 465 both, 467 both, 468 top, 469 top

Monsanto Company Records, University Archives, Department of Special Collections, Washington University Libraries, St. Louis, MO: 40/41

Courtesy of WeberHaus, Rheinau-Linx: 305

Courtesy of Larry Weinberg: 158/159, 160

© The Frank Lloyd Wright Foundation,Scottsdale: 164

Courtesy of ZenKaya Ecohomes, Pretoria: 376, 380

IMPRINT

Hohenzollernring 53
50672 Köln, Germany
www.taschen.com

Texts by:
Arnt Cobbers & Oliver Jahn, with additional updates by Philip Jodidio

English translation:
Maureen Roycroft Sommer, Bergisch Gladbach

EACH AND EVERY TASCHEN BOOK PLANTS A SEED!
Each year, we offset our annual carbon emissions with carbon credits at the Instituto Terra, a reforestation program in Minas Gerais, Brazil, founded by Lélia and Sebastião Salgado. To find out more about this ecological partnership, please check: *www.taschen.com/institutoterra.*
Inspiration: unlimited.
Carbon footprint: (almost) zero.

Printed in Bosnia-Herzegovina
ISBN 978-3-7544-0470-6

Page 1: Still from Buster Keaton's famous short film *One Week*, 1920

Pages 2/3: A heavy-duty Sikorsky S-64 Skycrane lifting a complete pre-fabricated house, measuring 28 feet by 44 feet, from the factory to its destination

Page 4: Cover of the magazine *Popular Science*, 1946

Pages 6/7: Richard Buckminster Fuller with the model of the Dymaxion House, c. 1929

Pages 40/41: The "House of the Future" at Disneyland in Anaheim, California, 1957